AF380797

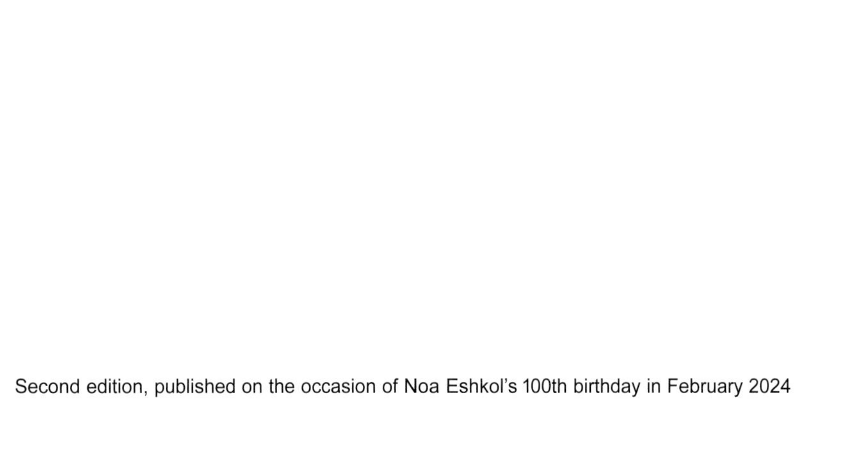

Second edition, published on the occasion of Noa Eshkol's 100th birthday in February 2024

Movement Notation

Noa Eshkol and Abraham Wachmann

KW Institute for Contemporary Art, Berlin
Verlag der Buchhandlung Walther und Franz König, Köln
In collaboration with Georg Kolbe Museum, Berlin

Foreword

This publication is the reissue of Noa Eshkol's seminal book *Movement Notation*, developed in collaboration with Abraham Wachmann and first published by Weidenfeld & Nicolson in 1958. Initiated by KW Institute for Contemporary Art and produced in collaboration with the Noa Eshkol Foundation for Movement Notation, this significant project coincides with what would have been Eshkol's 100th birthday: she was born on February 29, 1924, and passed away in 2007.

An Israeli performance artist and dance theorist, Eshkol devoted her life to the development of a notation for movement. Coined Eshkol-Wachmann Movement Notation (EWMN), not only did this notation serve as the basis for Eshkol's idiosyncratic and stripped-down choreographies, it also set out to record the movement of the body as such, extending beyond particular dance styles or even the human form. At the heart of Eshkol and Wachmann's interest lies the assumption that by studying movement, an understanding might be established as to how one movement evokes a certain feeling, while other movements produce entirely different emotions. As a milestone in discourses around the movement of the body, it has inspired and influenced performance art and dance of the generations to follow. Today, EWMN has long left the realm of the arts and has been applied to fields such as physical therapy, animal behavior, and medicine, its systematic procedure enabling new perspectives on the ways of thinking about, observing, and analyzing movement. It is therefore an honor to be able to bring this book back into circulation, expanding its international recognition and reintroducing it into contemporary contexts of notation, performance art, and dance.

In this spirit of preservation and contextualization, the reissue provides further insight into the history and development of EWMN. Accompanied by a contribution of early drawings, preliminary notations, and drafts that were carefully selected by the Noa Eshkol Archive, the original book *Movement Notation* is introduced through an extensive essay by Eshkol's student, longtime collaborator, and friend John G Harries.

Without the collaboration of the Noa Eshkol Foundation for Movement Notation, this publication would not have been possible; in particular, our thanks go to Mooky Dagan, Mor Bashan, Dror Shoval, Racheli Nul-Kahana, Noga Goral, and

Michal Shoshani. The foundation is a consortium of Eshkol's long-standing dancers, collaborators, and friends, as well as dancers who recently joined the Noa Eshkol Chamber Dance Group. Their devotion, which inspired the editorial process of this publication, has been instrumental in the preservation of EWMN. It is only through their efforts that this pivotal contribution to dance and performance art continues to exist, and we would therefore like to express our sincere gratitude to them.

At KW, the reissue follows a series of performances by the Noa Eshkol Chamber Dance Group that took place on August 25 and 27, 2023, including a workshop that gave insight into the theoretical and practical background of EWMN.

KW would like to thank Artis for their generous support of this publication as well as the performances at KW. Without their support, this project would not have been realized, and we are grateful for their commitment to fostering cross-cultural dialogue on Israeli art. Furthermore, we would like to thank neugerriemschneider, who generously supported the performances that took place at KW in late summer 2023.

I would also like to extend our gratitude to the Georg Kolbe Museum in Berlin, which will open in March 2024 an exhibition focusing on the life and work of Eshkol and her legacy in contemporary art and dance discourses with generous support by the German Federal Cultural Foundation. In particular, I would like to thank Kathleen Reinhardt, the museum's director, for her support of the reissue of *Movement Notation*.

In conclusion, I owe a deep gratitude to curatorial assistant Nikolas Brummer for producing the performances as well as developing this publication in collaboration with graphic designer Marc Hollenstein. Additionally, I would like to thank John G Harries for his insightful essay on the history of Eshkol's practice. We are also indebted to Anita Iannacchione, Jayne Wilkinson, and Z. Harris for their careful copyediting and proofreading.

Krist Gruijthuijsen
Director
KW Institute for Contemporary Art

John G Harries

Noa Eshkol and Movement Notation

To celebrate the centenary of the birth of Noa Eshkol, there could be no better way than the reprinting of the first publication of the unique method she developed with Abraham Wachmann for the notation of movement. In light of the dozens of books subsequently devoted to applications of the method in dance and other fields, the idea of reissuing the original textbook of Eshkol-Wachmann Movement Notation may appear strange. Many of these subsequent publications include full explanations of the method, and its development can be traced from one publication to another. The interest in republishing, however, lies precisely in the scope and the limitations of the original version of the method at a moment when it was nevertheless already fully capable of expressing dances of any style by virtue of being a movement notation rather than a dance notation. As an introduction to the study of the 1958 publication, it may be useful and perhaps interesting to provide an account of the developments that culminated in this first public step in the use of the method. It may also be of interest to illustrate the ensuing evolution of the method by indicating some of the changes that have taken place since it was first published sixty-five years ago.

Noa Eshkol studied dance in her native Israel in the years following World War II. Her instructor was Tehilla Roessler, one of the teachers of European modern dance then living and working in Israel. At this time, Noa became acquainted with the young composer Herbert Brün, who had studied with Stefan Wolpe at the Jerusalem Conservatory of Music. Herbert became her mentor, and instilled in her the attitude that no activity could be regarded as a fully fledged art unless it had a means of notation at its base. This prompted Noa to look for a method and teacher of such a system, and Roessler suggested that she should study Labanotation, the notation method of Rudolf Laban, who had recently opened a studio in England. Noa followed this advice, but was disappointed with what she found, and left to enroll in a modern dance course at the studio of Sigurd Leeder, hoping to find an alternative approach. It was there that I made her acquaintance; out of school, I became her student and one of the many people who often visited her at her home in London at that time. All of us were drawn into lively discussions—most frequently on the subject of the notation of dance. Herbert visited in the course of his return journey to Israel from further studies in the US, and he encouraged Noa to devise her own method of notation. In the discussions of what the character of a viable notation might be, Herbert maintained that the first and most important step in this task should be to find a basic element underlying all human movement. This advice led to the day when Noa entered her basement kitchen and proclaimed to Herbert, myself, and the resident cat that she had found a key element of all movement based on the human skeletal structure: the circle. This revelation was the initial insight from which a viable system of notation stemmed and developed over the years that followed.

Noa returned to Israel and began teaching. One of her students, Abraham Wachmann, contributed the spherical framework of a spatial system of reference for the coordination of the circular paths of the limbs in their movements identified by Noa as the basis of all human movement. A group of students took part in discussions and further helped develop what was by then a notation system in the making. A small performing group was formed—Noa herself and three others—which gave public performances of dances composed in the nascent system of movement notation using its symbols and concepts. The first drafts of a textbook explaining the system were written and included examples of notated dances—as the basis of the original book reproduced here.

In the years that followed, books were published containing revised explanations of the method as well as the notation of dances and other physical activities. Changes were made: some of the graphical signs originally employed were altered so as to be easier to write, or to reflect their meanings in a more direct way. Other changes were related to frequent, common combinations of movement, such as steps and jumps. The unraveling of verbal descriptions of such overall patterns of movement was essential in a notation capable of expressing not only generalized labels but also the exact physical nature of every movement event. For example, a term such as "step" is highly generalized and far from the aim of the notation to provide precise information. The movements of the limbs that produce a step could, however, now be precisely described in as much detail as required, with the amount of useful detail varying in different cases. The sign *S* was adopted to indicate a sequence and combination of movements that would result in the overall action of a step. The *S* represents the whole pattern of movement, to which can be added as much detail as required. Other overall signs include *W*, signifying a shift of weight, and *P*, to indicate passive movement of a limb caused by the movement of other parts of the body.

Further phenomena involved more extensive and significant additions to the writing principles foreshadowed in the earliest use of the notation, but became an explicit part of the method with the publication of a book on a zoological subject. In it, some movements of parts of the animal's body were defined and symbolized in relation to the body part that carried them—such as the ears in relation to the head—rather than to the overall system of reference. This option not only became a useful tool but also provided an alternative viewpoint and mode of reference in describing the integrated movements of chains of limbs.

As a consequence of the practical use of the notation, a verbal vocabulary has developed among those who employ it. This is not a trivial matter, as it allows for the distinct verbalization and discussion of phenomena revealed in the course of the practical usage of the notation. Prominent among these is the term "space chord," which is used to refer to the path traced by the combined movements of articulated limbs. No symbol is associated in the notation with a "simultaneous movement" or a "space chord," but these terms denote movement phenomena recognizable by anyone using the notation as a means to perform a movement. This vocabulary makes it possible to use precise, meaningful references in discussion or explanation, and therein lies its importance. Research carried out in 1968–69 at the University of Illinois was devoted to a computerized method of deriving space chords from instructions formulated in terms of EWMN, yielding paths of movement of limbs that created the phenomenon. These were analyzed and displayed in three-dimensional plots in Cartesian coordinates, and as EWMN coordinates with a base unit of a single degree. Such precision of course goes far beyond measurements that are relevant to the human body, but is significant in other areas where EWMN is applied, such as graphic art.

In choosing or designing the symbols of the notation, much consideration was given to the ease of writing them. It was intended that the notation should be above all writable, but—especially when reproduced in printed form—also readable. Experimentation with different techniques was part of a concerted effort to ensure clarity and legibility, finally met by the design of a computer program by Henner Drewes, appropriately named EW Notator, which provides the means of producing very clear printed scores composed in EWMN.

Today, the number of people in the world of dance who use a movement notation when composing their works is exceedingly small. The notion of movement literacy is not a preoccupation of many composers of dance and movement. Nevertheless, as Anne Hutchinson Guest found through extensive research, in every period since at least the fifteenth century, various attempts have been made to record and convey the structure of dances. Where notations have been used at all, it has usually been for the needs of documentation rather than composition. This approach is of course valuable, but documentation is only one facet of a fully functioning symbol system. To constitute a comprehensive system, a notation must also be capable of serving the purpose of composition, as does the notation of a verbal or musical language. This requirement involves being liberated from the set styles and sequences of movement upon which choreographers have long depended as organizational principles. A literate composer of movement can make choices among countless possible combinations of movement. Every composer will then be enabled to create a style of their own, without the need to adhere to any previously received style. The exploration and charting of new movement experiences can then be achieved by the use of a compositional tool based directly on the physical properties of the human body. This method affords free exploration of what is possible without abandoning responsibility for what is discovered.

The primary aim in creating EWMN was thus, in effect, to devise a language and a writing system that would make the composition of movement an art based on a symbol system comparable to the notation that supports Western music. This aim runs counter to approaches that regard dance as an entirely improvisatory activity. Anyone expecting that the new notation would be eagerly adopted by the entire dance world would have been sorely disappointed at a time when choreographers were increasingly turning to improvisational approaches, perhaps as a reaction to the previous era, which was dominated by classical ballet.

The idea that video recording can be used rather than notation has been raised in the past, and video can no doubt serve as an adjunct to a notation by providing a general picture of the appearance of a work. But as with music, compositions of any complexity are impossible to reconstruct at a more than superficial level by attempting to simulate a recording. Material of any depth can only be properly interpreted as a work created in movement through an understanding of the way it was originally conceived and produced. Analysis of movement through EWMN reveals and articulates the interrelation of the moving body and its spatial environment, a shifting correlation that characterizes our every physical action.

The first words of the introduction to the original textbook clarify that this is not a dance notation, but a movement notation—the implication being that it is intended to be applicable to any possible movement of the human body. In fact, its scope has proved to be wider still, with its application extending to the motor behavior of animals, motion graphics, or the education of children with learning difficulties. The continued use and exploration of the method in these and yet unthought-of fields will ensure the survival of EWMN as a living system rather than an interesting fossil in the evolution of dance and movement notation.

Noa's students who are literate in the notation and concerned with research, documentation, and composition have published books within the frameworks of the Movement Notation Society, the Jerusalem Academy for Music and Dance, and the Kibbutzim College of Education.

This reprinting of the first publication on EWMN provides the opportunity to study at source the initial formulation and basic principles of a unique method for anyone with an interest in the study, development, and use of a valid and comprehensive notation of movement.

Michal Shoshani and Humi Einbinder

Notes on *Promenade*—A Dance by Noa Eshkol

Movement Notation was written as a declaration of intent by its authors, presenting the vision of Eshkol-Wachmann Movement Notation and illustrating how it is translated into practical realization. The representation of a phenomenon as profoundly intricate as the movement of the human body inherently engenders challenges, with each facet necessitating a tailored theoretical understanding. Elucidating such intricacies has evolved into an extensive undertaking to clarify concepts and refine their symbolic representation.

Noa Eshkol and her working group were engaged in this endeavor throughout her lifetime. At one point, she decided to revisit the dances in *Movement Notation* in the context of considering the evolution of EWMN. The *Promenade* dance featured here with its "new" movement score (found on pages 93–94 of the original book) exemplifies a contemporary process of rewriting and updating EWMN in accordance with the changes it has undergone.

PROMENADE
BY NOA ESHKOL 16/11/23

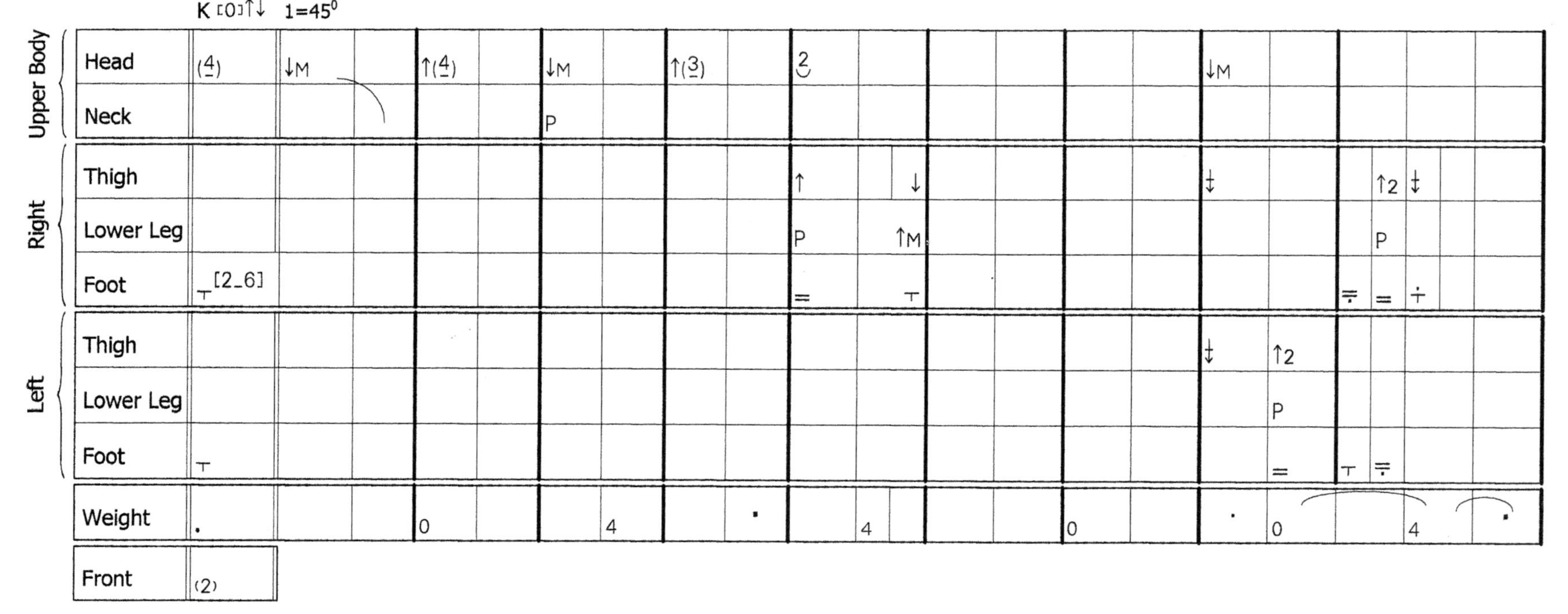

Upper Body	Head			⌒2										4 ∨		[4̄			2 ∨	[2̄
	Neck													P					P	
Right	Thigh	↟M		↑[ ]			‡	↑2										↟M		
	Lower Leg			↓				P	↑M											
	Foot			=	∸			=		⊤								± ⊤		
Left	Thigh	↟M					↑		‡	↑2 ⌒							↓M	↟M		
	Lower Leg						P↑M			P		↓					↓			
	Foot							⊤	╤	=		∸					= ∸	± ⊤		
	Weight			0	▪		0 ⌒						▪				4̇			
																		1 ◡	1)	

		1		2		3		4		5		6		7		8		9		
Upper Body	Head	[0]↑2		↓2		↑2	[6̄	2 ◡						[2↑M						
	Neck			P																
Right	Thigh													‡	↑1			‡M	↑M	
	Lower Leg														P					
	Foot				=	⊤									=	⊤				
Left	Thigh							↑	* ↑1					‡		* ↑M	↓	‡M	↑M	
	Lower Leg															P	P			
	Foot		=̇	⊤			=̇	=	⊤							=	⊤ =	⊤		
	Weight	2		6		2			•			2		•	2 ⁀		6	•		

Upper Body	Head	⌒2	(2̄									^6				[0̄
	Neck	P														
Right	Thigh				↑1			‡				‡			↓•		
	Lower Leg																
	Foot				=		⊤		=		.⊤			=	⊤		
Left	Thigh	↑[]					↑[]		‡								
	Lower Leg																
	Foot						=		⊤	=̣							
	Weight	2	•		1				2			•			6		
	Front	1)															

Re-notated by Michal Shoshani and Humi Einbinder
Typed in EW Notator, Henner Drewes's notation program, by Ein Ya Cohen

Mor Bashan and Dror Shoval

Prelude, 1940s–1950s: An Archival Capsule

The following capsule is a gallery curated from the eclectic contents of the Noa Eshkol Archive. Conceived to parallel the initial archival division titled "The Original/First Book, 1958," it also presents a new compilation of materials. Some of the items are arranged chronologically—taking advantage of the linear layout—while others are compiled thematically according to their subject matter. The capsule relates to Noa Eshkol's early years as a dancer, dance composer, and inventor, together with Abraham Wachmann, of Eshkol-Wachmann Movement Notation. The earlier pieces are from Eshkol's time in London, where she and John G Harries attended the Sigurd Leeder School of Dance and began to work together in 1948. From those days, there is a notebook they kept during the course of their anatomical and formal investigations into the movement of the human body, in an attempt to understand and organize movement so that a coherent language and notation would emerge. This was a point of departure from conventional dance styles. The underlying idea is reflected in the utopian school schedule, with its headings "Movement for the Sake of the Body" and "The Body for the Sake of Movement," and in the extract from a projected thirty-week tuition plan drawn up by Eshkol.*

The materials then follow Eshkol's trajectory from London to Israel, and from dancer to teacher, in the early 1950s. Photographs and scores from the mid-1950s correspond to her establishment of the Chamber Dance Group to perform dances composed in EWMN. By the late 1950s, she stopped dancing in the group to focus on teaching, composing, and publishing her notation. Archival records from the later 1950s focus on the promotion and publication of *Movement Notation*, including drafts, correspondence, and documentation of its first promotional exhibition as well as original illustrations featured in the book.

*See Noa Eshkol and John G Harries, *EWMN: Part I* (Holon: The Movement Notation Society, 2001).

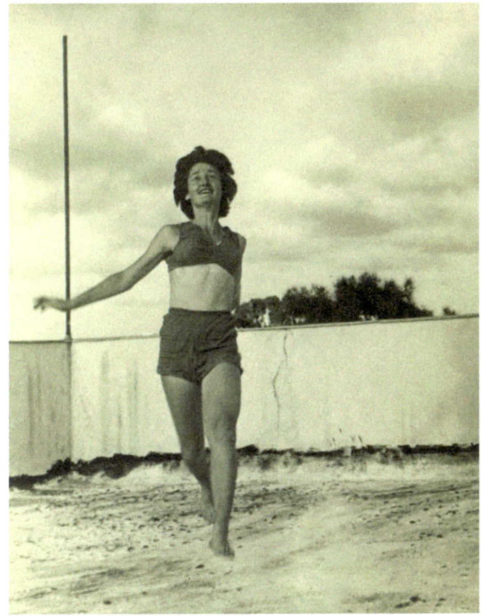

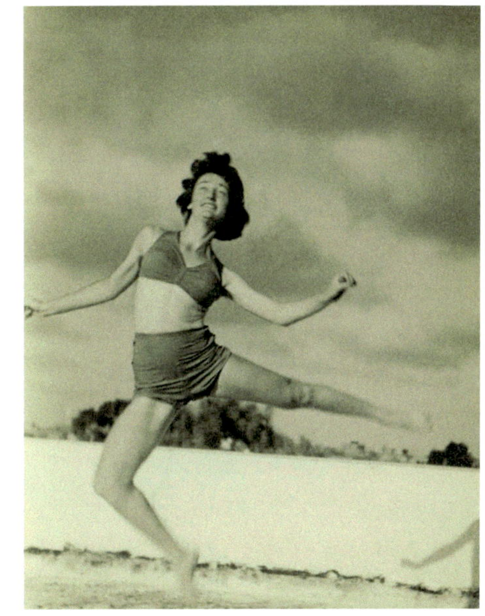

Private photographs of Noa Eshkol, with note on verso: "From Thilla Resler days—twenty-year-old Noa dancing, 1940++ [early 1940s]. The years of World War II. Noa the bouncy in vivace from here and andante from there," 1940–1945. Photos: Erde, Tel Aviv

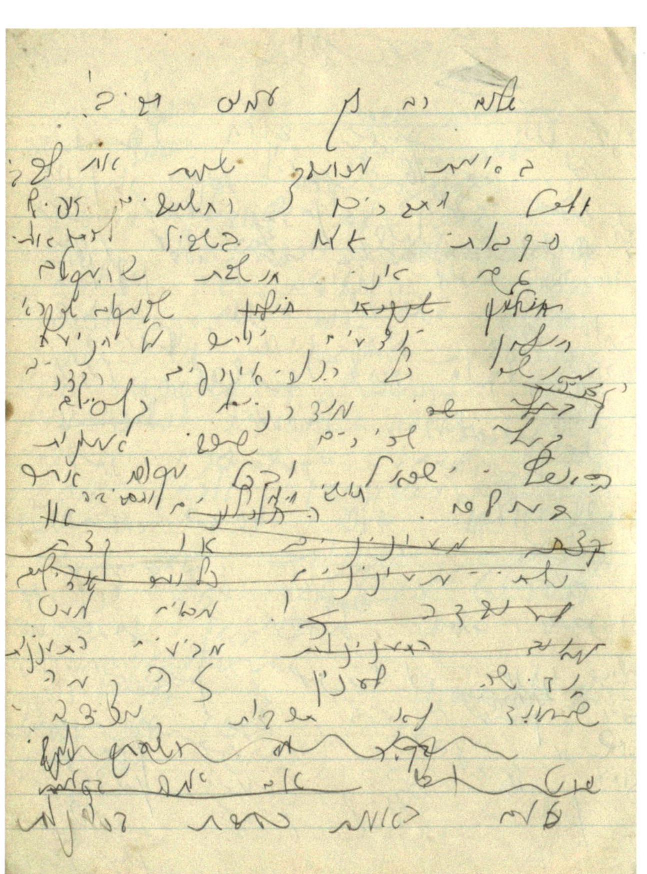

Draft of a letter from Noa Eshkol to Amos (probably Amos Kenan), announcing the invention of the movement notation system, 1954

Greetings to you, lovely Amos,

Really, your letter had warmed my heart, and I have even read it out loud to all my important friends, in order to take pride. I, too, think that in the place called Holon people know more about movement than all of the choreographers, modern and classical dancers with muscles (…) in the land of Israel and in every other place in the world.

The citizens of Holon show very little interest, which is very uncultured of them.

Once (…) you've written sincerely (…) that you can help the matter. A 16 mm film is not something I would be able to send in the near future because I don't have money from Shlomo—rich friends—and Dan would probably first of all—until he gets rich—film Inbal. And that is why the whole thing must remain as a plan for the future. But there's something important you can do: you probably know that Avraham'le [Wachmann] (a student of mine) and I developed a movement notation. We have improved, processed, and refined this notation, and wrote a book which explains the method. On February 1, we submit the notation to the Weitzman Institute of Science, and according to the contract, the book itself should be published on the first of June. The book is being published in English, because in Israel only Irena Guttery will buy it. There's a need to notify, distribute, and talk about the book's existence in the fitting milieus, if there are any. There's also a need for the book to be translated into (French, German)?

Maybe you can go to UNESCO and tell them they should organize an international conference of movement notation (there are a few crappy notations that exist) and invite everyone who has notation for lectures and demonstrations. Explain to them that it is a very important matter regarding means of communication, and for that reason, also for fraternity and understanding between the nations, the idea is practical.

In addition to that, I want to tell you that the notation is genuinely wonderful. On top of the fact that it annihilates the possibility of existence of all of the classical and modern dramatic, symbolic, and synthetic ballets—for the marvelous clean and immaculate movements are being hinted in it, movements which I am sure you sometimes see as well.

All of this shall not be told to dancers because they are certain that the notation doesn't serve but for them to be able to write their dances because they forget them (…) They do not know that they would need to write dances of a different kind, or maybe to become actors instead.

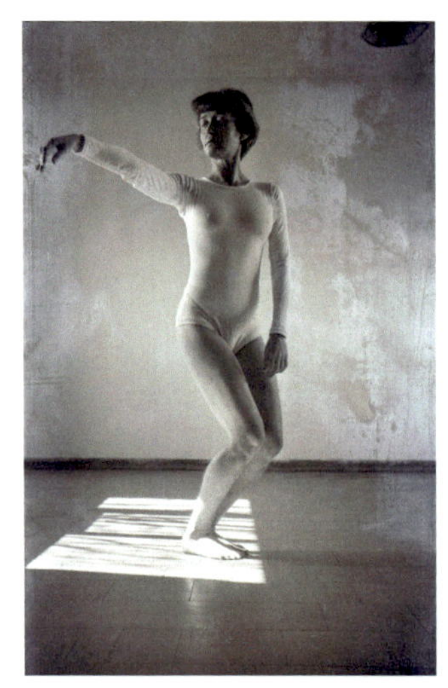

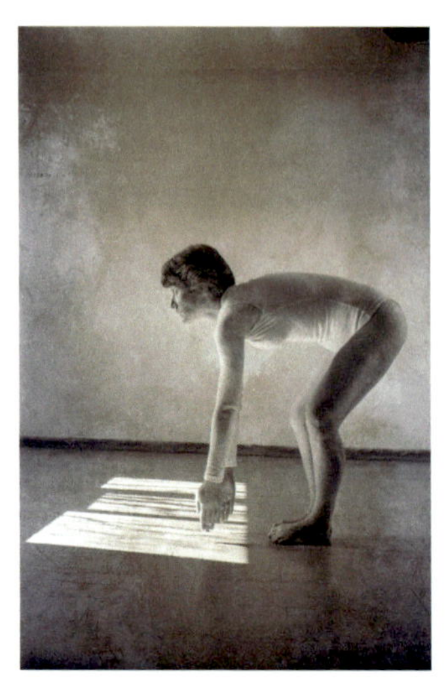

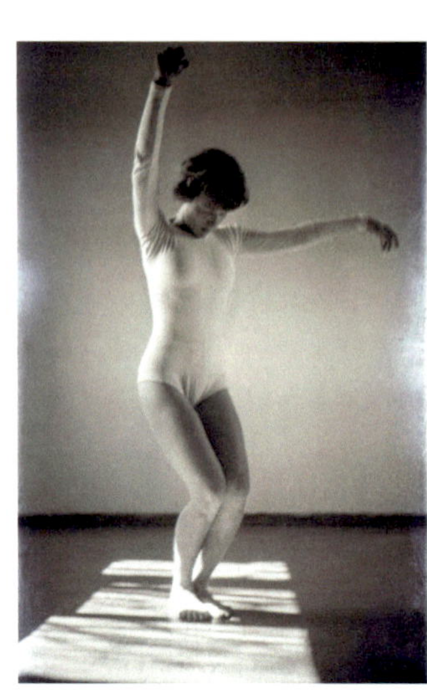

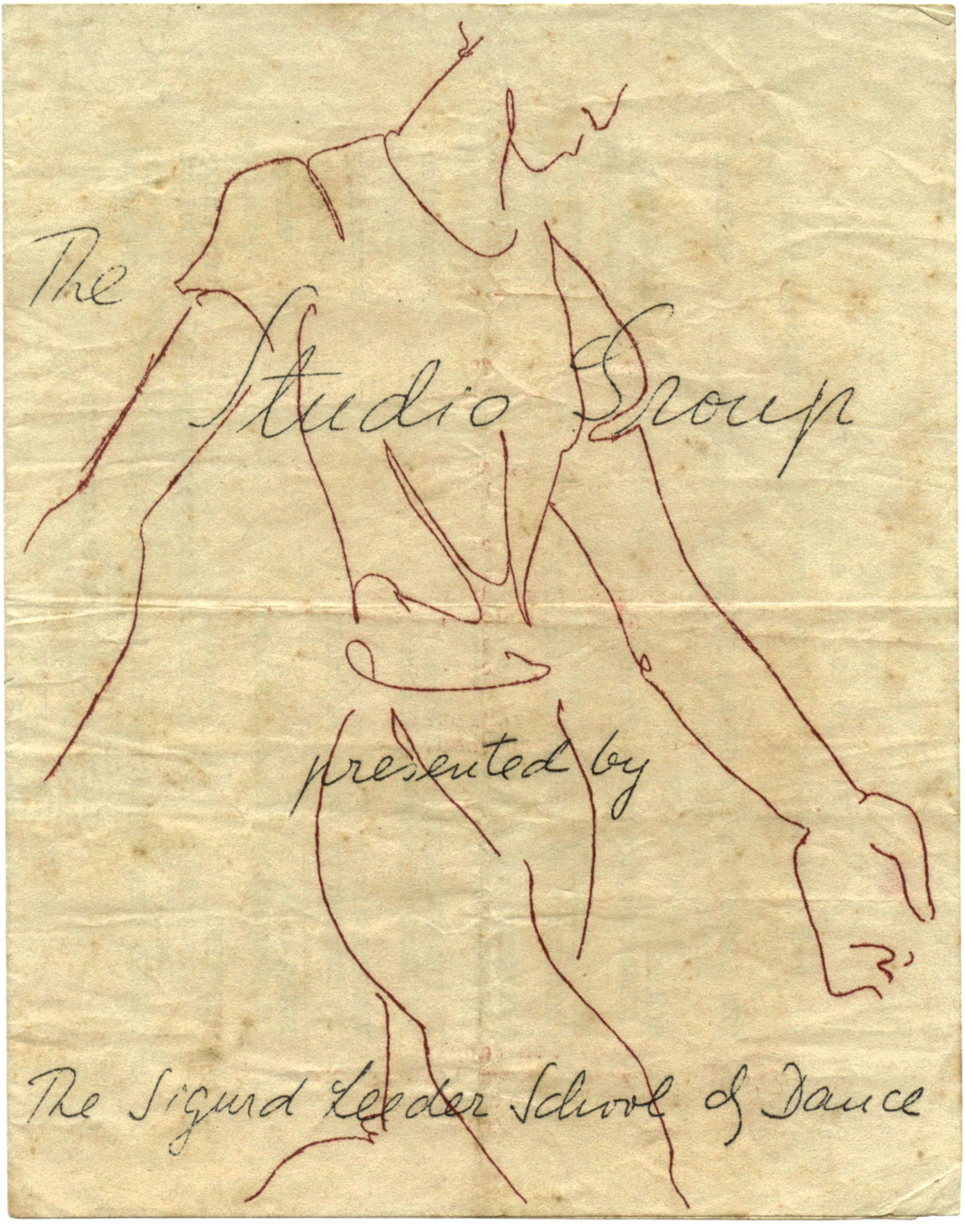

The Studio Group

presented by

The Sigurd Leeder School of Dance

Program cover of the Sigurd Leeder School of Dance, London, 1948–1950

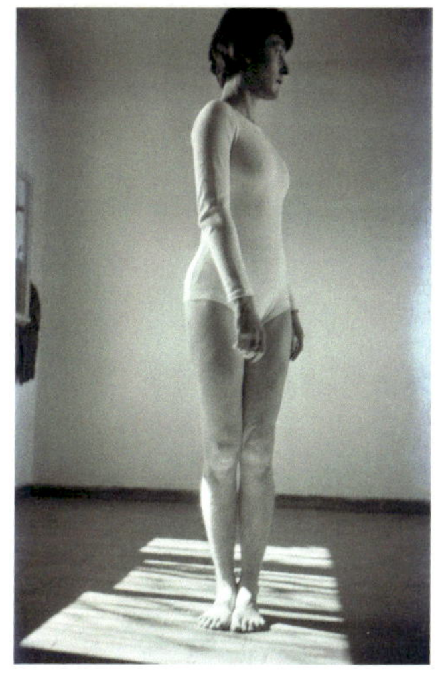

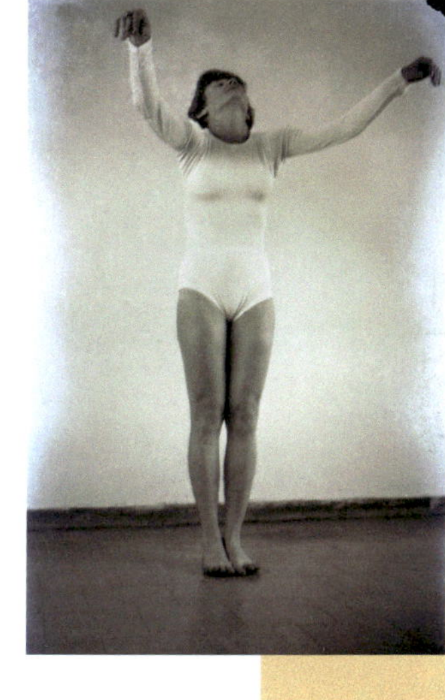

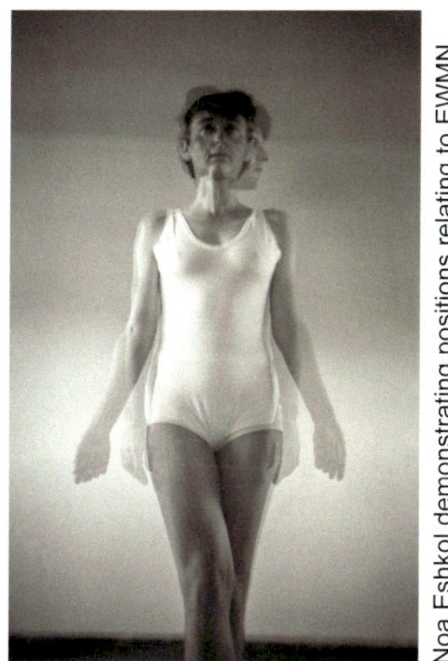

Noa Eshkol demonstrating positions relating to EWMN, Holon, 1948–1952. Photos: Herbert Brün

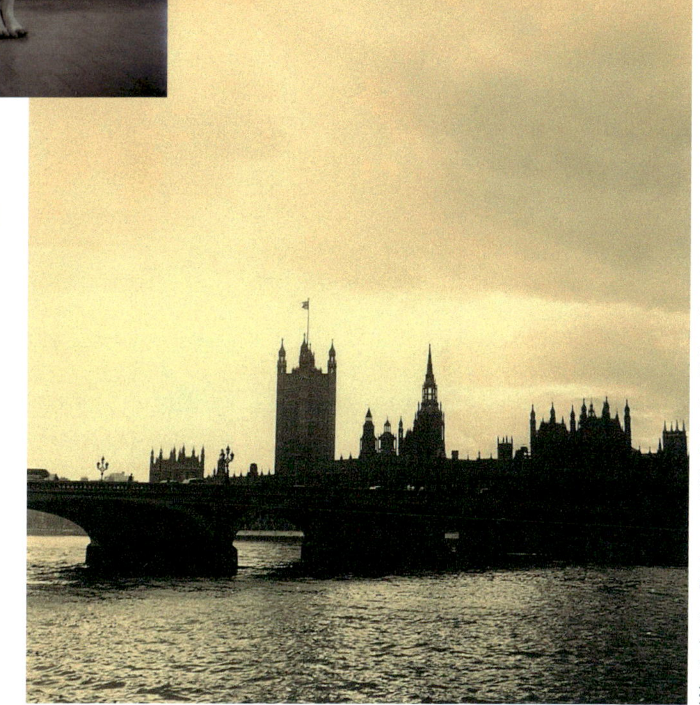

Westminster Bridge and Westminster Abbey, London, 1948. Photo: unknown

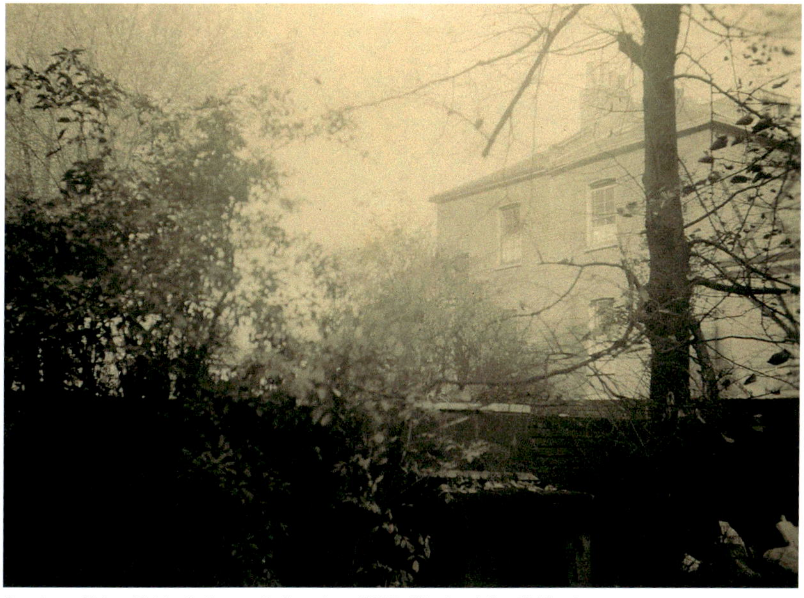

Garden of Noa Eshkol's house in London, 1948. Photo: John G Harries

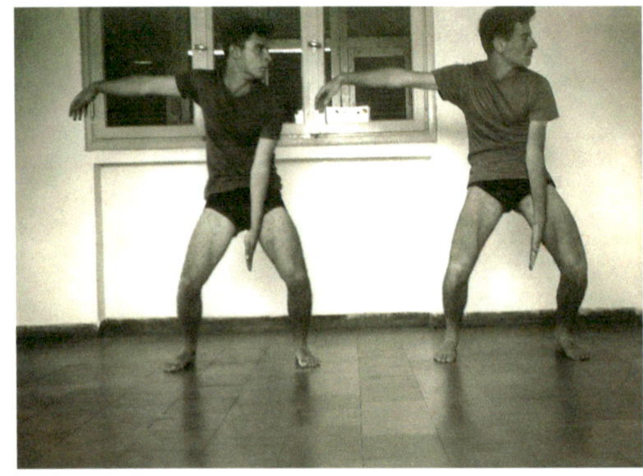

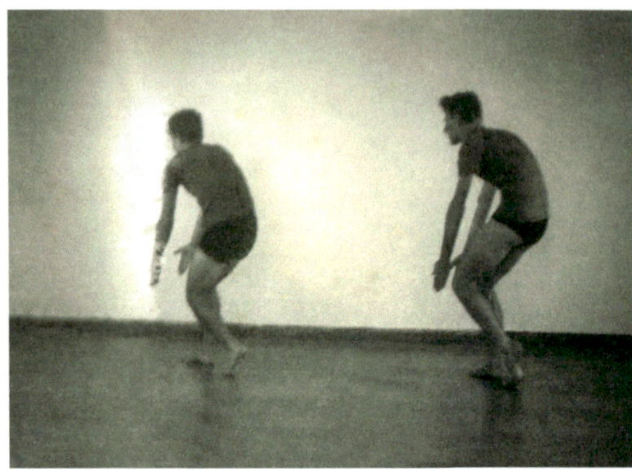

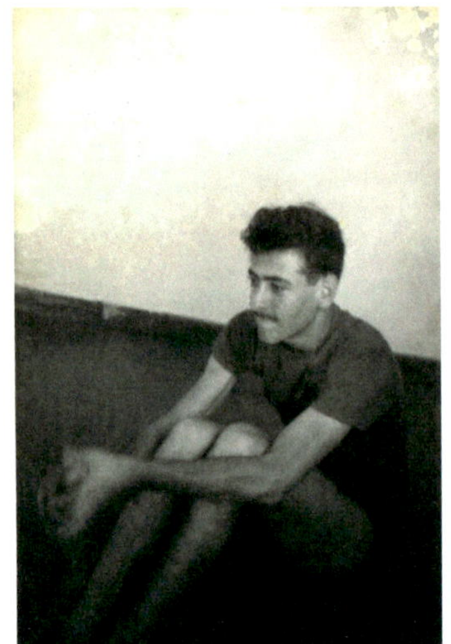

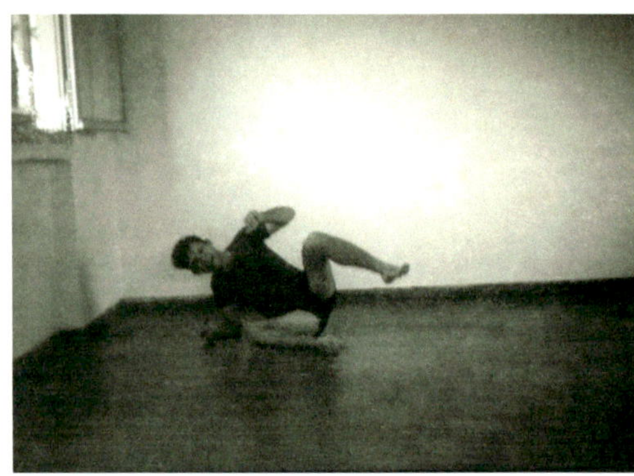

Abraham Wachmann, *David and Jonathan (Duet)*, 1951, performed by Amos Lev and Abraham Wachmann, Holon. Photos: Rami Carmi

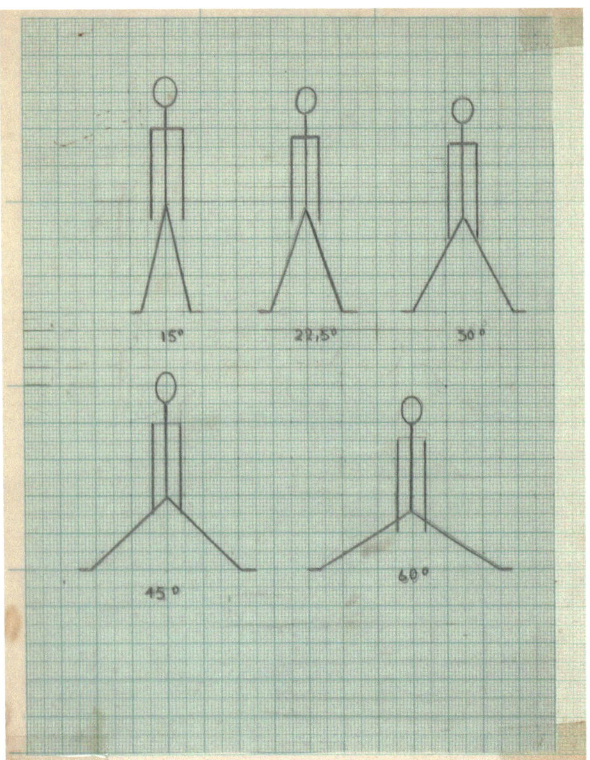

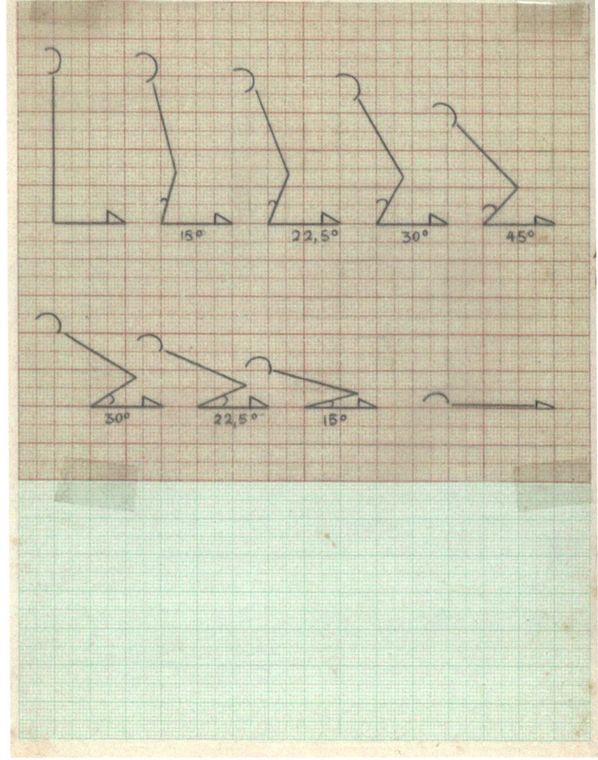

Notebook sketches showing the formal analysis of human skeletal movements by Noa Eshkol and John G Harries, London, 1950

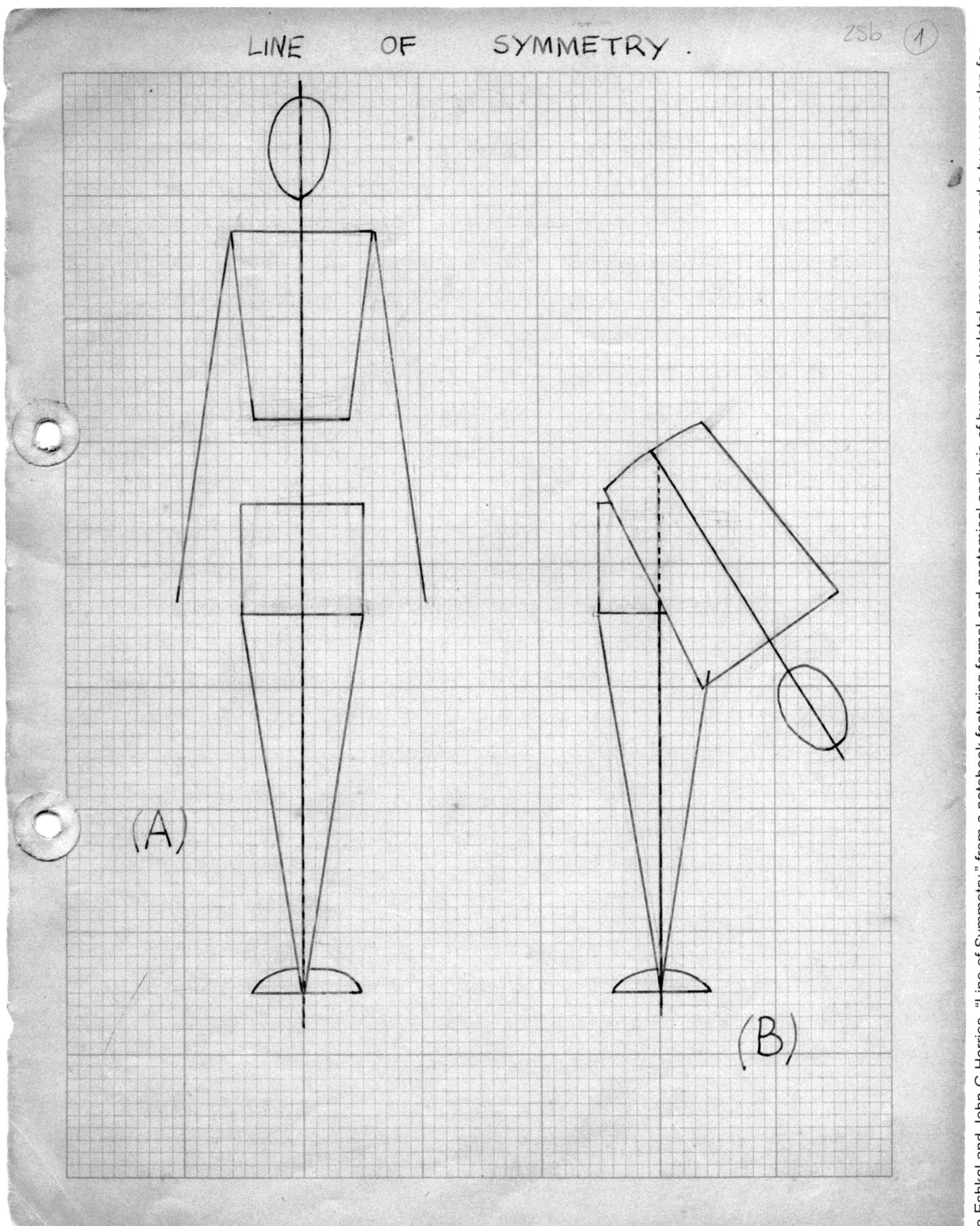

Noa Eshkol and John G Harries, “Line of Symmetry,” from a notebook featuring formal and anatomical analysis of human skeletal movements and a two-year plan for movement studies, London, 1948–1950

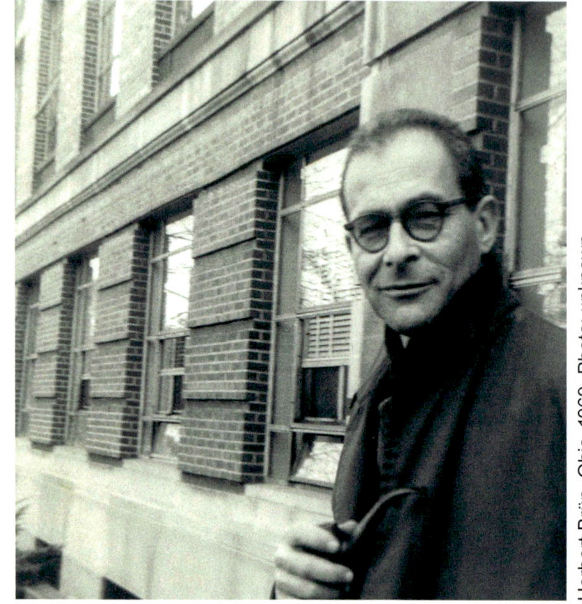

Herbert Brün, Ohio, 1969. Photo: unknown

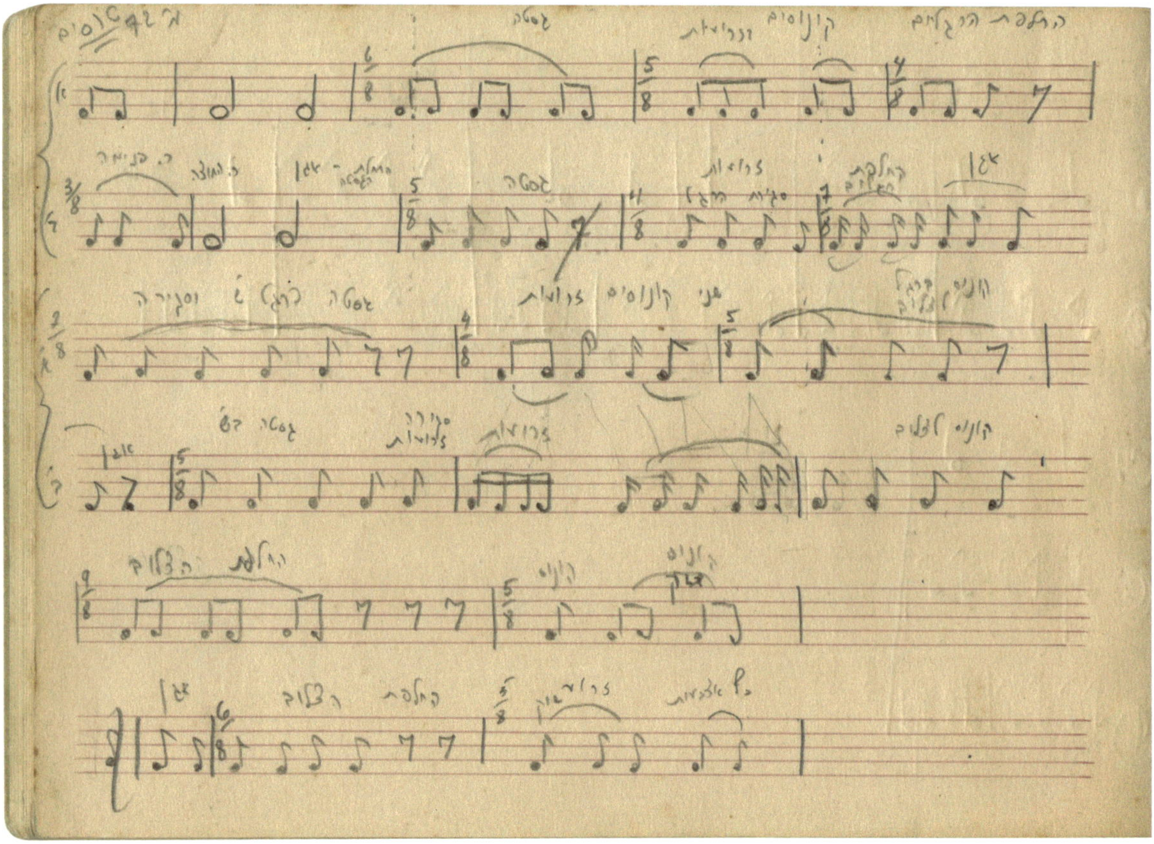

Musical notation for the dance *Peacocks* by Noa Eshkol, with a literal description in Hebrew of the movements, 1952–1958

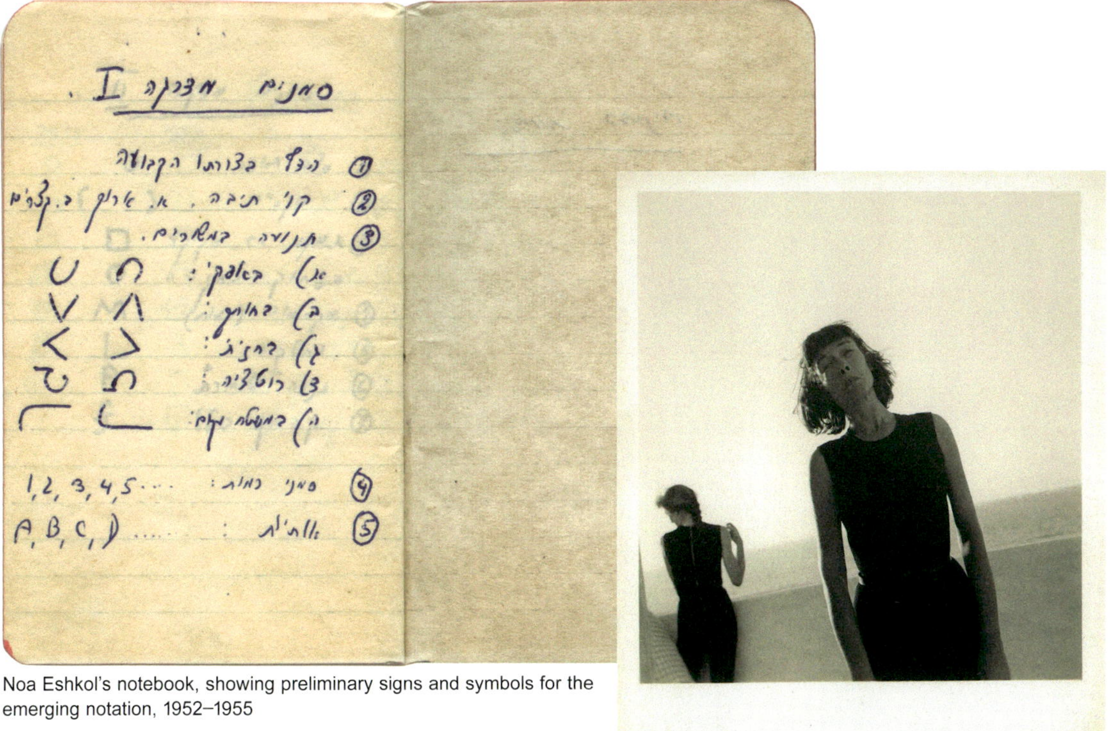

Noa Eshkol's notebook, showing preliminary signs and symbols for the emerging notation, 1952–1955

Chamber Dance, a dance cycle performed by The Chamber Dance Quartet—including Mirele Sharon (facing camera) and Noa Eshkol (facing away)—on the roof of Margot Klausner's house, Tel Aviv, 1955. Photo: unknown

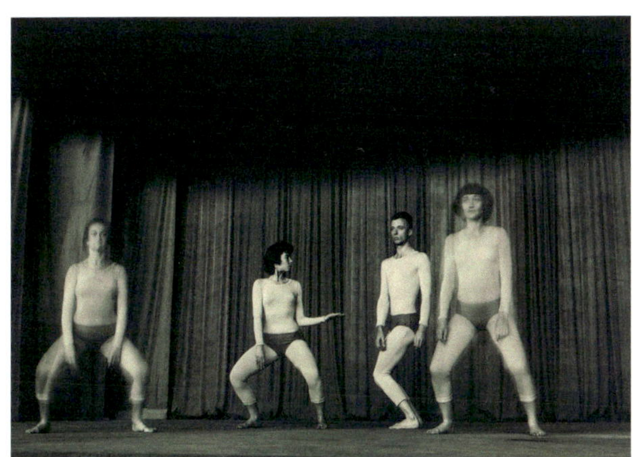

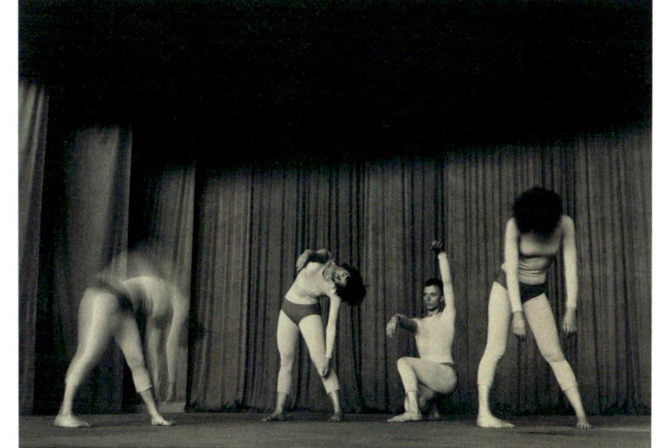

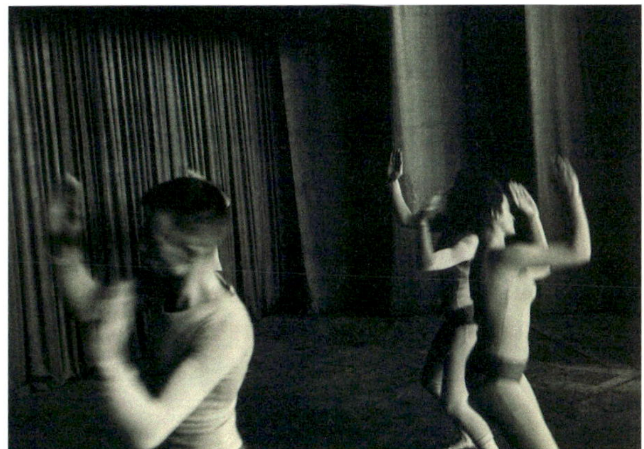

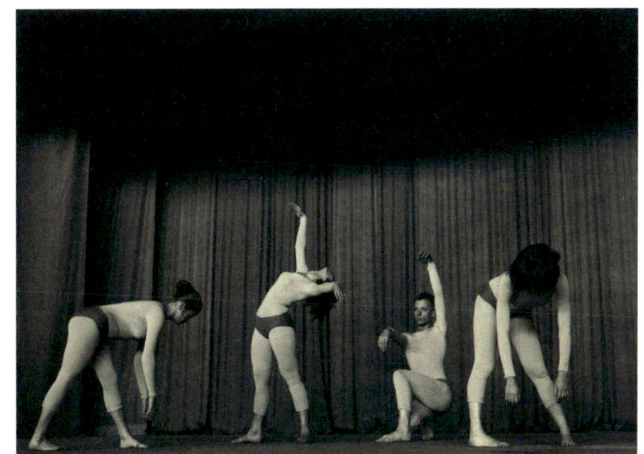

Plagues of Egypt by Abraham Wachmann (top left), *Perpetuum Mobile* by John G Harries (top and bottom right), and *Études* (bottom left), 1954–1956, performed by the Chamber Dance Quartet (Noa Eshkol, John G Harries, Mirela Sharon, Naomi Polani), Ohel Theater, Tel Aviv. Photos: T. Brauner

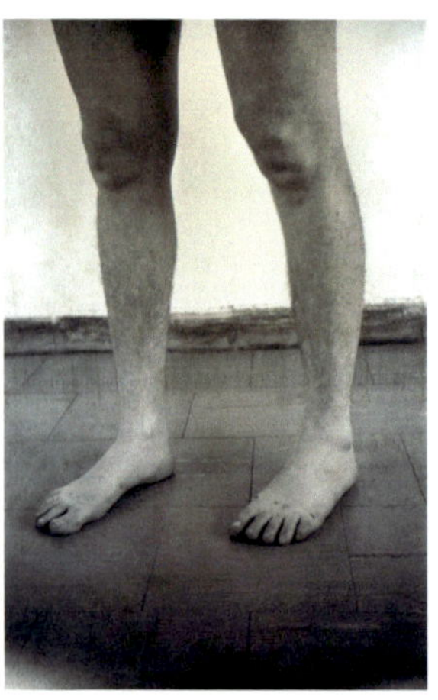
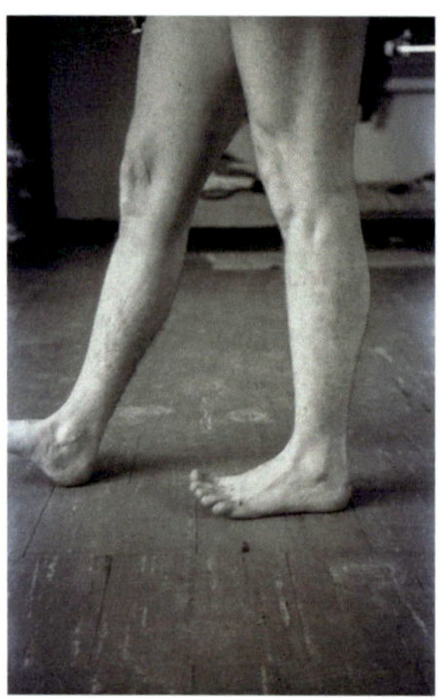
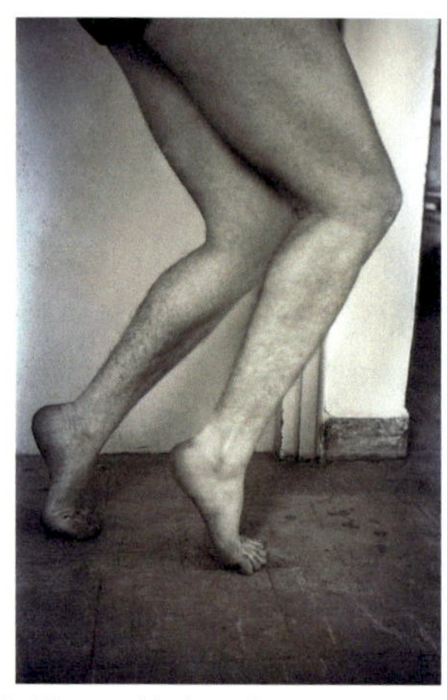
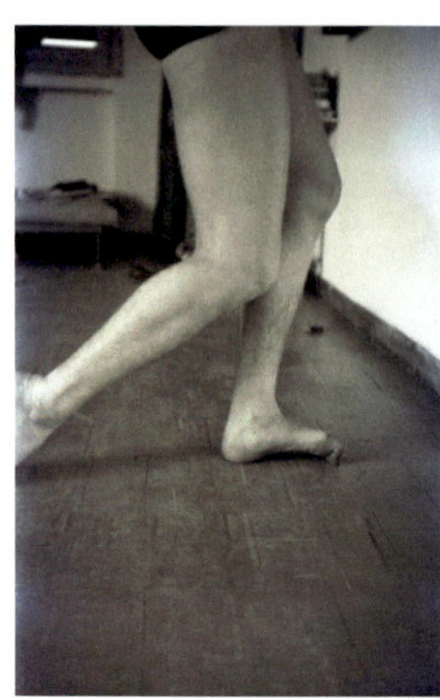

Noa Eshkol demonstrating positions relating to EWMN, Holon, 1948–1952. Photos: Herbert Brün

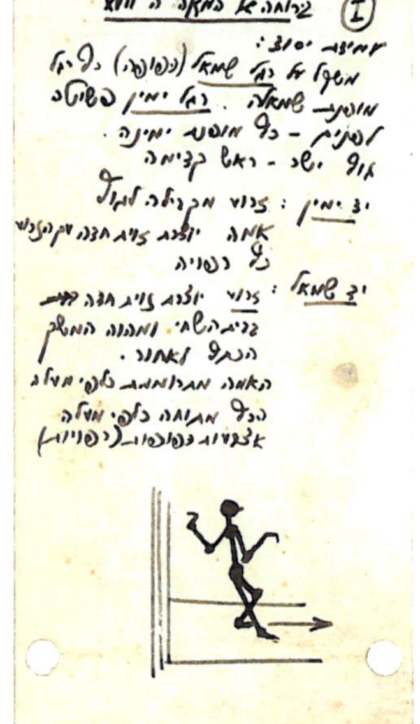
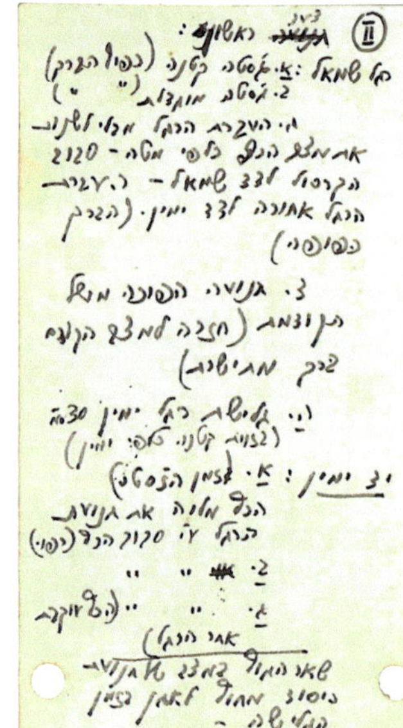
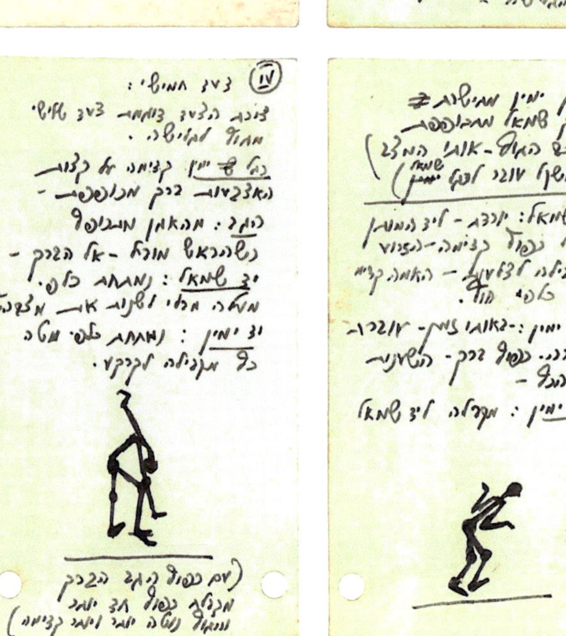
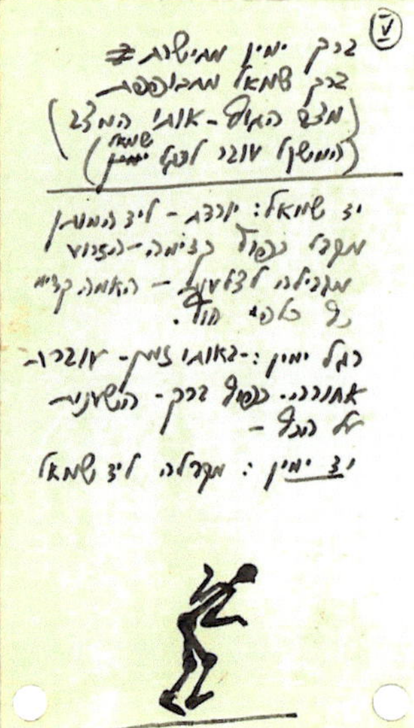
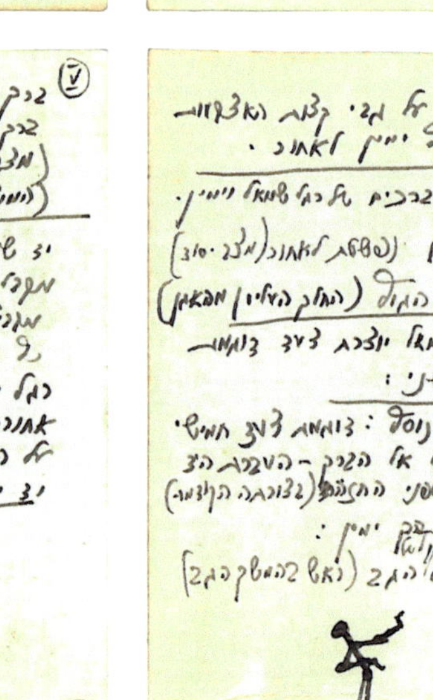
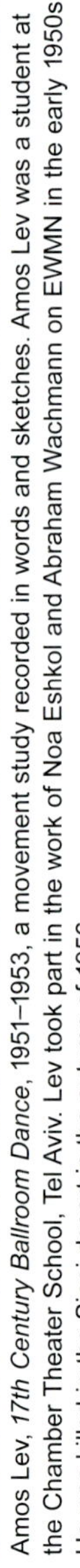

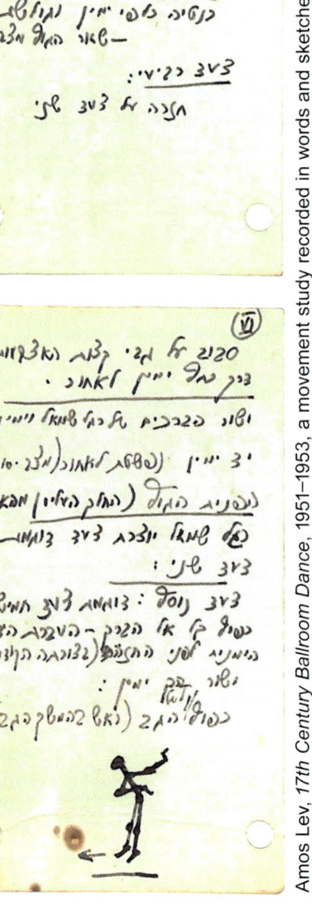

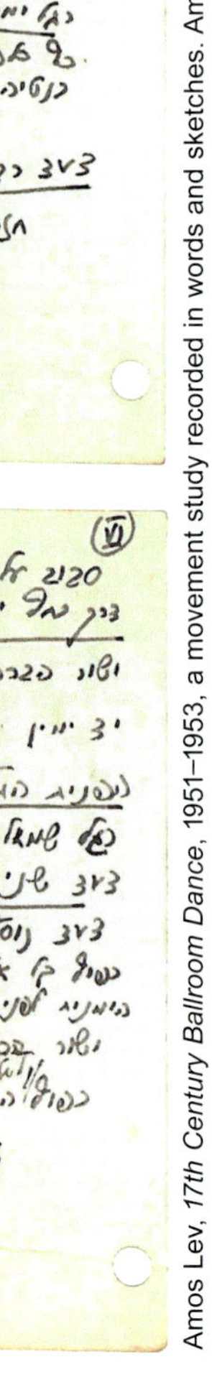

Amos Lev, *17th Century Ballroom Dance*, 1951–1953, a movement study recorded in words and sketches. Amos Lev was a student at the Chamber Theater School, Tel Aviv. Lev took part in the work of Noa Eshkol and Abraham Wachmann on EWMN in the early 1950s. He was killed in the Sinai desert in the autumn of 1956.

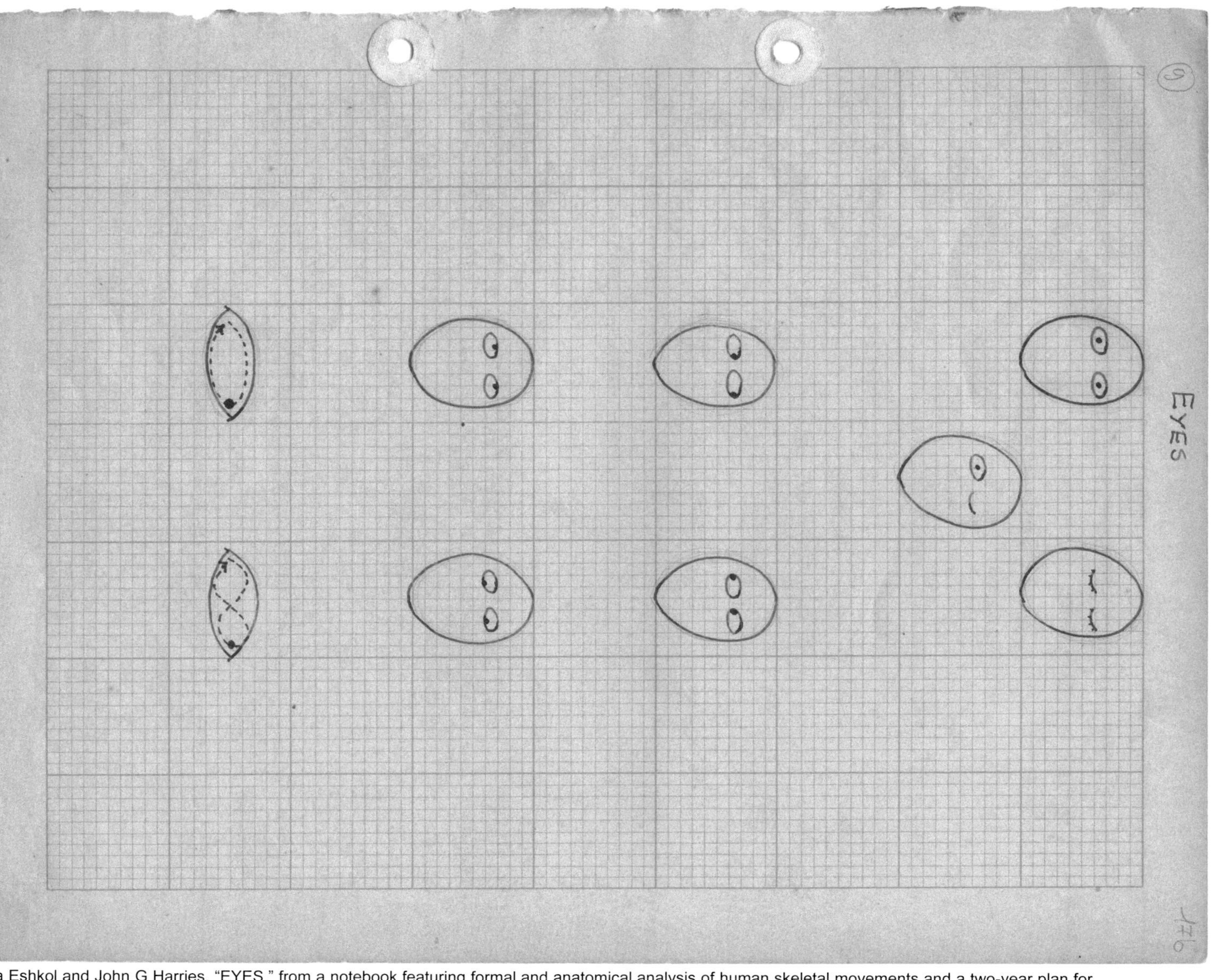

Noa Eshkol and John G Harries, “EYES,” from a notebook featuring formal and anatomical analysis of human skeletal movements and a two-year plan for movement studies, London, 1948–1950

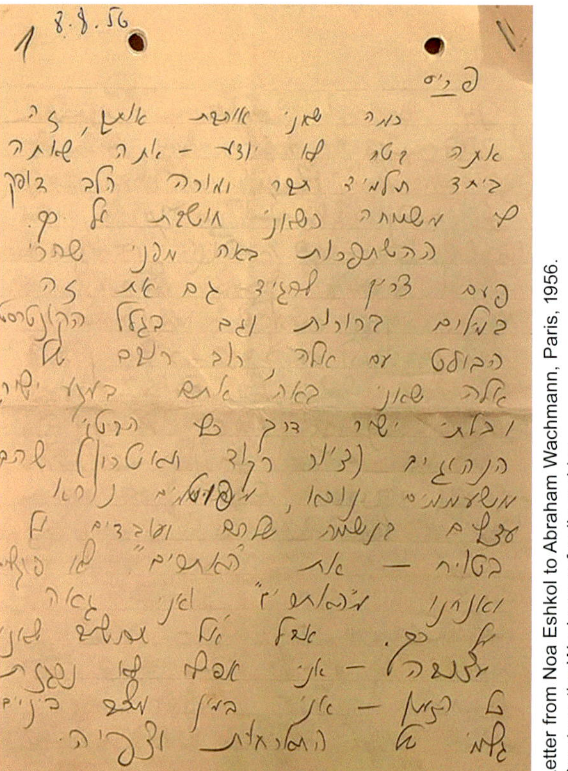

1 8.8.56

פריס

Letter from Noa Eshkol to Abraham Wachmann, Paris, 1956.
Courtesy the Wachmann family archive

Translator's note: The following document was translated on behalf of the Noa Eshkol Archive from a printed Hebrew copy of the original handwritten letter. The personal names appearing here were written in Hebrew letters in the original version, and therefore their transliteration into Latin letters was made by the translator and is not considered accurate. The punctuation was slightly altered. The version below is shortened from the original.

8.8.56
Paris

How much I love you, this you probably don't know—you, who are all together a student, a friend, and a teacher, my heart is beating with joy when I think about it.

This emotionality comes, for there comes a time when one should say this too, in clear words, and also because of the stark contrast with the majority of people with whom I come in direct and indirect contact, through the common means of expression (drawing, dance, theater), who are extremely boring, extremely fattened, lazy in their soul and go for what is safe; the "others" you don't often come across, and we are among "the others" and I am proud of it.

But don't think I'm sad, I am not even irritated all of the time—I am in some raw liminal state of sojourning and expecting.

And in the meantime, all sorts of things are being formed in my brain. It is now already clear to me (and it became clear with the thought of "axes of movement") what needs to be the nature of the next dances for them to serve the notation in a useful way. And the most wonderful thing is that "the relation between the axis of movement to the axis of the limb" and all of my most personal images—which are in part sentimental, memory, memories and literature, and different loves*—are making love between them and indulging one another. I miss you too!

Paris—Germany Darmstadt—Zurich—Paris. It is horrible when I think about the fact that you probably miss travelling and seeing, and I travel and go around in an almost complete indifference—you should know that I have only one thing in mind, and that is the book and the dance—even when I am not writing. When this changes by some magic way, I will write to you. Other than that, you should know that once something happens that will be valuable, I will let you know immediately—you can be assured.

All this occupation of a traveling sales agent, of a kind of commodity like ours, is "not so simple" (like Israel says) for sheer technical reasons; for instance, catching a person in Paris is a matter of some days (at least). One needs to learn about that person, find someone who knows him, try and arrange a meeting, attend the meeting, and hear from him about a number of other people who are much more suitable for a matter like ours and the whole thing starts anew. In addition to that, unfortunately the summer months here, and in any other place in Europe, are months of vacation for everyone who's worth something, and it is a real nasty business.

I am afraid I will have to stay some additional time—and there is no need to say that to provoke an internal spiritual "mental" interest in our business, *this* is almost unimaginable.

I will write to you here a *partial* list of some people I have met so that you can get some clue …

Darmstadt, Germany—especially the works of Herbert, who is an enthusiastic believer and loves the matter.
Pierre Boulez—the most important young French composer …
… Karlheinz Stockhausen (with whom, by the way, I fell in love).
Gottfried Koenig.
Matzke.

These three are young Germans from Cologne in their twenties and thirties who are extremely interesting. They are making electronic music. The last two understood our thing more than all the others I met. They were interested in it—genuinely, loved it, enjoyed it, and asked questions.

In electronic music there's a new notation and I think similar problematics … !!

… Switzerland—Zurich

"International Course for Dance." A collection of crazy people …
… I had met:

Mary Wigman—Germany, Berlin.

Anna Sokolova—America, New York. (Israel) …
… And to conclude,
In fact, I do not want to conclude. I do not want [to] because I cannot, [and] I am at the beginning of the way. One thing has become clear: we need a group here in Europe that can perform and demonstrate and that it would be possible to continue to work with.

…

… Pierre Boulez—promised to organize a performance and a demonstration in one of the most important cultural salons in Paris. He understood and agreed to write. His first question was whether the notation changes the face of the dance—can you imagine!

… My dearest,

I'm rambling on and on. I hope you get some kind of a picture. I really want [you to] write to me a lot—about everything—about you, about the work, about Relik, Degania, Gur, what are your thoughts. Don't pay attention if I am not writing.
… Send warm regards and loves to Dita, Shaya, Zalman (of course Relik), and Nahum, and a lot of special love to you. N.

* Translator's note: The repetition of "memory" and "memories" is found in the original letter in Hebrew.

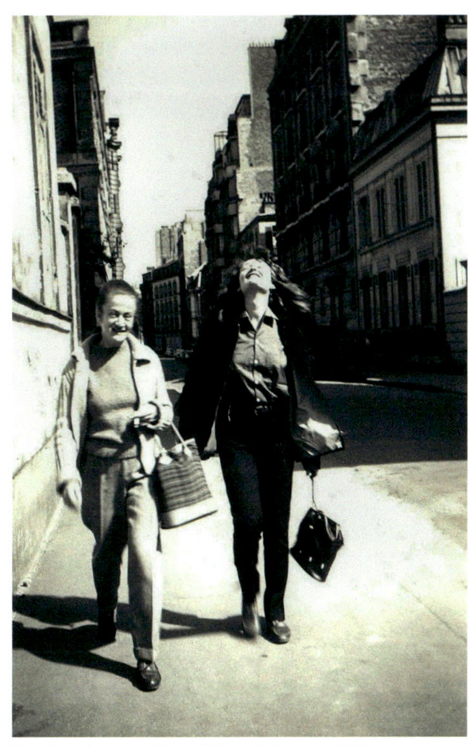

Noa Eshkol and Naomi Polani, Paris, 1956.
Photo: John G Harries

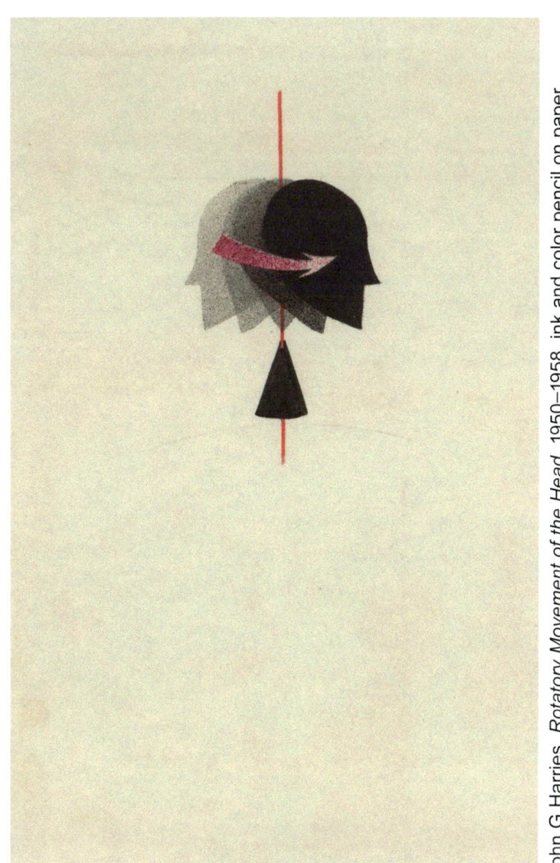

John G Harries, *Rotatory Movement of the Head*, 1950–1958, ink and color pencil on paper

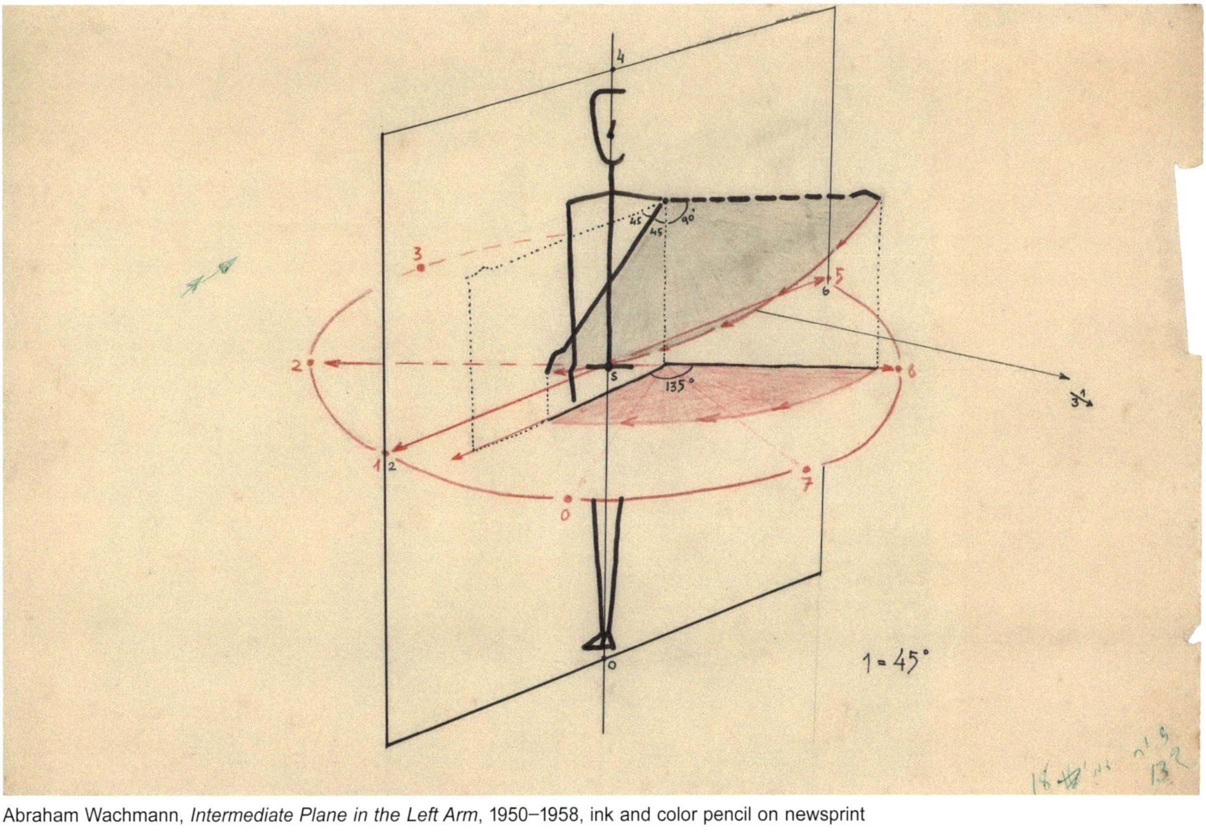

Abraham Wachmann, *Intermediate Plane in the Left Arm*, 1950–1958, ink and color pencil on newsprint

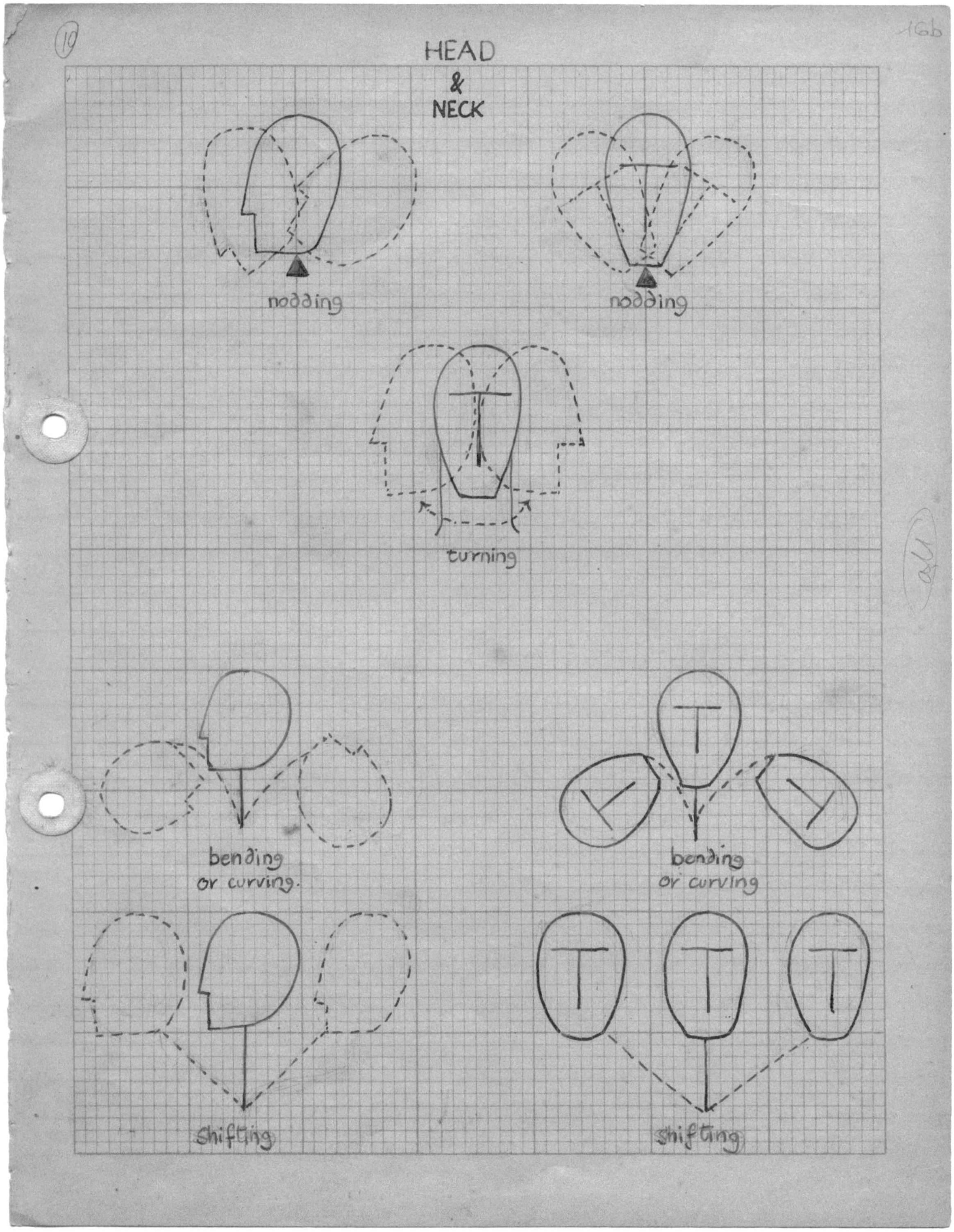

10 16b

HEAD
&
NECK

nodding

nodding

turning

bending
or curving.

bending
or curving

shifting

shifting

Noa Eshkol and John G Harries, "HEAD & NECK," from a notebook featuring formal and anatomical analysis of human skeletal movements and a two-year plan for

Dear Noa,

Have thot about you many times. As a matterof fact I've been waiting to hear from Chasseyah Levey to get your foot size. I want to send you and her each a pair of those Japanese peds that you liked. So let me hear from you.

I am writing to ask you if your notation panphlet has come off the press. I would like to buy several copies. Some one from the dance notation bureau read the report I wrote in the Hadassah News letter and wrote to me asking if I had a copy of it to send her. Do you know that Ann Hutchinsen is in England at the moment? When do you plan to come to thestates?

The news sounds awful and it is such a frustating feeling to be sitting here lapping up our own security and so helpless to change the brutal line of reasoning taken by our state dept.

Please give my love to mutual friends and warmest greetings from me,

Ann Halprin

April 10

FOLD SIDES OVER AND THEN FOLD BOTTOM UP
MOISTEN FLAP WELL AND APPLY PRESSURE TO SEAL
NO OTHER ENVELOPE SHOULD BE USED

Letter from Ann Halprin to Noa Eshkol, 1956

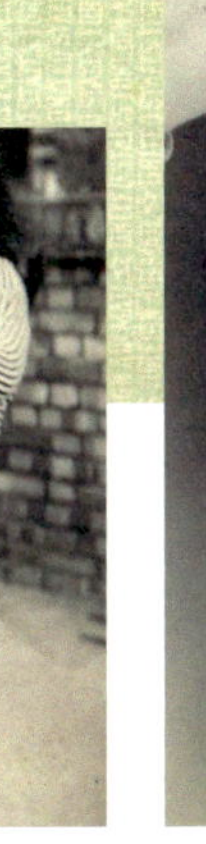

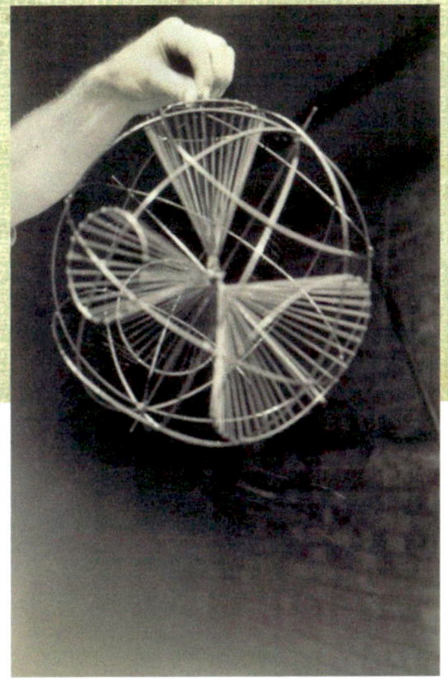

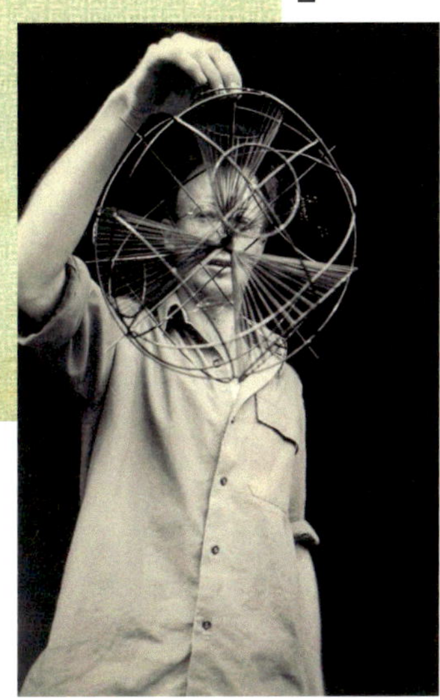

Noa Eshkol and John G Harries with the model of orbits in *The System of Reference*, London, 1956. Photos: Noa Eshkol and John G Harries

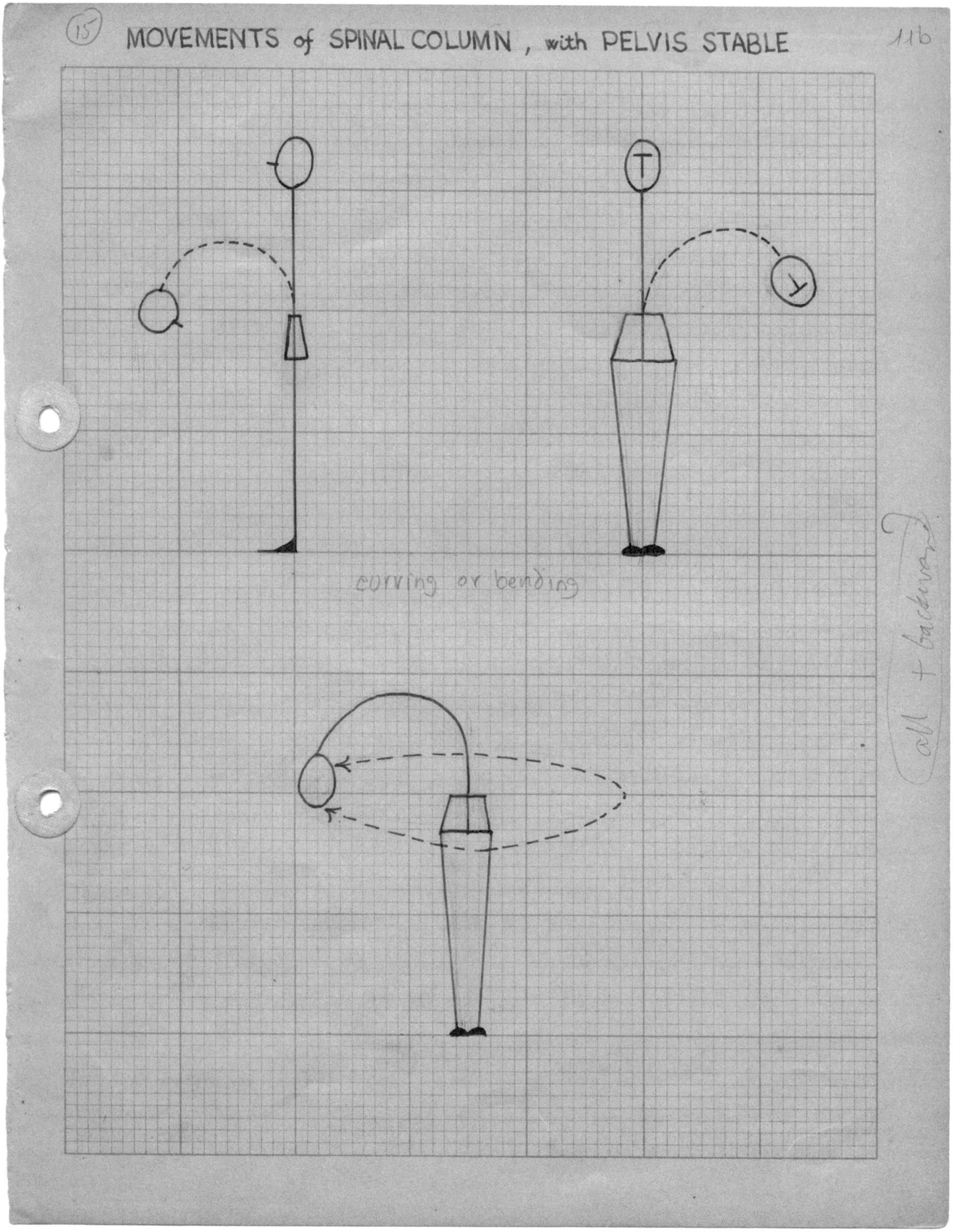

(15) MOVEMENTS of SPINAL COLUMN, with PELVIS STABLE 11b

curving or bending

all + backward

Noa Eshkol and John G Harries, "MOVEMENTS of SPINAL COLUMN, with PELVIS STABLE," from a notebook featuring formal and anatomical analysis of human skeletal

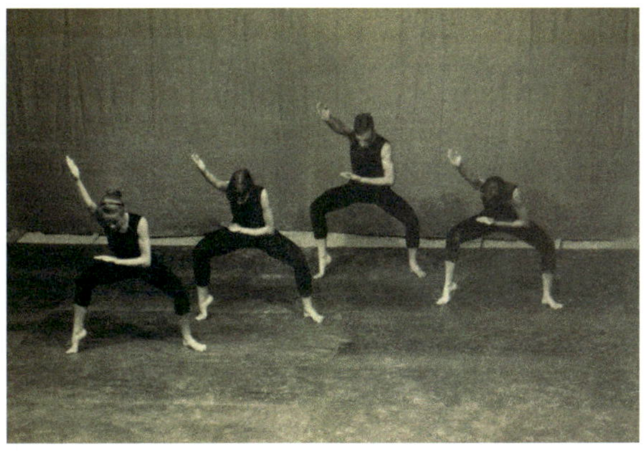

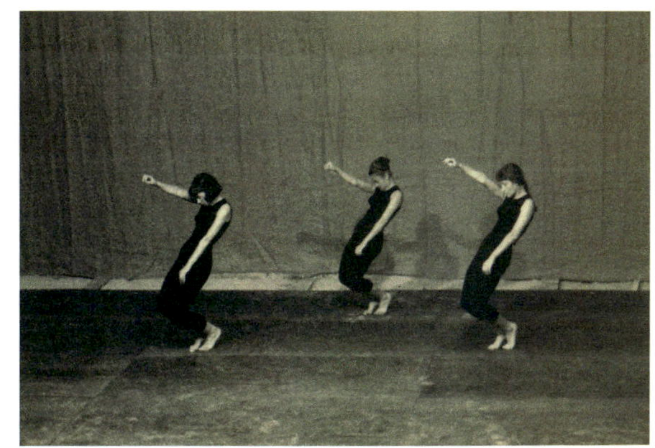

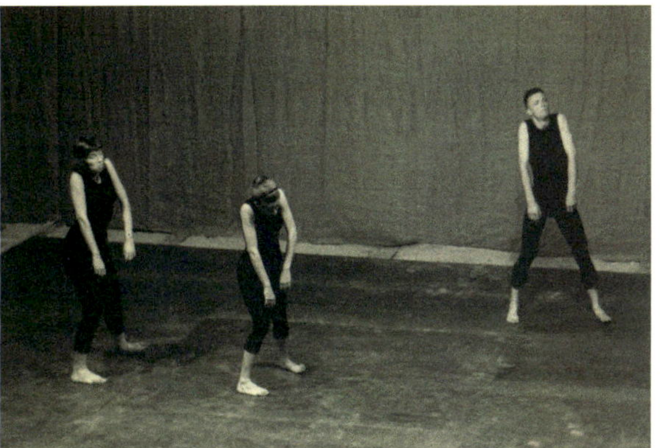

The Chamber Dance Quartet (Noa Eshkol, John G Harries, Mirela Sharon, Naomi Polani), Kibbutz Degania Bet, 1954–1956. Photos: T. Brauner

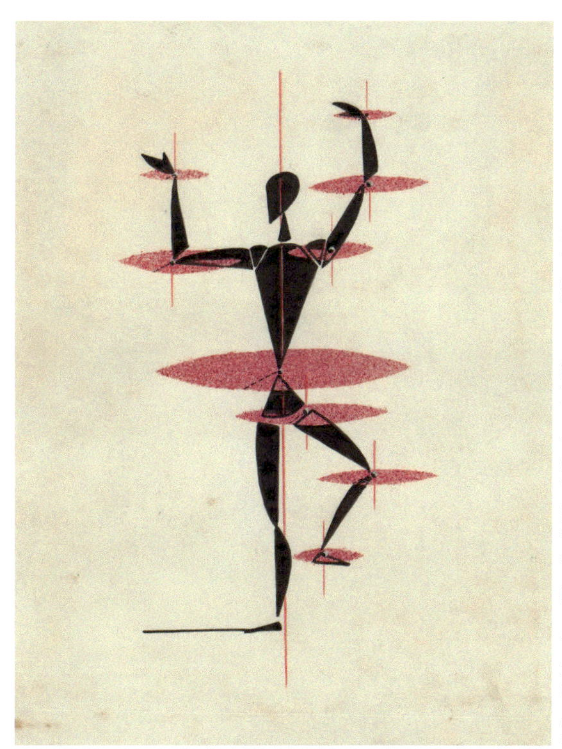

John G Harries, *The Individual Horizontal Planes of Each Moving Limb*, 1950–1958, ink and color pencil on newsprint

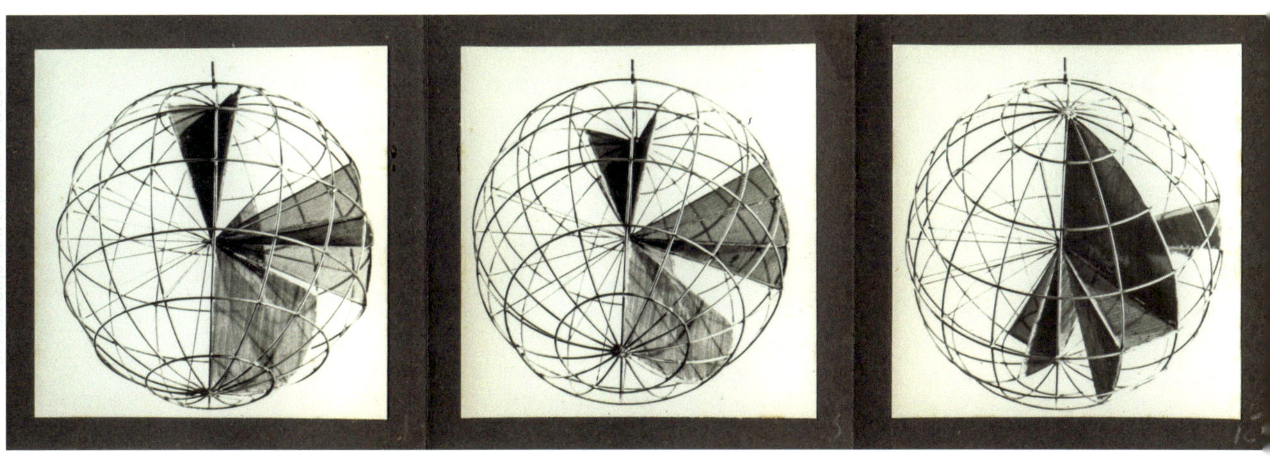

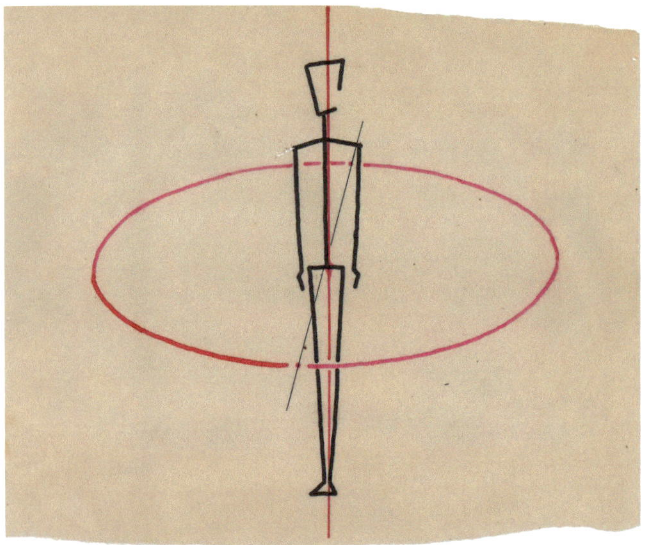

Abraham Wachmann, *The Horizontal Plane*, 1950–1958, ink on parchment

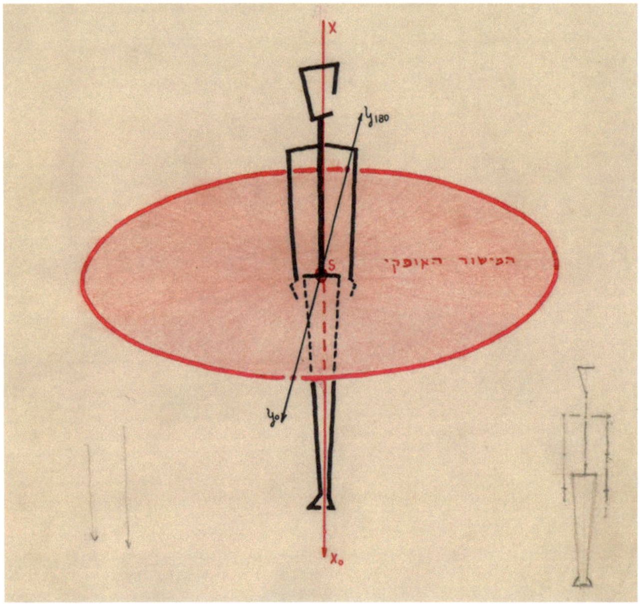

Abraham Wachmann, *The Horizontal Plane*, 1950–1958, ink and color pencil on parchment

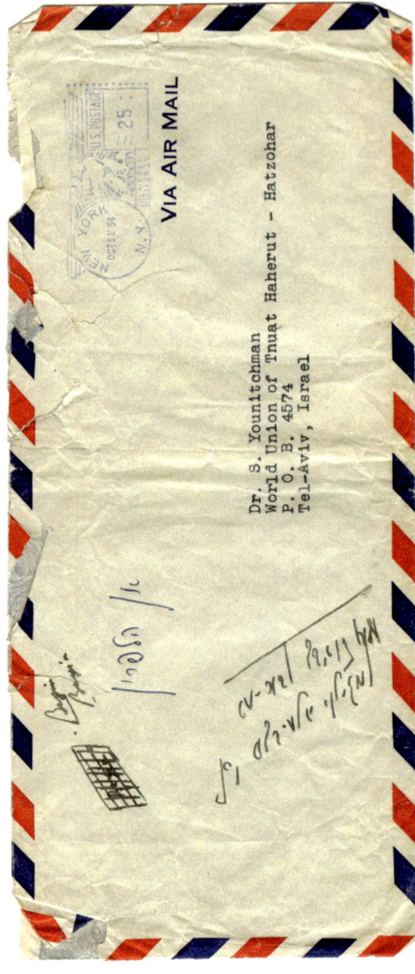

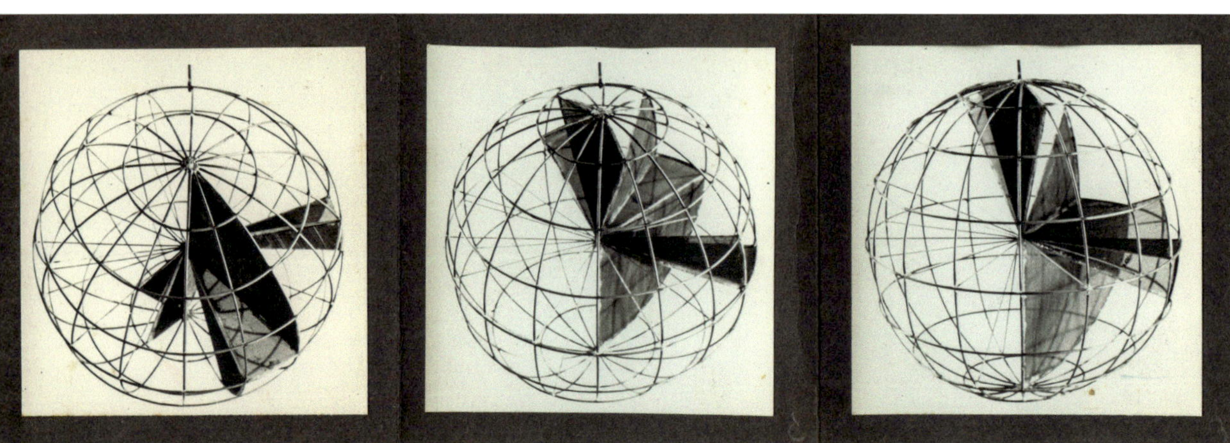

Pages from a fold-out book showing the model of orbits in *The System of Reference*, Holon, 1960. Design: Amos Hetz. Photos: Netta Harries

הסוכנות היהודית לארץ ישראל
THE JEWISH AGENCY FOR PALESTINE
16 EAST 66TH STREET, NEW YORK 21, N. Y.

TRAFALGAR 9-1300

Cable Address JEVAGENCY

October 11, 1954

Dr. S. Younitchman
World Union of Tnuat Haherut - Hatzohar
P. O. B. 4574
Tel-Aviv, Israel

Dear Dr. Younitchman:

I have been in contact with several well known dance authorities in this country to whom I have shown Miss Eshkol's letter about dance notation.

The enclosed copy of a letter which I have received from one of these authorities gives a specific suggestion which I believe Miss Eshkol might be wise to pursue. Will you be kind enough to forward the letter to Miss Eshkol?

Best wishes for a very happy New Year.

Sincerely yours,
Rose L. Halprin
Rose L. Halprin

RLH:DHT
Enc

COPY

HALPRIN-LATHROP DANCE SCHOOL
1831 Union Street
San Francisco 23

September 15, 1954

Dear Mrs. Halprin:

Ann has referred your letter of August 30th to me.

Since I have worked with Labanotation for several years I am of course prejudiced in its favor. It is good to know, however, that there is someone in Israel who is taking an interest with still a different notation. Any ultimate method will of course be a result of the vast amount of work and many points-of-view which are now in the process of developing.

I believe that Miss Eshkol should prepare a preliminary paper, describing the basic symbols, how they are used and in some way, show their application to various styles of dance movement. This should not require a complete book. If, for instance, she could present a page of writing which would describe a simple movement phrase in ballet, a similar one in folk style and something comparable in modern dance, this accompanied by a simple explanation of the fundamentals of the method, it would be possible to judge somewhat the extent of her research. The paper should be sent to educators and dancers everywhere in order to get reactions and to stimulate interest.

The textbook "Labanotation" which has been published in this country recently is the result of fifty years of research by Laban himself, fifteen years of work by Ann Hutchinson, the author of "Labanotation", and seven years of work on preparing the book itself. This textbook will no doubt go through many revisions.

I would not pretend to judge an entire notation system by the above suggested sample but of course, without some visual proof of its workability, it would be unwise to make any commitment.

My very best regards.

Sincerely,

(signed)

Welland Lathrop

Letter from the Jewish Agency for Palestine related to the release of the first book, *Movement Notation*, New York, 1954

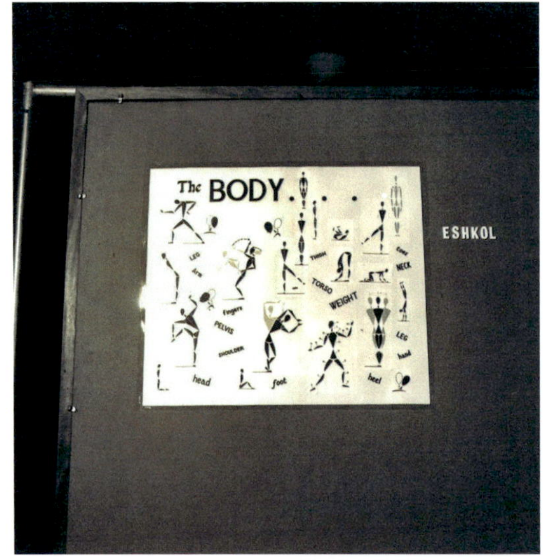

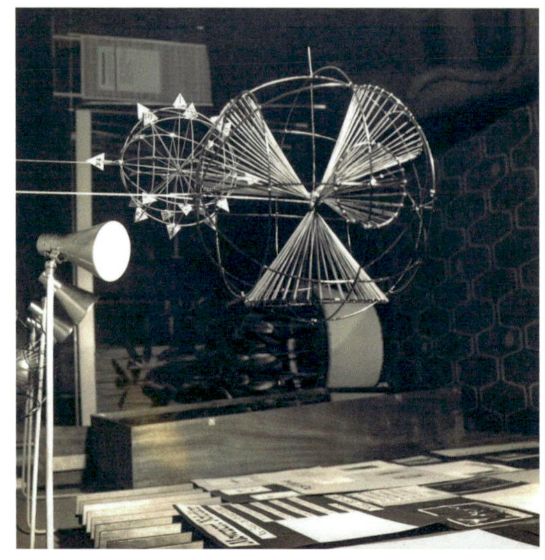

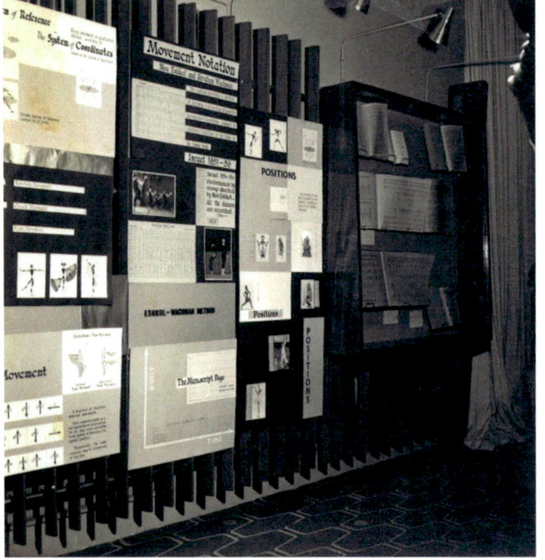

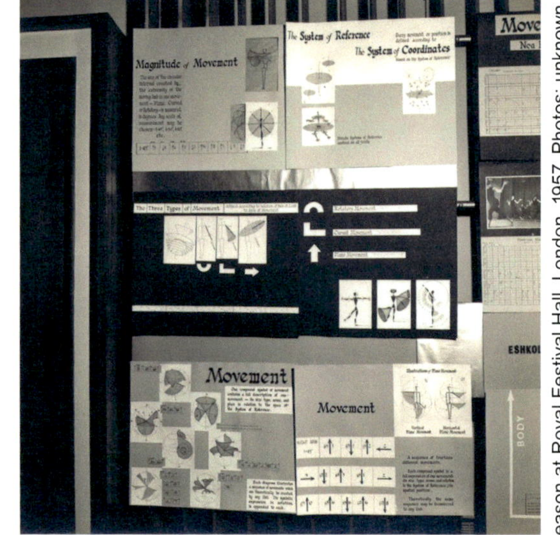

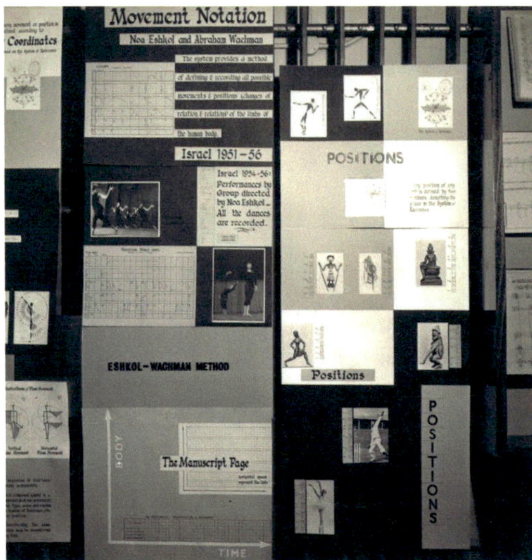

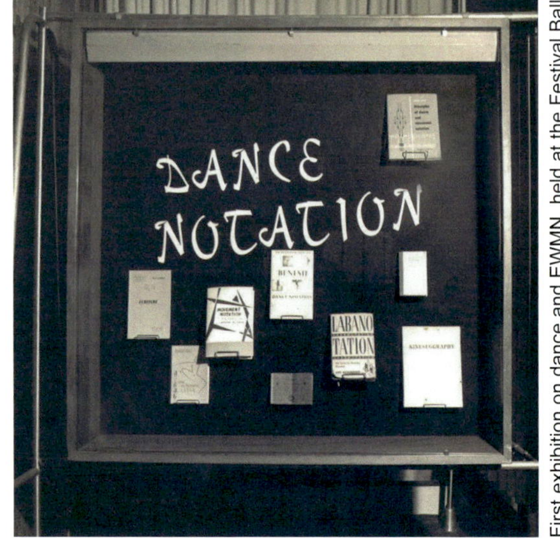

First exhibition on dance and EWMN, held at the Festival Ballet Season at Royal Festival Hall, London, 1957. Photos: unknown

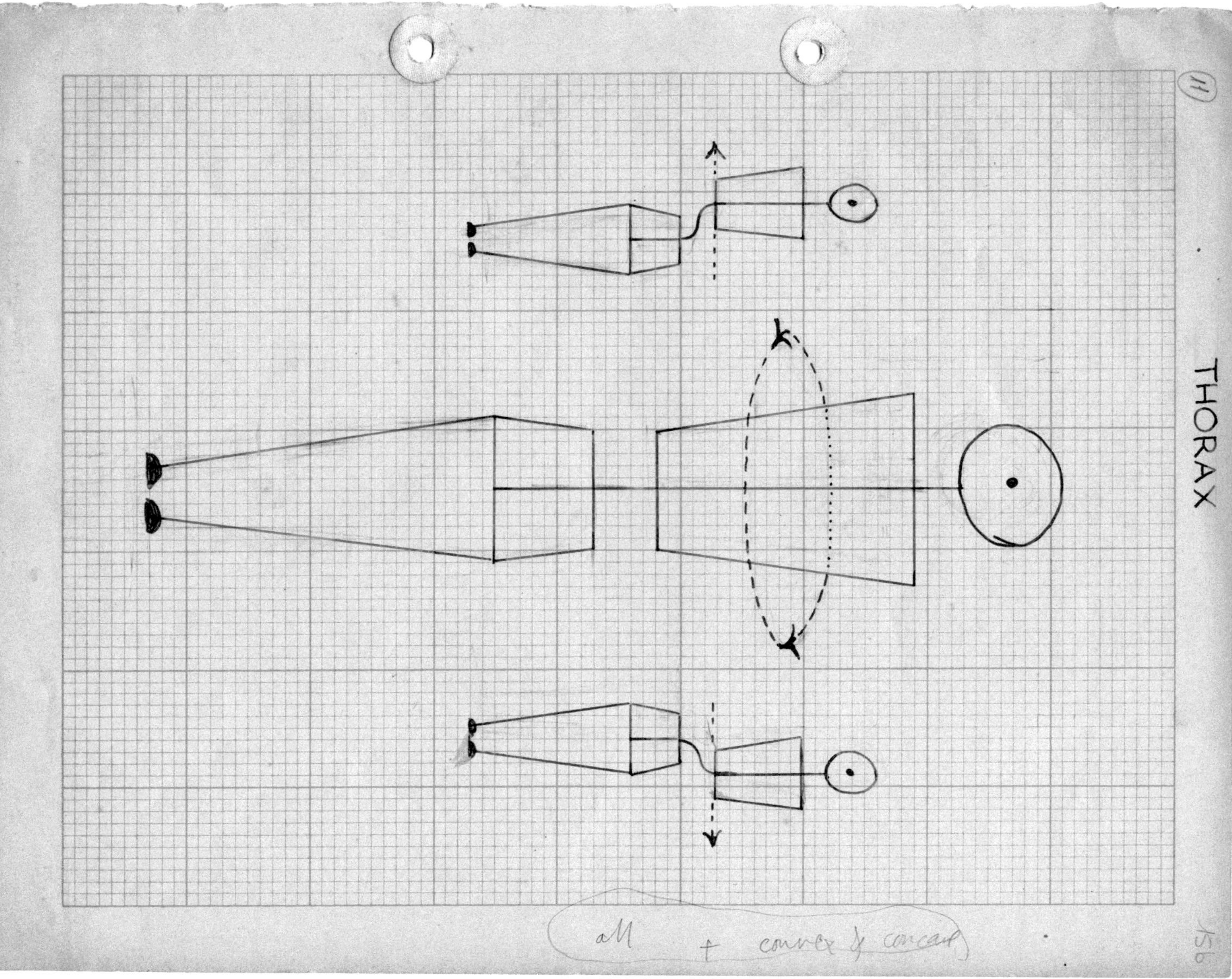

Noa Eshkol and John G Harries, “THORAX,” from a notebook featuring formal and anatomical analysis of human skeletal movements and a two-year plan for movement studies, London, 1948–1950

Abraham Wachmann, *The Influence of a Simultaneous Movement on the Change of Position of a "Light" Limb in Relation to The System of Reference*, 1950–1958, ink and collage on parchment

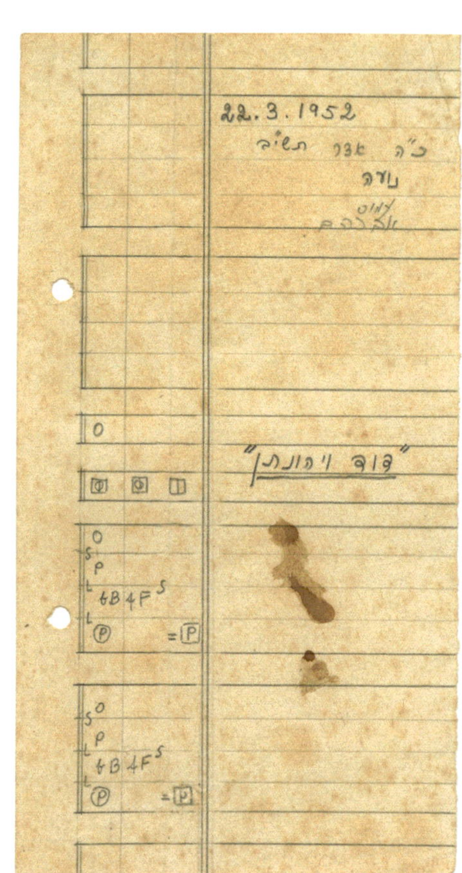

Abraham Wachmann, *David and Jonathan (Duet)*, 1952–1953, movement score notated using early movement notation signs and symbols, Tel Aviv

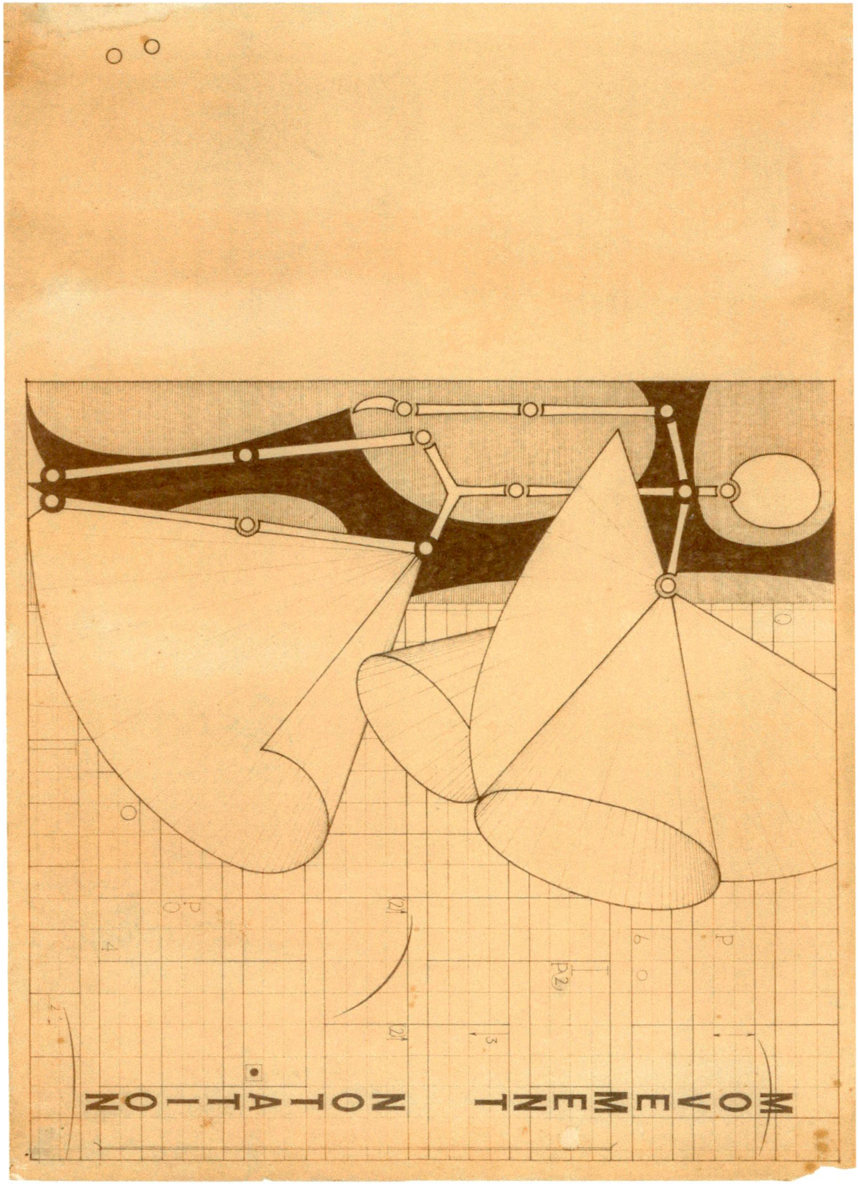

Abraham Wachmann, poster for *Movement Notation*, 1950–1960

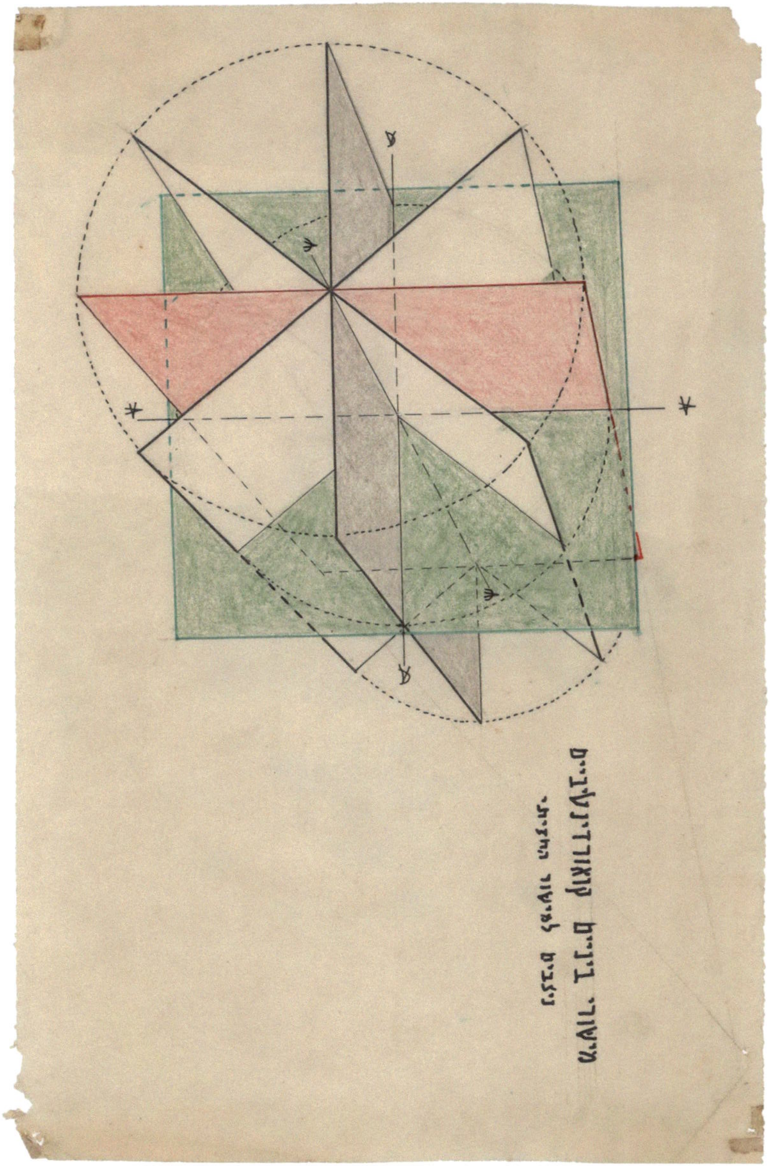

Abraham Wachmann, *Intermediate Coordinate Planes (Perpendicular to The Horizontal Plane)*, 1950–1958, ink and pencil crayon on parchment

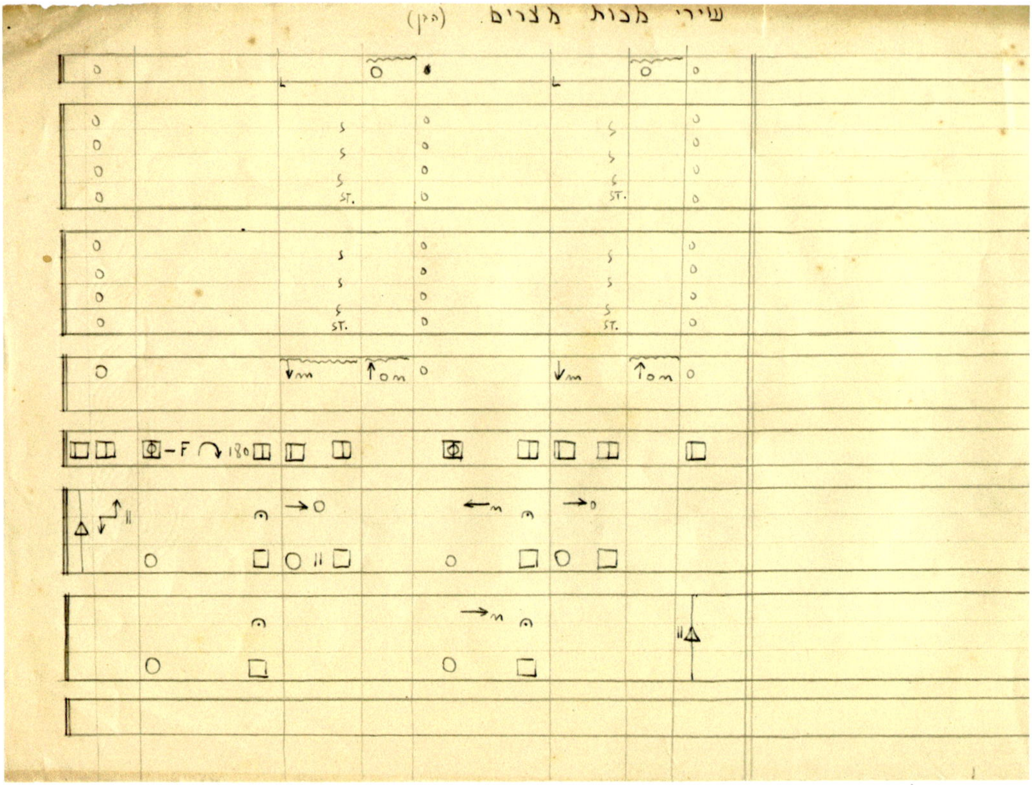

Abraham Wachmann, *Egyptian Plagues*, 1952–1953, movement score notated using early movement notation signs and symbols, Tel Aviv

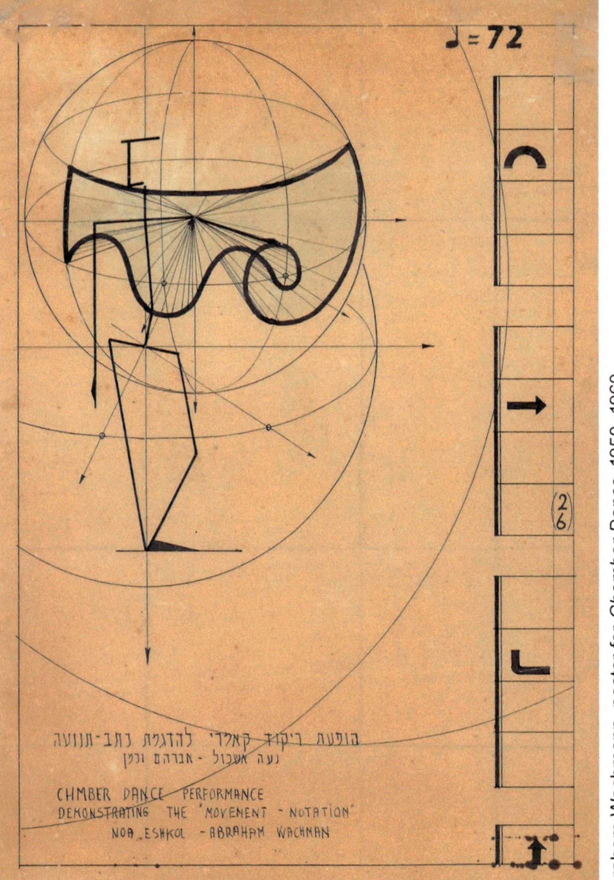

Abraham Wachmann, poster for *Chamber Dance*, 1950–1960

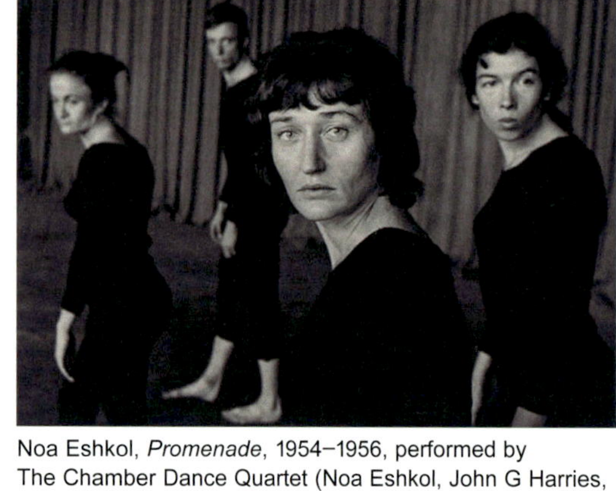

Noa Eshkol, *Promenade*, 1954–1956, performed by The Chamber Dance Quartet (Noa Eshkol, John G Harries, Mirela Sharon, Naomi Polani), Ohel Theater, Tel Aviv. Photo: T. Brauner

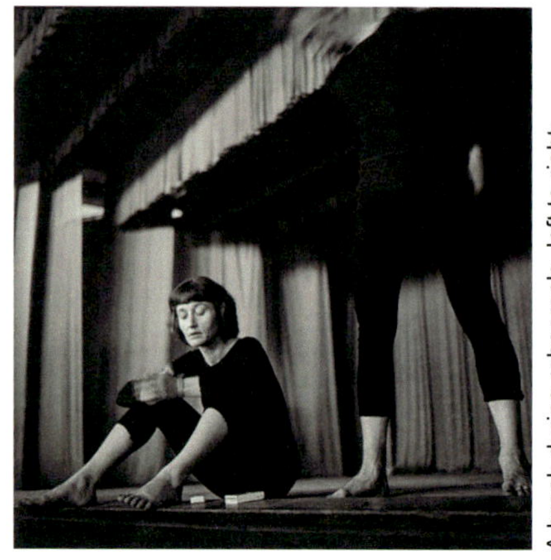

A break during rehearsals, left to right: Noa Eshkol, John G Harries, Photo: T. Brauner

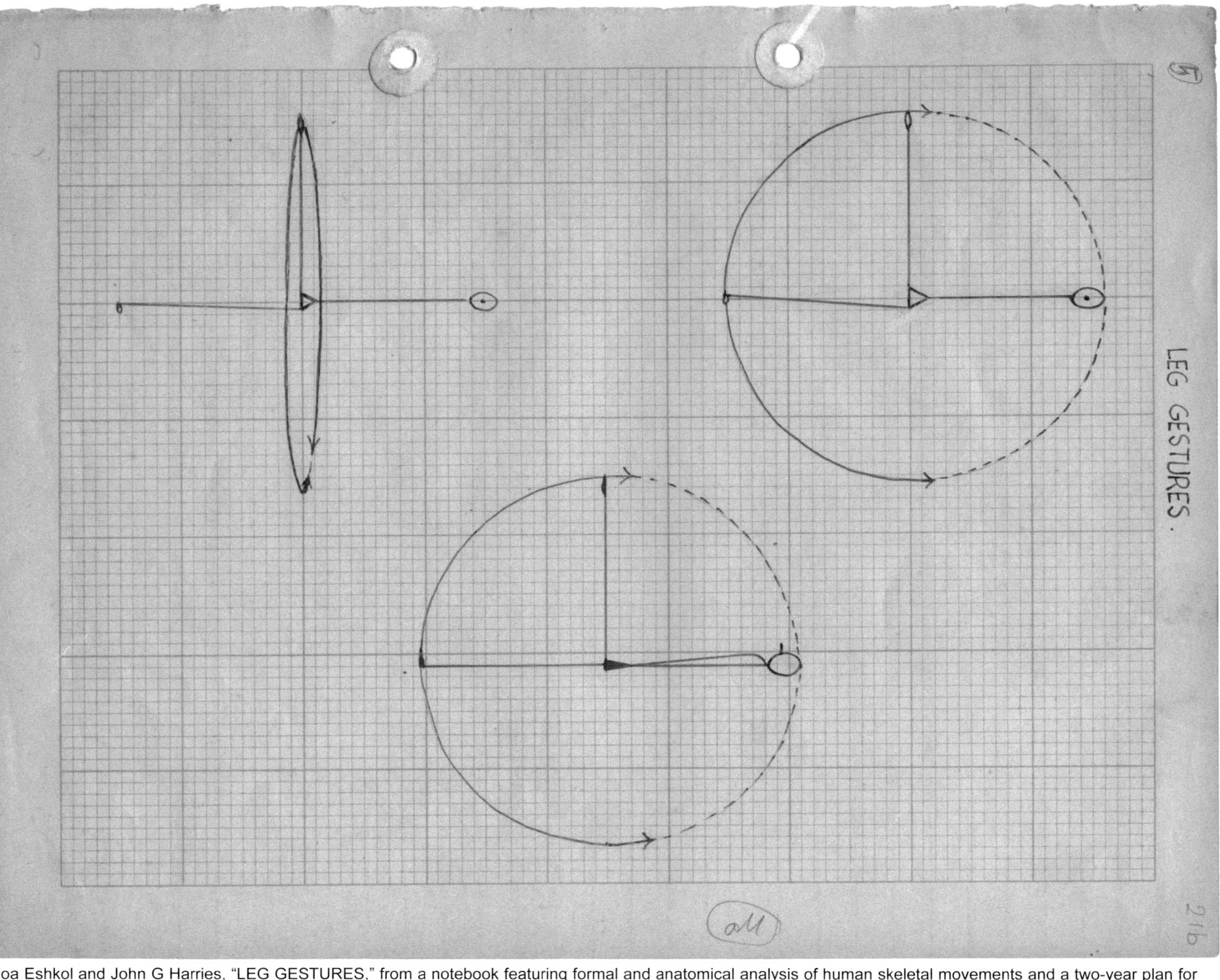

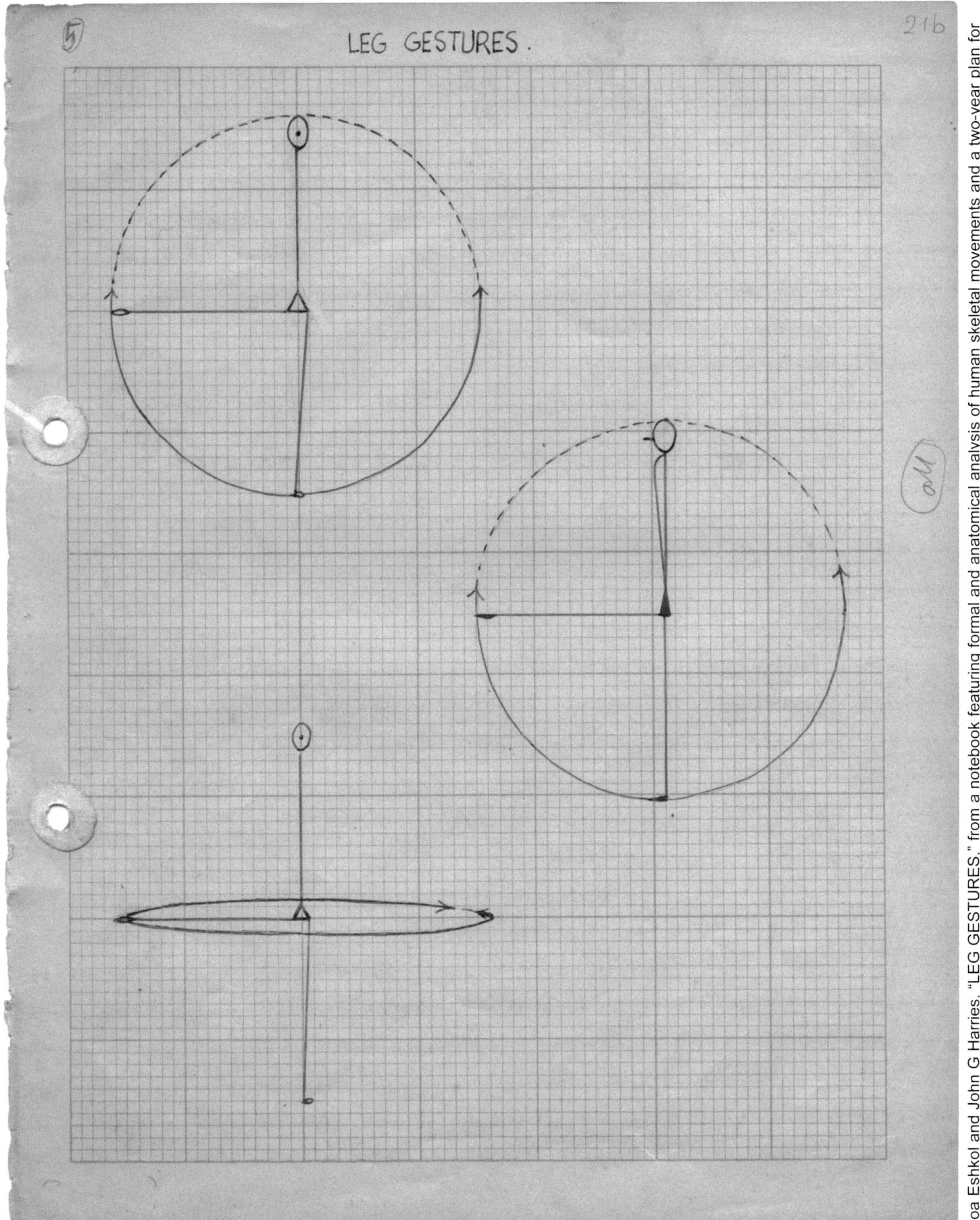

Noa Eshkol and John G Harries, “LEG GESTURES,” from a notebook featuring formal and anatomical analysis of human skeletal movements and a two-year plan for movement studies, London, 1948–1950

Shalheveth Freier
Ambassade d'Israel
143. Ave De Wagram
Paris, 17 ème

5. 10. 56.

Paris, 5.

Dear Mr. Delahaye ,

attached is the explanatory note on the movement notation of Noa Eshkol in as simple language as I could make it, with her guidance.

Before you send it out ,however,,to the various journals for reactions, I should draw your attention a little to the character and past history of this notation, so that you might form an idea of whom to enquire and what replies to expect.

The notation uses symbols on a ruled page to express every possible movement of the body, be it physical exercise or dance, much as do the notes in a musical score or letters ina book. Like these , the script is technical and there are no symbols for any of the multitude of emotional, muscular and other qualities which a composer past or cotemporary might care to attribute to a dance. The notation just tells you how to move and any additional significance a composer wishes to attach to the dance , he must write down verbally, as you put a"crescendo" or "piano" etc. in music.

A panel of professors of mathematics and the sciences of the Hebrew University and the Weizman Institute of Science as well as composers of music and dancers witnessed a demonstration of thi s notation by Noa Eshkol and her group. The mathematicians and the composers of music were of one mind, that this notation was both as concise as possible and at the same time visually suggestive. Those dancers who had an interest in writing down compositions and exact performance were similarly enthusiastic. Other dancers ,however, who rely on permanent improvisation and inspiration at any required moment felt they could do without this notation or any other.

It is necessary for you to know this in order to appreciate possible reactions. Whoever feels that intelligence must not encroach upon dance as it has on music and that dance is a set number of inspired movementsc clothed each time in a different costume, stage , and musical accompaniment, will not wish to bother with a general notation. Someone, however, who will explore the fulness of movement which becomes apparent through this notation, will wish for exactitude in performance and a means of composition which can be understood everywhere once the notation has bee n learned, will probably be much in favour.

To a layman like myself ,it seems that of all artists, dancers are the least inclined to admit alittle clear thinking into their art and that you will have no unequivocal response.

Above and opposite: Pages from a letter by Shalheveth Freier related to the promotion of the first edition of *Movement Notation*, Paris, 1956

A Movement Notation

Miss Noa Eshkol and Mr. Avraham Wachmann of Israel have invented a notation which allows any movement of the human body or any combination of movements to be written down.

It was the intention of the authors to devise a notation which could,depict all possible movement, use as few symbols as possible for this purpose,and yet choose the symbols in such manner as would allow the eyetto obtain a visual suggestion upof the intended movement,,upon reading the score. The notation, moreover , only tells you how to move and does not assign any particular quality, like "internal-external", "contraction -release" etc., to any movement sequence.

A general notation must be free from all stylistic preferences and interpretations which are a matter for the composer. There is ,in this sense, a striking resemblance between the proposed score for movement and a music score which by its very generality has served for the writing of all music hitherto composed.

The movement notation is written down on a ruled page. From bottom to top , the movable parts of the body are listed , and from [illegible] left to right , the page is divided into units of time whose length is indicated at the beginning of the composition

There are three principal types of movement into which each composite movement can be resolved.

a) movement about the longitudinal axis of a limb, indicated by the symbol ⌒

b) movement of a limb on a straight plane, indicated by the symbol ↑

c) movement of a limb on a curved surface, indicated by the symbol └

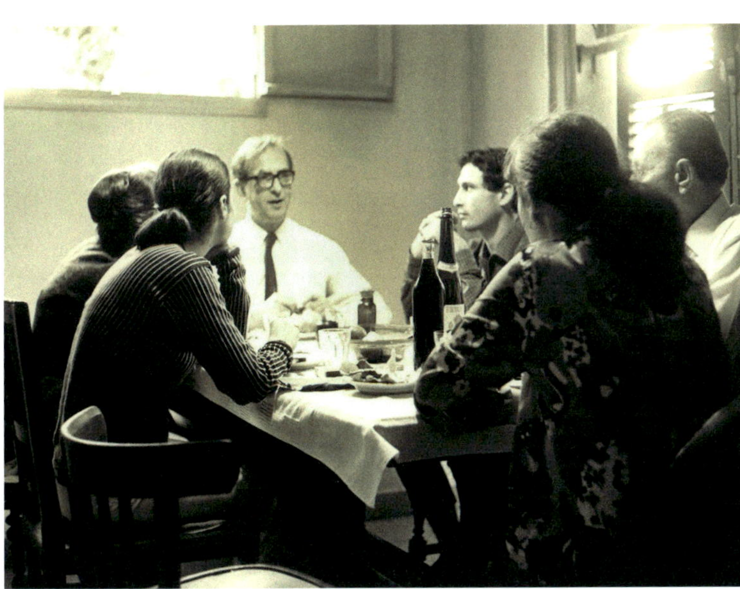

Photograph showing Noa Eshkol, Shmulik Seidel, Shalheveth Freier, and others, with note on verso: "Around the table in the back room—Leisure and Hospitality," 1969. Photo: unknown

25 (25) 16

30 weeks of movement lessons

1 Walking
2 Head movements
3 Walking & head movement & head positions
4 Walking & jumping
5 Jumping & head positions & head movements
6 Walking & turning
7 Turns & head positions & head movements
8 Symmetrical & asymmetrical arms movements.
9 Symmetrical & asymmetrical positions & movements with Head positions & movements
10. Symmetrical & asymmetrical arms positions & movements in walking & turning.
11 Symmetrical & asymmetrical arm positions & movements in jumping
12 Symmetrical & asymmetrical arms positions & movements with head positions & movements in walking.
13 Symmetrical & asymmetrical arms positions & movements with head positions & movents in turning and jumping.
14 Hands movement
15 Torso movement
16 Pelvis movement
17 Torso and pelvis movements
18. Torso and pelvis positions in walking - turning & jumping
19 Torso and pelvis movements in walking - turning & jumping
20. Torso and pelvis movements with symmetrical and asymmetrical

Noa Eshkol and John G Harries, "30 weeks of movement lessons," from a notebook featuring formal and anatomical analysis of human skeletal movements and a two-year plan for movement studies, London, 1948–1950

Our Ref.: SF/SA.-495

Paris, 18th December 1956

Mr. KARAM
Division of Relations with
Member States and National Commissions
U.N.E.S.C.O.
19, Avenue Kléber
P a r i s 16e

Dear Mr. Karam,

attached please find a copy of Noa Eshkol's suggested book on a notation for movement and dance, as well as the relevant drawings, a copy of the appreciations of her system by Miss An Hutchinson, President of the DANCE NOTATION BUREAU in the U.S.A. and by Mr. Haythorne, Chairman of the BRITISH DANCE NOTATION SOCIETY, as well as a brief note on the system.

I should also add, that from the literary point of view the book might require some editing, but I understand that it is on the merits of the system that a decision will be taken, primarily.

I have advised the Director General of the Israel Ministry of Education and Culture that I have brought the book to your attention, in order that it might be possible to arrange a meeting between the UNESCO experts and Miss Eshkol, while she is still in Paris, until the end of December, and have asked him to submit a proposal to UNESCO on behalf of his Ministry. From previous correspondence I have reason to believe that he is favorably disposed.

Thanking you once more for your friendly attention, I am

Yours faithfully,

Shalheveth Freier
Scientific Councillor

Letter from Shalheveth Freier to the Division of Relations with Member States and National Commissions, UNESCO, related to the publication of the first edition of *Movement Notation*, Paris, 1956

FIRST YEAR: Movement for the sake of the Body

	1ST. TERM	2ND. TERM	3RD. TERM
1ST. MONTH	Beginning of term:- Students' composition on their approach to Dance.	1st. Week (6 days): see table below; 2nd. Week, 3rd. Week, 4th. Week as 1st. Week	
2ND. MONTH			
3RD. MONTH			End of term:- Students' composition on their approach to Dance.

GYMNASTICS, LIGHT ATHLETICS, JUDO, ETC.

2ND. AND 3RD. MONTHS: SAME AS THE FIRST

3RD. TERM: SAME AS 2ND. TERM

1st. Week (6 days):

1	2	3
Gym. / History	Gym. / Physiology	Gym. / History

4	5	6
Gym. / Physiology	Gym. / History	Students' Compositions / Summary of Phys. & Hist.

2nd. Week, 3rd. Week, 4th. Week } as 1st. Week

SECOND YEAR: The Body for the sake of Movement

	1ST. TERM	2ND. TERM	3RD. TERM
1st. MONTH	1st. Week (6 days): see table below; 2nd. Week, 3rd. Week, 4th. Week as 1st. Week		
2nd. Month			
3rd. MONTH			1st. Week (6 days): see table below; 2nd. Week, 3rd. Week, 4th. Week as 1st. Week; Students' essay on their approach to Dance

2ND. & 3RD. MONTHS: SAME AS THE FIRST

2ND. TERM SAME AS 1ST. TERM

+ LESSON?

1ST. AND 2ND. MONTHS: SAME AS FOR 1ST. TERM

1st. Week (6 days) (1st. Term):

1	2	3
Anatomy with Gym. / Dance	History of Art / Dance	History of Music / Dance

4	5	6
History of Art / Dance	History of Dance Styles / Dance	Summary / Task

2nd. Week, 3rd. Week, 4th. Week } as 1st. Week.

1st. Week (6 days) (3rd. Term, 3rd. Month):

1	2	3
Dance	Dance	Dance
Compositions on History & Anatomy, & Dance Compositions		

4	5	6
Dance	Dance	Dance
Compositions on History & Anatomy, & Dance Compositions		

2nd. Week, 3rd. Week, 4th. Week } as 1st. Week

Students' essay on their approach to Dance

(178)

Noa Eshkol and John G Harries, “FIRST YEAR: Movement for the sake of the Body, SECOND YEAR: The Body for the sake of Movement,” a two-year plan for movement studies from a notebook featuring formal and anatomical analysis of human skeletal movements, London, 1948–1950

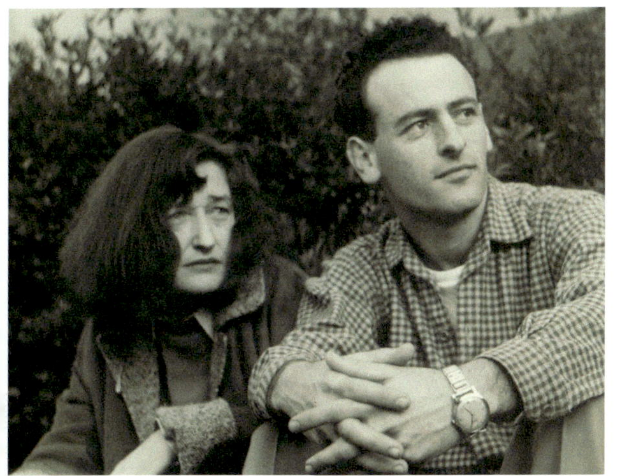
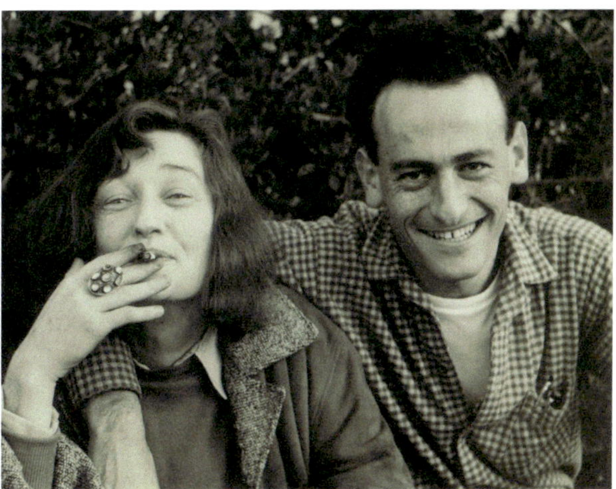
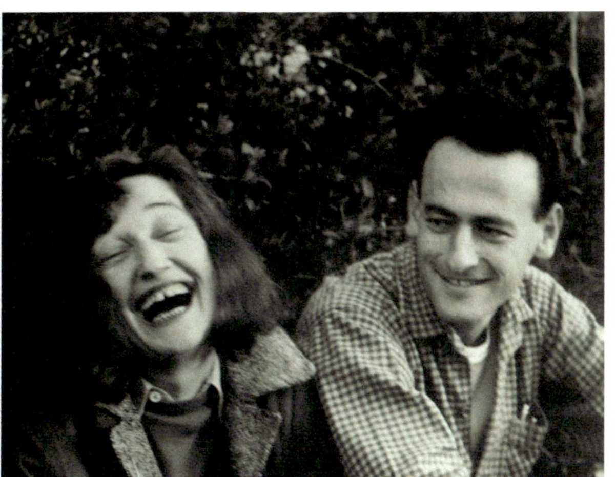
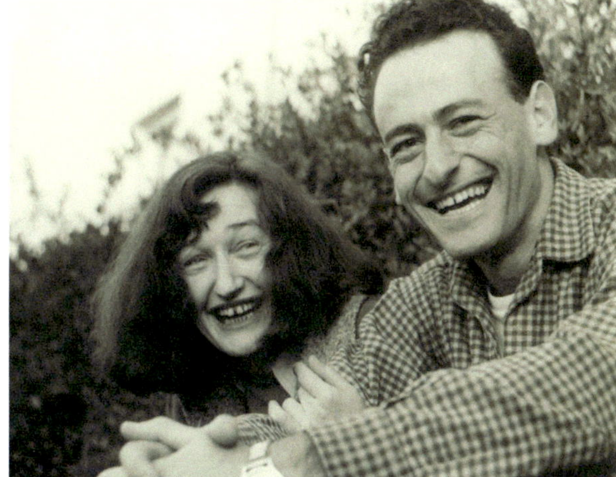

Noa Eshkol and Abraham Wachmann after the publication of *Movement Notation*, 1958. Photos: Zalman Einav

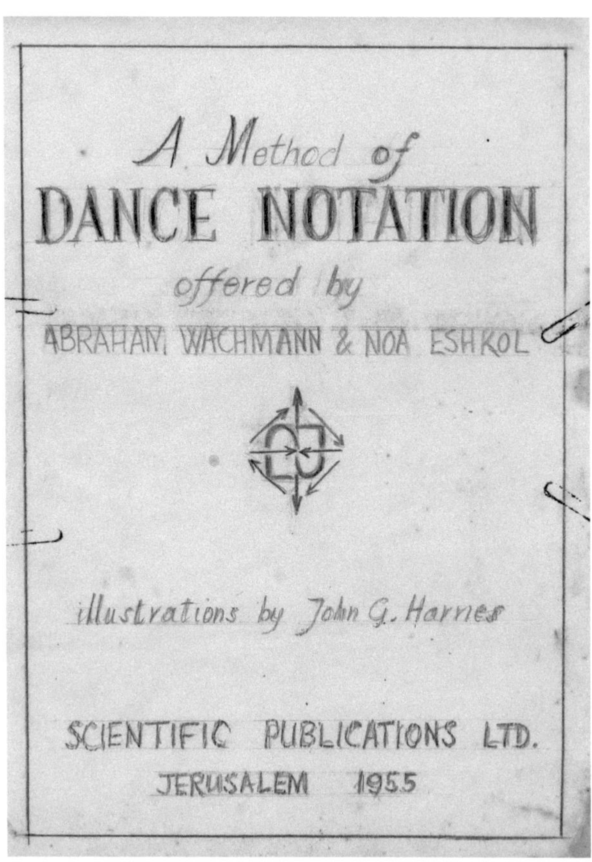

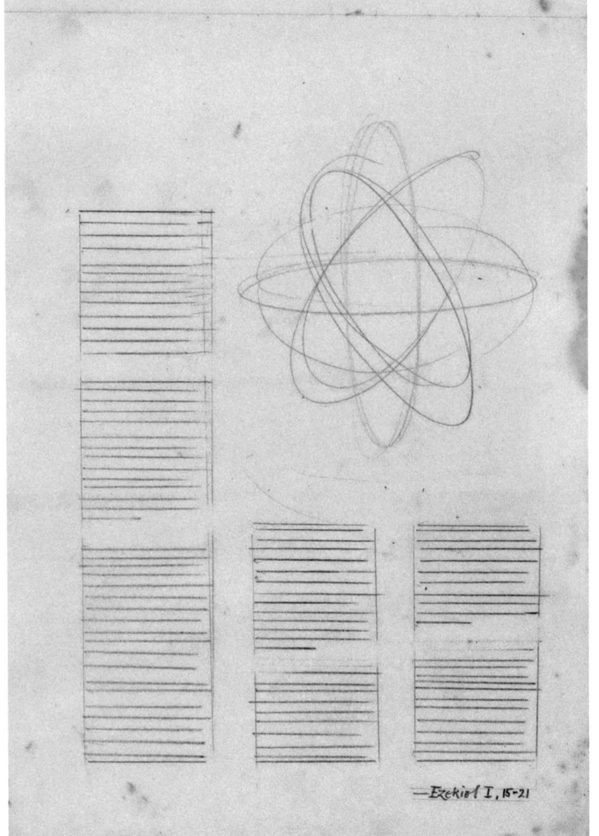

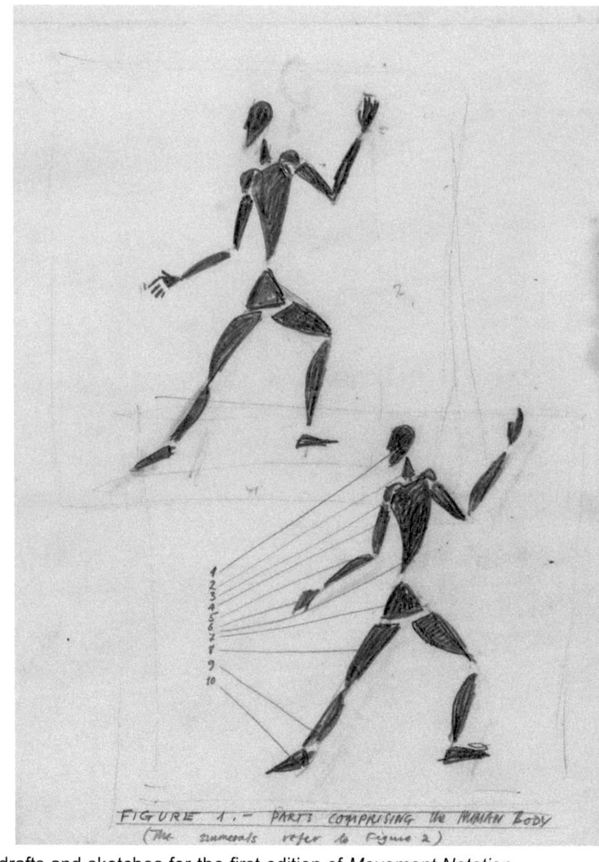

John G Harries, *A Method of Dance Notation*, 1955, preparatory design drafts and sketches for the first edition of *Movement Notation*

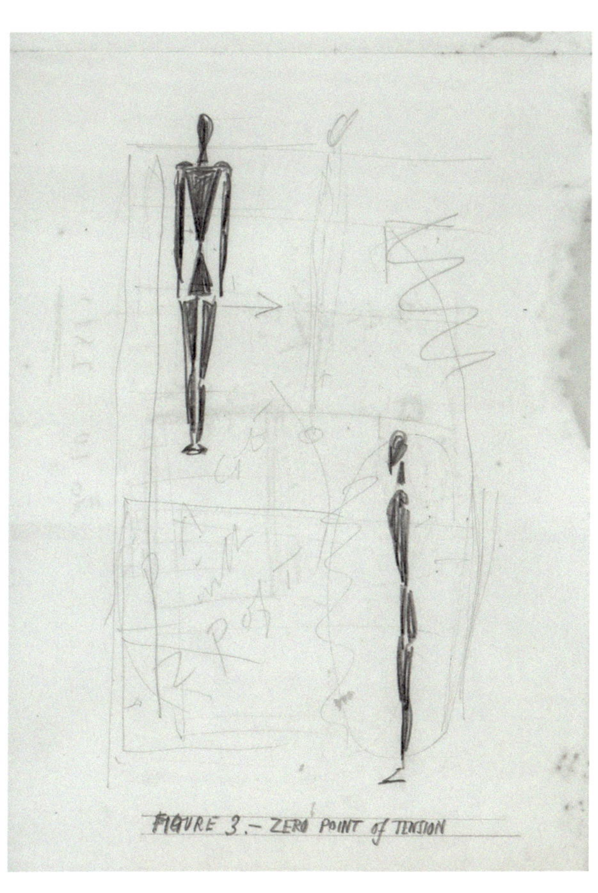

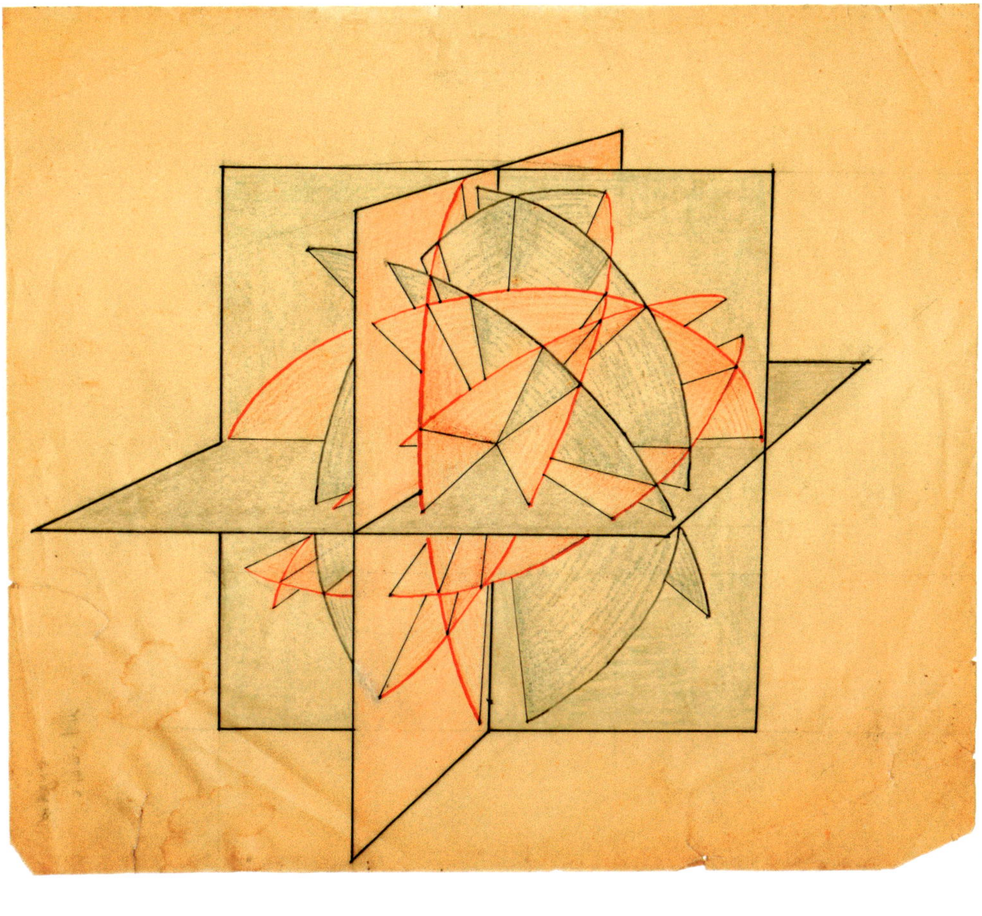

Abraham Wachmann, *The Spherical System of Reference* (early sketch), 1950–1958, ink on parchment

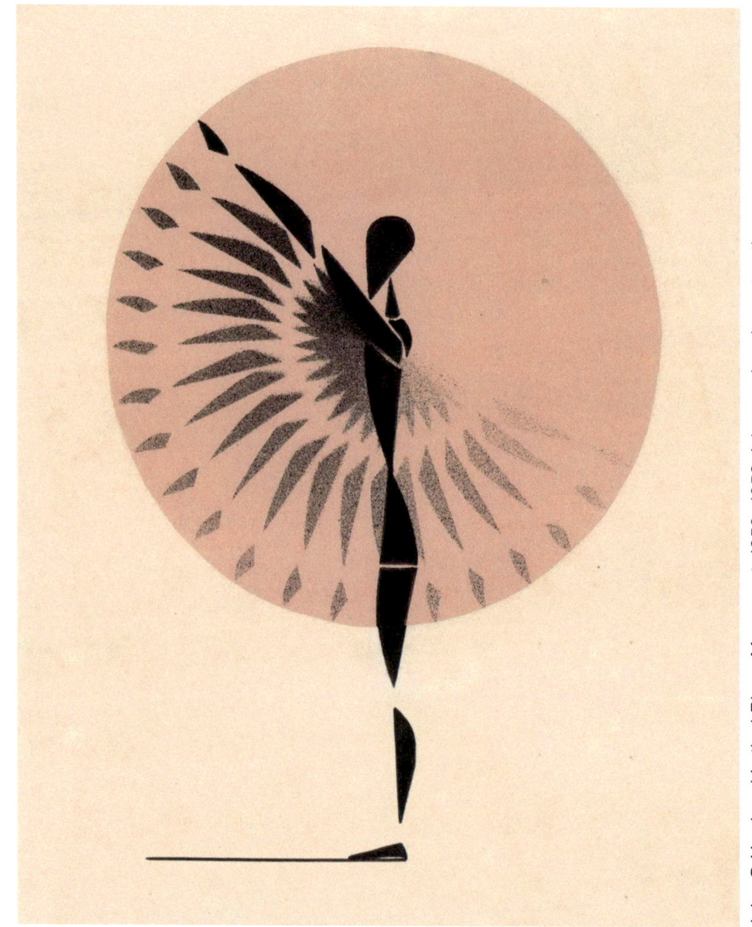

John G Harries, *Vertical Plane Movement*, 1950–1958, ink on colored construction paper

MOVEMENT NOTATION

MOVEMENT NOTATION

NOA ESHKOL

AND

ABRAHAM WACHMANN

Diagrams and illustrations by A. Wachmann and John Harries

WEIDENFELD AND NICOLSON

7 CORK STREET LONDON W1

First published 1958

PRINTED IN GREAT BRITAIN IN 11 pt. IMPRINT BY
J. W. ARROWSMITH LTD., WINTERSTOKE ROAD, BRISTOL
N. 6380

CONTENTS

ACKNOWLEDGMENTS

WE WISH to dedicate this system of notation to the art of movement, Dance.

The book, however, we wish to dedicate to the years of our happy and stimulating collaboration, 1951–56, during which the system was developed; also to all those who took part in this work, especially to John Harries, a member of the experimental dance group directed by Noa Eshkol, for his cooperation in the translation and graphic work of the book; to Naomi Polani for her active work in the group; and to Amos Lev who worked with us at the time of the conception of the original idea; he fell in the Sinai Desert in Autumn 1956.

We also wish to thank those friends whose moral and material assistance helped us to complete this work: Herbert Brün, Israel Liebertovsky, Geoula Dogan, and especially Shalhevet Freier, who gave his untiring efforts and unlimited patience on the weary journey which led to the publication of the book; and Mr Meyer Weisgal who by his sponsorship made that publication finally possible.

N.E.
A.W.

INTRODUCTION

TO BEGIN with, it must be pointed out that this notation is a *movement* notation and not a *dance* notation. The difference between these two conceptions is this: while the term 'movement' includes in its meaning all the possibilities of movement of the human body in their various manifestations, the term 'dance' indicates, in every period, a certain range of movements expressing the choice of a composer and dancer, and fulfilling the demands of a particular society in a certain epoch. In other words, while 'movement' is the name given to the material wherein all dance is wrought, the 'dance' is always the result of a specific way of treating that material.

Today the world of dance is compounded of a host of different approaches to the treatment of the world of movement, that is to say, of innumerable dance systems and dance styles. Every dance system regards itself as the one representing the best way of dealing with the material—movement. It is inevitable that each should deny the reason for the existence of every other system.

With every dance style or system is associated a special vocabulary of terms, technical and ideological, which is in every case necessary for the communication of that system from one person to another. Usually these special groups of terms do not remain within their own bounds, each in the particular style wherein and for which it was created, but are raised through years of persistent usage to the level of basic laws which propose to explain and define the world of movement in general. But these known 'basic laws', thriving in the world of the dance today, lose their power the moment an attempt is made to apply them to the explanation of dance styles for which they were not designed. Therefore the existence of a large number of sets of laws is a grave defect, and an unending source of obscurity and disagreement among those who actually work in the same creative field. This fact alone (the existence of a multitude of sets of laws) would not have been a negative one, had it been possible to create by their means order and system in the infinite possible combinations of movement; for their function lies in the potential capacity of creating order and system, although each in its own manner—a manner expressing a difference of outlook. In essence, then, all dance styles are closed units, with no standard of comparison between them.

These statements are proved by the fact that not one of the numerous sets of 'basic laws' has brought into being a comprehensive system of notation. The intelligibility and practicability of a system of notation should be measured by its ability to describe all the potential phenomena in a defined field of interest, independently of stylistic appearances which are characteristic and special.

A system of notation would have grown up naturally, had the field of interest (movement of the human body) been analysed in a homogeneous and consequential manner.

As far as this notation is concerned, any possibility of movement of the body which can be expressed, is 'important' and 'wanted', without prejudice and without taking into consideration the burden of emotional and stylistic notions which may be attached to any movement, and which lie outside the bounds of the world of pure movement. Therefore, there is in the outlook on the world of movement which this notation expresses, no place and no value for many of the concepts which are most used in the world of dance, such as 'expressive', 'aesthetic', 'internal-external', 'contraction-release', 'round' or 'straight' movements, 'space' as opposed to body. For these notions are annexed each to a special range of movements and are, each in a certain style of dance, the accepted conventions influencing creation and criticism. But all of them have been established from the point of view of dance, and not of movement.

It is apparent that, as in any defined field of interest, so in the world of movement, fundamental properties of the material may be discerned, which do not lose their significance in any stylistic frame. And it is inevitable that a notation—a set of signs capable of expressing, symbolising, 'standing in place of' any event—should reflect the point of view and method of analysis through which the events have passed on the way to their notation.

When a certain event raises our interest to the point where it becomes desirable to remember it, describe it, and above all to think and calculate or to compose within it—in short, to express it—then a fitting substitute is required for the actual event: this substitute is a symbol.

Any event which has not been provided with some symbol will remain fortuitous and unrepeatable. The symbol (or set of symbols) must be capable of expressing the chief properties and essence of the event, in a practical and possible manner, mainly for the purpose of thinking about and within this event, that is, for the purpose of composition.

It must be stressed that the notation offered here does not intend to warp the ways of any dance system or style, or to deprive the creator of the free use of imagination or personal expression. On the contrary, since the notation has been constructed in the wake of detailed analysis of the material, it opens new horizons of possibilities of dealing with this material, for it discovers and points out many facets of it which have remained until now unexploited. This investigation into the heart of the matter and the means of thought within it, stimulates the imagination of the dance creator and drives him to extract ideas hidden within the material which are thereby brought out from obscurity. Furthermore, and not less important, it is to be hoped that the notation will influence and advance the experiments which are made in the direction of the establishment, understanding and agreement about the laws of composition of the dance—laws which must consider and stand in close affinity with the fundamental properties of the material.

It is possible to write in the notation every visually discernible movement of the human body, and, therefore, all that has been composed in the world of the dance. However, for the recording of these dances, one would have to analyse them according to the given concepts of the notation, in spite of the fact that they have not been composed in consciousness of them. The analysis of these dances (period dances, national dances, theatre dances) which is made with the use of the concepts of this notation—concepts which are general and do not lose their significance in any frame of dance whatsoever—might bring about the understanding of the difference of structure between styles.

This difference is always the result of a different way of treating the world of movement. The difference of structure implies different conventions of composition, which are responsible for the special flavour and character of any dance style. These conventions are expressed symbolically in the record of a composition by characteristic formations and combinations of the notation symbols. This kind of expression which is at the same time an explanation, is factual and materialistic, as opposed to an explanation given by means of the word, which involves the danger of being entirely personal and based on the 'taste' of the explainer. A result of this may be that the critique of dances already existing and of those as yet uncreated, may turn from being utterly arbitrary and personal to being as far as possible objective.

The discussion of rules of composition for the dance, which begin to show themselves with the understanding of the fundamental properties of the material and the notation of it, can only follow the practical investigation of the notation itself.

CHAPTER 1

The Arrangement of the Page

(*a*) *The Body*
(*b*) *Time*

THE NATURAL events which are to be expressed in this notation are the potential relations and changes of relation between the parts of the human body.

Such relations will be called 'positions'.

A change of relation will be called 'movement'.

Considered from the point of view of its *structure* and its *ability to change*, the body is an instrument. But the aspect of the body with which the notation is concerned is its appearance, i.e. the body as a visual phenomenon. Although conditioned by its structure, the appearance of a body may constitute a separate field of interest, and it is this second aspect with which the notation is concerned. However, some knowledge of the structure of the body is necessary for those who wish to understand the notation. For dancers and composers, this knowledge should be a thorough one.

(*a*) *Body Line*

In writing movement, four dimensions must be taken into account—the three dimensions of the body (which is an instance of our three-dimensional space) and the dimension of time. The manuscript page must therefore be organized in such a manner that all these four dimensions may be given expression.

For the purpose of the script two lines, *T* and *X*, are drawn on a page, perpendicular to one another. The vertical line *X* represents the body. It is divided into equal sections, each section representing one part of the body. There are six groups of sections; with a gap separating each group from the next. The divisions are produced at right angles to *X* in the direction *T*, thus creating six groups of horizontal spaces on the page.

The page thus divided into horizontal spaces, by the extension in the direction *T* of the division of line *X*, represents the human body. (*See Fig. 1.*)

The manuscript page is divided into six groups of horizontal spaces. (*See Fig. 1.*) Starting with the lowest and reading upwards, these are as follows:

(1) A group of two spaces whose purpose will be explained at a later stage.

(2) A group of three spaces representing as a whole the LEFT leg:
- (i) The lowest represents the foot from the sole of the foot to the ankle;
- (ii) represents the lower leg, from ankle to knee;
- (iii) represents the thigh, from knee to hip-joint.

(3) The third group (the next above) represents the RIGHT leg in the same manner.

(4) A group of four spaces representing the body:
   (i) The lowest space represents the pelvis, from the hip-joints to the lowest lumbar vertebrae;
   (ii) The torso, i.e. the dorsal and upper lumbar vertebrae;
   (iii) The neck, consisting of the cervical vertebrae;
   (iv) The head, from the 'atlas' vertebra upward.

(5) A group of four spaces representing the RIGHT arm, including the shoulder.
   (i) The lowest represents the shoulder;
   (ii) The upper arm, from shoulder joint to elbow;
   (iii) The forearm, from elbow to wrist;
   (iv) The hand, from the wrist.

(6) The sixth group (next above) represents the LEFT arm in the same manner.

Note that most single limbs of the body lie between two joints.

In the notation the horizontal spaces represent the limbs. Note that for the convenience of reading and writing, we separate each group of horizontal spaces from the next by means of an empty gap.

(*b*) *Time Line*

In the same manner that the line *X* represents the body, line *T* represents the flow of time. Equal divisions are marked off along coordinate *T* and produced perpendicular to *T* in the direction *X*. These vertical columns represent equal units of time, following one another. They divide the flow of time into equal intervals as does a clock or a metronome.

This arrangement of the page—ruled with lines perpendicular to one another—is regarded as a symbol representing the body in time.

On the manuscript page line *X* symbolizes the three-dimensional body; line *T* symbolizes time-duration. *An event which can only be expressed as a relation body–time, is called movement, the material which this notation will describe and organize.* Most of the symbols which are to be written on the page, and included between these lines (and which will be explained later) express this event, which is called movement, and its character.

Dance is creation (or construction) consciously built from the material, movement, and it has rules of its own.

The various limbs of the human body are capable of moving more or less independently. The extent of the possibilities of movement of the limbs is a subject for study by anyone wishing to deal with the art of movement (dance). The active use of all the limbs, or the use of some only while the others remain passive, is a matter of choice for the composer.

There is one principle which must be borne in mind from the outset. This principle is, that there exists absolutely no hierarchy of importance among the limbs, although they differ in shape, weight, range of movement and place in the body, since as has been said above, the concern of this script is the ability of the limbs to stand in relation, and change their relation to one another, and this ability is possessed by each one of them. Even the specific functions of the various limbs which give them their significance in 'everyday life' (such as locomotion to the legs, 'working' to the hands, &c.) have no bearing on the parts of the body as conceived in the script; and of course none of the emotive or associative significance attached by different people to different limbs concerns us here, although they may have interest for the creator of dance. The active use of only certain parts of the body, as seen in different styles of dancing, is entirely a matter of choice.

In the analysis of movement of the body the particular shapes of the limbs will be disregarded and the movement of their longitudinal axes abstracted from them, the limbs being treated as straight lines. (*See Figs. 1, 2, 3.*)

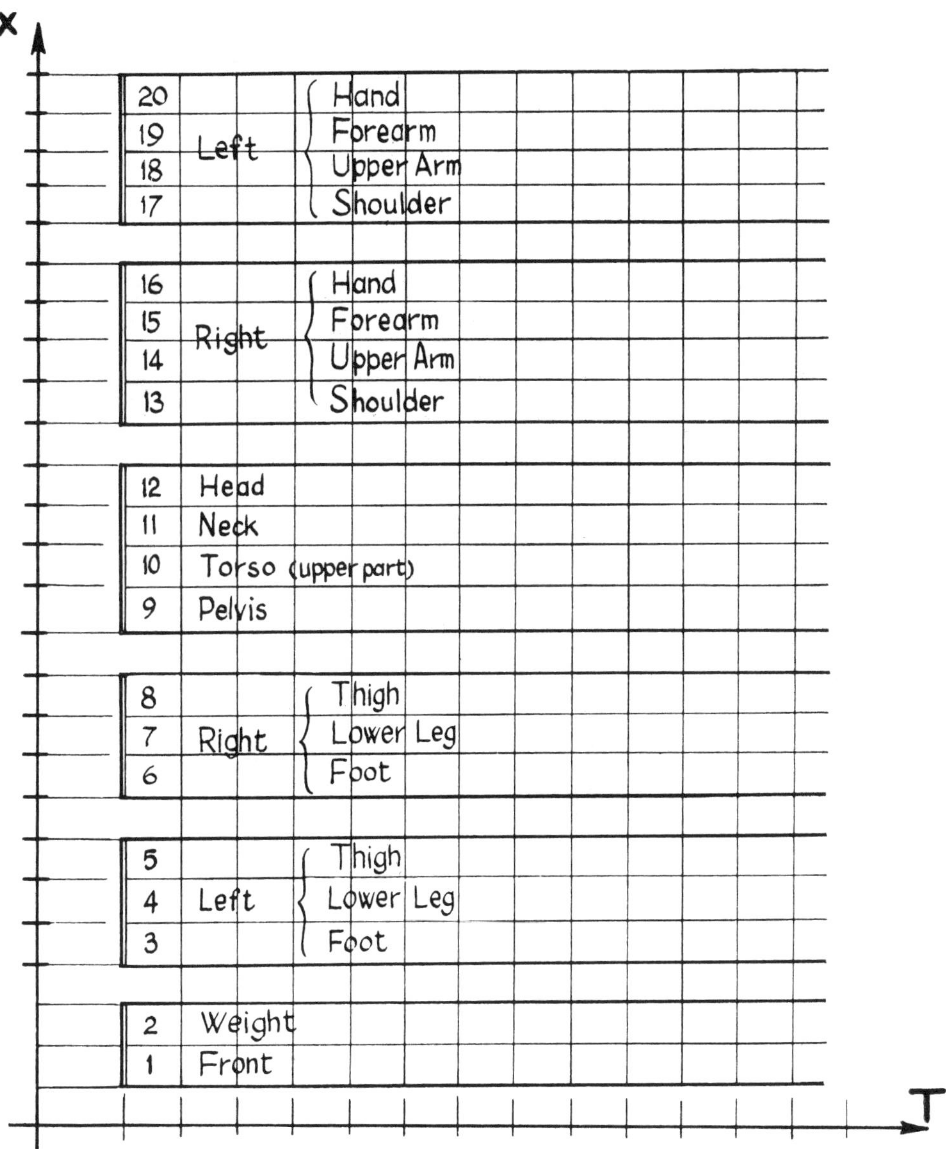

1. The Manuscript Page

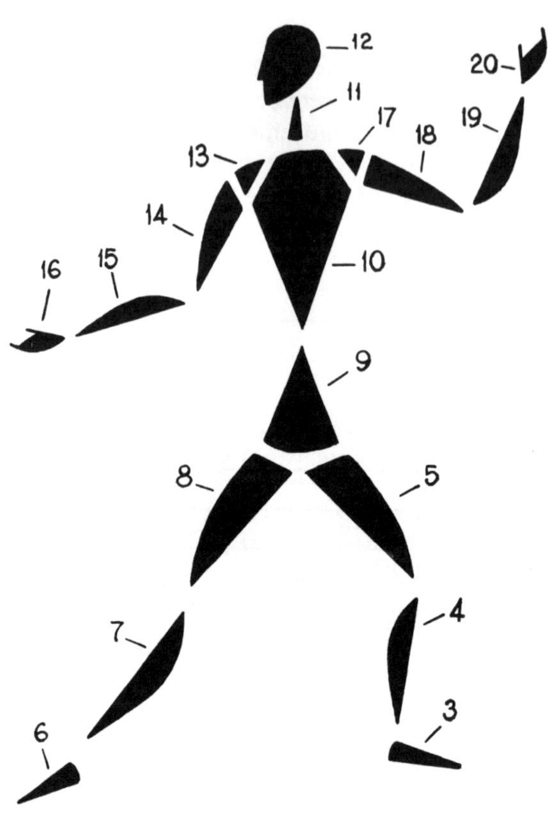

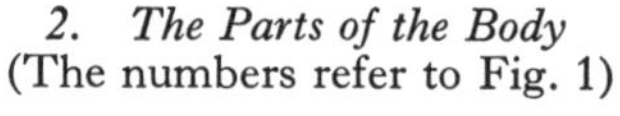
2. The Parts of the Body
(The numbers refer to Fig. 1)

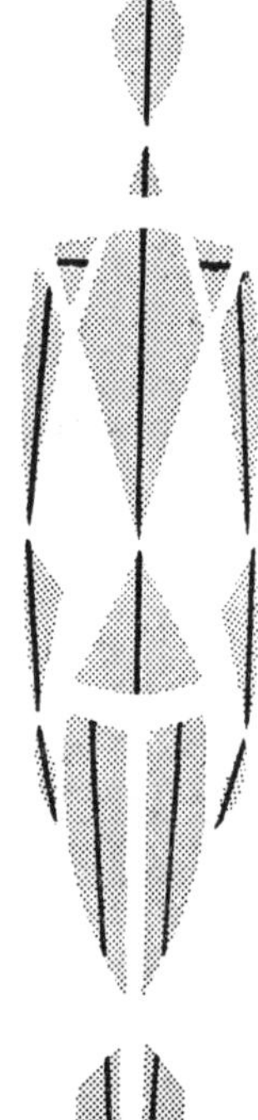

3. The Longitudinal Axes of the Limbs

CHAPTER 2

The Movement

OBSERVING the human body in motion, it seems as though its component parts may change their relations one to another in innumerable ways. An enormous number of words exist for the purpose of describing these different ways. Indeed, one might compile a whole dictionary consisting of words relating to movement. Some words are symbols for simple or complex everyday functional movements of the body; sitting, standing, lying and running: some denote a specific manner of performing functional movements; squatting, crouching, kneeling or stooping. Words like push, pull, wring, grasp, press or beat are also used to denote movements of the body, each with its particular character, although, properly speaking, they are descriptive of actions directed towards an external object. Other words describing the relations of shapes to one another are also used to describe movement of the limbs of the body, for instance to bend, straighten, curve, flex, extend or rotate. Furthermore there exists in every school and style of dancing a professional nomenclature, a selection of words which are names for particular movements of particular limbs, or for certain combinations of movements like 'plié', 'jeté', 'battement', 'contraction', 'release' or 'body wave'.

This is neither a complete nor an exact analysis of the relation between words denoting movement and movement itself. The intention here is only to point out that there exist innumerable ways of describing, expressing, relating or denoting movements of the body by means of the word. This very multitude of shades of expression is the richness of language but, on the other hand, it is an origin of confusion when, as in the present case, one is concerned to deal in an exact and unambiguous manner with one single aspect of movement.

The field of interest of this notation is the formal aspect of movement, and it is to be stressed that this is (according to the definition of movement given in the foregoing chapter) the formal aspect of the relations and *change* of *relations* between the parts of the body. Since the notation is used for dealing with the formal aspect of movement alone, it is therefore of no relevance for its construction and use to know why—from what cause and for what purpose—a movement is performed.

If the end result of a movement is of no interest, the fulfilment of its 'practical' purpose has no relevance to the notation. To give a crude example, one may raise an arm in order to push something, to strike somebody, to reach a high object, to pray or simply to express joy. All these are identical for the analysis of movement useful for this notation. What is of interest is the *manner in which* the arm is lifted, i.e. in what way the arm changes its relation to the other parts of the body.

The General Analysis of Movement

In consequence of the fact that every limb of the body is connected to its neighbour by a joint, the longitudinal axis of every limb (and therefore, every point on its longitudinal axis) will create some kind of arc while moving.

When the movement is circular—i.e. when every point on the longitudinal axis of the limb creates a circle or part of a circle—then the longitudinal axis of the limb moves about a certain axis which will be called the *axis of movement*. That is to say, every point on the longitudinal axis of the limb moves in a circle to the centre of which the axis of movement is perpendicular. The axis of movement must pass through the joint of the limb at which the movement takes place. Thus the *real* axis of the limb and the *imaginary* axis of movement both pass through the joint of the limb at which the movement takes place, and a certain angle exists between them. By observation of the angular relation between these two axes, the possibility is given of classifying all circular movements into three distinct types:

(1) Rotatory Movement.
(2) Plane Movement.
(3) Curved Surface Movement (which will be called 'Curved Movement').

(1) A Rotatory Movement is one in which a limb moves about its longitudinal axis. The longitudinal axis of the limb serves as the axis of movement. (*See Figs. 4, 5.*)

(2) A Plane Movement is one in which the longitudinal axis of the moving limb describes a plane. The longitudinal axis of the limb moves at right angles to the axis of movement. (*See Figs. 6, 7.*)

(3) A Curved Movement is one in which the longitudinal axis of the moving limb describes a curved surface. The longitudinal axis of the limb moves at an acute angle (less than 90 degrees) to the axis of movement. (*See Figs. 8, 9.*)

Thus no matter what kind of action the body may perform, and no matter what the final outcome of the change of relation between the limbs—whether they be flexed or stretched, to any degree, the actual process of movement, visually considered, may be described by means of these three types either singly or in combination.

Each type of movement has its distinct symbol, and these three comprise the main body of the symbols for movement used in the notation. The three symbols are:

(1) For a Rotatory Movement ∩
(2) For a Plane Movement →
(3) For a Curved Movement ∟

Their use will be explained in the succeeding chapters.

The moving parts of the human body are capable of deviating from a starting position, moving in any of the three manners of movement described above. But the mere classification of a movement into one of these three types would not satisfy the need for a complete description of the movement (the change of relation of one part to the others) from the aspect which is of interest for the notation: the visual aspect. For any part may produce in succession these imaginary planes and curved surfaces and rotations about its own axis, and these planes and surfaces may stand in endless different spatial and magnitudinal relations to one another.

It may be found that the same sequence of symbols of types of movement, for instance: ↑ |____ ∩ ↑ may represent on different occasions movement processes different in appearance, because of quantitative (magnitudinal) differences between the types, not designated by these symbols alone, and because of differences in their spatial relations.

This is seen clearly by comparing three actual examples all based on the above sequence. Let the sequence represent movements of the right arm, and the starting position of the arm be such that it hangs down straight at the side of the body.

Example (*a*) The first plane movement will be one in which the arm, with the palm facing downward, rises sideways creating a frontal plane, until it is held parallel to the ground and pointing to the right having moved through 90°. The second movement, which is curved, is such that the finger-tips trace a semi-circle, the straight arm rising and afterwards descending as if gliding over a dome, and at the same time moving towards the front of the body—so that the whole arm in its movement traces half a cone whose apex is at the shoulder-joint. The arm comes to rest, again at shoulder-level, but pointing straight forward. The third (Rotatory) movement is the turning of the arm through 90° on its own axis so that the palm faces towards the left. The final Plane movement is the lowering of the arm through 90°, resuming its opening position at the side of the body.

Example (*b*) For the second example it will be supposed that the arm is raised 135° instead of 90° in the first movement, i.e., a larger part of the whole plane, so that the second movement will begin from a position diagonally upward and sideways from the right side of the body. In this second movement a whole cone will be traced which lies between a point diagonally upward to the right of the body and forward from the shoulder, instead of the half-cone described in the previous example. The third movement will be a rotation of 180° instead of 90°. So that the palm faces upward. The final Plane movement will be a movement on the same plane as the first movement of the example, descending through 45°, the arm ending by pointing directly to the right from the shoulder.

Example (*c*) In the third example the same movements (as regards type and magnitude) will be performed, which were given in example (*a*), the sole difference being that the starting position of the arm is now raised sideways 45° from the side of the body (so that the first movement brings the arm through 90° to a position 45° *above* the horizontal, and so on).

In these three examples, the sequence of types of movement remained constant but changes in amount of movement and their spatial relation alter their appearance completely. In example (*b*) the magnitudes of the movements are changed and the placing of each movement in relation to the body and to the foregoing movement is altered. In example (*c*) the spatial relation of the starting position to the body is changed and as a result the spatial relations of all the movements are changed.

An indefinite number of variations might be based on the same sequence of types of movement, by changes of magnitude and spatial relation alone. From this it is seen that to indicate only the types of movement and their order is not sufficient for the full definition and expression of a sequence of movements.

For a complete analysis and description of any change of relation of one part of a body to the other, three stages will be found necessary:

(1) Analysis of the type of movement—whether it is Rotatory, Plane or Curved—and the relative order of the occurrence of these types. It may be found that one limb may move during a given stretch of time in such a way that the path of its sequence of movement consists at one instant of a Plane movement, at the next merging into a Curved movement, and all the while revolving about its own axis, and so on, in any possible order whatsoever.

The classification of movement into three types, which is a quantitative differentiation of the relations between the axis of movement and the longitudinal axis of the limb is sensually perceived as the qualitative differences between a plane, a curved surface, and rotation, created by a limb in the process of moving. These qualitative characteristics may be exploited in the composition of a dance.

(2) The second stage will be the spatial definition of these planes, curves and rotations according to one given system of reference (which will be described in the following chapter).

(3) The third stage will be concerned with what segment of a specific plane or curved surface, or how much rotation is performed in each part of a movement sequence consisting of the three types of movement using a definite method which will be described in the following chapter, also according to the system of reference which will be provided.

The three types of movement provide a classification by means of which the character of movements may be identified and their order in a sequence established. A given sequence of symbols may represent movement processes widely differing in appearance, because of differences of magnitude or of spatial relationship, or both; common to all movement processes represented by such a sequence of symbols is the order of appearance of the types of movement.

It should be noted here that the same sequence of types of movement may be performed by a limb other than the arm; when performed by a leg, for instance, the visual impression will obviously be radically different. Furthermore, the sequence might be distributed between more than one limb—the first movement being performed by the right leg, the second by the head, and so on.

4. *Rotatory Movement*

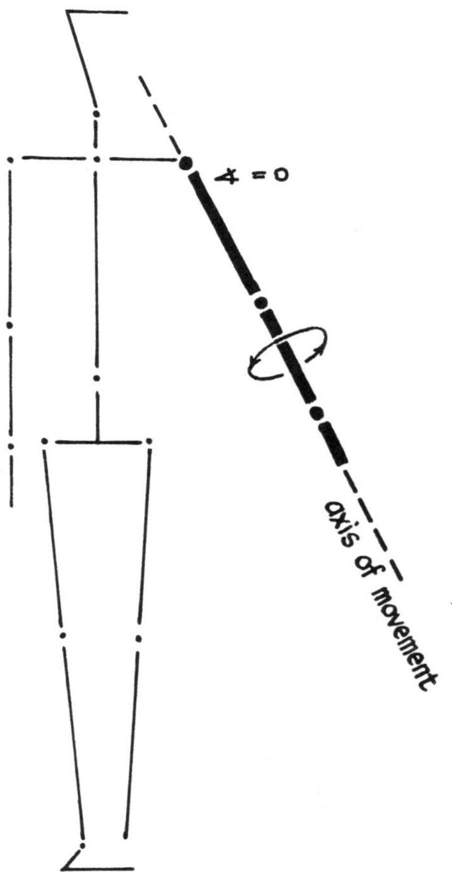

5. *Axis of Movement—Rotatory Movement*

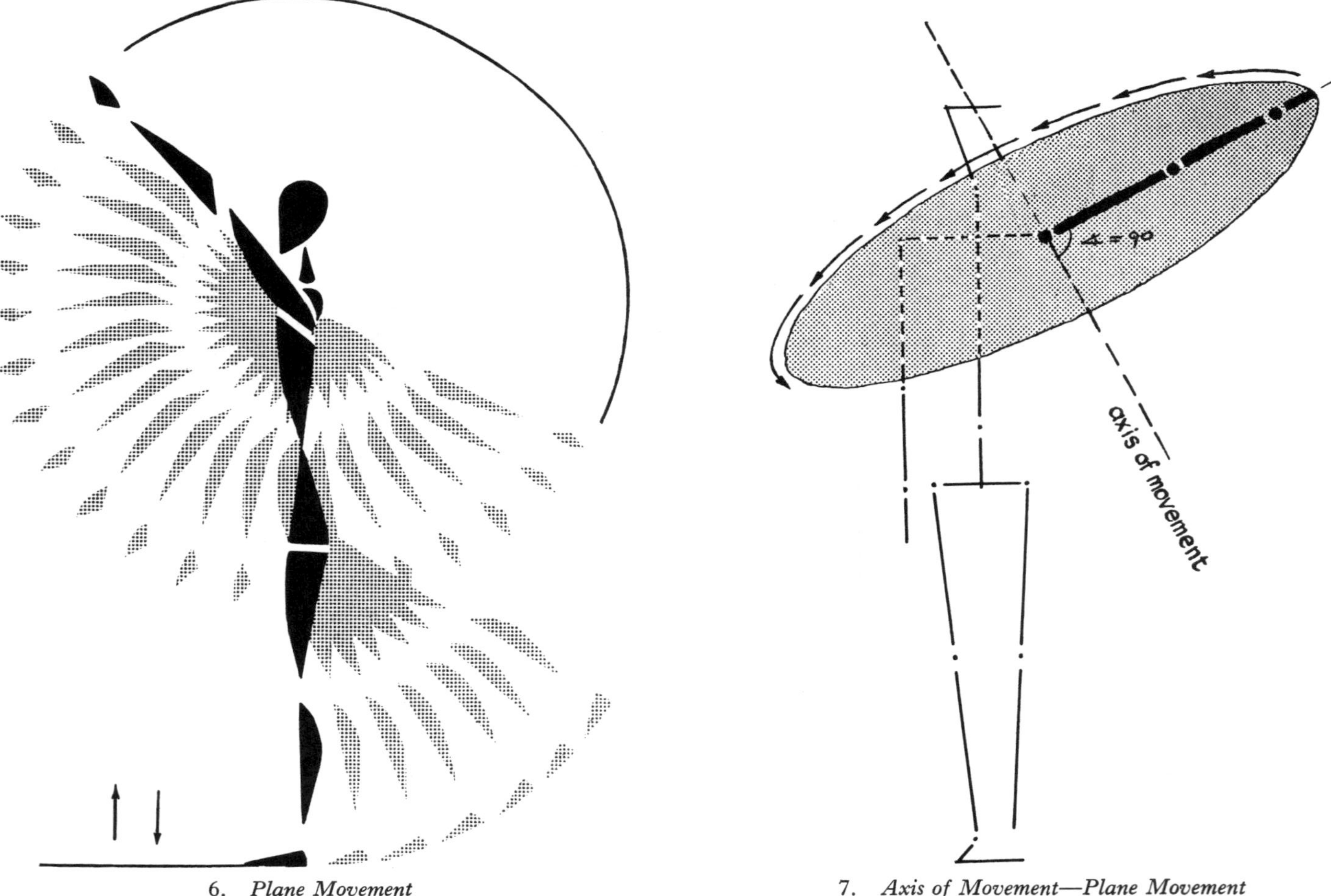

6. *Plane Movement*

7. *Axis of Movement—Plane Movement*

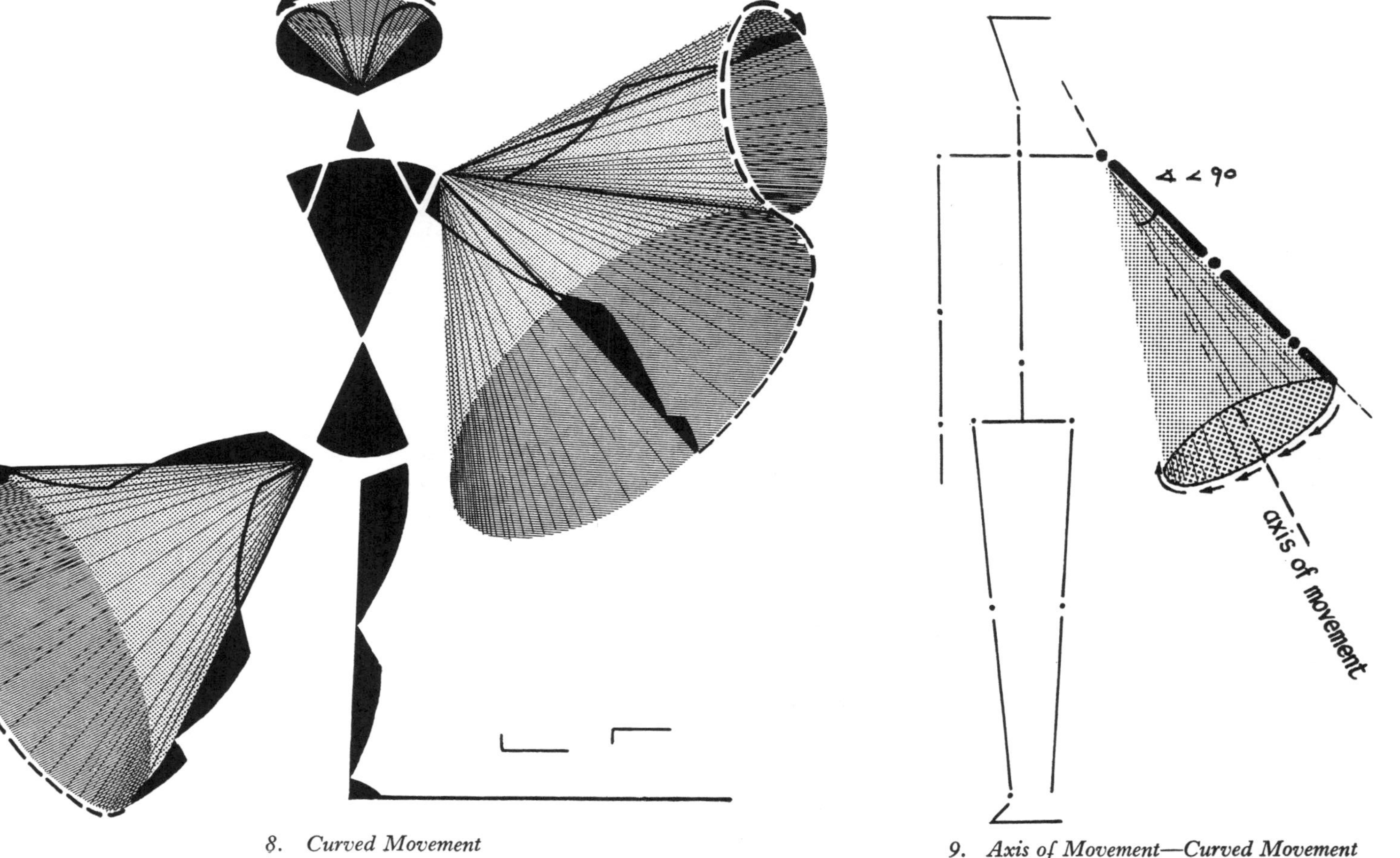

8. *Curved Movement*

9. *Axis of Movement—Curved Movement*

CHAPTER 3

Means of Analysis of Movement

IN THE LAST chapter it was explained why the indication of the types of movement and their order is insufficient for the full definition and expression of a sequence of movement. In the present chapter the method will be explained by which the spatial relations and amounts of movement in a sequence are to be established. These will be dealt with under the following headings:

(1) Division of the circle: 'Magnitude of Movement';
(2) Zero Position;
(3) The System of Reference.

(1) *Magnitude of Movement*

Since the movements of the limbs of the body are circular in essence any spatial scale chosen for the measurement of movement is bound to be based upon the relations of angles —that is, upon the division of the circle. The circular path (or the several circles) created by the extremity of one limb in its movement will be measured in degrees. Thus the division of the circle is a scale, and a basic aspect of this system of analysis and notation of movement. The surface enclosed by the circular movement of an extremity has no bearing on the measurement of magnitude of movement—the movement of a limb tracing a complete single cone will have the same magnitude regardless of the size of the cone.

For the purpose of the notation of movement, the division of the circle into 360 degrees is too minute, since the eye is incapable of perceiving and the limb of performing any movement of only one degree. Therefore, for the measurement of the amount of movement, the circle is divided into larger sections. The circle may be divided into larger or smaller sections according to the necessity arising from the specific movement sequence to be notated; that is to say, according to the smallest interval produced in a given movement composition.

Before every movement sequence or composition, a 'Scale of Magnitude' will be fixed (i.e. it will be decided into what sections the circle is to be divided), thereby establishing the smallest unit of magnitude required for the notation of the particular composition. The choice of the size of this unit of magnitude is theoretically unlimited. The smallest unit will always be signified by the numeral 1. Thus, for example, where 1 represents 45 degrees, 2 represents 90 degrees, and so on. (*See Fig. 10.*)

The Scale of Magnitude is written at the beginning of any composition by indicating the smallest unit of magnitude of which every amount of movement may be expressed as a multiple, thus: 1 = 30°, 1 = 15°, 1 = 10°, and the like. The Scale must be chosen so that it is possible to express the magnitude of *every movement in the composition* as a multiple of this unit.

Accordingly, all numbers appearing attached to the symbols of movement in the manner to be explained in the following chapter, will give the amount of movement in degrees.

A maximal movement is one in which a limb moves until obstructed from further movement by the limit imposed by the construction of the joint; it is represented by the letter M written in place of the numeral.

A minimal movement is a movement of lesser magnitude than that expressed by a single unit of the Scale decided upon. It is indicated by the omission of any numeral representing magnitude.

With the provision of a method of measuring the magnitude of a movement, it is possible to begin to describe movement.

For example, the series 2, 4, 16, where 1 = 45°, might be interpreted as a sequence for the right arm. If the arm began hanging straight down at the side of the body, the first movement might be a Plane movement to the side, the arm rising to shoulder level: creating by its movement one quarter of a complete circular plane, the extremity of the limb (i.e., the tips of the fingers) tracing a curved path, 90 degrees of a complete circle. In the second movement, a Curved movement in which the movement of the arm creates half of the surface of a cone, the extremity traces a path which is 180 degrees of a complete circle. The third might be a movement in one of the directions which allow the arm to pass twice over the 360 degrees of a complete plane, the extremity twice tracing the same circular path.

Again, the same sequence of amounts could be interpreted in a completely different way, by making the first movement a Rotatory Movement of the arm through 180 degrees; the second a Plane movement passing forward and up until the arm is vertically upward, the extremity tracing a curved path of 180°; and the third a curved movement tracing, twice in succession, a conical surface, the extremity passing twice over the same circular path. (Notice that the third cannot possibly be a Rotatory movement of the arm, since the limb is incapable of turning fully on its own axis, twice in succession, in one direction.)

The same sequence from the point of view of magnitudes and types of movement could be performed, the limb starting from a different position relative to the rest of the body, or the sequence could be performed by another limb, or distributed among various limbs, and so on in apparently endless variations—always remaining faithful to the original basic sequence of magnitudes: 2, 4, 16. Such a series may serve as the framework or theme of a movement composition.

Three possibilities now suggest themselves, for the organization of series which can form the basis for potential movement compositions:

(1) A series (that is, the order in time) consisting of the distribution of movements among the various limbs of the body—indicating only the limb producing each movement, without defining either its type or magnitude. (*See Ex. 1.*)

(2) A series of types of movement, indicating only the order in which they appear, particularizing neither the magnitudes of the movements nor which of the limbs perform them.

(3) A series of amounts of movement, without indication of the types of movement, and without designating by which limbs the movements are produced.

Furthermore, the possibility exists of utilizing all logical variants and derivatives of these series. The series of magnitudes 2, 4, 16, might be interpreted as a progression in which each term is the square of the preceding term, and a series beginning with the magnitude 3, and continuing 9, 18, would be a legitimate transposition producing a logical variation. (*See Ex. II*).

(2) *Zero Position*

Since the aim of the notation is to describe changes within the human body—changes of the relations between its parts—one fixed and unchanging formal position of the body is necessary. This position serves as the prime starting position for the description of every process of change. This position is called Zero Position. Thus any deliberate bodily event which is seen by the naked eye and which directs the body away from this zero position, we call movement, and this event stands in a relation to zero position—a relation which can be written. Zero position serves, for the purpose of notation, as a 'constant', a reference-position which provides an unchanging point of reference for all the changes of relation described. This remains true even if the actual physical position does not itself appear in the course of a given movement process.

Description of Zero Position

It has been decided that the position of the body which is identified as Zero Position, is:

Erect vertical standing posture;

Legs straight, closed together, feet parallel;

Weight of the body distributed equally on its base, the feet;

Body 'relaxed'—i.e. with no muscular effort influencing the skeleton, in excess of that necessary for normal standing;

Arms hanging at the sides of the body, relaxed, palms towards the body.

In other words, the Zero Position may be described as the standing position in which the parts of the body are arranged one above the other with every limb from top to bottom placed as nearly as possible over the centre of gravity of the limb beneath, so that the posture requires a minimum of muscular effort.

Any position might have been selected as Zero Position; this particular one has been chosen for its neutrality.

Zero position is represented in writing by the following complex of symbols:

In all the horizontal spaces on the manuscript page which represent the various limbs, the symbol ○ appears, except in those of the feet, in which the symbol □ appears, signifying contact with the ground. (The use of this symbol will be explained later). In the second space from the bottom appears a blocked-out zero: ●, denoting that the weight of the body is distributed equally on both feet. (The use of this symbol will also be explained at a later stage.) (*See Fig. 11.*)

(Note: In the first examples of written sequences of movement, Zero Position will always serve as the starting position.)

(3) *The System of Reference*

The System of Reference is an imaginary construction by means of which the spatial and magnitudinal relations of movement will be defined. This construction must be three-dimensional, since its purpose is to define the position and change of position of the axis of the limb in three-dimensional space. The simplest construction giving this possibility consists of three axes perpendicular to each other. For the purpose of the notation a plane and an axis perpendicular to it have been chosen, equivalent to three axes perpendicular to one another.

It is to be imagined that through the centre of the body in Zero Position there passes a plane parallel to the ground, which will be called the Horizontal Plane, and an axis *X* perpendicular to this plane, which coincides with the long axis of the body (since both are perpendicular to the ground). The point at which the axis *X* passes through the Horizontal Plane will be considered the centre of the body and will be called *S*. The lower end of the axis *X* will be given the number 0 and will be written *X*0. In Zero Position a line *Y* on the Horizontal Plane passes from front to back (in relation to the body), cutting coordinate *X* at *S*; the forward end of this line will be given the number 0 and will be written *Y*0.

Every line on the Horizontal Plane passing through the point *S* becomes a coordinate if we give the amount of its deviation from *Y*0, which is zero coordinate, according to a chosen scale of magnitude. The Scale of Magnitude at the beginning of a work of movement will usually indicate the scale of the radial division of the horizontal Plane of the System of Reference. The 'System of Reference' consists of the Horizontal Plane—with its potential coordinates which may be produced by *any* radial division of the horizontal circle—and axis *X*, as they are related to the body in Zero Position. According to this System of Reference, all movements and positions will be analyzed or produced. *(See Figs. 12, 13.)*

Private Systems of Reference

The relation of the moving limbs to the System of Reference

Were the body so built that all the joints connecting its limbs coincided at *S*, the centre of the body in Zero Position, then the method of locating the path traced by the moving limb relative to the System of Reference would have been direct and the main System of Reference as suggested would have been sufficient. That is to say, the movement of any limb could be described by means of a coordinate or combinations of coordinates built on the System of Reference, since the limb itself or its horizontal projection could be identified with a coordinate. But since the joints of the limbs do not in fact coincide with *S* but are at some distance from the centre, it must be imagined as if every separate limb carries with it a private System of Reference. The point *S* in the private System of Reference of a limb will then be the imaginary centre of the joint around which that limb moves. All these private Systems of Reference will be considered permanently parallel to the main theoretical System of Reference. This parallel relationship—Horizontal Plane to Horizontal Plane, axis X to axis X, *Y*0 to *Y*0—is preserved, no matter in what relation the limb stands towards the others, whether it be in Zero Position or in any other position whatsoever. Thus a limb always moves within the limits of its own private System of Reference, and there is no necessity to suppose fixed 'absolute' positions in 'outside' space towards which the limbs move. *(See Fig. 14.)*

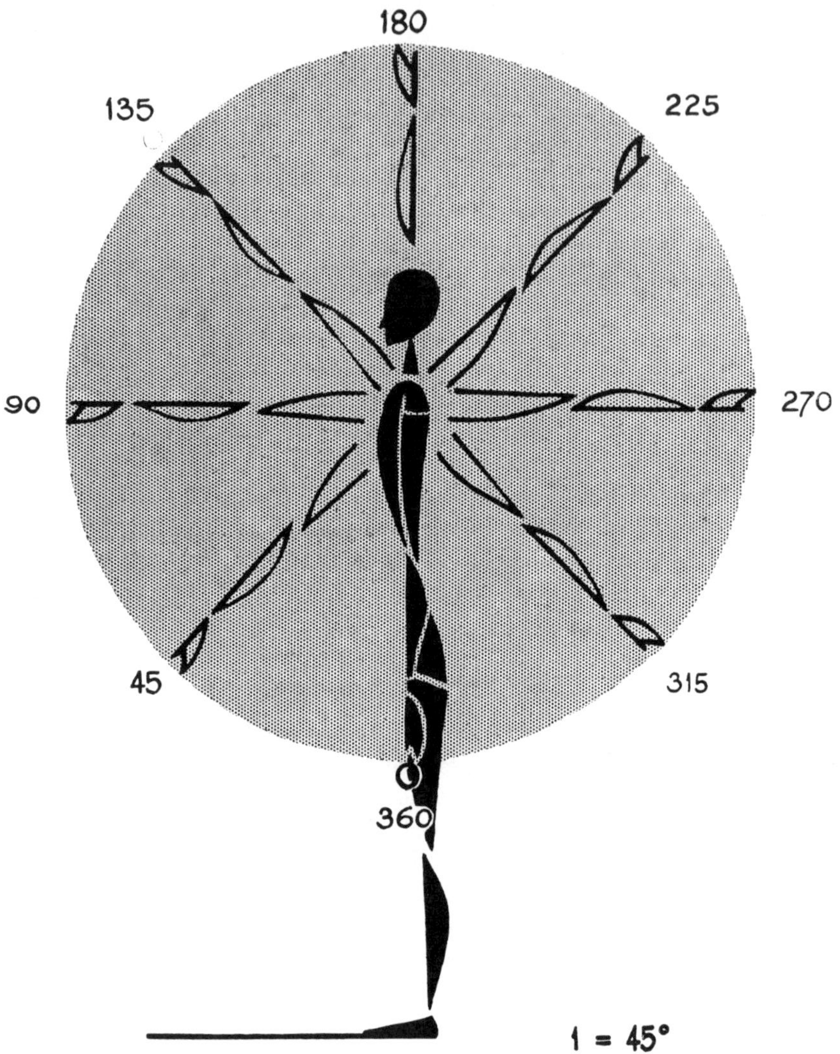

10. A scale of Magnitude: 1 = 45°

From	0 to 45°	= 1
,,	0 to 90°	= 2
,,	90 to 225°	= 3
,,	90 to 270°	= 4
,,	135 to 360°	= 5
,,	90 to 360°	= 6
,,	0 to 315°	= 7
,,	0 to 360°	= 8
,,	0 to 360° × 2	= 16
		&c. ...

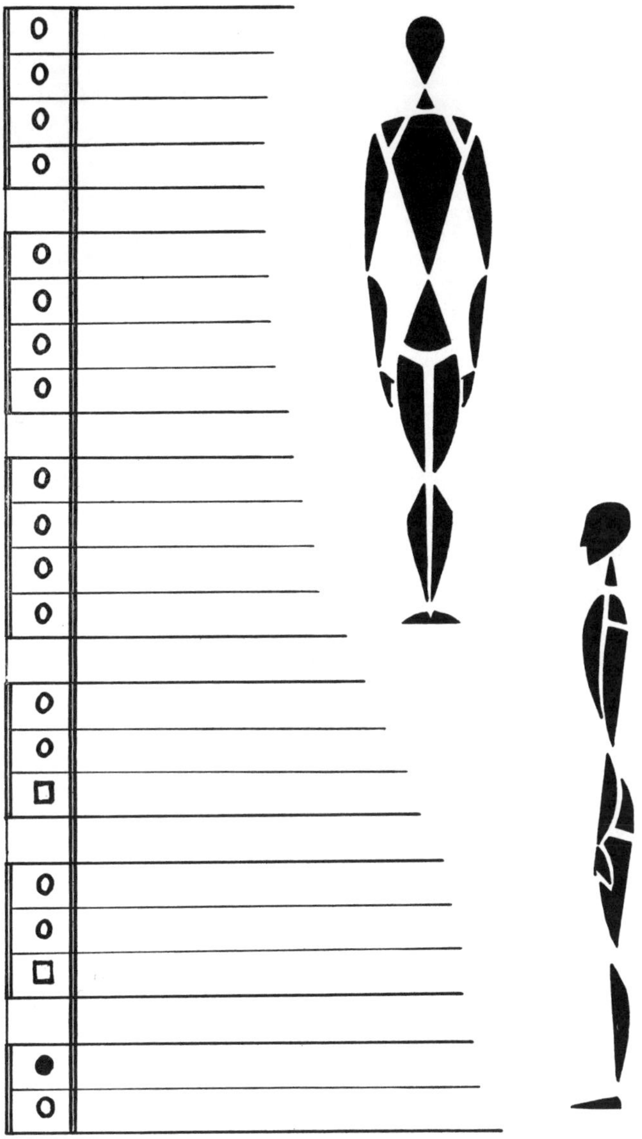

11. Zero Position

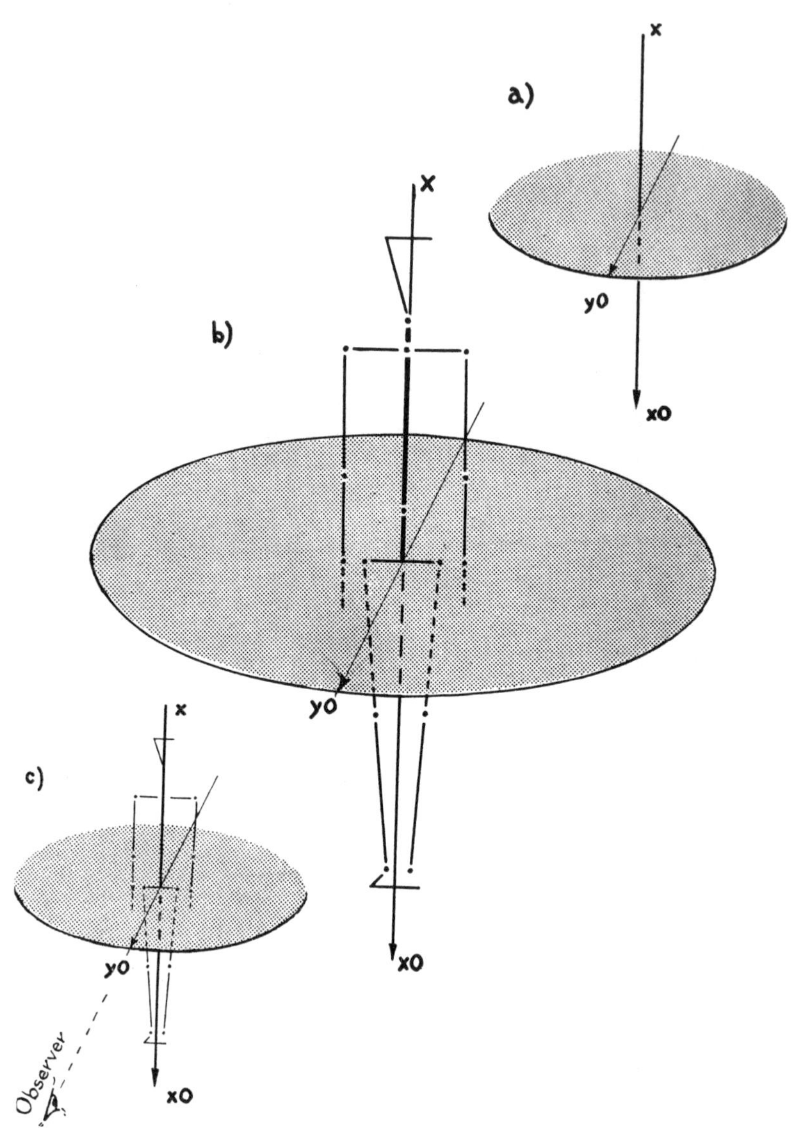

12. The System of Reference

(a) The System of Reference, composed of Horizontal Plane, coordinate *Y* on the Horizontal plane, and axis *X* vertical to the Horizontal Plane.
(b) The body in Zero position 'inside' the System of Reference. The front of the body faces in the direction *Y*0 and the longitudinal axis of the body coincides with axis *X* of the System.
(c) The body 'inside' the System of Reference; *Y*0 of the System points towards an observer, and the frontal surface of the body therefore also faces the observer.

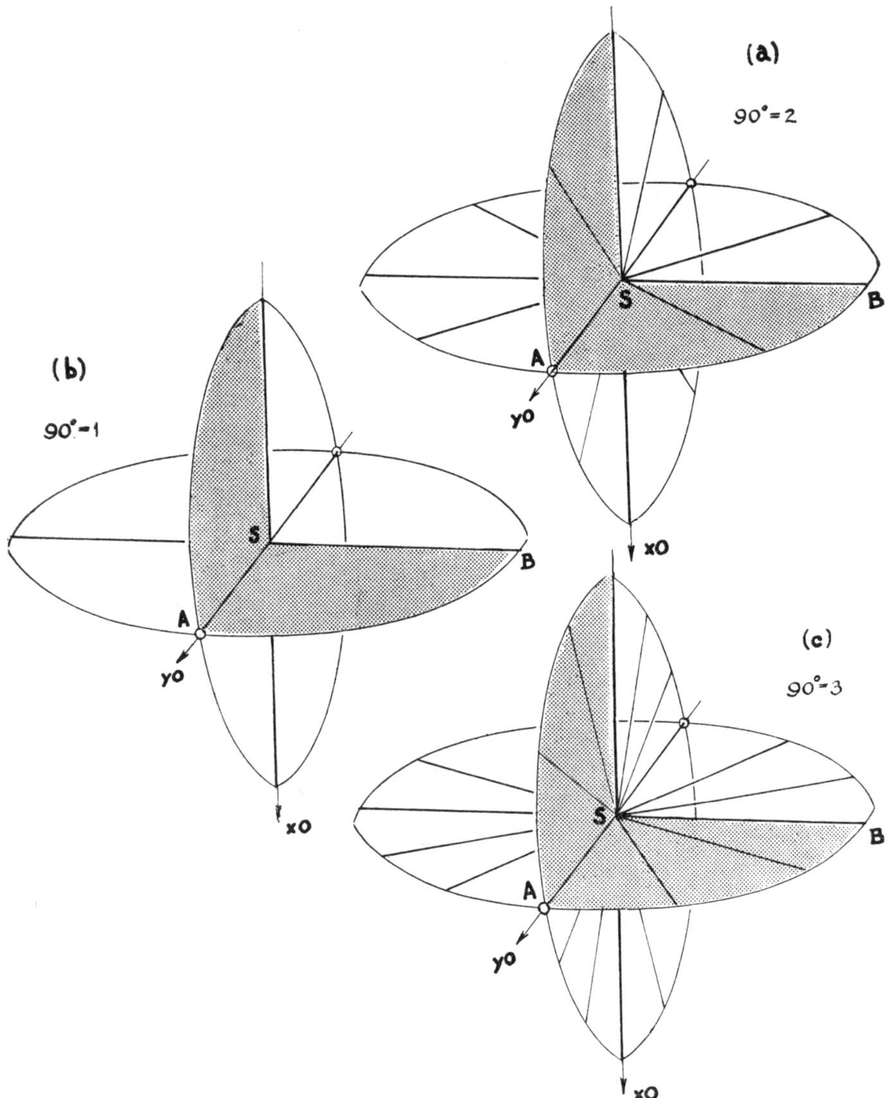

13. Three different Radial divisions

These serve as three scales of magnitude of movement, and consequently also give the division of the Horizontal plane of the System of Reference.

In all three figures, the section *SAB* is 90° of the Horizontal plane.

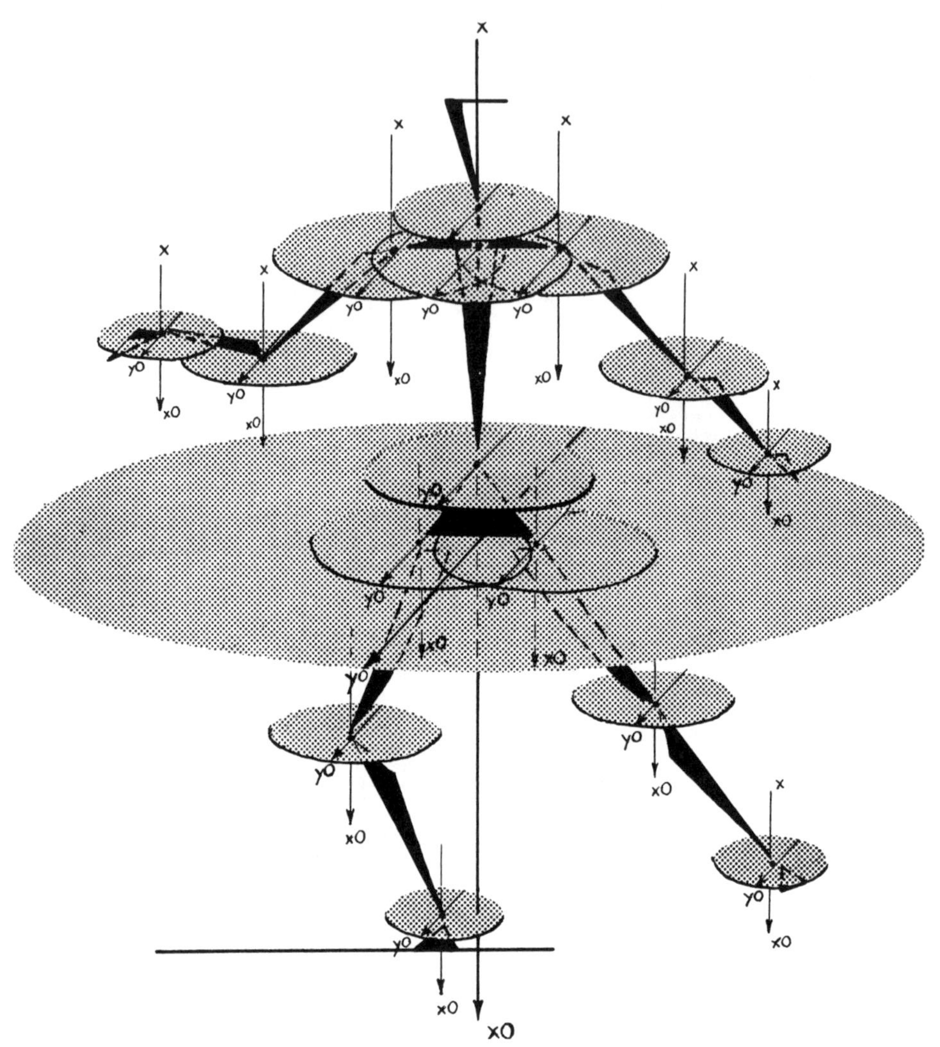

14. The Main and Private Systems of Reference

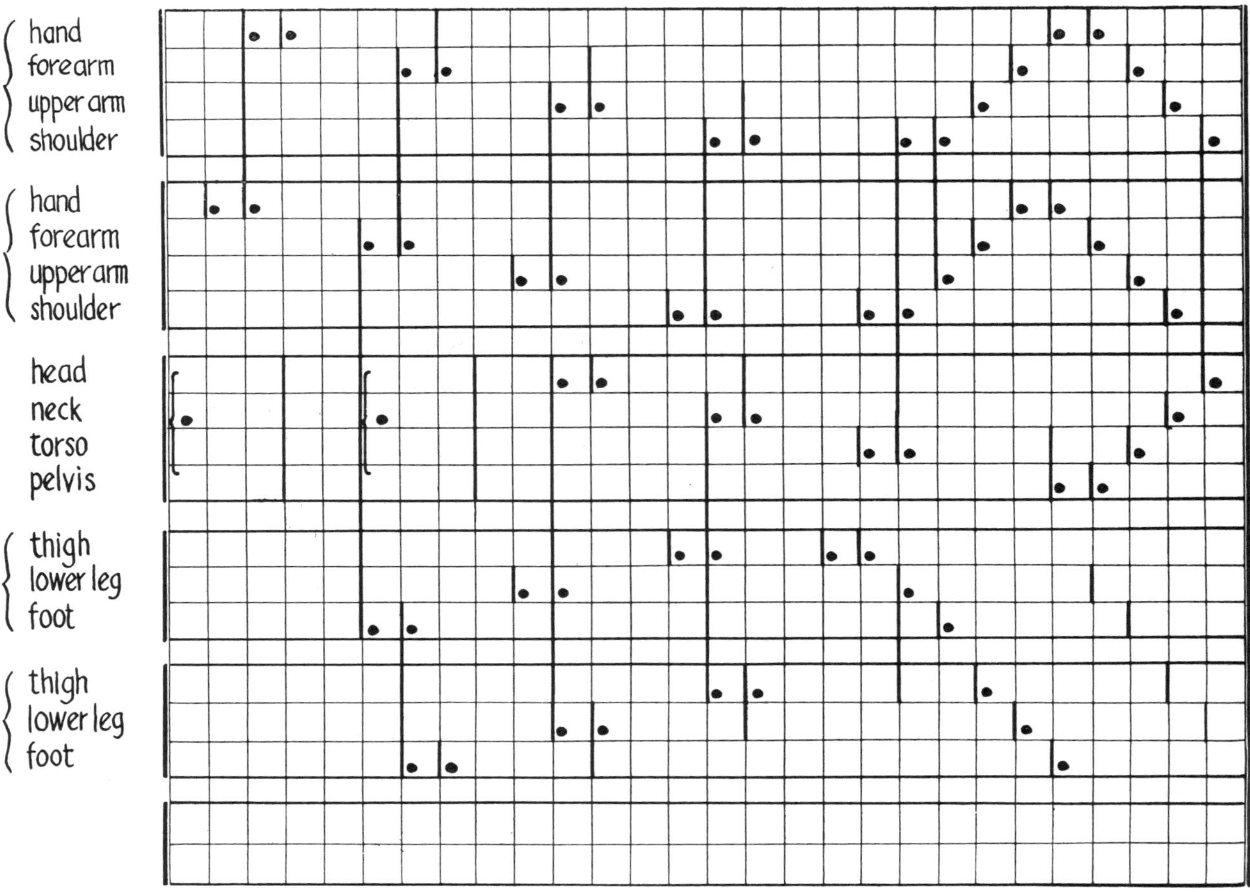

Ex. I. The order of appearance and duration of the movement of the limbs. In this example the dots on the manuscript page stand in place of symbols of movement. A pattern has been constructed which signifies the order of the active part taken by the various limbs in the course of a given work. An analogy can be made with the entrances and duration of the activity of the instruments of an orchestra. (The duration of a movement is represented by the space between the heavy lines.)

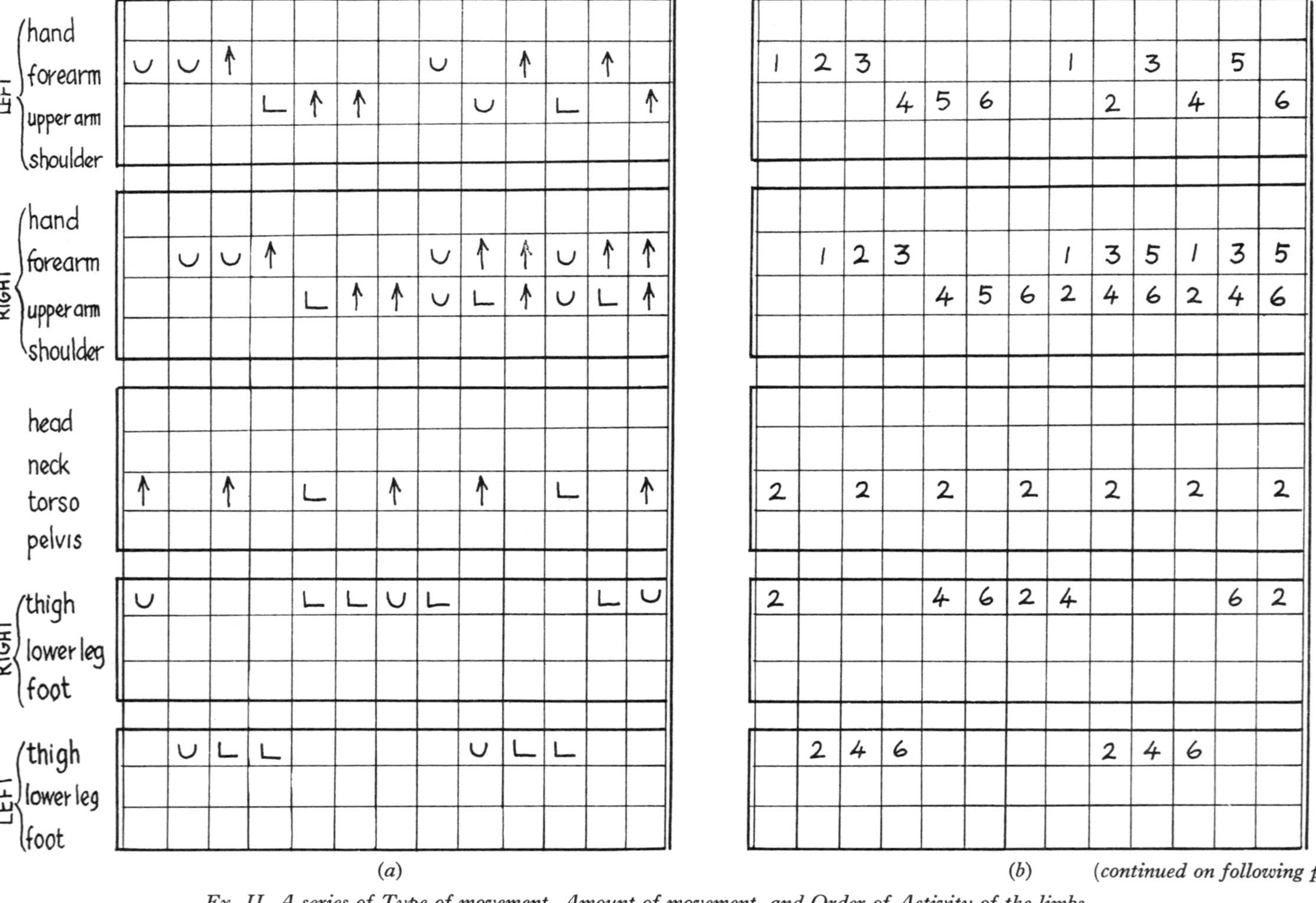

(a) (b) (continued on following page)

Ex. II. A series of Type of movement, Amount of movement, and Order of Activity of the limbs

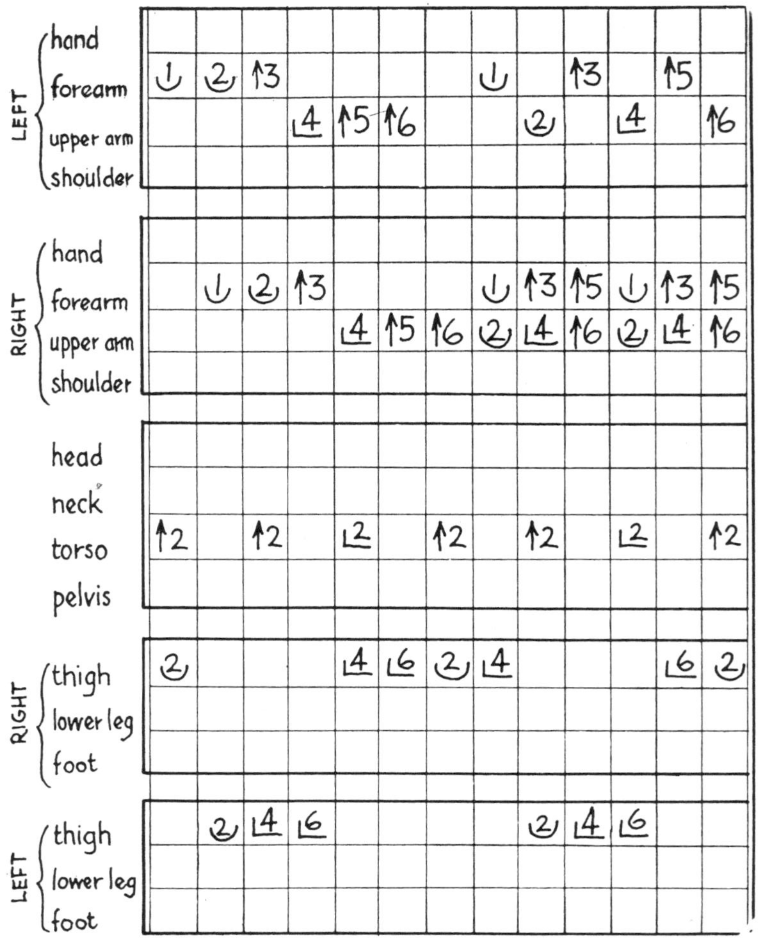

		1	2	3	4	5	6	7	8	9	10	11	12	13
LEFT	hand													
	forearm	∪1	∪2	↑3					∪1		↑3		↑5	
	upper arm				└4	↑5	↑6			∪2		└4		↑6
	shoulder													
RIGHT	hand													
	forearm		∪1	∪2	↑3				∪1	↑3	↑5	∪1	↑3	↑5
	upper arm					└4	↑5	↑6	∪2	└4	↑6	∪2	└4	↑6
	shoulder													
	head													
	neck													
	torso	↑2		↑2		└2		↑2		↑2		└2		↑2
	pelvis													
RIGHT	thigh	∪2				└4	└6	∪2	└4				└6	∪2
	lower leg													
	foot													
LEFT	thigh		∪2	└4	└6					∪2	└4	└6		
	lower leg													
	foot													

(*c*)

Ex. II. (*cont.*)

(*a*) In the arms, the series ∪ ∪ ↑ L ↑ ↑ (Rotatory – Rotatory – Plane – Curved – Plane – Plane) appears. In the left arm, the symbols appear in succession; in the right, two or more appear simultaneously, as 'chords'. In the upper torso, the series ↑ ↑ L (Plane–Plane–Curved) appears at regular intervals of time. The series ∪ L L (Rotatory–Curved–Curved) is distributed in alternating fashion between the two legs.

(*b*) Three series of amount of movement: the arms produce movements regularly increasing in amount by one unit from one to six. The movements of the torso remain of equal amount, recurring at regular intervals of time: 2–2–2 . . . &c. The movements of the legs are of the amounts 2–4–6 recurring in this same order.

(*c*) The two series (*a*) and (*b*) are combined.

CHAPTER 4

The Law of 'Light' and 'Heavy' Limbs

THE BODY may be seen as an orchestra in which every limb is used as a separate instrument. Though in some respects independent, these instruments, being interconnected, influence one another by their movements.

Consider, for example, a limb which is connected at both ends to other limbs—the forearm. The forearm is connected at one end to the upper arm, and at the other to the hand. When the upper arm moves, it carries with it the forearm and the hand connected to it; that is to say, it changes the relation of the forearm and hand to the other members of the body. However, if the hand moves, it does *not* carry the forearm with it. The forearm does not carry the upper arm, but it does carry the hand.

For the purposes of the present analysis, the degree of interdependence of the limbs will be described by using the terms 'light' and 'heavy' (although not in the customary sense of actual weight). Thus a limb which carries another will be referred to as 'heavier' than the 'lighter' limb, which it carries.

In Zero Position, the feet form the base by which the body is anchored to the floor, and a movement of the lower leg relative to the base will naturally carry the rest of the body with it. Thus the 'heaviest' limb will be that nearest the base, the next above it being relatively 'lighter', though 'heavy' as compared with the next again, and so on. This hierarchy of 'light' and 'heavy' limbs holds good for all cases in which there is a contact of the body with the floor; whatever limb may perform the function of base, whether it be the foot, knee, hands, or even head, the limb nearest that base will be 'heavy' relative to those further away, and those furthest in order from the base will be the 'lightest'. (*See Fig. 15.*)

In the case where one leg is raised from the ground, the lower part of the standing leg remains the 'heaviest' limb, the thigh being 'lighter' than the lower leg, and the pelvis 'lighter' than the thigh. The thigh of the raised leg will be its 'heaviest' part (though 'light' relative to the pelvis), the lower leg 'light' as compared with the thigh and the foot the 'lightest'. (*See Fig. 16.*)

In a jump, when the whole body loses contact with the floor and is suspended in the air, the 'lightest' limbs are those of the periphery—i.e., head, hands and feet—and the 'heaviest' those nearest the centre of the body. Chest and pelvis are regarded as equally 'heavy' and either may be described as moving relative to the other. (*See Fig. 17.*)

Thus the limbs are divided into *relative* classes—'heavy' limbs and 'light' limbs. Every limb is 'heavy' in relation to any limb which it carries while moving, and 'light' in relation to any limb by which it is being carried. The terms 'light' and 'heavy' may therefore be used of *any* limb; they indicate whether the limb *moves actively* or *moves passively.*

The law of 'Light' and 'Heavy' limbs states that *when a certain limb moves, it carries with it the 'lighter' limbs.*

The 'lighter' limbs change their relation to the System of Reference passively, as a result of the movement of the 'heavier' limbs. Nevertheless, a 'lighter' limb, at the same time that it is being carried by a heavier limb, can also move independently, and this will not contradict the law just stated; the path which that limb creates while moving is then the result of a double movement. In fact, it may be the result not only of a double movement, but of three or four movements, as, for example, when the hand moving independently, is at the same time being carried by a separate movement of the forearm, which is at the same time being carried by the upper arm, also moving independently, but which is again carried by a movement of the shoulder. Usually, in such cases, the movement of each part is analysed and written as if the 'heavier' limb were at rest, i.e., without reference to the simultaneous movement of the 'heavier' limb.

Any fixed angles between the limbs, that is, any shape formed as a result of a previous movement, is carried intact by the heaviest limb, the whole shape (position) changing its relation to the System of Reference as one unit. In such cases, only the movement of the heavy limb is actually written. (*See Figs. 18, 19 and 20.*)

It should be remembered that any limb may be at the same instant both 'heavy' and 'light'; or it may change during a sequence of movement, being at one moment 'heavy' and afterwards becoming 'light', or vice versa.

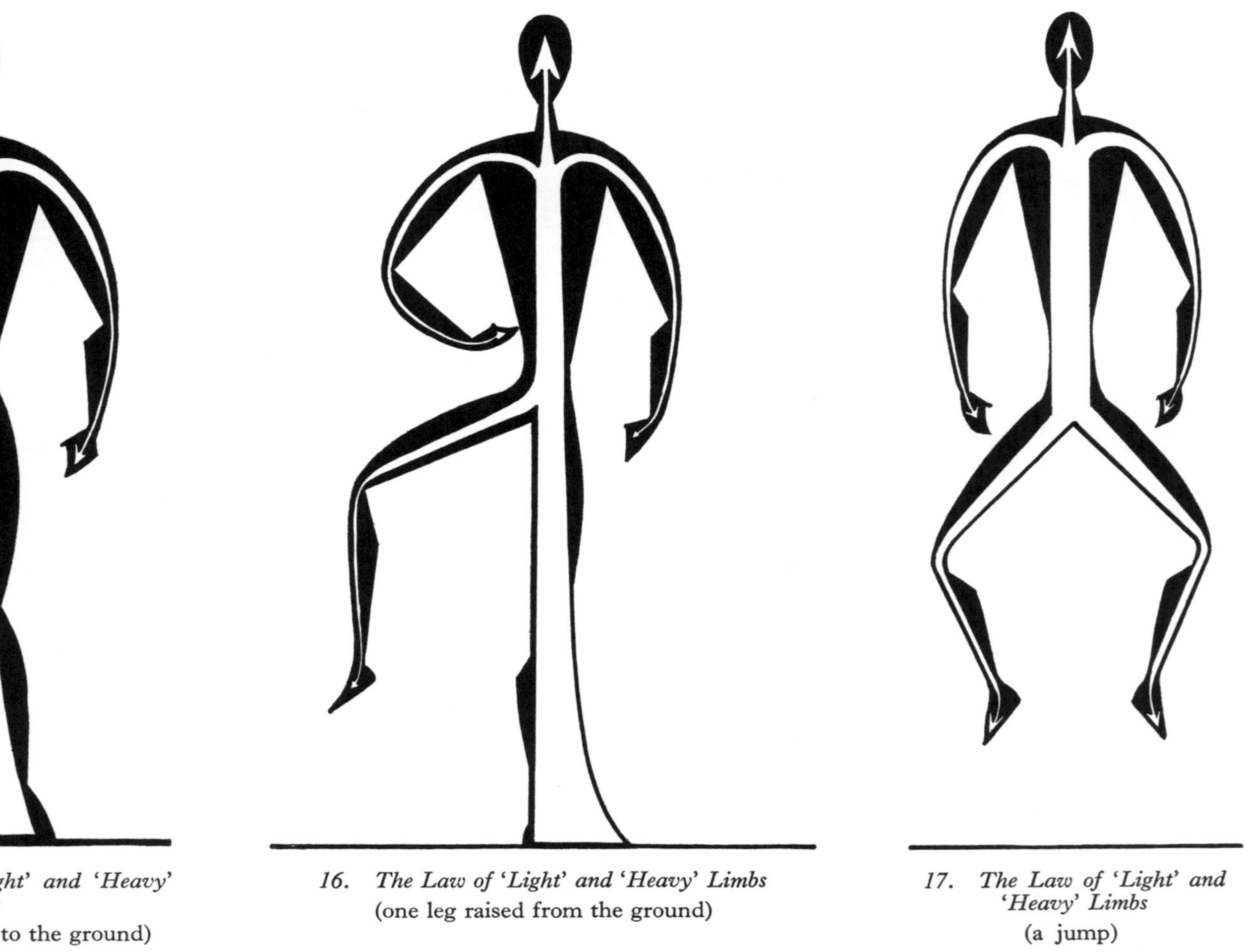

15. The Law of 'Light' and 'Heavy' Limbs
(both feet anchored to the ground)

16. The Law of 'Light' and 'Heavy' Limbs
(one leg raised from the ground)

17. The Law of 'Light' and 'Heavy' Limbs
(a jump)

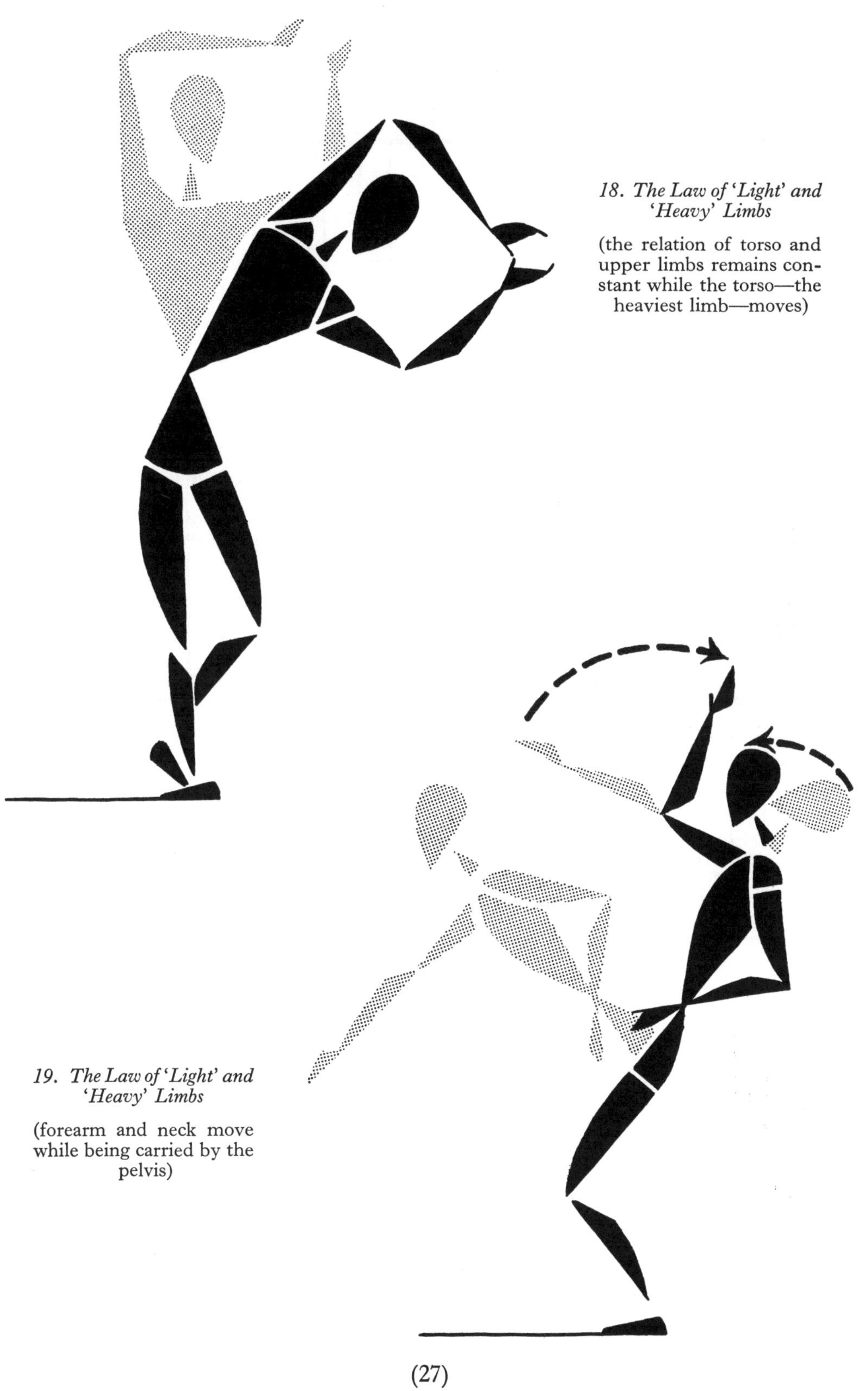

18. The Law of 'Light' and 'Heavy' Limbs

(the relation of torso and upper limbs remains constant while the torso—the heaviest limb—moves)

19. The Law of 'Light' and 'Heavy' Limbs

(forearm and neck move while being carried by the pelvis)

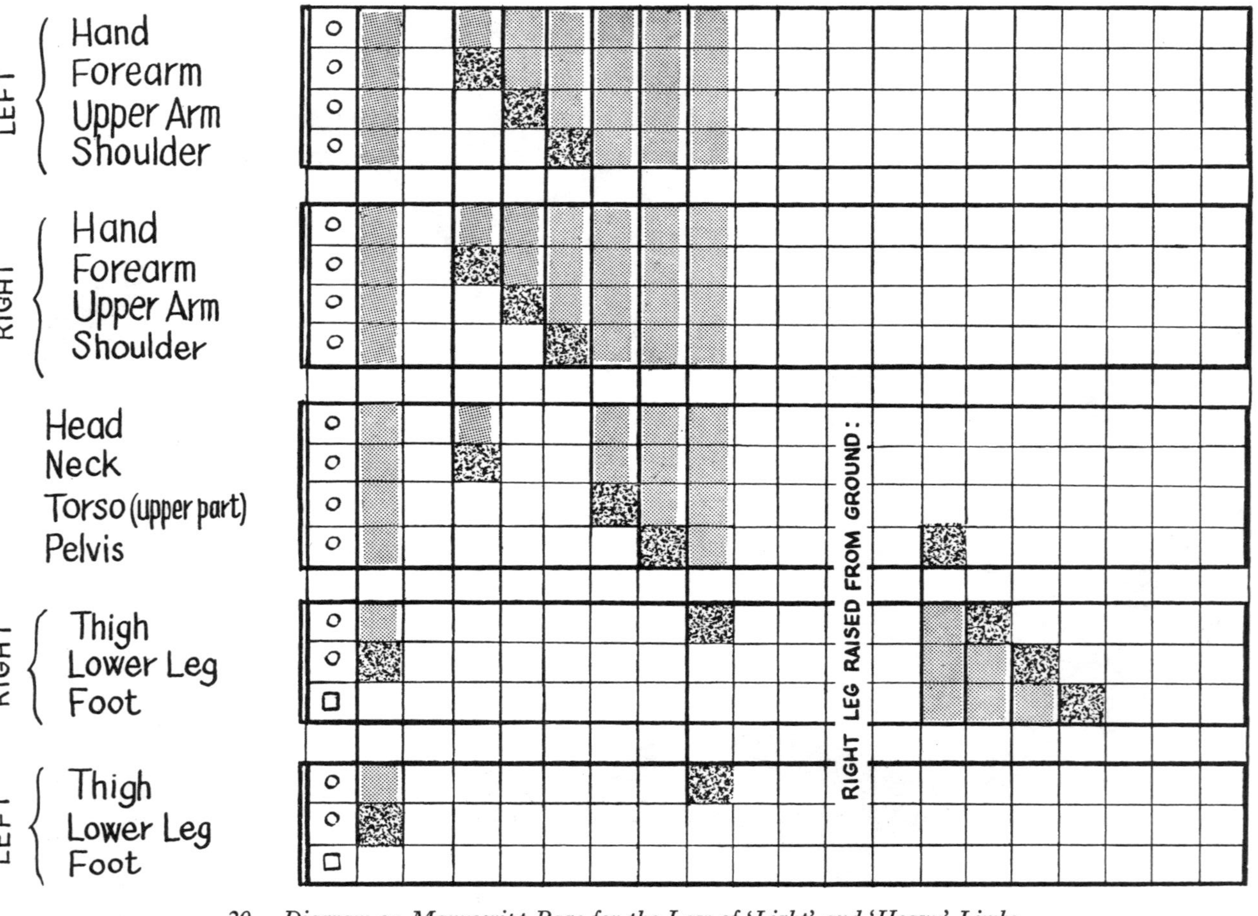

20. Diagram on Manuscript Page for the Law of 'Light' and 'Heavy' Limbs

In each time-unit column, the dark shaded portion represents the movement of the 'heavy' limb, and the lighter continuation of it represents the passive movement of the 'lighter' limbs which are carried by it.

It should be noted that the legs (when both are on the ground and supporting weight) and the arms, are paired members, and are equal in respect of 'heaviness' in spite of their representation being one above the other on the page.

CHAPTER 5

Rotatory Movement

A ROTATORY movement is a movement in which a limb (any limb) moves about its longitudinal axis, the longitudinal axis of the limb serving as the axis of movement. The theoretical longitudinal axis of the limb remains in the same position during the movement. From the point of view of an observer, the limb while moving changes the side facing towards him, without, however, changing the position of its longitudinal axis in relation to the other limbs. (*See Figs. 4 and 5.*) Since in Rotatory movement the longitudinal axis of the limb coincides with the axis of movement, the axis of the limb does not change its relation to the System of Reference.

In Zero Position the longitudinal axes of all the limbs are perpendicular to the Horizontal Plane (apart from the longitudinal axes of the shoulders and feet, which are parallel to the Horizontal Plane; both of these cases will be dealt with in later chapters). Therefore in Rotatory movement in Zero Position, every point on the moving limb moves on a horizontal plane, either clockwise or anticlockwise. The sense of a Rotatory movement in Zero Position is determined by looking at the Horizontal Plane from above, a clockwise movement being referred to as *positive*, an anticlockwise, as *negative*. (*See Fig. 21.*) These are fixed in relation to the axis of movement, which coincides with the longitudinal axis of the limb. Whether these axes be in positions other than Zero Position, or in movement, these directions remain in fixed relation to the axis of the limb.

The sign for a positive (clockwise) Rotatory movement is: ∩

The sign for a negative (anticlockwise) Rotatory movement is: ∪

The amount of rotation (magnitude of movement) is the amount of deviation of the limb, from the moment it leaves *any starting* position, and up until the end of its movement. (It must be remembered that the Magnitude of movement is an interval and does not refer to fixed positions.) The number expressing the magnitude of movement is written within the sign; for example:

∩2				2∪		∩3	1∪			2∪	
		∩1			∩1			2∪			

(*See Fig. 22.*)

Had the body been made up of parts of uniform size and shape, such as equal cylinders, Rotatory movements would have had very little formal significance. But since each part of the body is completely different from every side, the whole form of the body changes from the point of view of the observer, while its parts rotate. For instance, the head, when rotated through ninety degrees from Zero Position, is seen by an observer as being in profile instead of in full face. Again, the formal aspect of a movement may be entirely changed by Rotation of the moving limb; bending of the legs after outward Rotation through ninety degrees will have an entirely different appearance from bending of the legs in Zero Position, and will be in fact that of a first position *plié* in Classical Ballet.

Since in Rotatory movement the position of the limb in relation to the System of Reference remains constant, Rotatory movement may occur simultaneously with any other type of movement. For instance, the right arm may be imagined as being raised from Zero Position forward to shoulder level, the arm being gradually turned so that the palm of the hand faces upward instead of inward. A Plane movement has then been performed simultaneously with a positive Rotatory movement of 90 degrees.

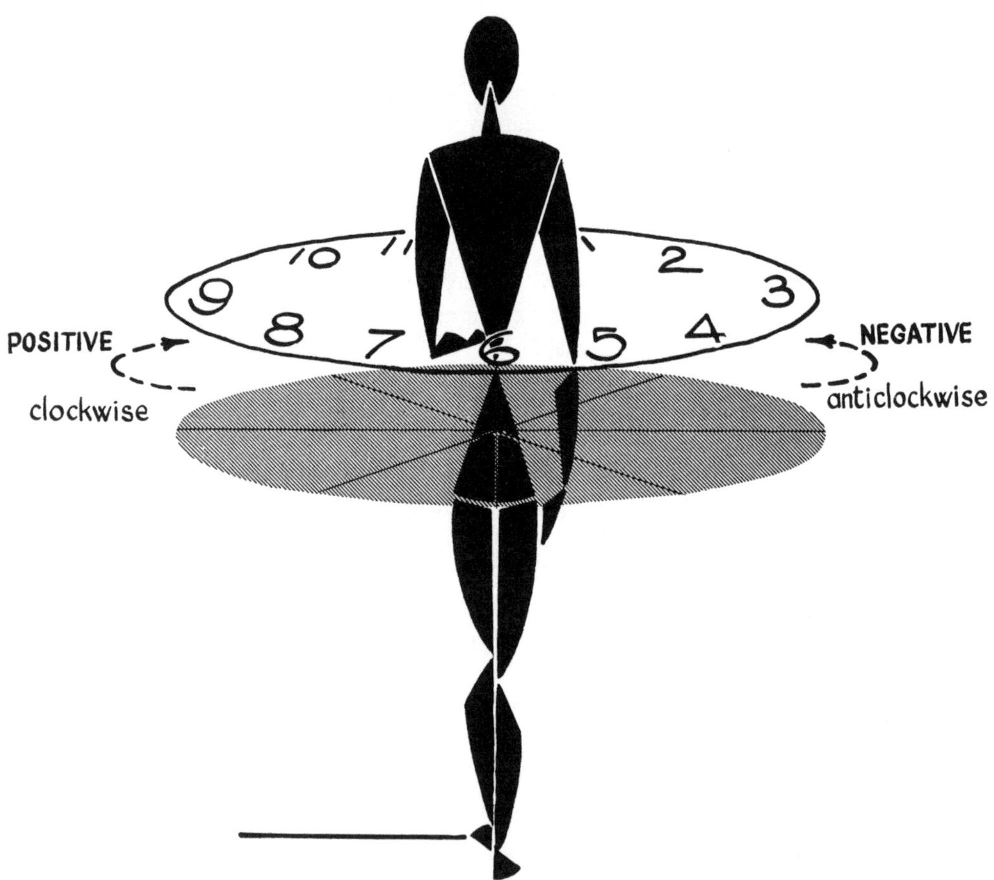

21. The Horizontal Plane

Sense and amount of Movement are determined by looking down onto the plane.

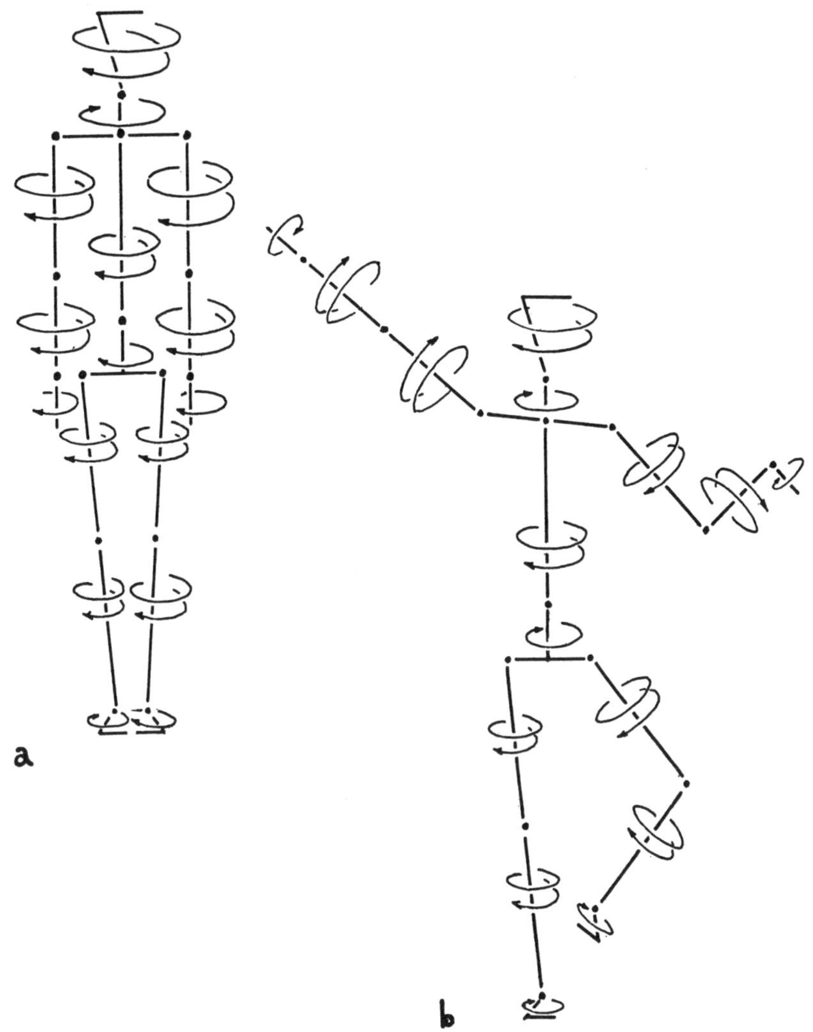

22. Sense of Rotatory Movement

(a) Rotatory movement in positive sense when all limbs are in Zero Position, indicated by horizontal spirals.
(b) Showing the spirals as if carried by the limbs to whatever position the limbs move.

CHAPTER 6

Plane Movement

A PLANE MOVEMENT is one in which the motion of a limb (the longitudinal axis of the limb) produces a plane. The axis of the limb moves perpendicularly to the axis of movement. (*See Figs. 6 and 7.*)

Plane movements are classified as follows:

(1) A horizontal movement in which the moving limb produces a horizontal plane. (*See Fig. 23.*)

(2) A vertical movement in which the limb produces any plane perpendicular to the Horizontal Plane; (axis X of the System of Reference is common to all such planes). Planes of this kind will be called 'Vertical Planes'. (*See Fig. 24.*)

(3) A complex movement producing an Intermediate Plane: a combination of horizontal and vertical movement, the limb producing any plane not included in (1) or (2) above. (*See Fig. 25.*)

The written sign denoting any plane movement whatsoever will be an arrow.

(*a*) *The Analysis and Writing of Horizontal Plane Movements*

A movement producing a horizontal plane is one in which the longitudinal axis of any limb produces a plane parallel to the Horizontal Plane of the System of Reference. The sign for a movement in a horizontal plane is an arrow pointing either to the right or to the left. These two directions on the page denote the two possible senses of movement in any horizontal plane, positive or negative. In order to decide the sense of a Horizontal Plane movement, a fixed angle of observation of the horizontal plane is chosen: the bird's-eye view, looking from above downward on any horizontal plane. The positive sense will then be given the sign $\rightarrow$ and the negative, the sign $\leftarrow$. (*See Figs. 21 and 23.*)

The magnitude of a movement in a horizontal plane is indicated by giving a measurement in degrees (by means of the given scale) of the amount of deviation of the moving limb from its starting position, that is, indicating the size of the horizontal section produced by the horizontal movement, or in other words, the horizontal interval produced. (*See Fig. 23*).

Thus the sign for a Horizontal Plane movement will always consist of two symbols: (i) the *arrow* indicating the kind of movement, (plane) the *way it lies in relation to the page* indicating the classification within that kind (horizontal plane), and the *direction of its head*, the sense of the movement positive or negative; (ii) the numeral, indicating the magnitude of movement.

e.g.: $\overset{1}{\rightarrow}\ \overset{2}{\leftarrow}\ \overset{4}{\rightarrow}$ &c.

(b) *The Analysis and Writing of Vertical Plane Movements*

A Vertical Plane movement is one in which the motion of any limb produces a vertical plane—any plane perpendicular to the Horizontal plane. The sign for a movement producing a vertical plane will be an arrow pointing either upward ↑ or downward ↓.

In order to analyse and write a movement producing a Vertical plane, three things must be verified:

(1) With which coordinate on the Horizontal plane the horizontal projection of the vertical plane coincides. By this the relation of the vertical plane to the System of Reference is established.

Any line on the horizontal plane which passes through *S*, the centre of the body, to (*Y*) may become a coordinate if its amount of deviation from *Y*0 be indicated. (*See Fig. 24.*)

The horizontal projection of a Vertical plane coincides with two coordinates having an angle of 180 degrees between them. The horizontal coordinates are numerically denoted according to their deviation from *Y*0 in a positive sense only, and each plane thus has two numbers, those of the two horizontal coordinates (standing in a relation of 180 degrees to one another) with which it coincides; so that, for example, a movement of the arm, rising forward from Zero Position towards *Y*0, may be correctly written either as a movement in a vertical plane identified as coinciding with coordinate 0—or as a movement in the vertical plane coinciding with coordinate 4, where the scale is $1 = 45°$. To denote the projection of the Vertical plane it is sufficient to indicate one of the two coordinates with which it coincides.

The coordinate of the Vertical plane will be indicated by means of a number, in brackets. A Vertical plane whose horizontal projection coincides with coordinate *Y*0 will be indicated by (0). If the scale of the written composition is $1 = 45°$, then the number 1 or 5 (according to choice) will indicate a plane which deviates forty-five degrees from a Vertical plane whose coordinate is 0. The number 2 will denote twice this amount of deviation, and so on according to the agreed scale, the coordinates being always in numerical order and read in the positive sense

e.g. (1)↑   (2)↑   (6)↑   &c.

(2) The size of the section of the Vertical plane (the vertical interval) produced by the movement will be denoted by a number, indicating the amount of movement according to an agreed scale which may or may not coincide with the scale by means of which the coordinates have been established. This number will always appear, without brackets, at the right side of the arrow.

(2)↑2   (2)↑4   (0)↑5   &c.

(3) The sense of movement. In a Vertical plane movement, there are again two possible senses of movement. The shortest way from *X*0 to the horizontal coordinate which denotes the plane, and the continuation of this way, is called the *positive* sense. The long way from *X*0 to the horizontal coordinate denoting the plane is called the *negative* sense.

The positive sense is indicated by an arrow pointed upward in relation to the manuscript page: ↑; and the negative sense by an arrow pointed downward: ↓.

The complex symbol which indicates a movement producing a plane will always be comprised of three units:

(2)↑3   (4)↓1   (0)↑2   &c.

The arrow denotes the kind, classification within the kind, and sense of the movement. The number in brackets on the left indicates which specific vertical plane is produced (according to a given scale). The number at the right side shows the size of the section of specific plane produced (again according to a given scale). (*See Fig. 26.*)

(*c*) *The Analysis and Writing of Intermediate Plane Movements*

(*See Fig. 25.*)

An Intermediate Plane movement is one in which the movement of the limb produces an intermediate Plane.

An Intermediate Plane is any plane which is neither a Horizontal nor a Vertical Plane. Any plane whose relation to the Horizontal Plane is other than perpendicular is an Intermediate Plane.

As the possibility is given to define the position of any line by two projections of that line, so it is given to find the position of any limb (its longitudinal axis) by two projections of that limb:

A projection on the Horizontal Plane. This projection coincides with a certain horizontal coordinate, and this coordinate is called horizontal coordinate of the limb in the given position.

A projection on a Vertical Plane. The limb, in whatever position it may be, lies on a certain vertical plane. The coordinate of the vertical plane is the same as the horizontal coordinate of the limb. The position of the limb on the specific Vertical plane coincides with the projection of that limb on the Vertical plane. The position on the Vertical plane is determined by its deviation in degrees from X0 in the positive sense. This vertical projection gives the Vertical coordinate.

These two coordinates, the Horizontal and the Vertical, are sufficient to define the position of a limb in relation to the System of Reference.

The moment that a limb moves, it begins to change continuously either its Horizontal coordinate or its Vertical coordinate, or both of them. In a Horizontal plane movement, the limb changes only the Horizontal coordinate, in a Vertical plane movement only the Vertical coordinate is changed.

In a movement producing any intermediate plane both the horizontal and the Vertical coordinates change.

It is given, then, to write a movement creating an intermediate plane by denoting the change of the two components of the movement—the Horizontal and the Vertical. However, it has been chosen, for reasons which will partly be explained later, to write an Intermediate plane in a different manner.

A System of Reference constructed on the Scale $1 = 45°$ contains 26 coordinates, and each of these may serve as the axis of movement of a Plane movement (in which the axis of the limb moves at an angle of 90° with the axis of movement). As there can be only one relation of 90° to one axis of movement, there is therefore a total of twenty-six planes in such a System. Since one-half of the coordinates is complementary to the other half (i.e. half the coordinates continue the lines of the other half, on the other side of *S* at an angle of 180°), the same plane is common to a coordinate and its component, leaving a total of thirteen planes.

When once the radial division of the Horizontal Plane of the System of Reference has been established (by means of a given scale) then the planes given within the space of the System are also known. Where the scale is $1 = 45°$, these are as follows:

One *Horizontal Plane*, whose axis of movement is X of the System of Reference.

As many *Vertical Planes* as there are coordinates on the Horizontal Plane (not counting their complements)—in this case four. The axis of movement of each is the horizontal coordinate which is at an angle of 90 degrees to the horizontal coordinate denoting the plane. Each Vertical Plane coincides with one coordinate on the Horizontal Plane, and its complement: e.g. the Vertical plane, which runs forward and backward dividing the body symmetrically, coincides with Horizontal coordinate 0, and its complement 4.

Twice as many *Intermediate Planes* as there are Vertical Planes, their axes of movement being coordinates on vertical planes.

In a System of Reference built according to a scale of 1 = 45° only eight axes are found which belong (are perpendicular) to Intermediate planes. That is to say, among all the Intermediate planes which it is possible to perform and write in a scale of 1 = 45° by denoting shift of the horizontal and vertical components of the movement, it is possible to express only eight, in the manner which will be described, i.e. by the coordinates of the system. (In the examples given in this book only such planes will be dealt with.)

For the purposes of analysis intermediate planes may be considered as Horizontal, Vertical Planes as tilted. The amount of tilting of the Vertical plane necessary in order to reach the required intermediate position is decided as follows. The Vertical plane is identified according to the horizontal coordinate with which it coincides. Counting in the positive sense, a second horizontal coordinate is found which lies at an angle of 90° with that of the plane. The Vertical plane now moves around its own coordinate which is the axis of movement of axis X of the plane so that $X0$ moves towards the coordinate which lies at 90° to it, moving in the positive sense. Thus, if the Vertical plane is based on the horizontal coordinate 1 (1 = 45°), then the movement will be in positive sense towards coordinate 3, which is at 90° to coordinate 1. If it is based on coordinate 2, then $X0$ moves in positive sense towards 4, and so on.

The amount of movement of $X0$ (i.e., the amount which the Vertical plane shifts) is expressed by numbers from the given scale. Thus if the scale is 1 = 45°, a shift of 1 gives an Intermediate plane, a shift of 2 would make the tilted plane coincide with the Horizontal plane, a shift of 3 would again give an Intermediate plane, and a shift of 4 would return it to vertical. Thus each Vertical plane, when tilted through the degrees given in the scale 1 = 45°, yields two possible Intermediate Planes, and a total of eight in the whole System of Reference.

The Intermediate Plane may thus be identified and written by means of two numbers:

The first (which is written as the lower) indicates the Horizontal coordinate on which is constructed the Vertical Plane.

The Second (written above the first) is a number indicating the amount of shift of the Vertical Plane (read as a positive movement of its lowest point $X0$) away from $X0$.

An arrow pointing either up ↑ or down ↓, indicating (a) that it is a Plane movement and (b) the sense of movement. The sense of an Intermediate Plane movement is determined according to the sense of its horizontal shift.

Two numbers at the left-hand side of the arrow e.g. $\genfrac{}{}{0pt}{}{2}{(3)}\uparrow$. The lower number, which is in brackets, identifies a Vertical Plane by means of its Horizontal coordinate (as was done in the case of Vertical Plane movement). The upper number without brackets indicates the amount which this Vertical plane has shifted in order to coincide with the required Intermediate plane, the shift always being in the positive sense from $X0$. It is to be imagined that axis X of the Vertical plane moves in a Plane movement, in the positive sense (carrying with it the whole plane); around an axis of movement which is the horizontal coordinate which denotes the plane.

A number at the right-hand side of the arrow indicates the magnitude of movement, again judged according to the horizontal shift, e.g. $\genfrac{}{}{0pt}{}{4}{(8)} \downarrow 6$.

N.B. From Zero Position the limb may move only in one of the Vertical planes. To create a Horizontal plane the limb must be in a position on a horizontal plane. To create an Intermediate plane, the limb must be in any position other than perpendicular to the Horizontal plane. (*See Exs. III and IV.*)

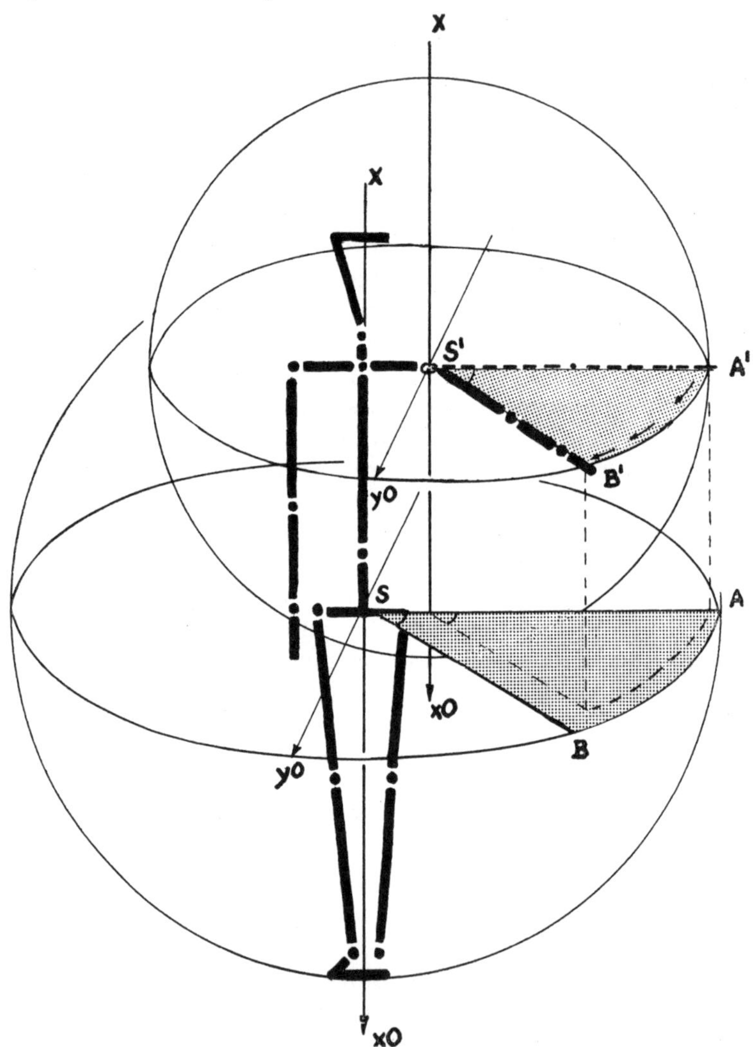

23. *Horizontal Plane Movement*

The left upper arm, acting as 'heavy' limb, carries the whole arm in a movement from *A'* to *B'*, creating a 45° section of the Horizontal plane of its private System of Reference. The analysis of movement is carried out according to the private System of Reference of a limb, but all private Systems are reflections of the main System and thus the plane section created by the movement of the arm is reflected in parallel fashion by *SAB* in the Main System. When the scale is 1 = 45°, the movement will be written $\xrightarrow{1}$.

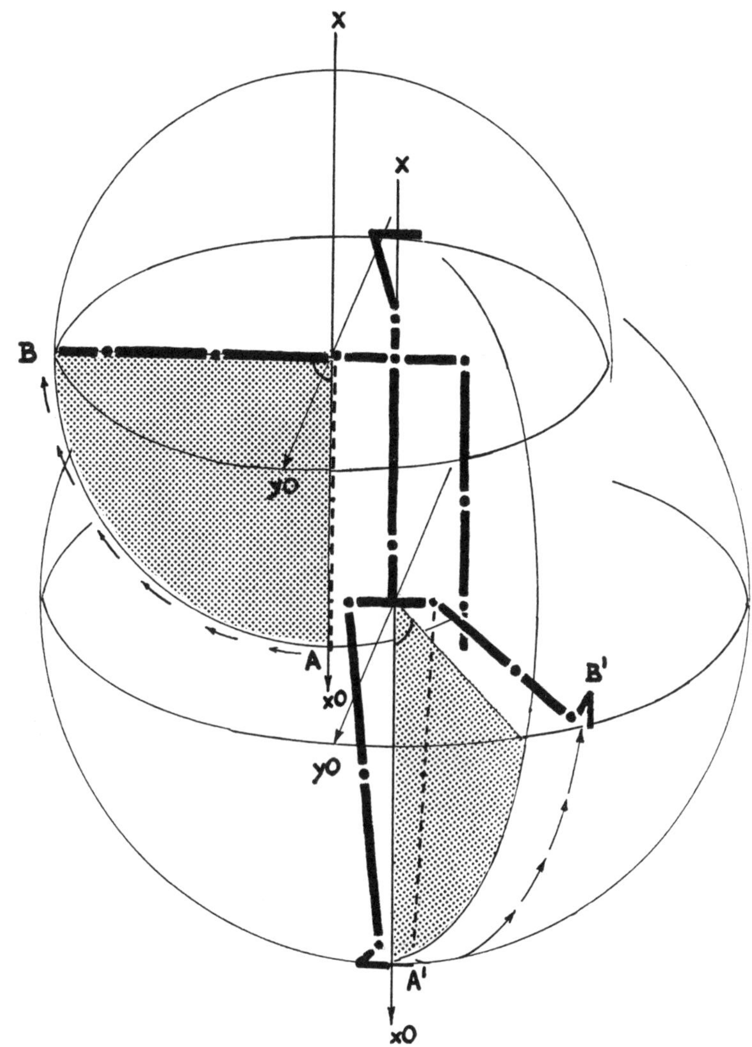

24. Vertical Plane Movement

The right arm creates in its movement from *A* to *B* a 90° section of a vertical plane. Should the coordinates on the Horizontal plane have been fixed according to a scale in which 1 = 30°, the movement of the arm would then be a positive movement in a vertical plane of which the horizontal coordinate is 3, the movement would then be written: (3) ↑ 3.

The left leg moves in a positive direction from *A′* to *B′* creating a 90° section of a vertical plane of which the horizontal coordinate is 11. This movement is written: (11) ↑ 3.

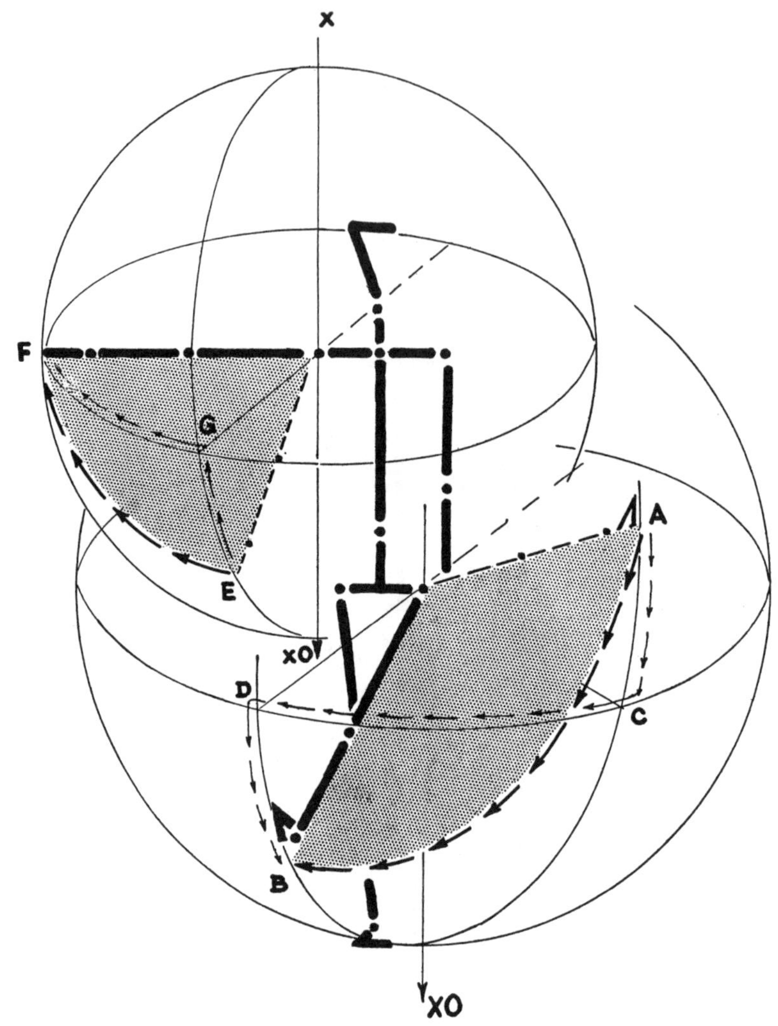

25. Intermediate Plane Movement (1)

The left leg moves from *A* to *B* in an Intermediate plane. The horizontal shift of the movement is from *C* to *D* in a positive sense. The vertical shift is equal to the two sections *AC* and *DB* in the negative sense. The resulting movement is therefore in an Intermediate Plane.

The right arm moves from *E* to *F*. $GF = 90°$ and $EG = 30°$; there is both a horizontal and a vertical shift and the movement is an Intermediate Plane movement. The arm creates one quarter of the Intermediate Plane which would result from tilting the Vertical plane 3 (when $1 = 30°$) so that its lowest point rises 60° in the positive sense. If $1 = 30°$, the movement is written $_{(\frac{1}{3})} \uparrow 3$.

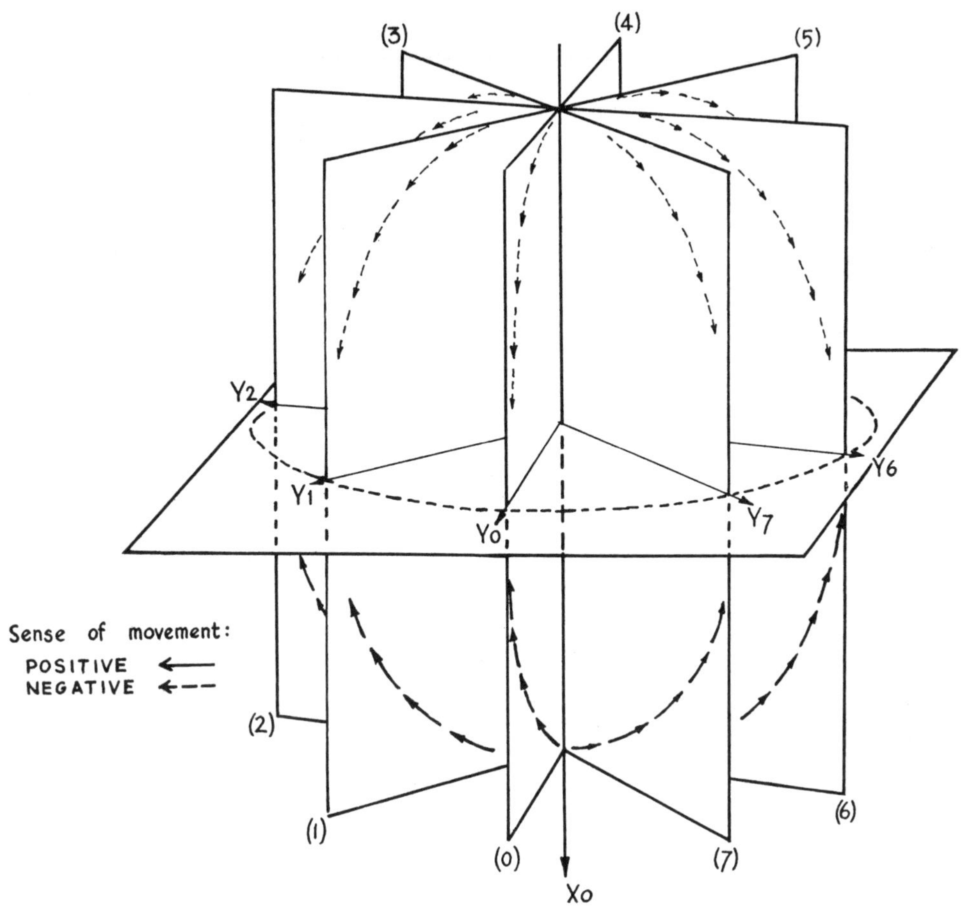

26. Horizontal Plane and Vertical Planes, with sense of movement in the Vertical Planes

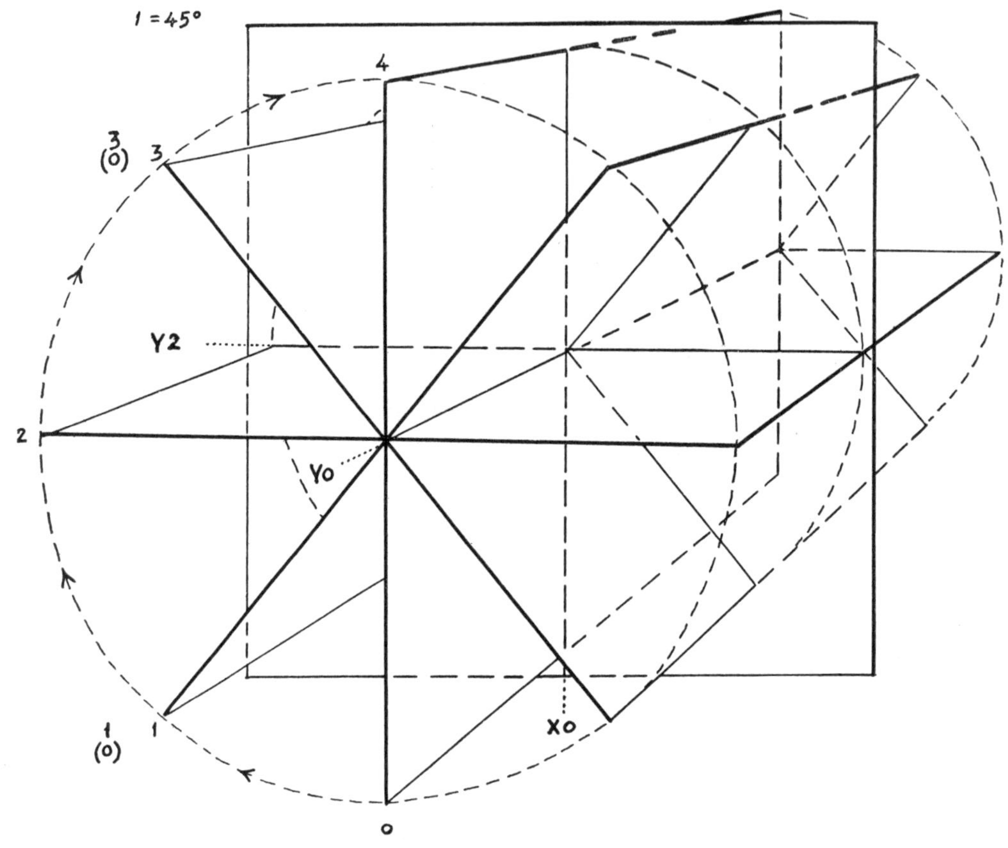

27. Horizontal Plane, Vertical Plane, and Intermediate Plane

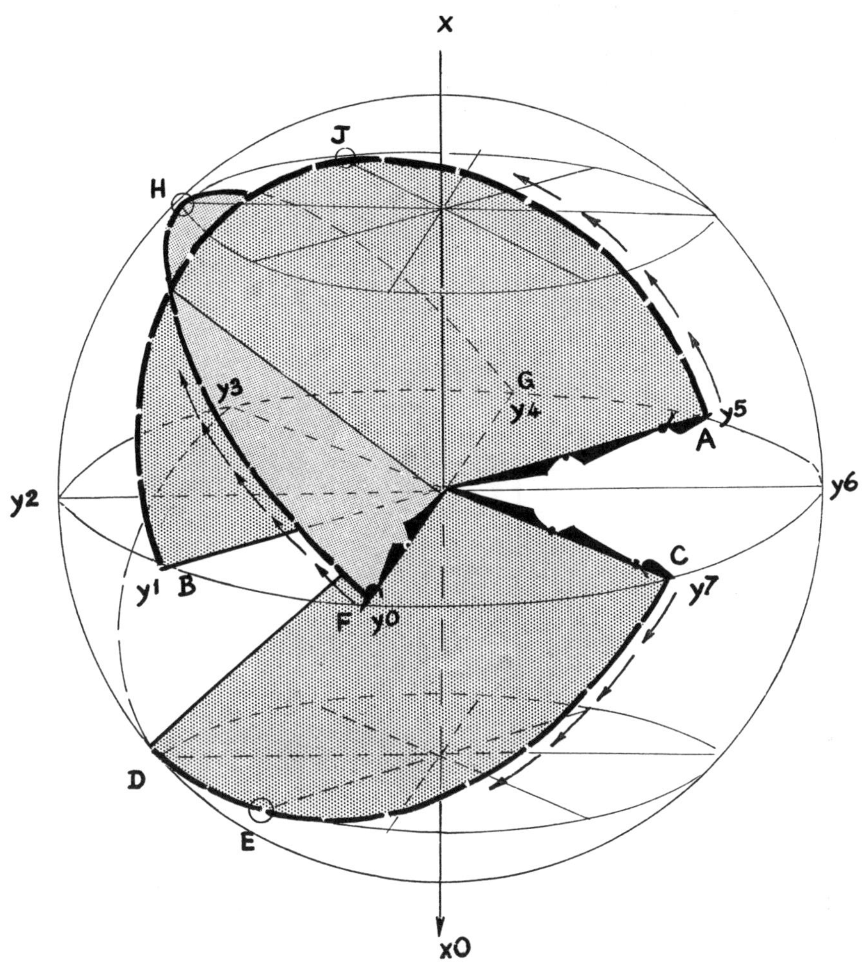

28. Intermediate Plane Movement (2)

The diagram shows three arms moving in Intermediate Plane movements. The arm which moves from *A* to *B* creates a section of the Intermediate plane $(\frac{1}{1})\uparrow$; the Intermediate Plane is denoted as the Vertical plane (1), tilted 45° in the positive sense. The amount and sense of the movement are established according to the horizontal shift. The movement is therefore written $(\frac{1}{1})\uparrow 4$, when the scale is 1 = 45°.

The movement of the second arm, from *C* to *D*, creates a section of Intermediate plane $(\frac{1}{7})\uparrow$; this plane is regarded as the Vertical plane (7), tilted 45° in the positive sense. Amount and sense of movement are established according to the horizontal shift, and the movement (when 1 = 45°) is written $(\frac{1}{7})\uparrow 3$.

The third arm creates, in its movement from *F* to *G*, a section of Intermediate plane $(\frac{1}{0})\uparrow$. The Intermediate plane is regarded as the vertical plane (0), tilted 45° in the positive sense. The amount and sense (in this case negative) are, as always, established according to the horizontal shift. When 1 = 45°, the movement is written $(\frac{1}{0})\downarrow 4$.

1 = 45°

LEFT ARM	o	(0)↑1	(0)↓1	(0)↑8	(0)↓8	(7)↑1	(7)↑1	(7)↑1	(7)↑1			(7)↑4
RIGHT ARM	o	(0)↑1	(0)↓1	(0)↑16		(1)↑1	(1)↑1	(1)↑1	(1)↑1	(1)↑4		
TORSO	o									⌣2	⌢2	⌢2

	(6)↑1	(6)↓1	(6)↑8	(6)↓$\overset{\frown}{8}$	(5)↑1	(5)↓1		(5)↑8	(4)↑1	(0)↑5	(0)↓4	
	(2)↑1	(2)↓1	(2)↑16		(3)↑1	(3)↓1	(3)↑8		(4)↑1	(0)↑5	(0)↓4	
⌣2										(0)↓1	(0)↓1	(0)↑2

(6)↑2	$\overset{1}{(2)}$↑2	$\overset{1}{(2)}$↓2	$\overset{1}{\rightarrow}$	$\overset{3}{(7)}$↑1	$\overset{3}{(2)}$↓2	$\overset{2}{\leftarrow}$						
(2)↑2	$\overset{1}{(2)}$↓2	$\overset{1}{(2)}$↑2	$\overset{1}{\leftarrow}$	$\overset{1}{(1)}$↓1	$\overset{1}{(2)}$↑2	$\overset{2}{\rightarrow}$						
(0)↓1			(0)↓1			(0)↑2	⤒	(1)↓2	$\overset{2}{\leftarrow}$	(7)↑2	⤒	(0)↓1

(continued on following page)

Ex. III. Plane and Rotatory movements of the Arms and Torso

LEFT ARM								(6)↑1	$\overset{3}{(1)}$↑1	(7)↓1	(5)↑2	(7)↓2
RIGHT ARM								(2)↑1	$\overset{3}{(1)}$	(7)↓1	(1)↑2	(3)↓2
TORSO	↑	2	(0)↓1	2	2	↑	(0)↑2				$\overset{2}{\rightarrow}$	(1)↑2

Ex. III. (*cont.*) This example is designed as a simple exercise in reading, and has no compositional significance. It consists of a succession of movements such as are ordinarily used in gymnastic exercises, but which might appear within any movement composition. By the convention adopted in this notation method, whenever no indication is given, it is assumed that the limbs remain in Zero Position; therefore only those limbs which are active are represented on the written page. For the most part the movements are given the same time value: for this example the rhythmical value is of no importance, and the duration of each movement may be read as is convenient. Theoretically, this succession of movements might be transferred to any other parts of the body, although of course this is not always possible in practice, since the more limited range of movement of certain limbs would prevent the performance of some movements.

1 = 45°

RIGHT LEG:	ZERO POSITION	(0)↑1	(0)↓1	(0)↑2	1 →	(1)↓1	(1)↓2	(1)↑1

(2)↑1	(2)↑1	(2)↓3	(2)↑3	1 →	(7)↑4	(3)↑1	(3)↑1	(3)↑1	(3)↑1

1 →	(0)↑4	(4)↑4	(0)↑5	(4)↑2	(0)↑1	5 →	← 6	1 →	(0)↓2

Ex. IV. Movements of the Right Leg. A simple reading exercise consisting of twenty-seven movements The time values are arbitrary and may be modified at will. No indication being given for the rest of the body, it is assumed (according to the convention adopted) to be in Zero Position. An interesting exercise would be the transference of this example, unchanged, to the left leg. Although in relation to the System of Reference the new sequence would be identical with the original, it will be found that the movements would be different in their relation to the rest of the body: movements and positions which were 'open' will become 'closed' (*croisée*, in the terminology of the Classical Ballet). It would also be interesting to observe the result when the same sequence is performed by the thigh, but with the lower leg flexed in relation to it, throughout. Again, the leg might be rotated through 90 degrees in the positive sense, and remain so throughout the sequence; the same movements would then assume the appearance of the Classical Ballet style.

CHAPTER 7

The Rhythmical Organization of Movement

ROTATORY AND PLANE MOVEMENT, introduced up to now, offer by themselves a wide field for the composition of movement, and a general and technical explanation of the notation of body time recommends itself at this point.

Up to now, only the three-dimensional (spatial) relations of movement have been dealt with, but the element of time was already implied, since the notion of 'earlier' and 'later' is involved in any process of movement. It is in fact inseparable from the other elements, but when the necessity arises for symbolization, the time element must be abstracted from the organic whole and dealt with separately.

On the manuscript page, coordinate *T* represents the flow of time. The coordinate is divided equally, and the equal spaces resulting from the division represent equal time-units. These smallest units of time may be of any single value whatsoever, as measured by the metronome or clock; they have no meaning except as units of measurement of duration. These equal units can be built into larger or smaller groups. By means of this grouping a time-pattern is created, and such a pattern may serve as a model by which events of any kind (including the change of relations of the limbs) may be organized and represented in their order of appearance and duration in time.

The movement symbol is written in the horizontal space allotted to a limb (writing from left to right). The length of time during which the movement continues is measured by the number of small units of time, counted from where the symbol is written—which is always immediately following a bar line—up to the next bar line. The bar line traverses the horizontal space or spaces allocated to one or more limbs. It marks the amount of time during which the limbs change their relation to each other—by the enclosure of a certain number of the small time-units, the amount of time during which the movement takes place is defined.

Some written symbols, being larger than others, occupy more space on the page, but the duration of a movement is always indicated by the number of columns representing small time-units between one bar line and the next, regardless of the size of the symbol. In the following example, *both* the movements represented have a duration of two time-units:

$\overset{\frown}{2}$				
(2) ↑ 8				

It is possible with the help of small time-units and bar lines to create time patterns on the manuscript page. In fact, it is theoretically possible to create as many divers simultaneous 'polytime' patterns as would be allowed by the number of horizontal spaces allocated to the limbs. However, as far as the notation of the rhythmical value of movement is concerned, this division provides only the most general programme of time division of any sequence of movement. The full rhythmical meaning will appear only when the complete movement signs (indicated kind and amount) are written within the groups of time-units comprising the pattern.

The *same* time pattern (as expressed by the division of the page by the bar lines and the small time-units) may have a completely different rhythmical meaning when differing movement signs are distributed within it. For a movement of one limb, taking place in the same length of time, will be faster when it is of larger magnitude and slower when it is of lesser magnitude. The rhythmical meaning of a movement sequence consists of the relation between fast and slow movement. This relation of fast and slow, relations of speeds of movement, may be the result of the different sizes of limbs producing the same amount of movement within the same time limits; or it may be produced by changing, within the movement sequence of one limb, the amount and kind of the movements, while the time allocated to each single movement remains constant; or again, by changing the amount of time allocated to the same movement.

The speed of a moving limb is the result of the size of the path which it traverses in a given time, and is expressed by the full movement sign and the time-units attached to that sign.

'Empty' columns on the manuscript page which are included between two bar lines and contain no symbols, signify that a certain set of relations of the limbs to one another—the position of the limbs implied in the previous bar—is preserved during the given time. In a dance composition this is usually called a 'pause'.

When it is wished to indicate the absolute speed of a written composition, the value of the small time-unit is indicated at the beginning of the written composition. If, for example, each unit is to be equivalent to one beat of a metronome set at 60, this is written as □ = ♩ = 60.

It is sometimes found desirable to change the value of the small units during the course of a written work, either for convenience of writing, or in order to reflect an actual change of rhythmical character. In such a case, the first indication of the value of the time-units is given as, for example, □ = ♩ = 80, and each unit will then be understood as equivalent to one beat of a metronome set at 80. If it is then required, at a certain point in the composition, to give to each unit half the time-value, the indication □ = ♪ is written at that point in the written work, at the bottom of the page, beneath the lowest horizontal space. Two units will then be equivalent to one metronome beat. Similarly, if it is required to double the time-value originally given, so that each unit becomes the equivalent of two beats of the metronome, the indication □ = 𝅗𝅥 is given at the appropriate place. The new value holds good until a further indication is given of change of value of the time-unit.

Time is inseparable from movement, even when one movement alone is conceived; since it contains the idea of transition, it contains automatically the idea of time. When attention was drawn to the various possible series (of amount, type of movement, and distribution among limbs—see Chapter 3), in each of them a corresponding time series was also implied, since the idea of 'earlier' and 'later' was involved. However, from the present chapter it becomes clear that it is possible to build another series, one consisting of durations of time itself. This series, like the others, contains the idea of order of certain units—in this case, units of amount of time. This fact is important, because such a series, like the others, can serve as the framework for a composition, and by taking into account the possibility of building such a series a means of composition comes into being, because a method of organizing the material (movement) is provided, which is based on the characteristics of that material. This series can be combined with the others in all possible permutations.

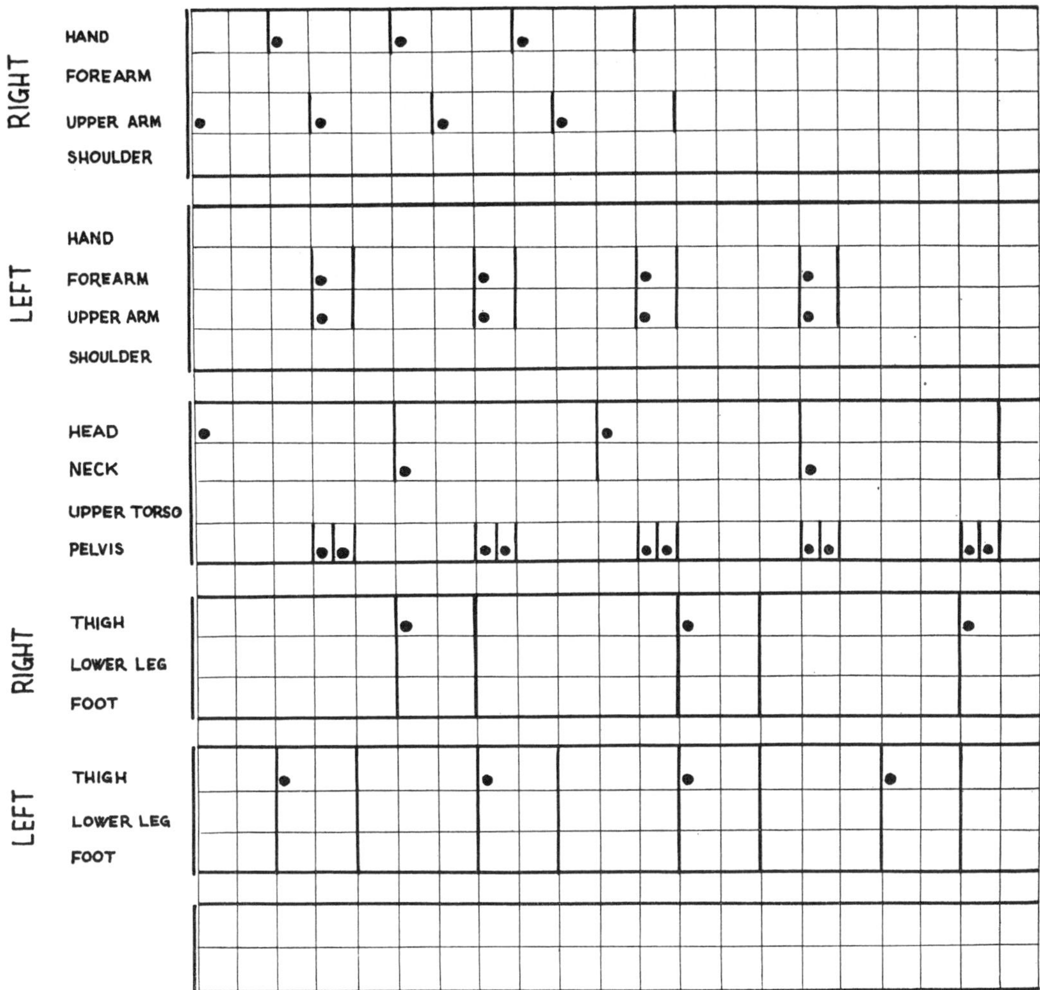

Ex. V. Time Pattern. In the right hand and upper arm, movements follow one another without a pause; each of them has the duration of three time units. In the left upper arm and forearm, movements occur of one unit in duration, separated from one another by pauses of three units. The head and neck alternate in movements of five units' duration, one moving while the other remains in a fixed position. The pelvis has movements of one unit in duration, appearing in pairs—two movements, followed by a pause of three units. The right leg remains in a fixed position throughout five units of time, and moves during two: this is repeated thrice. The left leg produces movements of two units duration, separated by pauses of three units.

It can be seen that the movements and positions of each limb occur in a pattern in which a certain regularity may be discerned. Although these patterns, as they stand here, do not indicate the actual speed of the movements—since amount and kind of movement are not indicated—nevertheless the possibility of creating them suggests that they may be used in order to create a coherent composition.

This example and Ex. I are not essentialy different, except that they emphasize different aspects of the notation: in one case that of the order of appearance of activity in the limbs, and in the second case, the pattern of the duration of this activity.

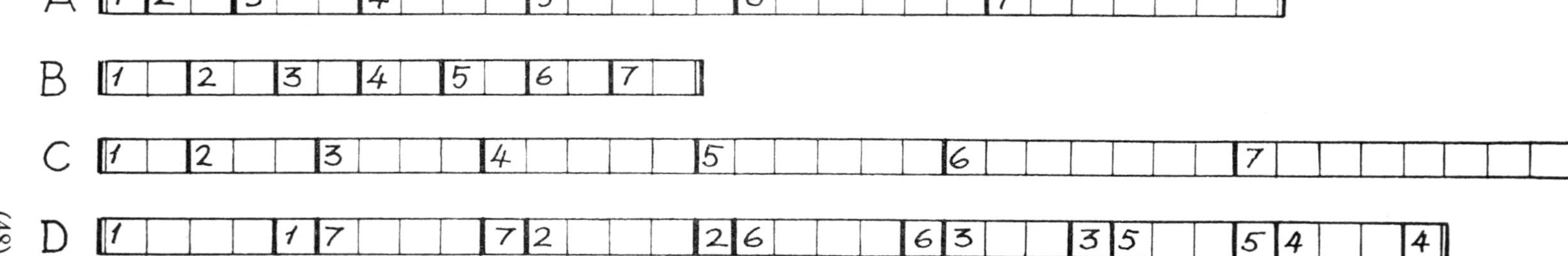

Ex. VI. Speed of movement. In this example the numbers represent the size of the movement, the smaller unit being 1. In *A* the speed of the movements is constant, since the size of the movements increases together with their duration. In *B* the speed increases in the ratio 1, 2, 3 ... 7. If the sequence be read in reverse order, the speed of the movements decreases. In *C* the speed of movement increases but at a lesser rate than in *B*, as the relation between size of movement and time units is different from that in *B*. *D* is a sequence of movements of unequal speeds.

CHAPTER 8

Positions

THE SYSTEM OF REFERENCE provides for the definition of movement; that is, the definition and measurement of the *change* which takes place when a limb travels from one position to another.

The System of Reference also provides the possibility of defining the *position* of a limb (a line) included in the space of the System.

A position is an unchanging state.
A movement is a state of change.

It is possible to define the actual change, from the point of view of the *amount* of change taking place, by making use of one or two components of any movement:

(1) A Horizontal component (the amount of horizontal shift), which is measured by the section of the Horizontal plane which the projection of the limb creates in its movement.

(2) A Vertical component (the amount of the vertical shift), measured by the section of the vertical plane created by the projection of the limb while moving.

For the analysis of the amount of movement alone, a system of reference would have sufficed which, without any of the special numerical signs which have been affixed to the radial divisions (coordinates) of the System used, such as *Y*0, *X*0, *X*2 or *Y*3. By means of such a system it would have been possible to *measure the amount of movement*, but no idea could have been given of the specific spatial relations of the limbs to one another at any given moment. It would be possible to see the movement of a limb as deviation relative to a given starting position, and simply to count the number of radial divisions of the System and to express the movement as a deviation of so many degrees from that starting position.

In this kind of analysis the place of the moving limb within the space of the System is neither indicated nor located; so the System would be a *measuring* System. However, since in the System of Reference absolute numbers have been affixed, progressing from *Y*0 in the positive sense and from *X*0 in the positive sense (according to any chosen scale) it is possible to locate the position of a limb within the space of the System. At every instant, whatever the position of a limb, it is possible to define the horizontal and vertical projections of that limb and to identify their projections by means of the appropriate coordinates. Thus, for the definition of any position of a limb at a given instant, two numbers are sufficient; a number expressing its horizontal deviation from *Y*0 and another expressing its horizontal deviation from *X*0. In such cases the System serves as a *defining* System.

The two aspects of the Systems of Reference—as a 'measuring' system and as a 'defining' system—provide two ways of writing any movement:

(1) By writing the actual path of movement, giving the starting position of a limb, and thereafter writing the kind of movement and amount of movement;

(2) By writing the starting and final positions of a limb and, between them, the kind and sense of movement (but not the amount of movement).

In the first case (since it is a result of the movement) the final position of a limb will be inferred. In the second case, the amount of movement is a result which can be inferred. (*See table given below.*)

N.B. The foregoing applies when the movement is of *one* limb only. Cases in which several limbs move simultaneously will be dealt with later.

In the analysis and writing of Plane movement the System of Reference was used mainly for the measurement of the *amount* of movement of a moving limb, after the plane created by the moving limb (Horizontal, Vertical, or Intermediate) had been defined, and after the sense of movement had been established. For the definition of the plane which a limb produces in its movement, however, use is made of the principle of writing of position in order to locate the plane in relation to the System of Reference.

Any position is represented by two numbers, written one above the other. The numbers which represent positions are enclosed within brackets to distinguish them from the numbers which signify amount of movement, $\binom{2}{2}$ $\binom{1}{4}$ $\binom{0}{0}$ $\binom{4}{0}$ $\binom{3}{6}$, &c. The upper number expresses the vertical coordinate; the lower number, the horizontal coordinate. N.B. in the writing of Intermediate Plane movement, the two numbers on the left side of the arrow also define a position—but in this case, the new position of coordinate *X* of a shifted Vertical plane, and not the position of an axis of a limb. (To distinguish this from the notation of the position of a limb, only the lower number is enclosed in brackets: $\genfrac{}{}{0pt}{}{2}{(4)}$ $\genfrac{}{}{0pt}{}{1}{(3)}$ &c.)

Every position of a limb can be written in two ways; either according to that coordinate with which its horizontal projection actually coincides, or by using the coordinate which lies at 180° to it—i.e. its complement. For example, the position of an arm held straight forward, parallel to the ground, could be written as either $\binom{2}{0}$ or $\binom{6}{4}$ when $1 = 45°$. For the definition of positions, half the number of coordinates would have sufficed; but the use of all is permissible. However, when the position is comprised of connected limbs which are in one plane, it is preferable to use only one coordinate (and not a coordinate and its complement); this coordinate should be that which coincides with the horizontal projection of the 'heavy' limb (*See Figs. 29 and 30.*)

$1 = 45°$

Starting Position	Movement Sign (Including Amount of Movement)	Resulting Final Position	Starting Position	Movement Sign (Including Final Position)	Implied Amount of Movement
(0)	(0) ↑ 2	$\binom{2}{0}$	(0)	(0) ↑ $\binom{2}{0}$	2
(0)	(0) ↑ 16	$\binom{0}{0}$	(0)	(0) ↑ $\binom{0}{0}$ + (0) ↑ $\binom{0}{0}$	16
$\binom{1}{0}$	(0) ↓ 3	$\binom{6}{0}$ or $\binom{2}{4}$	$\binom{1}{0}$	(0) ↓ $\binom{6}{0}$	3
$\binom{2}{1}$	(1) ↑ 7	$\binom{0}{1}$ or $\binom{0}{0}$	$\binom{2}{1}$	(1) ↑ $\binom{0}{0}$	7
$\binom{1}{7}$	$\genfrac{}{}{0pt}{}{3}{(1)}$ ↑ 2	$\binom{3}{1}$	$\binom{1}{7}$	$\genfrac{}{}{0pt}{}{3}{(1)}$ ↑ $\binom{3}{1}$	2

The Rotated State of a Limb

For the exact definition of the position of a limb, it is not enough to state the relation of its longitudinal axis to the System of Reference, because even in one fixed position the limb may turn about its longitudinal axis, thereby changing the side facing an observer, the axis of the limb meantime not changing its position. Therefore, for the complete definition of a limb's position, it is necessary to define its 'rotated state' in the given position. For this purpose it is necessary to imagine the limb as being brought to Zero Position—its 'rotated state' remaining fixed as that of the position analysed. The amount of rotation, positive or negative, necessary in order to bring the limb into its present 'rotated state', is ascertained by comparing the two 'states of rotation': that of Zero Position and that of the given position.

An example will make this imaginary process clear;—a position in which the arm is held directly upward with the palm facing forward. To determine the rotated state of the limb the amount of Rotatory movement must be judged which would bring it from Zero Position (by rotation) to a position in which the palm faces forward—in this case 90 degrees. This whole process of 'bringing the limb to zero position' is a purely imaginary act, since it is not always possible to avoid rotation of the limb in moving it from one position to another.

The Rotated state of a limb is then expressed by a Rotatory movement sign positive or negative—with the amount of movement—enclosed in brackets, this sign being placed together with the positional sign.

When a positional sign appears without a Rotatory movement sign, the rotated state of this limb will be identical with its rotated state in Zero Position.

Starting Position

The occasions which require the use of positional signs will be discussed each in its appropriate place; one application however, will be dealt with immediately, namely that of *Starting Position*. This is the position from which a sequence of movement begins. Starting Position is not necessarily identical with Zero Position. Starting Position may consist of any possible constellation of relations between the limbs of the body. It is indicated at the beginning of any composition, all the numbers expressing positions of the limbs being enclosed by brackets. Immediately following this, a double bar line is drawn, traversing the whole page. The vertical columns in which the Starting Position is written do not express time units and are not taken into account as part of the duration of the movement sequence. (*See Figs. 31, 32, 33 and 34.*)

Hitherto, systems of movement notation have been positional notations, in the sense that they have generally consisted of signs for fixed directions and fixed positions of the limbs; a series of such positions is recorded, and according to an accepted convention the performer passes from one position to another by means of movement. However, the fact that such a convention is possible indicates that a hard-set style is being relied upon for the interpretation of the notation, which does not take into consideration the infinity of different ways in which it is possible to pass from one position to another. A positional notation can therefore never be a sufficient and complete form of movement notation.

Since it is possible to move from one position to another in an endless number of ways, a series of positions cannot in itself constitute a dance. But when the movements are defined, by means of which the positions are reached (as they may be defined by the use of Symbols of movement), then such a series may be exploited as a subject or motif in a dance—just because of the very diversity of movement which can give a series its significance in the composition. The positional series is, then, another means of composition—which may fruitfully be combined with those series already mentioned (Chapters 7 and 10). (*See Examples VII and VIII.*)

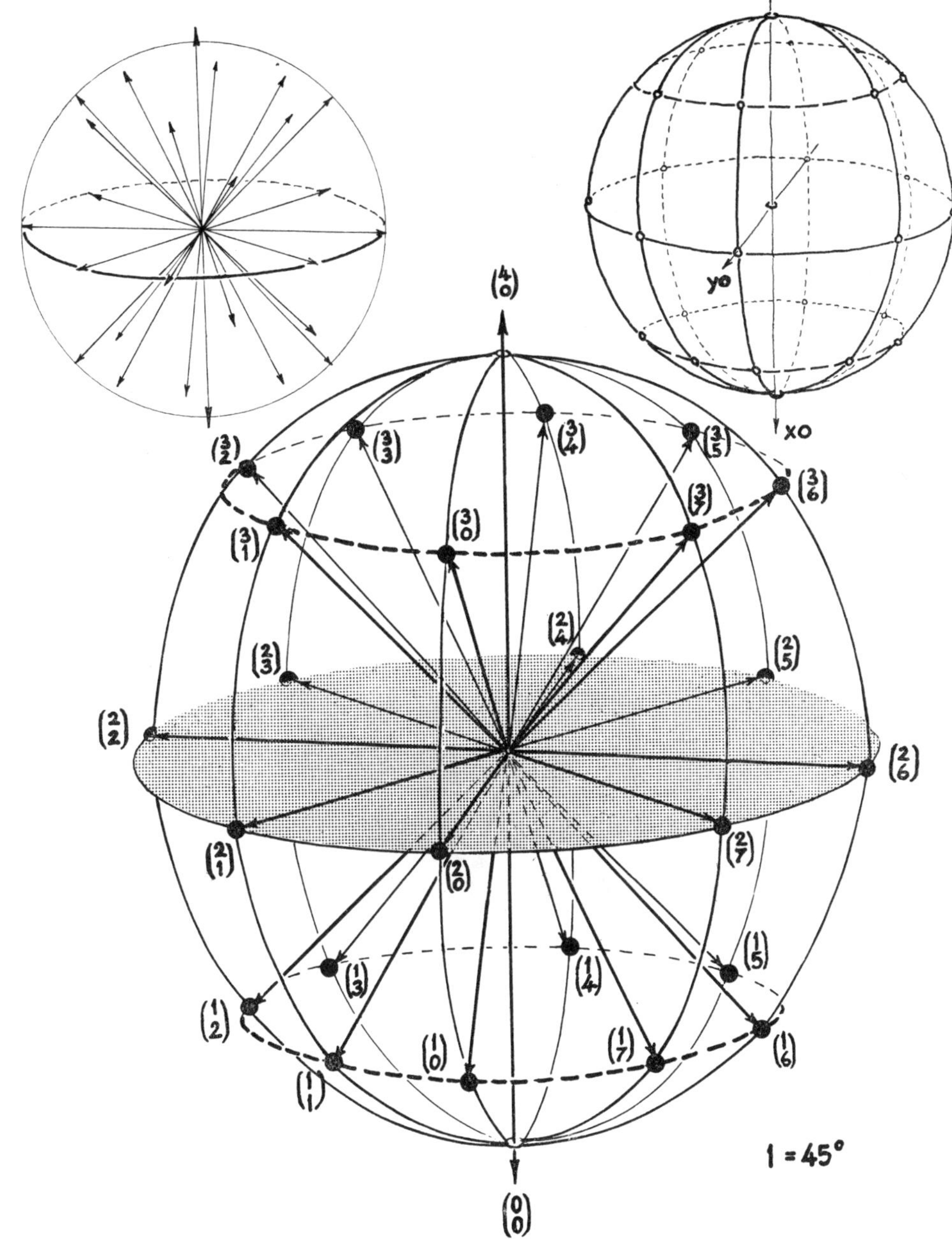

29. The Coordinates Constructed on the System of Reference

The diagram provides a more concrete illustration of the two aspects of the notation—the analysis of movement and the analysis of position—and the connexion between them. The System of Reference with all the coordinates built upon it, contains in itself two elements: movement-sections, and coordinates. Once a scale of division of the Horizontal Plane of the System of Reference has been chosen, the number of coordinates within the space of the System of Reference is finite. (A coordinate is a line in the space of the System which is defined according to its horizontal and vertical projections.) When, for example, the scale of division of the Horizontal plane is 1 = 45°, then the number of coordinates, including $\binom{0}{0}$ and $\binom{4}{0}$, will be twenty six. On the other hand, the number of possible movement sections is much greater.

In the diagram, the upper left-hand figure shows only the coordinates, built on a scale of 1 = 45°. The right-hand upper figure shows the curves of the horizontal and vertical movement sections only. Every short curve (separated from the next by circular points) is a curve of 45°. In combination, certain of these curves form the Horizontal Plane and Vertical Planes.

The large central figure shows a combination of the two smaller systems, and is the System of Reference in its entirety, when 1 = 45°. Without the coordinates it is impossible to define planes of movement, and without the existence of Planes of Movement, the coordinates remain unrelated one to another.

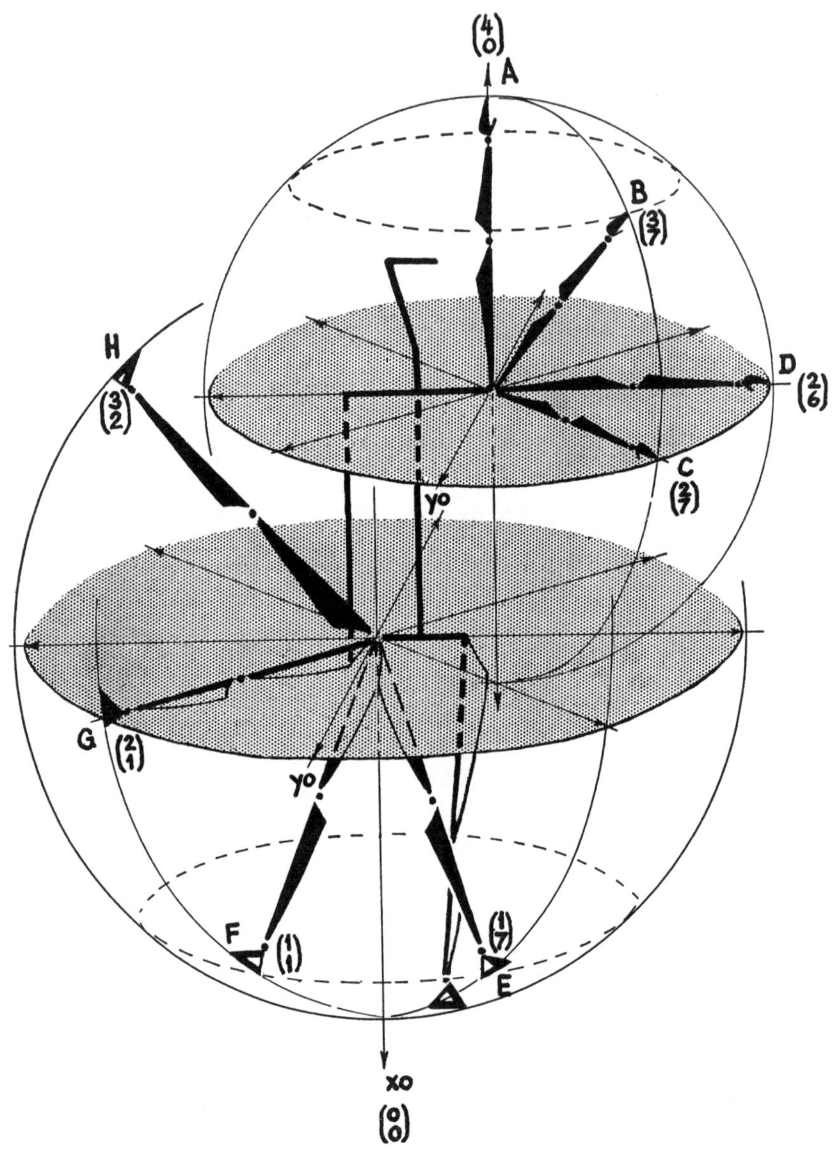

30. A Sequence of Positions of One Arm and One Leg

The scale: 1 = 45°.

Position of the Arm: A—$\binom{4}{0}$, *B*—$\binom{3}{7}$, *C*—$\binom{2}{7}$, *D*—$\binom{2}{6}$.

The positions *B* and *C* are identical in respect of their horizontal coordinates. The positions *C* and *D* are identical in respect of their vertical coordinates. Hence it is possible to infer that a movement from *B* to *C* (and from *A* to *B*) will be a vertical movement, since between these two positions there is a vertical difference and horizontal parallelism. A movement from *C* to *D* will be a horizontal movement, since here there is a horizontal difference and a vertical parallelism.

Position of the leg: E—$\binom{1}{7}$, *F*—$\binom{1}{1}$, *G*—$\binom{2}{1}$, *H*—$\binom{3}{2}$.

As in the positions of the arm, it can be seen that a movement from *E* to *F* will be a horizontal shift (a horizontal cone), a movement from *F* to *G*, a vertical movement, and from *G* to *H* a movement in an intermediate plane, since between *G* and *H* there is a difference in both their horizontal and vertical coordinates.

31. *Analysis of a Position of the Whole Body*

(The limbs in relation to the System of Reference). In this analysis, only the positions of the longitudinal axes of the limbs are written, without indicating their rotated state.

In the diagram, all the longitudinal axes of the limbs are in one plane, that plane of which the horizontal projection coincides with the horizontal coordinate (2), or (6) which is the complementary coordinate of (2). Coordinate (2) will be used here. Thus, the horizontal projection of all the limbs is identical with the horizontal coordinate (2). But the vertical projection on this plane is different in various limbs, and the numbers indicating the shift of the limb from $X0$ in positive sense will be different in the different limbs.

In the middle figure, the circle enscribing the System of Reference represents the vertical plane (2) with all its coordinates.

The notation of the position of the axis of a given limb is performed by writing the sign of the coordinate to which that limb is parallel in the space of the System of Reference, and will always consist of two numbers, the lower indicating the horizontal projection of the limb, and the upper the vertical projection.

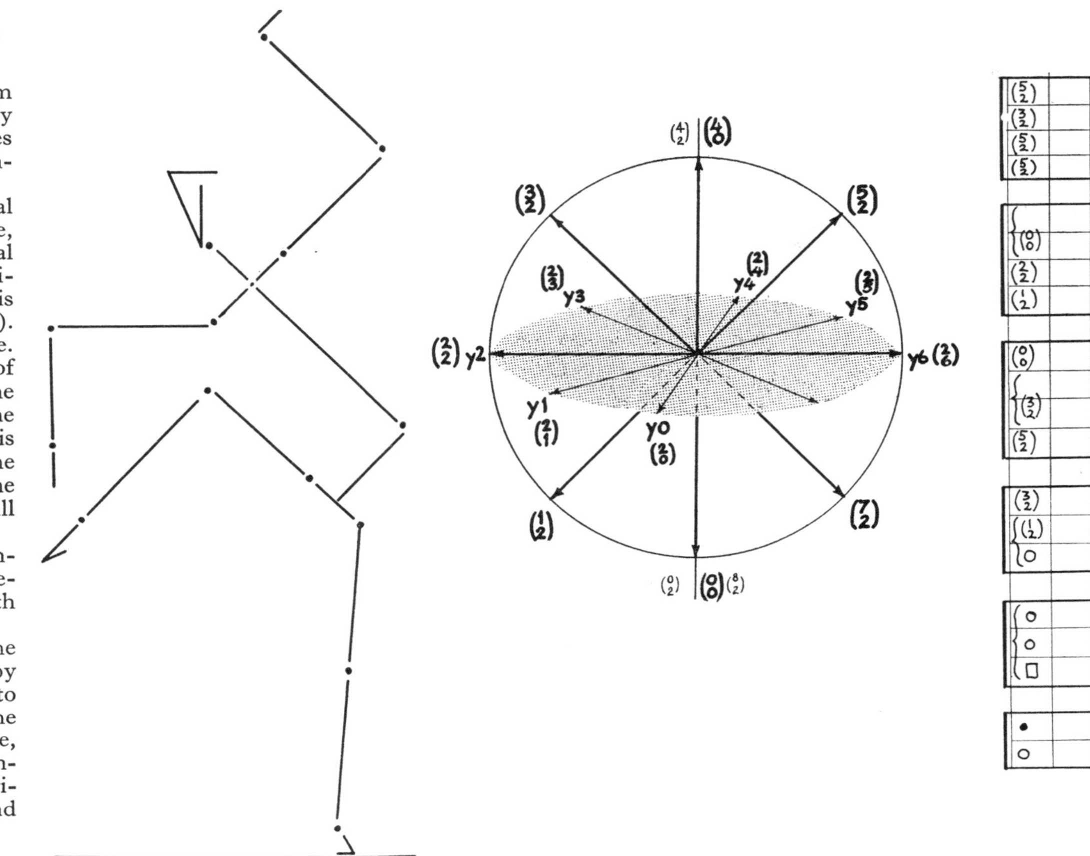

E

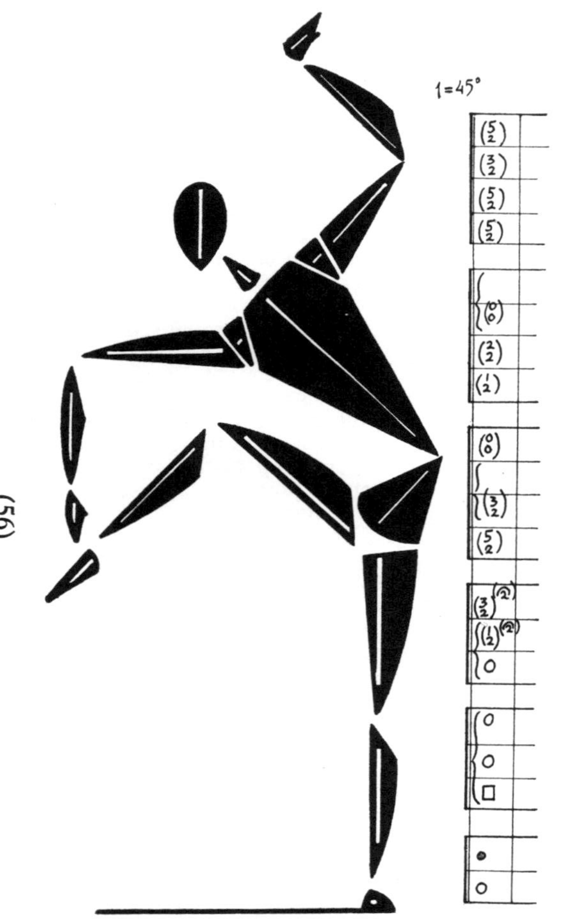

32. Analysis of a Position of the Body

The position is the same as that of Fig. 31 with the addition of the rotated state of the limbs.

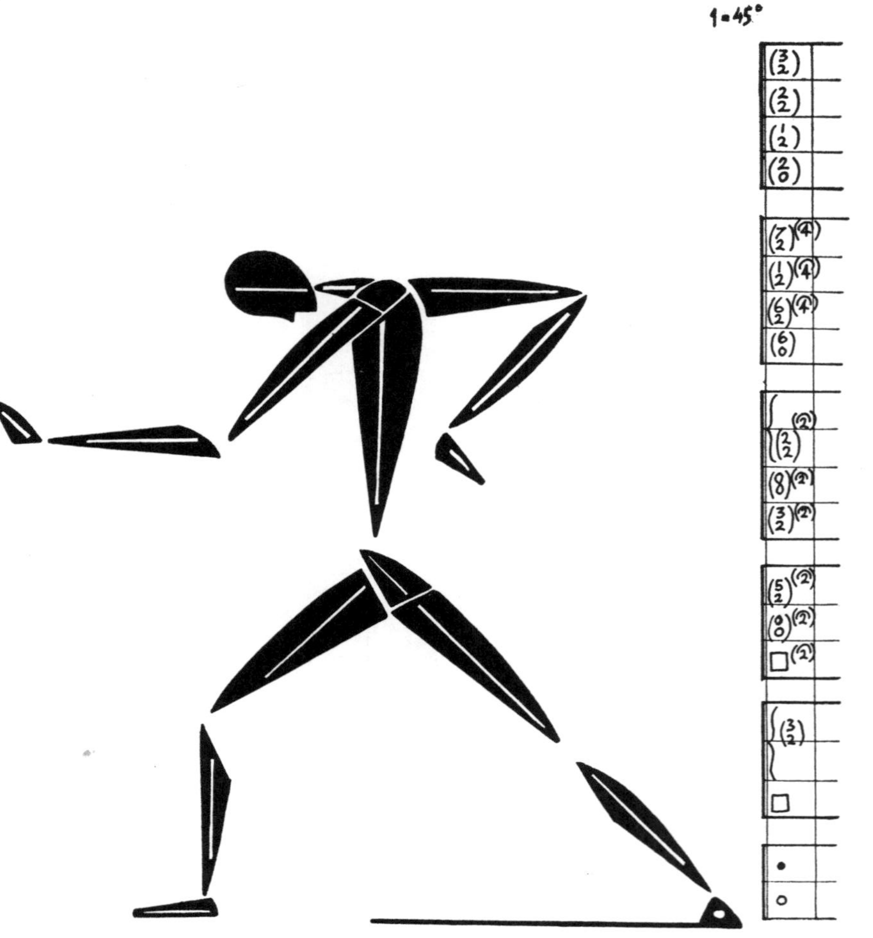

33. Analysis of a Position of the Body

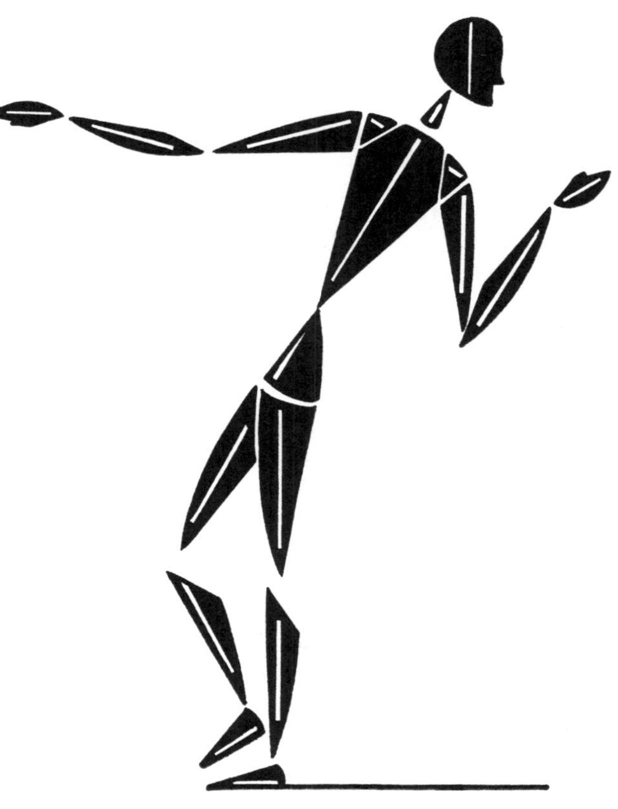

34. Analysis of a Position of the Body
Note that the scale here is 1 = 15°.

1 = 15°													
LEFT ARM	0							(0/0)					
	0					(18/0)	(12/0)	(6/0)(6)	(6/12)(6)				
	0	(21/6)	(13/6)	(13/6)(12)	(6/0)(6)	(12/0)	(18/6)	(18/6)	(6/0)	(6/21)(6)	(9/0)(6)	(3/3)	(3/3)
	0												
RIGHT ARM	0							(12/0)				(6/9)(3)	(18/3)(9)
	0					(18/0)	(0/0)	(6/0)(6)	(12/0)(6)			(12/9)(3)	(12/3)(9)
	0	(3/6)	(6/6)	(6/6)(12)	(12/0)	(12/0)	(6/6)	(6/6)	(0/0)	(6/3)(6)	(3/0)(6)	(18/9)	(6/3)
	0												
RIGHT LEG	0	(0/0)(6)	(13/6)(6)	(13/6)	(1/0)(6)	(1/0)	(15/6)(6)	(6/0)	(3/6)	(15/6)(6)	(3/0)	(10/6)*	(6/3)(6)
	0						(12/0)(6)			(0/0)(6)	(0/0)		(18/6)
	□	□(6)	□(6)	□	□(6)	□	□(6)			□(6)	□		
LEFT LEG	0	(0/0)(6)	(11/6)(6)	(11/6)	(23/0)(6)	(23/0)	(9/6)(6)	(0/0)	(15/0)	(9/6)(6)	(8/0)	(14/6)	(15/0)
	0						(12/0)(6)		(9/0)				(9/0)
	□	□(6)	□(6)	□	□(6)	□	□(6)	□	□	□(6)	□	□	□

Ex. VII. Thirteen Positions of the Body. (Note the scale: 1 = 15°). The whole torso remains in Zero Position in all the positions, and is therefore not represented on the page, The first four positions are broadly described below.
(1) All the limbs are in Zero Position.
(2) The legs are in "first position", and the arms midway between the "first" and "second position" of Classical Ballet.
(3) The feet are a small pace apart, the legs turned out; the right arm extended to the right side, horizontal to the ground; the left arm raised almost to the left side of the head.
(4) Similar to the third, except that the feet and legs are parallel to one another and the arms rotated so that the palm of the right hand faces upward, and the palm of the left hand towards the right.
Note.—In position 12, the single asterisk indicates that the right leg crosses in front of the left.

1:45°

		1	2	3	4	5	6
RIGHT	FOREARM	$\binom{3}{0}$	$\binom{6}{2}$	$\binom{1}{0}$			$\binom{4}{7}$
	UPPER ARM	$\binom{1}{0}$	$\binom{2}{0}$	$\binom{1}{0}$	$\binom{2}{7}$	$\binom{3}{1}$	$\binom{2}{7}$
HEAD		$\binom{2}{\smile}$	$\binom{4}{0}$	$\binom{0}{0}$	$\binom{2}{4}^{(\overset{\frown}{2})}$	$(\overset{\frown}{2})$	
TORSO		$\binom{1}{0}$	$\binom{2}{0}$	$\binom{2}{0}$	$\binom{5}{4}$	$\binom{3}{7}^{(\underset{\smile}{1})}$	$\binom{6}{2}$
RIGHT LEG (THIGH)		$\binom{1}{0}$	$\binom{2}{2}$	$\binom{6}{0}$	$\binom{1}{4}$	$\binom{1}{1}$	$\binom{2}{2}$

Ex. VIII. Six positions of the Body. The first two positions, broadly described:

(1) The right leg is raised forward and the torso tilted down towards it. The head is in profile. The arm is raised forward with the forearm at an angle to the upper arm.

(2) The right leg is raised sideways, parallel to the ground, and the torso tilted forward parallel to the ground. The right arm is raised forward and flexed at the elbow.

Note that the upright position $\binom{4}{0}$ of the head is that of Zero Position. In Zero Position all the limbs apart from the arms, shoulders and feet, are in $\binom{4}{0}$. In the following position the head is lowered so that its top is towards the ground—$\binom{0}{0}$.

The left leg remains in Zero Position throughout, and therefore (in accordance with the convention established) does not appear in the written notation.

CHAPTER 9

Curved Movement—Conical

A CURVED MOVEMENT is one in which the motion of the longitudinal axis of a limb produces a curved surface. The longitudinal axis of the limb moves at an acute angle (less than 90°) to the axis of movement (*see Figs. 8 and 9.*) Any curved movement may be regarded as creating the surface, or part of the surface, of a cone whose apex is in the joint of the moving limb. A distinction will be made between a cone on a circular base and a cone on an elliptical base. *A Conical movement* is the name given to a curved movement in which the extremity of a limb describes a perfect circle, or part of a perfect circle. (*See Fig. 46–1*, following Chapter 15.)

The Analysis of a Conical Movement

In order to analyse a conical movement, three things must be verified:

(i) The size and relation of the imaginary cone to the System of Reference.
(ii) The amount of the movement.
(iii) The sense of the movement—positive or negative.

(i) *Size and relation of the Cone to the System of Reference.* The relation of a cone to the System of Reference is established by defining the circular base of the cone. The starting position *A* is given, either by means of positional signs, or as the consequence of preceding movements. A second position, *B*, is defined (according to its vertical and horizontal coordinates), such that the straight line joining *AB* will be a chord on the base of the cone produced (or part of which will be produced) by the moving limb. In Conical movement the chord chosen will always be a diameter of the base of the cone. The chord *AB*, a straight line which is known, since it joins two known coordinates, will define the position of the base of the cone in the System of Reference, and the distance between *A* and *B* will define the size of the cone. Position *B* will be expressed by two numbers included in brackets.

An example will help to make the method clear. Suppose a movement of the right arm, which creates three quarters of a cone, beginning from a position *A*, in which it points directly forward from the shoulder, parallel to the ground. Let it begin the cone by rising and moving to the right, the finger-tips tracing a circular path, and the whole arm a curved surface, until the arm points upward and forward in a forty-five degree diagonal towards the right, and continues, in the same manner, descending until it points directly to the right at shoulder level and—still creating a curved surface—finally reaches a position downward and forward in a forty-five degree diagonal to the right. The axis of the cone of which three quarters has been produced in this movement lies parallel to the ground in a diagonal of forty-five degrees to the right: position $\binom{2}{1}$ when $1 = 45°$. (Throughout the movement each point on the limb remains at a fixed distance from the axis of movement.)

In the example given, the starting position of the limb was $\binom{2}{0}$. The position B, which lies on the same plane as the starting position and the axis of movement, is $\binom{2}{2}$. Thus the position of the cone in relation to the System of Reference will be concisely expressed: $\underline{|\binom{2}{2}\;}$; this symbol must be understood in conjunction with the starting position of the limb.

In a conical movement, point B, the end of the diameter by which the size and relation of the cone is defined, may not ever be reached, since only a quarter of a cone may be produced; or it may be passed one or more times, since the same cone may be produced more than once in succession.

(ii) *Amount of Movement.* The magnitude of movement in a Conical movement is expressed as the section of the circumference of the base which is traced by the extremity of the moving limb: the amount in degrees of this circular path is given according to the scale of the composition.

(iii) *Sense of Movement.* Looking from the apex of the cone towards its base the movement of the extremity of the limb is classified as either positive, when it is clockwise; or negative, when it is anticlockwise.

When a Conical movement is such that the axis of the cone is vertical, and the base parallel to the ground, it is sufficient that the sign should consist of two units—the sign of Curved movement, and a numeral within it expressing amount of movement; for example: $\underline{|\;2\;}$. Further indication of its relation to the System of Reference is redundant, since in a given position of a limb, only one axis of movement can be perpendicular. Thus only one cone can be performed when the axis of movement is known to be perpendicular and the starting position is given (either by positional signs or as the result of preceding movements). In all other cases, the sign of a Conical movement is made up of three units:

(1) The sign of a Curved movement, positive $\underline{|\quad}$ or negative $\overline{|\quad}$.

(2) The positional sign (two numbers in brackets) written inside the sign of the curved movement $\underline{|\binom{2}{3}\;}$. This gives the relation of the cone to the System of Reference. When understood in conjunction with the position which precedes the movement (a position not indicated in the symbol, but known already, being either the inevitable result of the previous movements—or the starting position of the whole composition).

(3) A number indicating the section of the cone actually produced by the movement.

$$\underline{|\binom{2}{3}\,3}$$

(*See Figs. 35, 36, 37 and 38* and *Examples IX, X and XI.*)

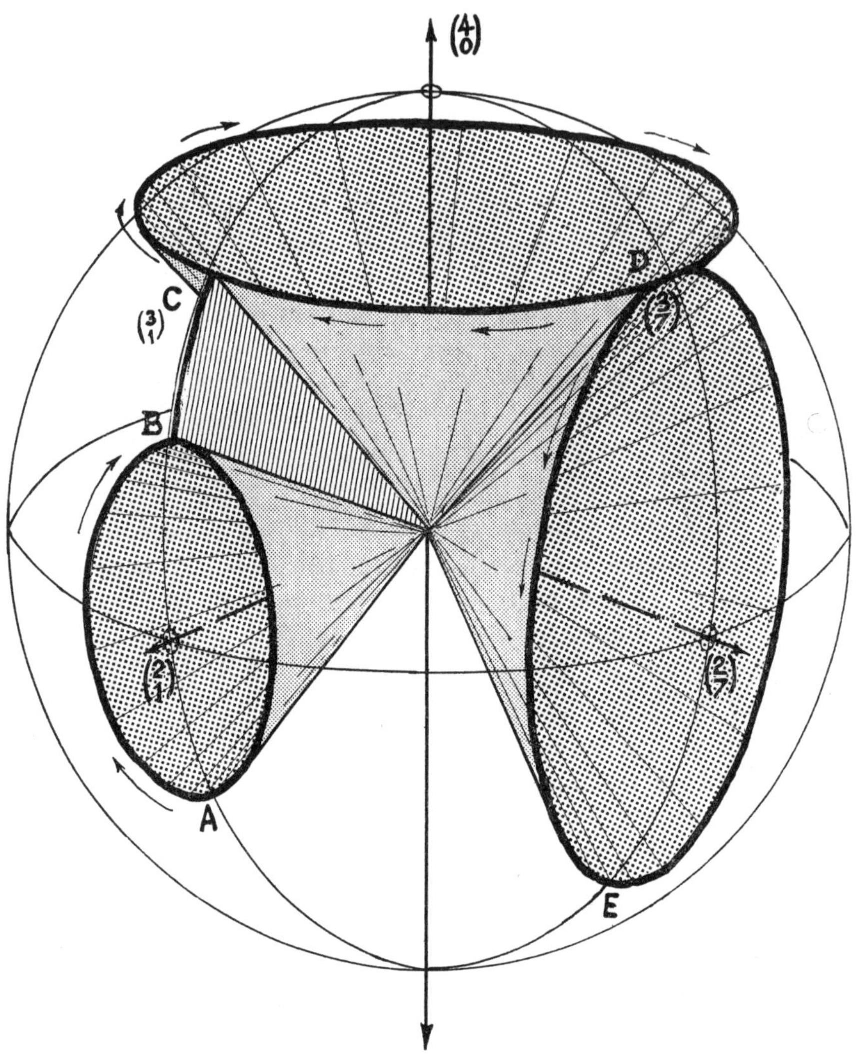

35. Conical Movement

In this diagram a limb is imagined as moving from *A* to *E*. The path of movement is divided into four parts for purposes of analysis. (1) A movement creating a cone of which the base is perpendicular to the Horizontal plane; the diameter of the circular base of the cone is *AB*. (2) A vertical movement from *B* to *C*. (3) A movement creating a cone in which the base is parallel to the Horizontal plane. (4) A movement creating a cone of which the base is perpendicular to the ground; the diameter of this cone is *DE*.

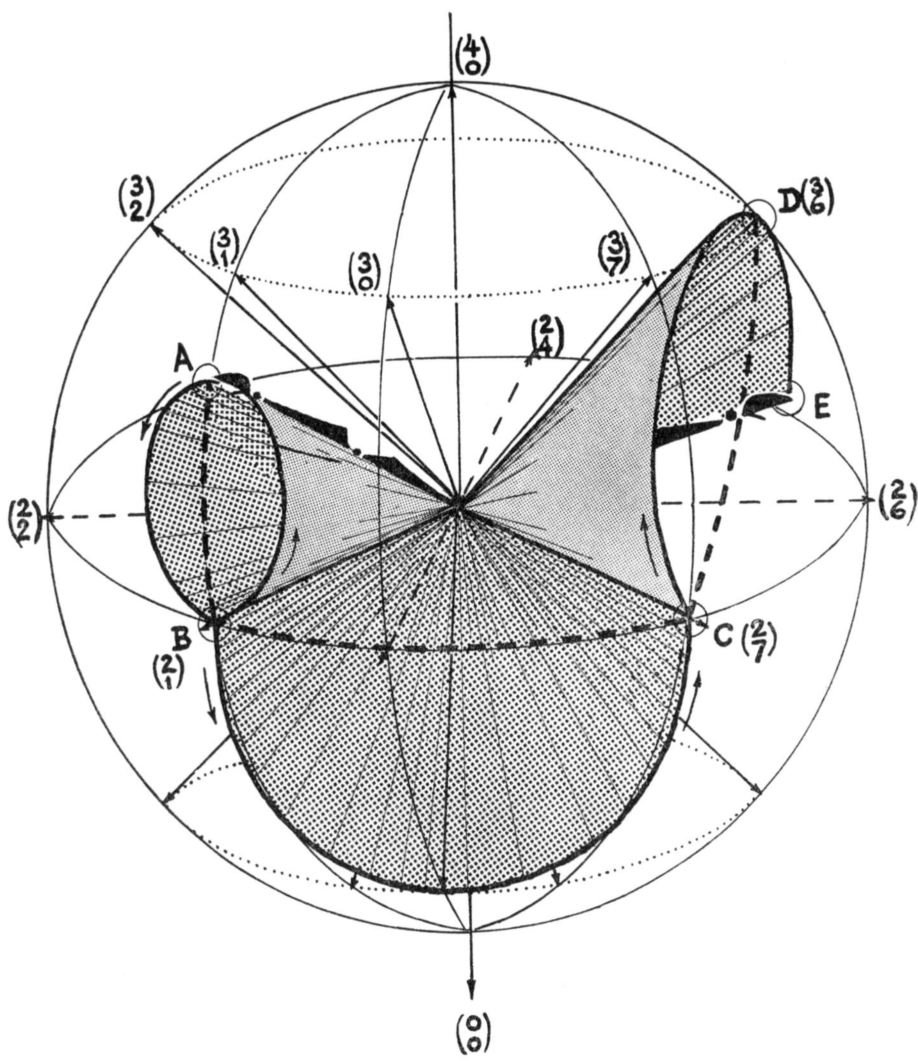

36. The Path of a Conical Movement: The amount and relation of these curves to the System of Reference

The limb leaves point *A* and moves by way of a curved surface to point *E*. The path of movement is divided into three parts, each of which will be analysed:

(1) The movement of the limb creates a cone (the diameter of which is perpendicular to the ground. The position *A* of the limb is given; the position *B* is $\binom{2}{1}$; the relation of the base of the cone to the System of Reference is thus defined. The amount of movement is 360° +180°, or a cone and a half; the movement is in positive sense. If the scale is 1 = 45°, the movement will be written $\underline{|\binom{2}{1}\ 12}$.

(2) At the end of this movement the limb arrives at *B* and continues by creating half a cone from *B* to *C*. The amount of movement is 4; the position of the limb at *C* is $\binom{2}{7}$; the diameter of the cone is parallel to the Horizontal Plane; and the sense of the movement is positive. The movement will be written thus: $\underline{|\binom{2}{7}\ 4}$.

(3) The limb moves from *C* to *E*; the diameter is *CD*, which lies at an angle to the Horizontal Plane; the amount of movement is 6; the position of the limb at *D* is $\binom{3}{6}$; the *sense of movement* negative. The movement will be written thus: $\overline{|\binom{3}{6}\ 6}$.

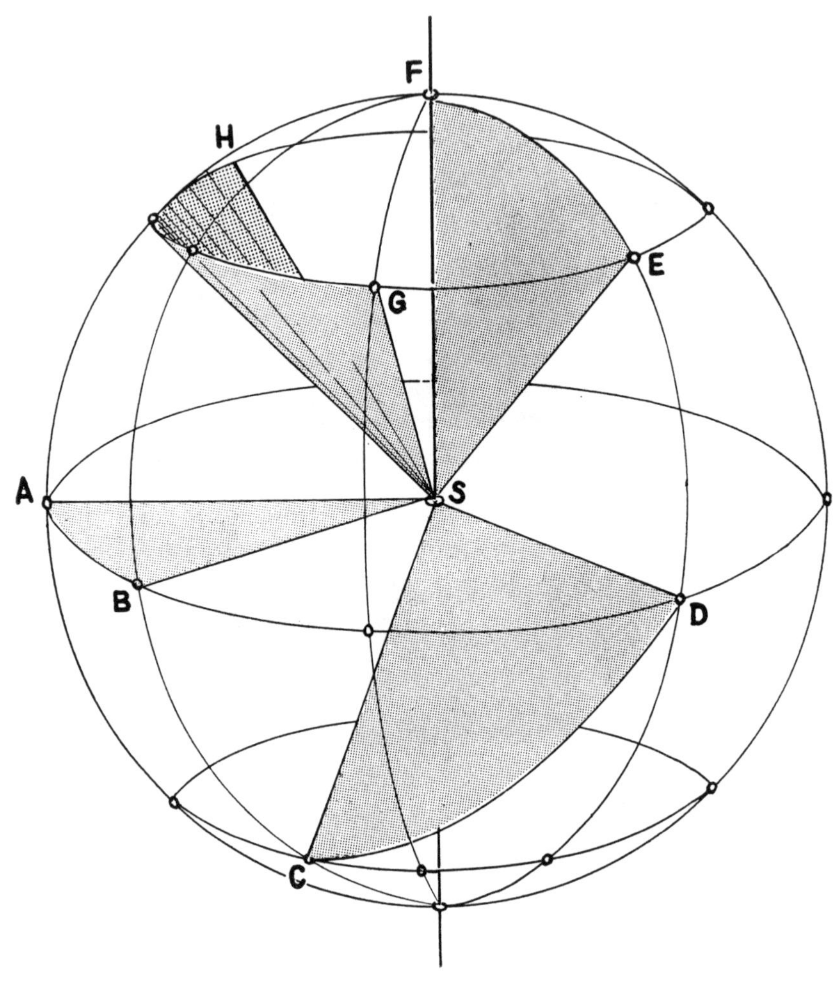

37. Movement Sections (or Intervals):

Horizontal:	*SAB*
Vertical:	*SFE*
Intermediate plane:	*SCD*
Curved:	*SGH*

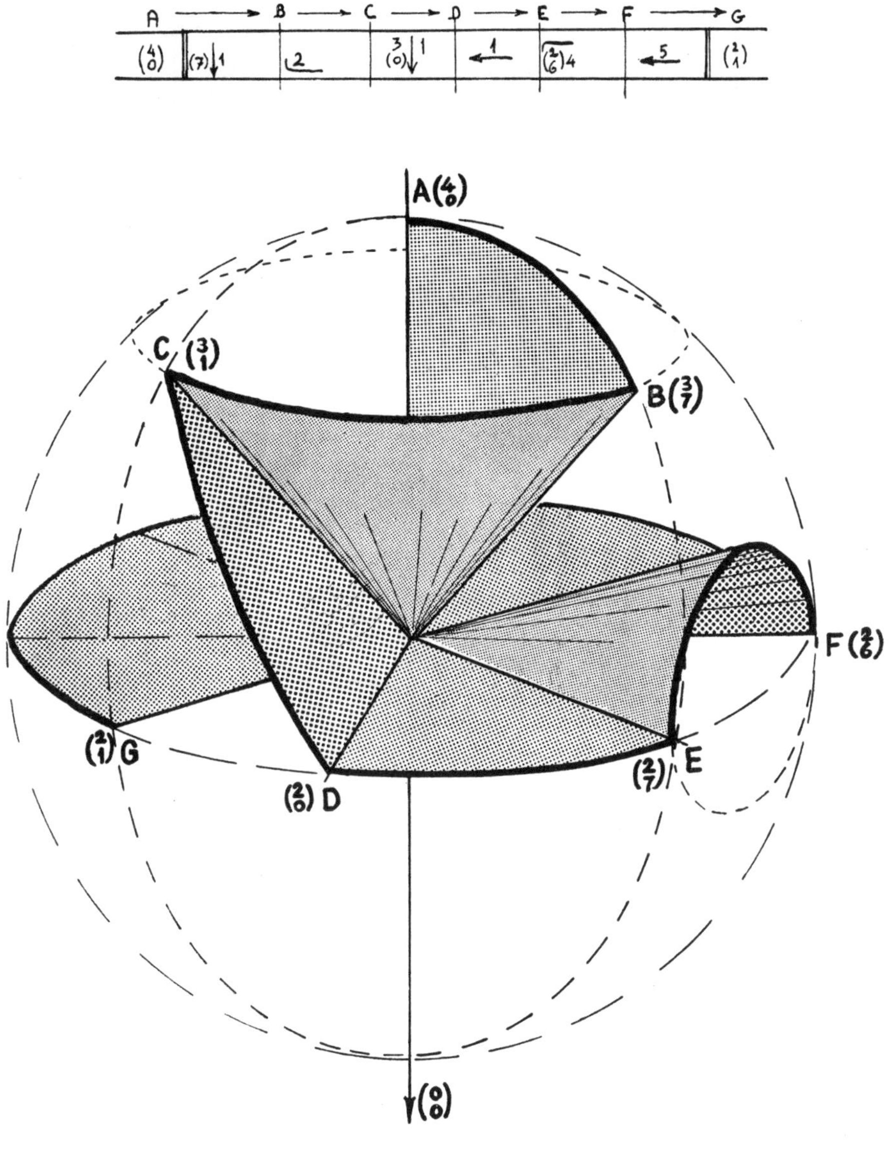

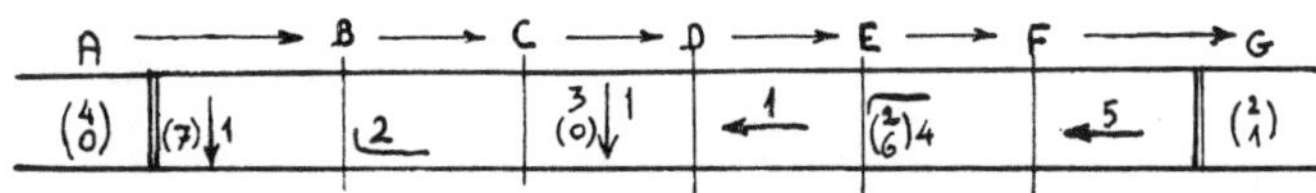

38. A Sequence of Movement

It is imagined that the limb starts its movement at *A* and finishes at *G*. The whole path is analysed in 6 parts, the proper sequence of which is written by means of movement and positional signs in the upper part of the diagram.

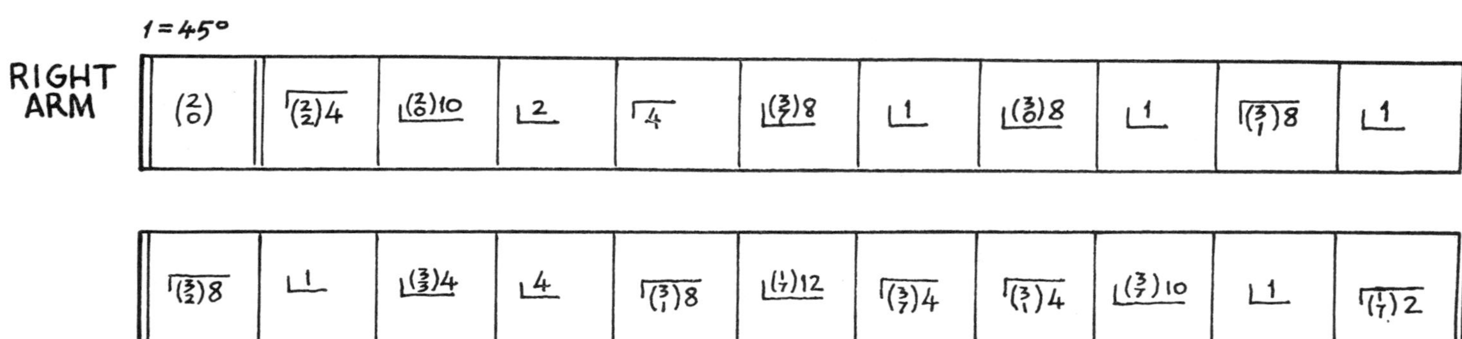

Ex. IX. Twenty-one conical movements of the right arm. A simple reading exercise with no compositional significance. Since the movements are all of equal time value, while the amounts of movement are varied, the speeds of movement are also various. It may be found interesting to perform the whole exercise with the forearm set at different fixed angles to the upper arm.

1 : 15°
RIGHT ARM

Ex. X. A sequence of twenty-five conical movements, different from Ex. IX in that a smaller scale has been provided for the construction of the System of Reference, thus making possible the definition and writing of much smaller intervals. This allows for movements which are more "complicated", in the sense that a more subtle sensibility is required in order to perform and discern them. The smallest interval usually employed in dance and gymnastics is 45°, anything smaller being regarded as "in between"—an undefined deviation. In the present notation such "complications" involve only a quantitative difference in the analysis.

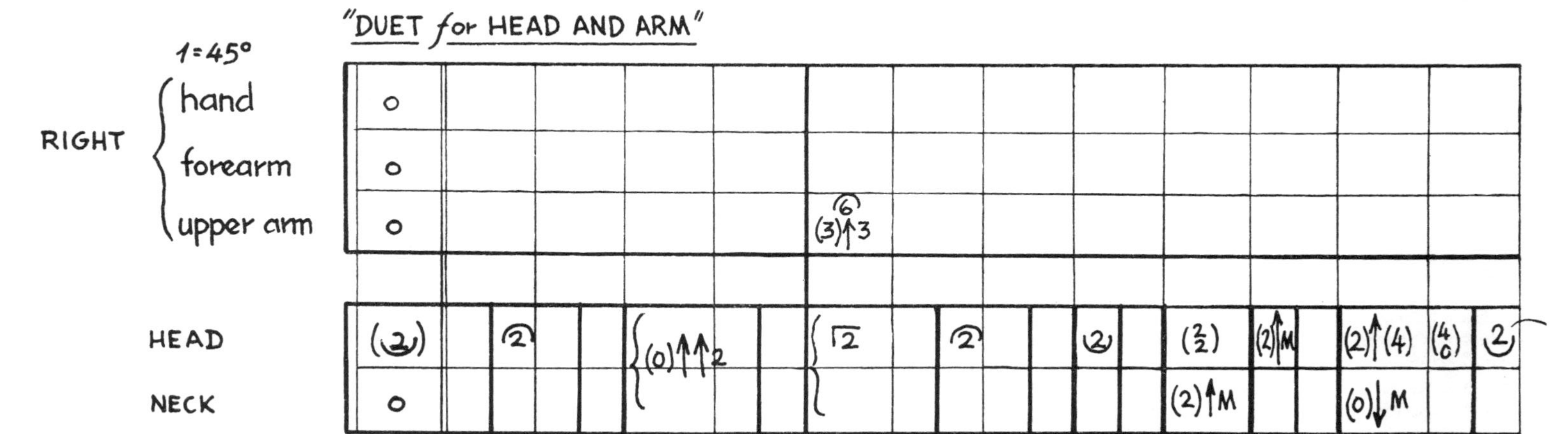

(Continued on following page)

Ex. XI. Part of a dance performed by the Chamber Dance Group directed by Noa Eshkel.

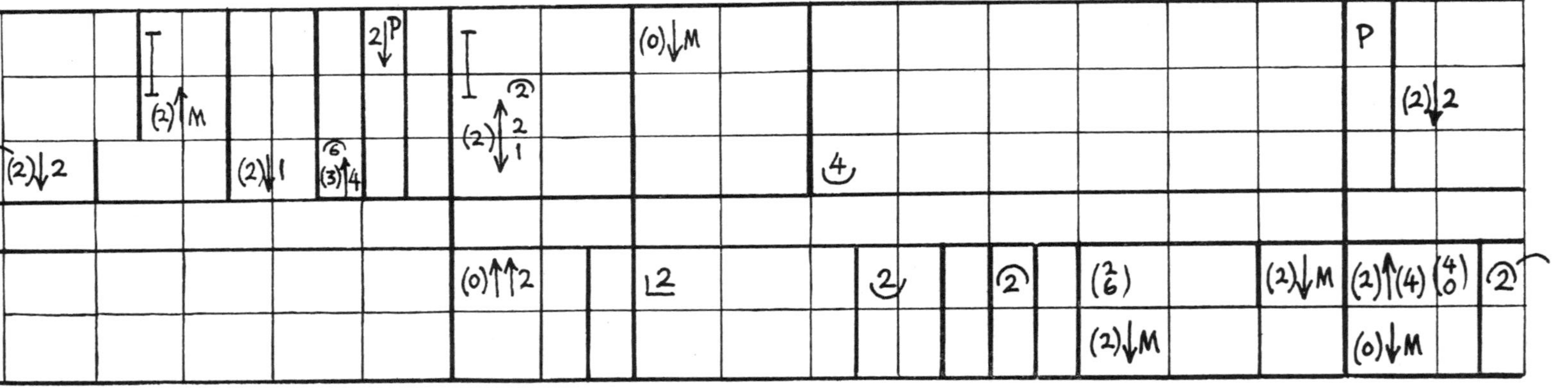

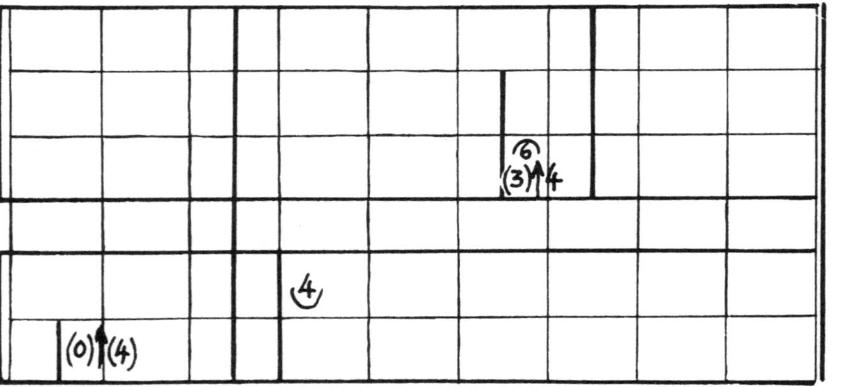

Ex. XI. (*cont.*). The sign I indicates that the longitudinal axes of the parts in whose spaces it lies are brought into one straight line. The sign P indicates that muscular tension is released in a limb, and the force of gravity allowed to act upon it causing a movement of a dropping character (see Chapter 20).

CHAPTER 10

The Contact of the Feet with the Ground

IN ZERO POSITION, the sign indicating that the feet are in contact with the ground will be a square: □. Whenever the foot loses contact with the ground, i.e. is lifted in the air, although the physical fact is always the logical result of a movement in some other part of the body, such as the hip, thigh, or lower leg, for the sake of clarity and convenience the sign ○ will be written in the space representing the feet. Similarly, when the foot is brought into contact with the ground again the sign □ will be written in the appropriate place.

Since, from a visual point of view, the movement of the feet is very small in comparison with other movements, to facilitate the writing of movements of the feet and the specific manner in which they meet the ground, the sign representing them will be fixed and permanent. That is to say, wherever the lower leg moves the System of Reference of the foot will be carried with it, not necessarily in parallel relation to the main System of Reference. Thus, regardless of position, 'stretching' of the foot will always be denoted by the sign ↓, as it would have been written had the movement been performed in Zero Position; likewise, flexing the foot will always be indicated by ↑, and so on appropriately. A lateral movement is always in a horizontal plane →, ←, a conical movement is written in the usual manner for conical movements, except that the position of the base is not indicated. A rotatory movement to the right is positive, to the left negative.

Rotation of the foot takes place (as in all limbs) about its longitudinal axis. However, as has been noted, the longitudinal axis of the foot in Zero Position is not, like that of other limbs, vertical, but parallel to the Horizontal Plane. Rotation is nevertheless *always* a movement about the longitudinal axis of *the limb*.

The variety of possibilities of contact of the foot with the ground, that is, the variety obtained by different sides and parts of the foot coming into contact with the ground, will be expressed by the two main signs for 'contact' and 'absence of contact' enclosing numbers.

In Zero position, when the feet are in parallel positions on the ground, the actual sides of the feet face in various directions, and each side may be identified with a coordinate on the Horizontal plane. Thus the front part of the foot may borrow the number 0, since it coincides with the coordinate *Y*0 of the Horizontal plane, the heel—number 4, &c.

Raising of the Foot from the Ground

(1) Raising of the whole foot ○.
(2) Raising of the heel only ④.
(3) Raising of the front part of the foot (the ball) ⓪.
(4) Raising of the toes ⊙.
(5) Raising of the right side of the foot ②.
(6) Raising of the left side of the foot ⑥.

Lowering of the Foot from the Air into Contact with the Ground

(1) Lowering of the whole foot □.
(2) Lowering of the heel alone [4].
(3) Lowering of the ball of the foot [0].
(4) Lowering of the extreme end of the toes [·].
(5) Lowering of the toes and heel [4̇] (forming an arch).
(6) Lowering of the right side of the foot [2].
(7) Lowering of the left side of the foot [6].
(8) Lowering of the back of the foot [I].

These symbols indicate a physical fact, namely, which side of the foot is to come into contact with the ground. They are movement signs because they indicate the inevitable movement which must be performed in order to achieve the particular kind of contact. However, they are *secondary* movement signs because they do not express exactly the relation of the movement to the System of Reference but only suggest it.

The laws applying to the writing of bar lines remain valid for these signs.

When a foot is once indicated as being in contact with the floor, it is unnecessary to repeat the sign in subsequent bars; the foot remains in contact until a sign is written to indicate the contrary. The converse applies to the sign indicating that the foot is in the air: it remains so until a sign is given showing that it comes into contact with the ground.

Should any particular composition or style involve greater precision and subtlety in the movements of the feet than is allowed for by the method described in this chapter, then the feet may be treated in the manner prescribed for all the other parts of the body. Where this is the case, the method used should be indicated at the beginning of the work.

The Sign L (*'Loose Contact'*)

It should be noted that when the foot is in contact with the ground, it does not necessarily support the weight of the body.

Loose Contact is the name given to the contact of a part of the body with some object (usually the floor) when that part does not bear the weight of the body. When the sign of Loose Contact appears in the horizontal space of a limb, that limb is relieved of weight, but remains in contact with the object, so that it is possible to draw the limb over the object's surface without abandoning the contact.

(*See Example XII.*)

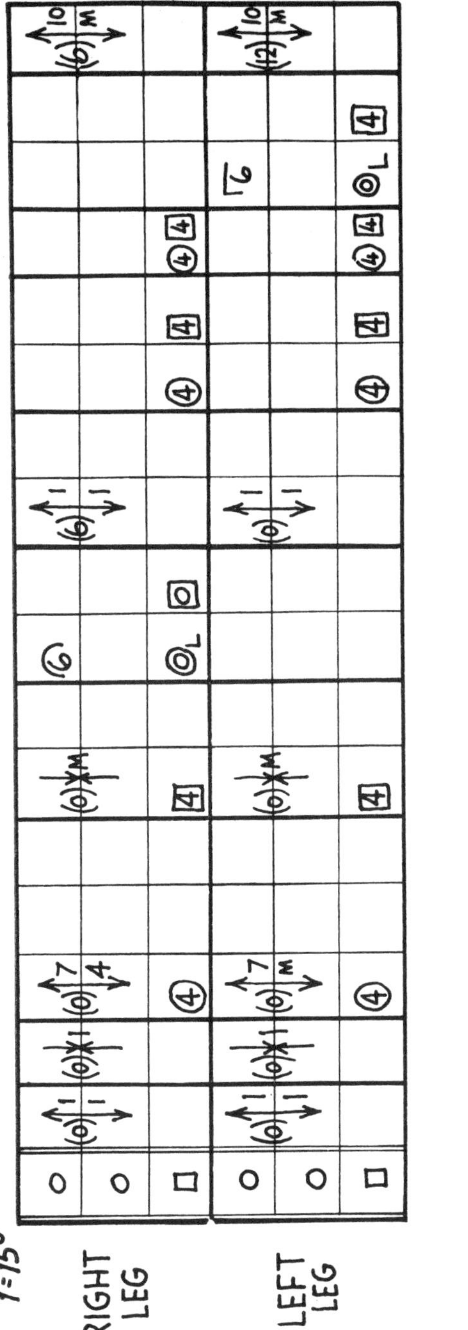

Ex. XII. Leg movements and contact of the foot with the ground.

(continued on following page)

F

(3)✕M	(3)↕3							(3)✕M		(3)̆ (0)↑3				(0)↑3			(0)↑2
	④	[4]		④	[4]					L				L			L
(3)✕M	(3)↕3					⌐3						(0)↑3				(0)↑2	
								(0)↑M									
	④	[4]	④	[4]	④	L		L	[4]			L				L	

Ex. XII. (*cont.*) The contact of the foot with the ground is either the whole foot, the ball of the foot, or the heel, in changing order. The numbers within the signs of contact, which, by a convention, indicate which part of the foot is involved in the contact, are derived from the coordinates of a scale of 1 = 45°, and not 1 = 15°—the scale adopted in this example for the notation of the movements of the legs.

CHAPTER 11

The Weight

THE BASE of the body is that limb which is in contact with the ground and supports the weight of the body. The projection of the centre of gravity always moves within the bounds of the base. If the projection of the centre of gravity passes outside the bounds of the base, the body loses its equilibrium and falls. During every movement, even the smallest, there is a shift of the centre of gravity. The present notation is not concerned with the shift of the centre of gravity as a mechanical phenomenon, but the notation does define as 'shift of weight' a certain kind of movement, namely one in which the body as a whole changes its relation to the base in accordance with the Law of 'Light' and 'Heavy' limbs. From an anatomical point of view, the movement occurs in the joint between the limb or limbs performing the function of 'base' and the limb next above it; in standing, the joint would be the ankle, the base of the body the foot, and the moving limb the lower leg; when kneeling, the knee joints, the base being the lower leg, and the moving limb the thigh, and so on.

In Zero Position that movement will be seen to take place between the feet (which are anchored to the floor) and the lower legs, and the whole body will be carried by the movement of the lower leg. (In practice, slight adjustments of the body are necessary in order to preserve the relations between its various parts.)

The 'shift of weight' concerns the notation when it is a visual phenomenon in which the whole body changes its relation to the base, whatever part of the body may form the base. When the base is maximal, as when the whole body lies on the floor, such a movement is practically impossible, since when it lies on the floor, the whole body *is* the base, according to the definition given above, and therefore no shift of weight can be performed.

The movement is written in a space specially reserved for this purpose, since to write it (for example) as a movement of the lower leg from Zero Position in relation to the foot, would not sufficiently emphasize the visual effect which is seen in the resulting movement of the whole body.

Equal distribution of the weight of the body on the whole base is indicated by a filled in zero ●, in the second space from the bottom of the page, the space reserved exclusively for shift of weight. When the weight is shifted —that is, when a Plane movement is created by the part nearest the base, the whole body being carried by it—the projection of the longitudinal axis of the body on the *Horizontal Plane* is seen to coincide with one of the coordinates, and this *horizontal* coordinate is indicated by a number, determined according to the scale of the composition, counting in the positive sense.

●		0		●	2		4	●	7		5	●

When the weight is shifted in a continuous manner, moving through the range of co-ordinates without returning to a state of equally distributed weight, a conical movement of the whole body results, and this is indicated by using the sign of a conical movement, with base parallel to the ground; the amount of the cone created is represented by a number inside it. An additional number in brackets follows, indicating the horizontal coordinate with which the projection of the centre of gravity of the body coincides at the end of the movement. 2 (6) 4 (5) 1 (2). (*See Fig. 41.*)

Rotatory movements do not involve a 'shift of weight' in the sense of the definition used here, and therefore never appear in the space allotted to 'shift of weight'.

The magnitude of the movement is normally to be understood as the greatest possible without incurring loss of balance. A lesser amount is hardly perceptible because the amount of movement possible is very small. When loss of equilibrium is intended, the letter M is written above the number indicating the 'direction' of the movement; a falling movement results:

M M
1 0 &c.

All the laws relating to the use of bar lines are valid for movements of shift of weight, whose symbols indicate movements no less than do the other movement signs.

Every movement incurs a shift of weight; it is particularly important in movements involving transport. It is, however, not necessary to indicate every shift of weight—especially when it is understood from the description of the movements of the limbs. If, for instance, from a position of standing on both feet, one is then lifted, it is clear that the weight is to be shifted completely onto that which remains in contact with the ground. The writer or composer need write a shift of weight only when it is a motivically used visual phenomenon, or when it is essential to the technical understanding of the movement. When it occurs as a compositional motive, then it must, of course, be indicated, like any other movement forming part of a composition—even though it may be technically unnecessary to write it.

All the limbs not directly connected with the base may move independently while a 'shift of weight' is being executed.

(*See Figs. 39 and 40.*)

The Jump

The jump is the physical action in which the body remains for a certain time in the air, completely losing contact with the ground; the body loses its base. This physical phenomenon is the result of movements in some parts of the body, which are always indicated in the written script. A jump is not in itself a movement but a physical occurrence, the result of certain kinds of movement. For instance, when a leg is raised, its route being exactly described in relation to the System of Reference, and the second leg is then also lifted, without returning the first to the ground, the resulting phenomenon will be a jump. Since the notation is concerned with describing movement from a visual point of view only, it disregards all muscular actions necessary in order to produce a jump. However, to facilitate the understanding of what is written, the fact of the occurrence of a jump will be noted in the horizontal space provided for changes of weight, by the sign ⊡. This is a combination of the sign □, indicating contact with the ground, and the sign ○, indicating absence of contact. Whatever part of the body served as the base before the jump (in most cases the feet), will at the same time receive the sign ○.

When the body does not descend on the same place on the ground which it left, the direction in which it travels during the jump is expressed by one of the horizontal coordinates, i.e., by a number obtained by means of the usual method of division of the Horizontal plane according to the scale given at the beginning of the work. This number is written above the sign of the jump in the 'Weight' space.

1 2 6
⧇ ⧇ ⧇

The size of any jump is determined by the time provided for its execution. A short given time will naturally produce a small jump, and when the given time is longer, the jump will be accordingly larger.

It should be noted that all the limbs may move in the air in precisely the same manner as when the body is in contact with the ground; but it should be remembered that in a jump the 'heaviest' limbs are either the torso (in relation to the upper part of the body), or the pelvis (in relation to the lower part). (*See Fig. 17.*)

It must also be borne in mind that when the body travels in any indicated direction, the System of Reference is carried with it, and *does not turn* in that direction.

There are some positions from which it is impossible to jump without a preparatory movement such as a bending of the knees, and some jumps from which it is impossible to land without a concluding movement. It is, for example, almost impossible to land with straight legs from a high jump.

When the preparatory and concluding movements are of an unusual character, or have a motivic value within a composition, then the exact movements must be written. Where they are not indicated in detail, natural movements of preparation and conclusion, proportionate to the size of the jump, will be understood.

(*See Fig. 42 and Examples XIII, XIV, XV.*)

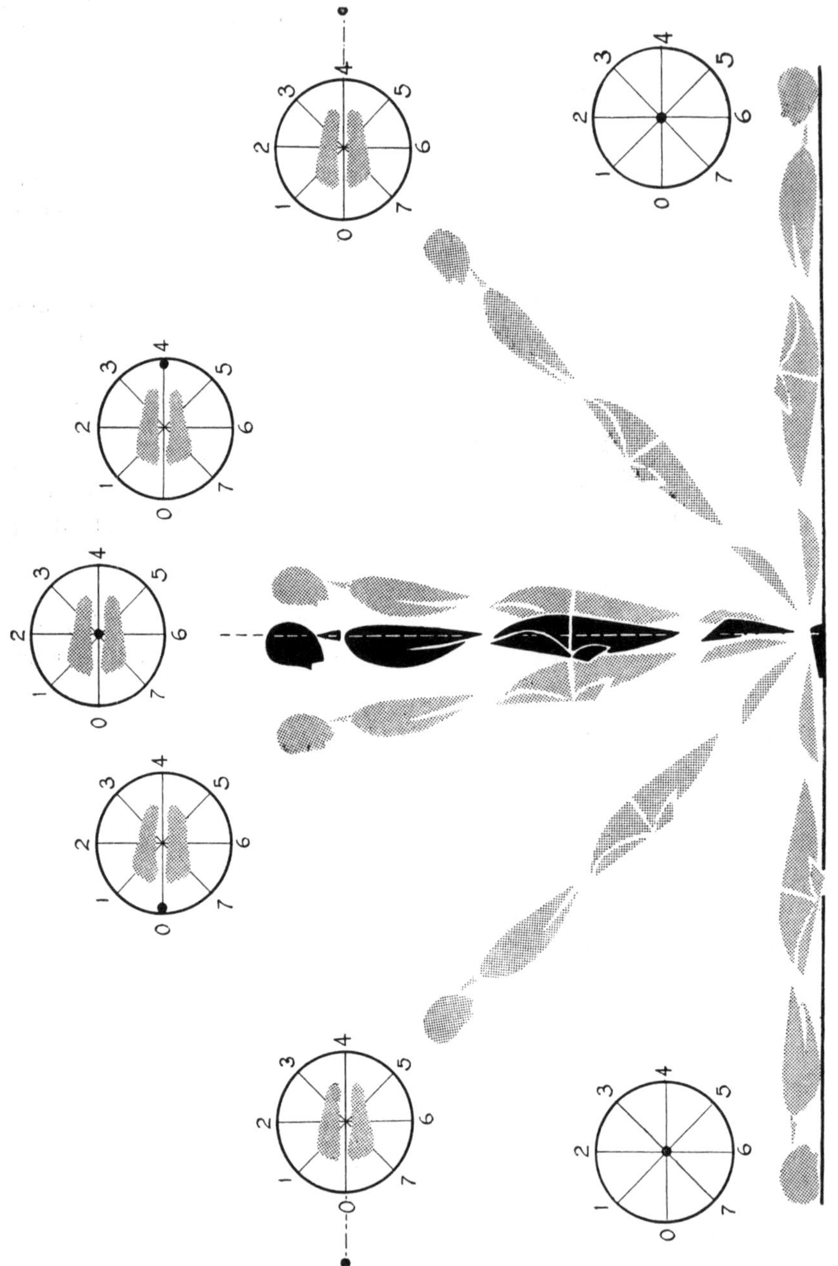

39. *Shift of Weight in Coordinate (0)*
The vertical plane (0) is created in this movement

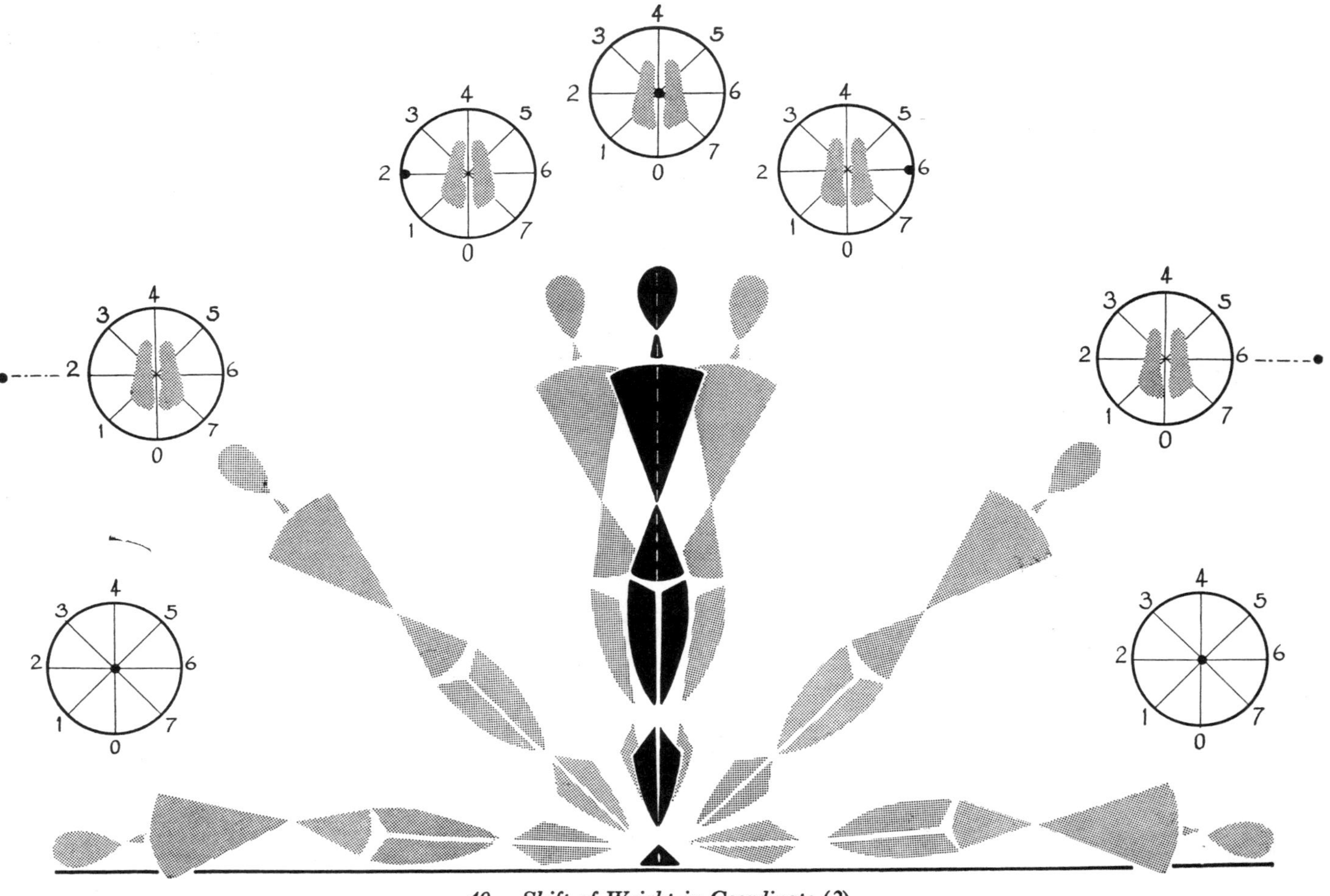

40. Shift of Weight in Coordinate (2)
The Vertical plane (2) is created in the movement

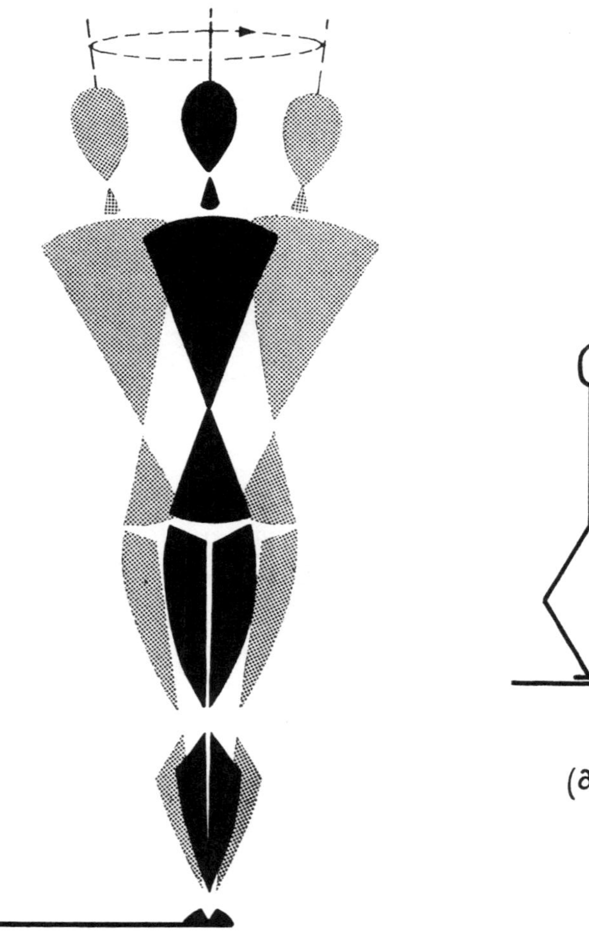

41. *Conical Shift of Weight*

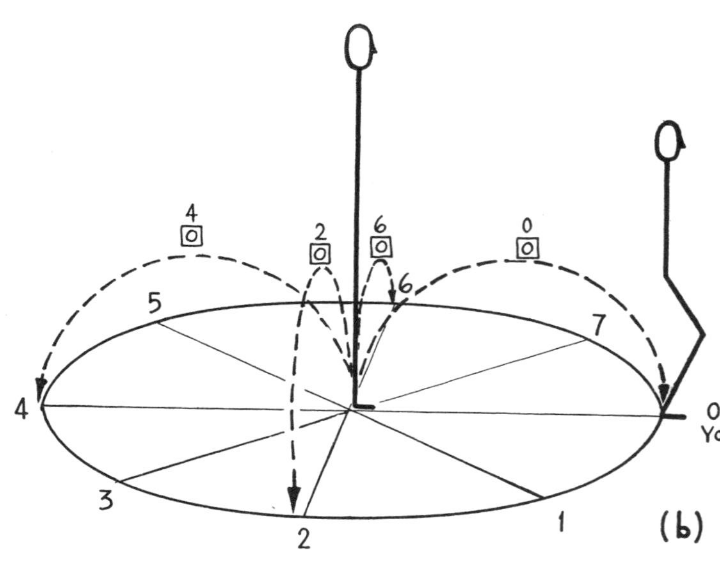

42. (*a*) *A Jump* (*b*) *The direction of a jump*

1=45°

WHOLE TORSO

RIGHT LEG

LEFT LEG

WEIGHT

(continued on following page)

Ex. XIII. Shift of weight, and maximum shift of weight resulting in a falling movement of the whole body.

Ex. XIII. (*cont.*) Note that the torso is given only one horizontal space, indicating that the whole torso is regarded as a single lever, movement occurring at the hip-joint only; there is no movement between the small component parts of the torso. It will be noticed that in the space allocated to the torso both movement signs and positional signs are used: positional signs are used in combination with a "falling" movement; the positional sign indicates that position which is to be arrived at, at the end of the "falling" movement. In this way the amount of "fall" is defined.

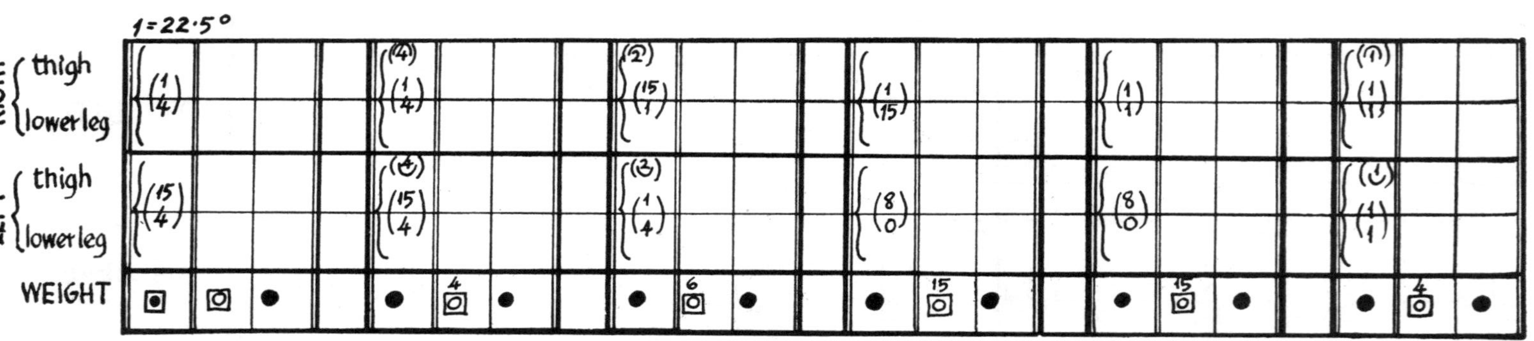

(*continued on following page*)

Ex. XIV.

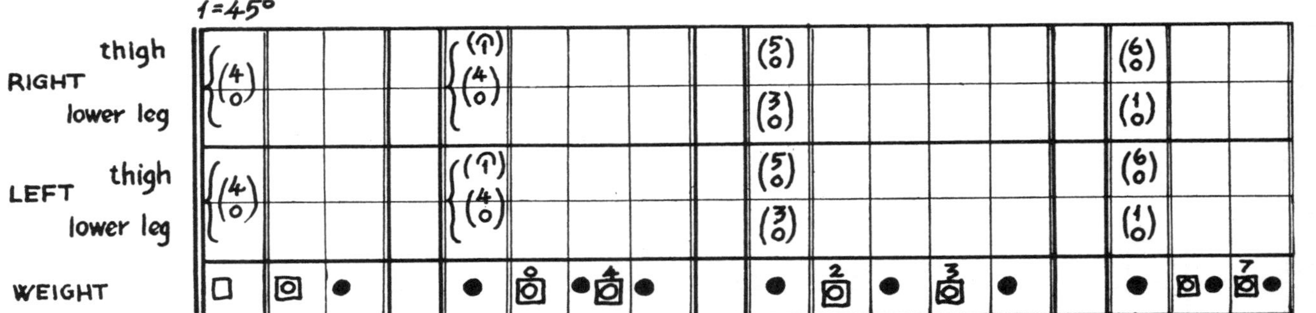

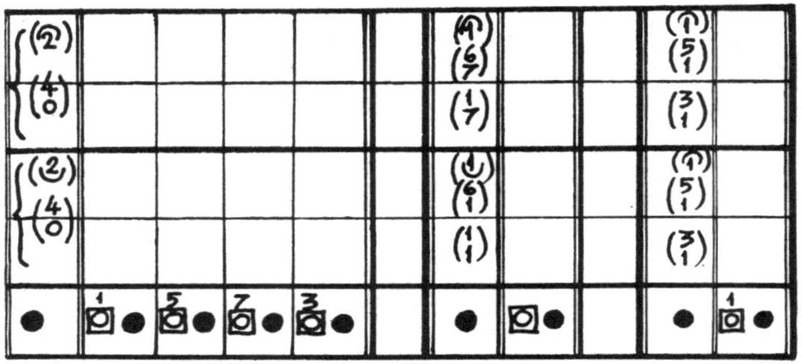

Ex. XIV. (*cont.*) Each section begins with a position, and this is followed by a series of jumps. The given position is retained both in the air and on the ground. The notation is abbreviated: the movements of preparation and recovery necessary for the execution of a jump, are not written; and contact of the feet with the floor is not indicated. This is a possible and legitimate way of using the notation, suitable for the writing-down of certain folk dances, simple dances for children, and the like.

The first line of jumps is written with the scale 1 = 45°, and the second with the scale 1 = 22.5°. In most of the jumps the body travels in a direction indicated by a number written above the jump sign; but it should be noted that there is no *notation* of the body.

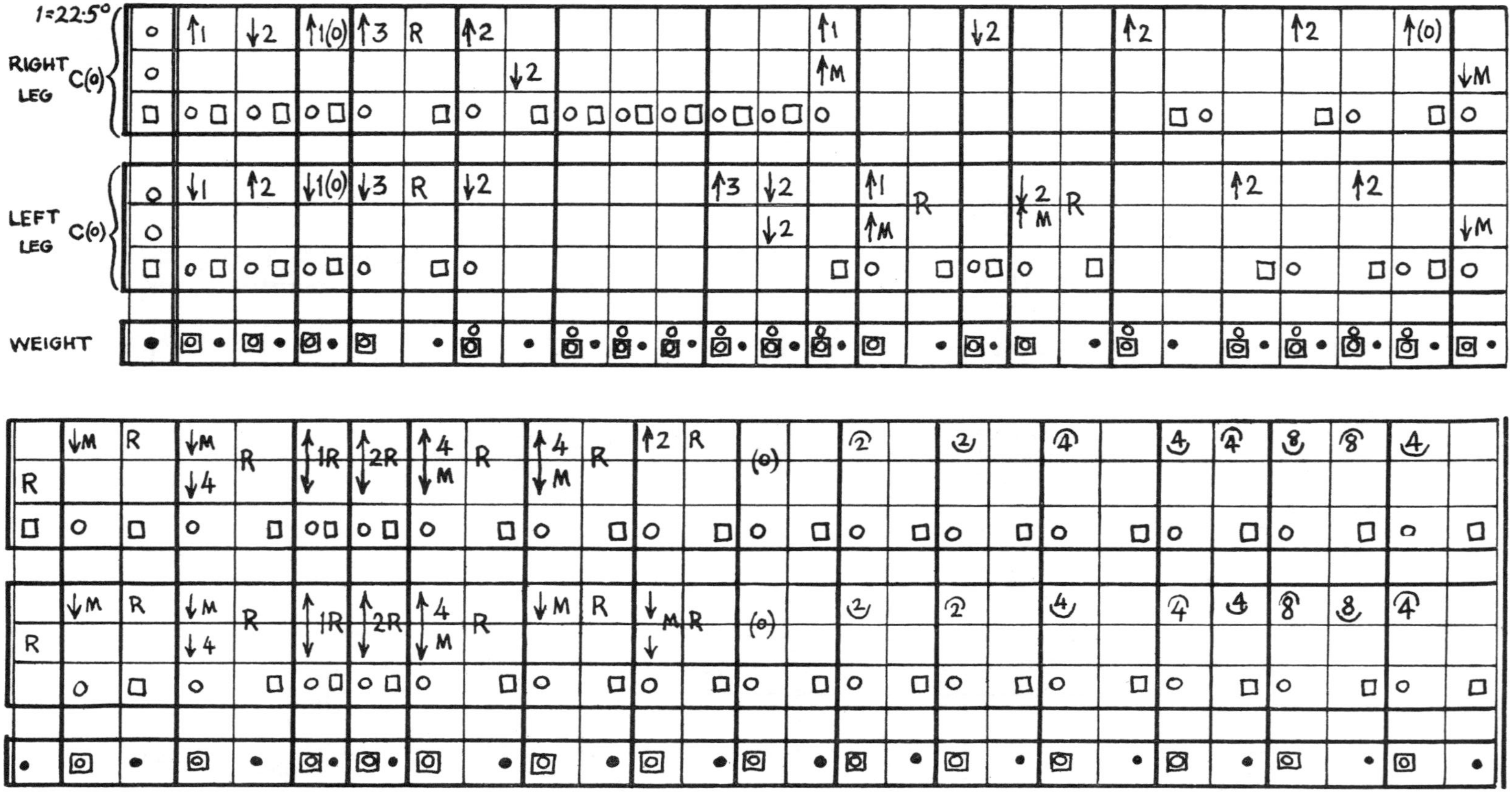

1=22·5°

RIGHT LEG C(o)

LEFT LEG C(o)

WEIGHT

Ex. XV. Jumps. A sequence of thirty-four jumps constituting a simple reading exercise; the given time-values are arbitrary. It should be noticed that the sign *C(o)* appears at the beginning of the notation. This denotes that all plane intervals created belong to coordinate plane (*o*). The number which normally precedes the arrow in Plane movements is therefore unnecessary, unless a different plane is created—which must then be indicated in the usual manner.

The sign *R* also appears in the notation. This is explained fully in a later chapter; here it should be understood as meaning reverse movement—i.e. the reversal of the immediately preceding movement: the same path is retraced by the limb, this time beginning at the end, and returning to the starting position of the original movement.

Note that preparatory motions physically necessary for the performance of a jump are not notated.

CHAPTER 12

Turns — Rotation of the Base

A TURN is a rotation of the base (the limb which is in contact with the ground). Being the 'heaviest' limb, its rotation will carry the entire body with it.

Turning is a simple Rotatory movement. It is, however, extraordinary in that it creates what may be regarded as a new joint—an articulation between the body and the ground.

This rotation is seen as a continuous and uninterrupted change of the side of the body presented to a given point, the observer. The rotation may consist of a whole turn—that is, the movement may be continued until the same side of the body which was presented to the observer before the turn, again faces him; or a greater or lesser amount of turning may occur.

No matter what position the body assumes, zero position or any other, a rotation of the base always takes place about an axis vertical to the ground, i.e. a parallel to $X0$, or $X0$ itself. The feet need not necessarily perform the function of base, This can be done by any other part of the body which makes the act of rotation physically possible.

Since turning is a movement which involves the whole body as one unit and cannot be described as a movement of any one limb, it is therefore written in a space allotted to this kind of event exclusively. This is the lowest space on the manuscript page. The sign used is that of Rotatory movement, positive or negative as appropriate, and the amount of movement within the sign $\overset{\frown}{8}$, $\overset{16}{\smile}$, $\overset{\frown}{2}$ &c.

A rotation of the base is always made possible by a 'loosening' of its contact with the ground. Therefore a sign L is introduced in the space allotted to the limb which forms the rotating base, indicating that its contact with the ground has become 'loose', in addition to the rotation sign in the lower space.

If the limbs move in an independent manner during a turn, their movements are represented in the usual manner, in relation to the System of Reference, as if the System were turning about coordinate X in exactly the same amount, sense and duration as those of the turn of the body, so that there is no change of relation between body and System.

(See Examples XVI and XVII.)

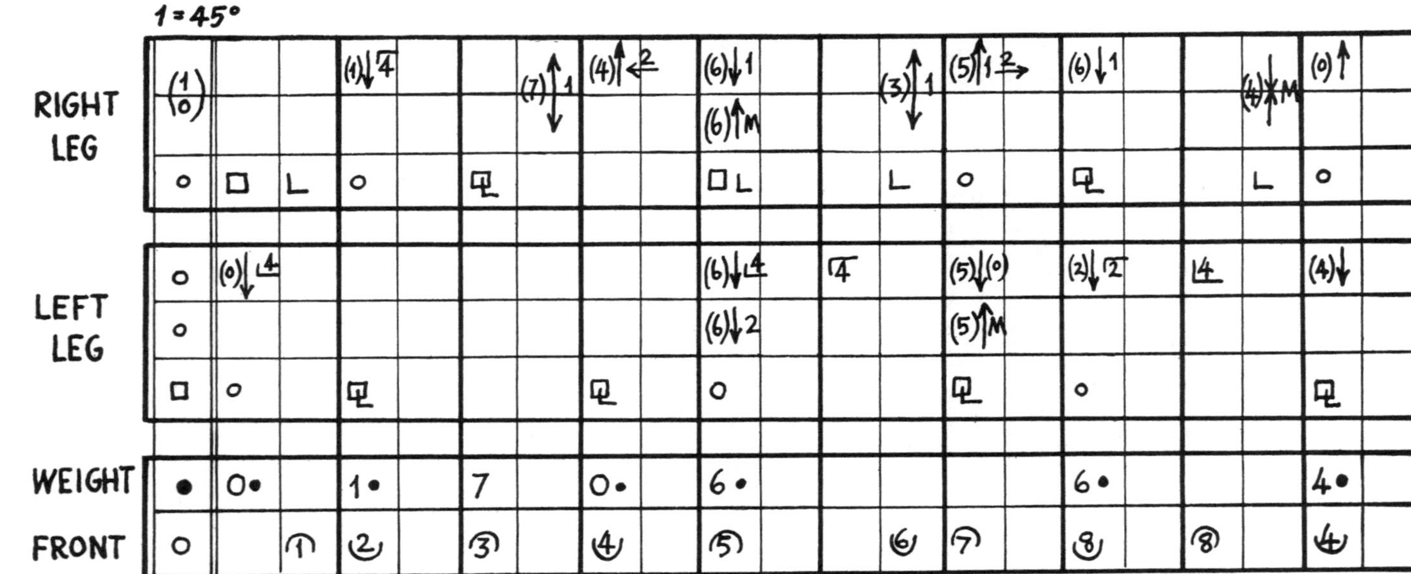

Ex. XVI. A sequence of movements including rotation of the whole body (*turns*). Note that the frontal surface of the body will be 'facing' in a new direction at the conclusion of every turn.

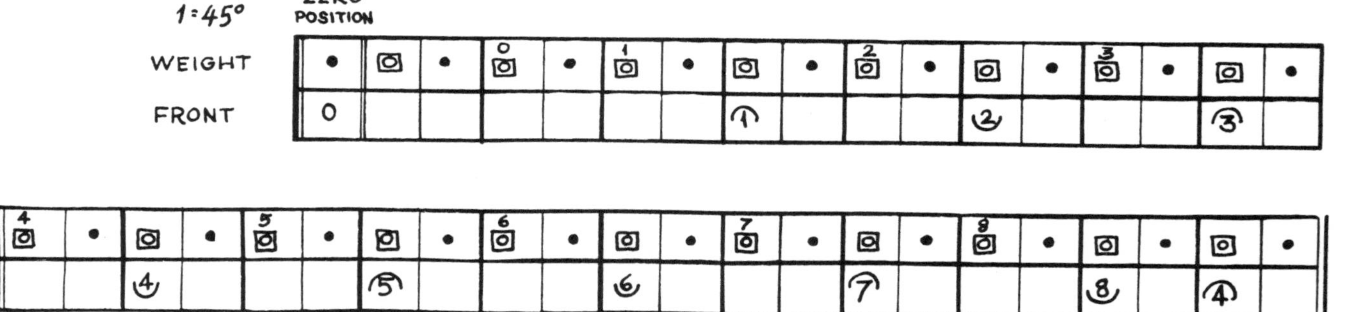

Ex. XVII. Turns in the air. As in Ex. XIV, the possibility is seen of abbreviating the notation. Only the signs for the jumps, and for the direction of transport during the jumps, are given in the Weight space; and, in the Front space, the signs for the turns. It may easily be imagined that such abbreviated writing would be suitable in sequences, such as are encountered in children's dances, or folk dances, in which the position of the body remains unchanged throughout the jumps. The second example consists of *four jumps of differing speeds*.

These examples show the typical appearance of the Weight and Front spaces within a work which includes jumps during which turns are performed.

CHAPTER 13

The Front — Change of Front

THE PRESENT MOVEMENT NOTATION is intended to serve as a dance notation, for the writing of compositions which are constructions in a defined material, movement—constructions designed to be seen when performed by the human body. Since dances are designed to be seen, the angle of observation on a moving human body is of essential importance, because the same sequence of movement defined according to the System of Reference would appear as completely different visual phenomena when seen from various angles. The composer, intending to present to the eye something definite, is obliged to indicate from what angle of observation he wishes the dance to be seen, and must therefore be able to express it.

Had there been no rotatory movement, mainly that of the base, carrying the whole body, in all the various possible ways—that is to say, had there been no possibility of turning a different side of the body towards the observer—then both the relation between mover and observer (i.e. between the moving body and one fixed point of observation), and all the changes of relation occurring within the body and seen by the observer, would have been fully expressed by the sequence of symbols denoting the analysis of movement according to the System of Reference. In other words, a sequence of movement repeated exactly, so far as the relations between the limbs are concerned, would appear to the observer as identical on every repetition, and would, in fact, be represented by an identical sequence of movement. However, the fact of the existence of rotatory movement allows the possibility that the same sequence of movements (change of relations between the limbs), when repeated before and after a rotatory movement may no longer appear as identical to an observer whose position has not changed. Were the same movements to be represented in the same way both before and after the turn, this would involve giving the same symbols to two events which from the point of view of the observer are entirely dissimilar.

For instance, consider a sequence of movement for the left arm, beginning from Zero Position with the front facing directly towards the observer. The left arm is raised in a Plane movement to the side until it reaches shoulder level: 2 $\downarrow$ 2; the observer sees the whole of the plane created by the movement of the arm. Next, a conical movement creating half a cone, the arm moving in the positive sense ascending and then descending, until it points straight forward: $|\underline{\binom{2}{0}\ 4}$; the observer will see the open end of the cone, which is towards him. There is, from the observer's point of view, a graduated foreshortening of the arm up to the end of the movement, until it is finally seen 'end-on'. A Horizontal Plane movement follows, in the positive sense, the arm moving at shoulder level until it is in the forty-five degree diagonal across the body to the right: $\overset{1}{\rightarrow}$; part of the performer's body is obscured from the observer by the arm. A negative Rotatory movement of 90° reveals the back of the hand to the observer: $\overset{2}{\circlearrowleft}$.

Suppose that the performer turns 90° to his right, presenting his left side to the observer, and repeats precisely the same sequence of movements (in relation to the body).

The observer will, in the first Plane movement, see the whole outer side of the arm, which becomes continuously foreshortened until seen 'end-on'. In the Conical movement, the form of the outer surface of the cone is now seen by the observer; in the second Plane movement the arm will again become foreshortened, but this time it will not obscure the body to any great extent. In the Rotatory movement which follows, the back of the hand appears.

What is seen by the observer in the two performances of the sequence, is changed—although all the movement signs remain unaltered, and the full sequence in both cases would be written in the same way thus:

$$(2) \downarrow 2 \qquad |\underline{\tbinom{2}{0}\,4} \qquad \overset{1}{\rightarrow} \qquad \overset{2}{\smile}$$

The notation might have been based on a method of analysis in which one limb, or one point in the body, served as a constant point of reference for the analysis of the movements of all the other parts. But then the relation—and change of relation—of the moving body to the observer, would not have been expressed, although it might have been inferred. The same signs would always represent the same changes of relations between the limbs, even though performed at different angles to the observer, and therefore seen by him as different phenomena. The everyday application of this principle of analysis may be seen in the use of terms for the orientation of movement such as 'forward—backward'; 'central and peripheral' movements, 'high movement—low movement', &c. For example, 'Central' is understood as movement which brings the limbs towards the centre of the body, and usually involves some form of flexion, 'peripheral' indicates movement of the limbs away from the centre of the body, and implies extension no matter what may be the position of the body—facing the observer, or with the back turned to him, or lying on the floor, &c.

Had the analysis of movement been based on a point outside the body for example, the observer—the symbols would then have expressed all changes occurring in the moving body as changes of relation between the body and that point. The relation of mover to observer would then be fully expressed. But the *identity* of what is (from the point of view of relations between the parts of the body) the same sequence of movements, when they happened at different angles to the observer, would not have been expressed at all; for, whenever performed at a new angle to the observer, the same movements would have to be written in a different manner. This principle of analysis, by which movements are referred to fixed points outside the body may be seen in practice in the use of phrases such as 'raise your arm towards the left wall'; 'lift your face towards the ceiling', &c.

Considering these two methods of analysis in terms of the System of Reference, it will be found that in the first case, the System remains as if fixed to the body, and with every turn of the body, the System of Reference also turns, the coordinate *Y*0 of the System changing its angle to the observer to the extent that the front of the body changes its relation to him. The same sequence of changes of relations between the limbs would then have been represented before and after the turn by the same symbols. That is to say, the interrelations of the limbs would have been expressed, but the rotation of the body and of the System of Reference would have to be expressed by an *additional* sign.

In the second case, the System of Reference is imagined as remaining permanently fixed, with the coordinate *Y*0 pointing towards the observer. The difference as seen by the observer between the same sequence of movements before and after turning would be expressed by the difference between the sequence of symbols, expressing the movements of the limbs before the turn, and the symbols used to express the same movements after the turn. The change of relation of mover to observer would have been inferred from the *difference* between the symbols in the two cases; but, because of this very difference, the written symbols would not show that the movements of limb in relation to limb were the same in both cases.

For the expression of the threefold relationship of mover, System of Reference, and observer, both methods of analysis of movement are valid, the difference between them being the degree of emphasis laid upon one aspect or the other.

Both methods of analysis are incorporated in this system of notation, in the manner now to be described.

This threefold relationship of mover–system of Reference–observer, which is explained as (i) *Zero position of the body*—the limbs in the relations to one another which were described in Chapter 2 (*See Fig. 11.*); (ii) *Coordinate Zero Position*; that is, the body in Zero Position of the body 'placed inside' the System of Reference in such a way that the co-ordinate *Y*0 of the System passes through the body from the back forwards; see Chapter 3; (iii) The coordinative Zero Position related to the observer in such a way that that coordinate *Y*0 of the System of Reference is directed exactly towards the observer. This constellation of Body, System of Reference and Observer is referred to as *Absolute Zero Position.* (*See Fig. 12.*) The direction in which the coordinate *Y*0 points in Absolute Zero Position co-incides with the direction towards which the front of the body faces, and is called the 'Front'. 'Change of Front' is the name given to the procedure of turning and fixing the co-ordinate *Y*0 into any direction other than that in which it points in Absolute Zero position. That is to say, in a Change of Front the System of Reference is rotated about coordinate X so that the direction of *Y*0 is no longer that of Absolute Zero position, but is turned to a new direction. This rotation of the System of Reference is an act of reorientation, performed for the purpose of the analysis and writing of movements. From the moment that it is performed, *all changes of relation of the limbs are analysed according to the new direction of the System of Reference.* (*See Fig. 43*).

The Change of Front (the rotation of the System of Reference about coordinate *X*) is expressed by means of a number. This number indicates (according to the scale given at the beginning of the composition) the Horizontal coordinate with which *Y*0 coincides after the rotation of the System. The direction of *Y*0 in Absolute Zero position is known and is noted by the number 0, and the given scale of the composition provides a division of the Horizontal plane by coordinates numbered in the positive sense from *Y*0. The numbers furnished by the division provide as many directions as may be required.

Change of Front is an intellectual act which may technically be performed at any chosen moment in the course of a movement composition.

Even when no rotation of the body takes place, a Change of Front may be written, and from that point onward, all movement signs on the manuscript page are to be understood in relation to the new direction of *Y*0. The Front may thus be continually changed, despite the absence of any turning movement in the body, and the symbols by which the same movements are represented will be continually changing, because of the shifting of their point of reference. Used in this manner, however, the Change of Front is a purely formalistic procedure, and does not mirror any event in reality. This kind of Change of Front would be seen only when read, or, as an actual physical phenomenon, if the observer could be caused to move in relation to the mover (as in fact happens in certain film shots).

Since it is customary for the dancers to move, and not the audience, the Law of Change of Front states, that *Change of Front cannot be used unless some Rotatory movement in some part of the body precedes it* (not necessarily of the whole body). However, even when rotation of the whole body and its base takes place, the composer is not obliged to write a Change of Front, although in such a case an overwhelming motivic reason should be provided. He may or may not make use of the possibility, depending upon the way in which he wishes the composition to be understood.

Change of Front is written in the lowest horizontal space on the page and is represented by a number only. The number indicating Change of Front denotes one of the fixed Horizontal coordinates—that is, a fixed direction. The number indicating Rotation of the whole body is written in the same horizontal space, but always appears together with the sign of Rotatory movement. The latter number denotes an *amount* of movement; it does not appertain to fixed directions, but indicates intervals only. For example: If the whole body rotates in the positive sense from Front 2 (1 = 45°), the amount of movement being $\underset{2}{\frown}$, then the new front will be 4. If the rotation of the body were $\overset{14}{\smile}$ (i.e. one and three-quarters of a circle in negative sense), the new front would again be expressed as 4. Again, if the starting position were at Front 3, and the movement $\underset{1}{\frown}$, the new front would once more be 4.

The 'Front' indication should be included in the notation of every 'Starting position'.

Almost all the remaining examples in the book could serve as examples of the principle of Change of Front.

(*See Examples XVIII, XIX and XX.*)

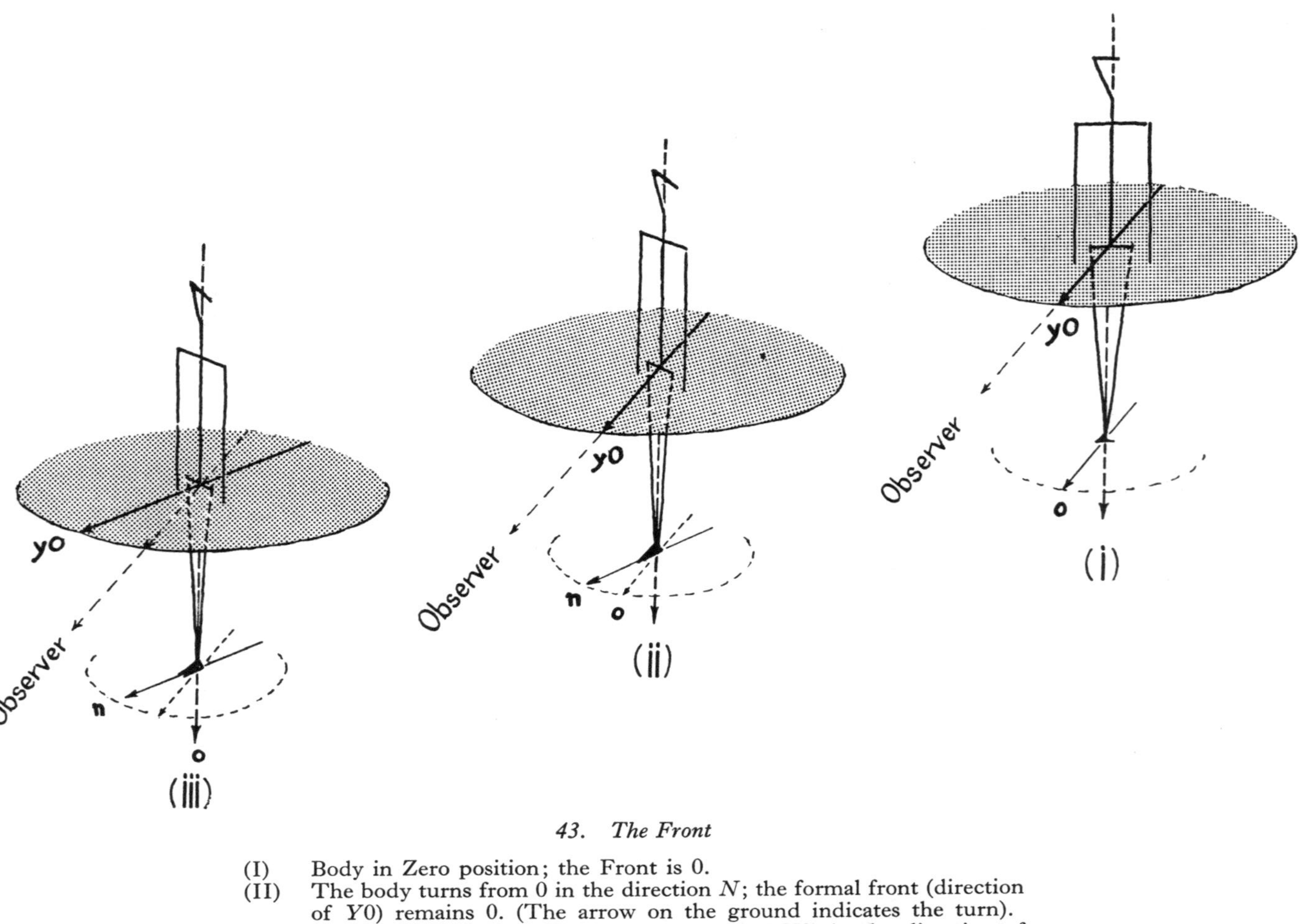

43. The Front

(I) Body in Zero position; the Front is 0.

(II) The body turns from 0 in the direction *N*; the formal front (direction of *Y*0) remains 0. (The arrow on the ground indicates the turn).

(III) A change of the formal Front (direction of *Y*0) in the direction of the turn of the body.

A (ORIGINAL)

RIGHT ARM	0	(0)↑1	⌊1	(1)↑1	1→	(2)↓1	⌊(1/4)8	(2)↑3	(3)↓16	(4)↑12
FRONT	0									

B

RIGHT ARM	0	(7)↑1	⌊1	(0)↑1	1→	(1)↓1	⌊(1/3)8	(1)↑3	(2)↓16	(3)↑12
FRONT	0	1								

C

RIGHT ARM	0	(6)↑1	⌊1	(7)↑1	1→	(0)↓1	⌊(1/2)8	(0)↑3	(1)↓16	(2)↑12
FRONT	0	2								

D

RIGHT ARM either (i)	0	(0)↓1	⌊1	(1)↓1	1→	(2)↑1	⌊(7/4)8	(2)↓3	(3)↑16	(4)↓12
RIGHT ARM or (ii)	0	(4)↑1	⌊1	(5)↑1	1→	(6)↓1	⌊(1/0)8	(6)↑3	(7)↓16	(0)↑12
FRONT	0	4								

E

RIGHT ARM	0	(1)↑1	⌊1	(2)↑1	1→	(3)↓1	⌊(1/5)8	(3)↑3	(4)↓16	(5)↓12
FRONT	0	7								

Ex. XVIII. One sequence of movement interpreted in six different ways. In *A* (the original) the sequence is interpreted in the most obvious way. The body and System of Reference are in Absolute Zero Position (i.e. *Y*0 coincides with a line running from the back forwards through the body, and is directed towards the observer).

In *B*, *C*, *D* and *E*, the body remains as in the original, but the System of Reference is rotated so that *Y*0 no longer points towards 0, but towards the direction indicated in the Front space immediately after the starting position. Since the System of Reference, in relation to which all movements are analysed and written, has been reorientated, the same movements must now be notated in a different manner. The new notation will be identical with that which would have been used had the Front number remained unchanged and the body been rotated the same amount in the opposite direction from the reorientation of the System of Reference.

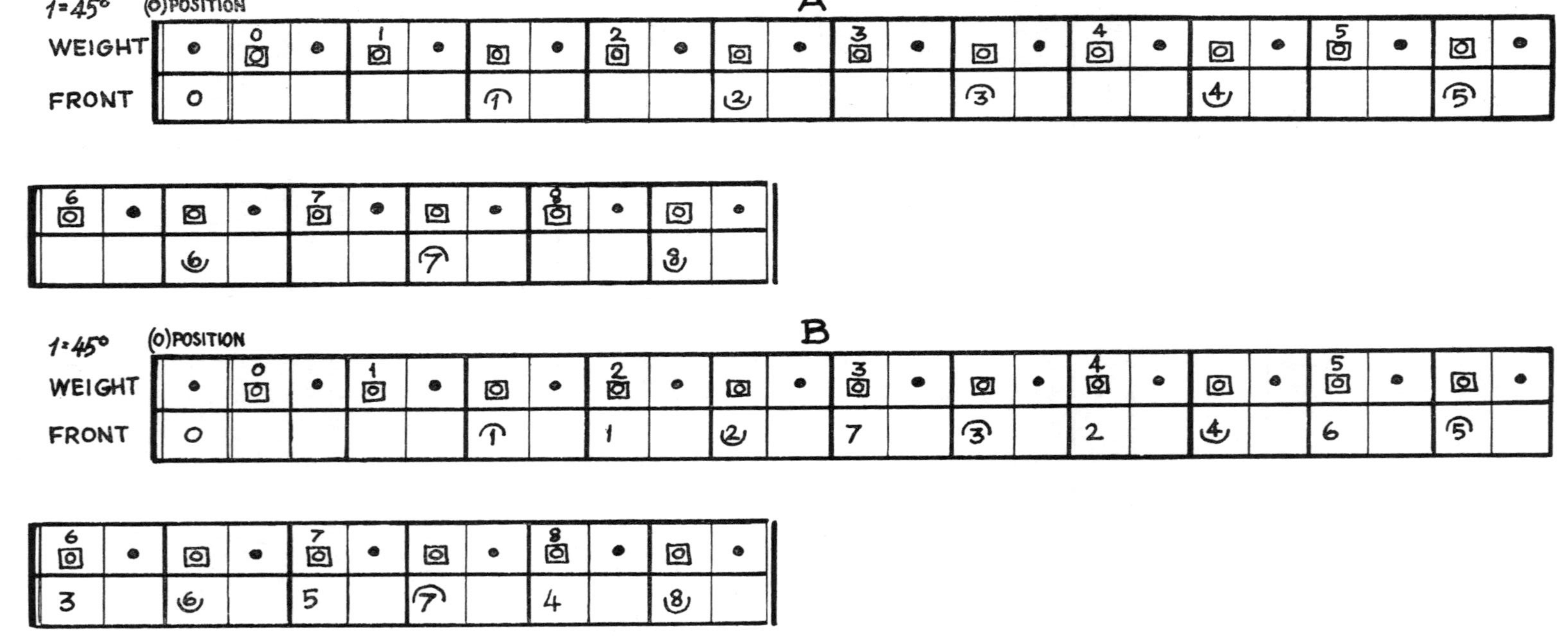

Ex. XIX. Two sequences of jumps, with transport of the Body and with turns in the air. The two sequences start from Absolute Zero Position. In the first sequence, all that is notated is related to *Y*0 of Absolute Zero Position, although the turns cause the frontal surface of the Body to face in all the directions provided by the System of Reference in which 1 = 45°. In sequence *B*, however, a change of front is introduced after each turn, making *Y*0 of the System of Reference coincide with the new direction in which the frontal surface of the body faces.

The resulting movements should be compared.

In both *A* and *B*, the first turn brings the body into direction 1 relative to *Y*0 of the System of Reference, that is, facing into the right forward diagonal. In the jump that follows, there is a difference between the two sequences. In *A*, the body is carried towards direction 2 relative to *Y*0 of the System of Reference, i.e. sideways in relation to the observer. In *B* there is a change of front and *Y*0 is reorientated to coincide with the new direction in which the front of the body faces, which is 1. The direction 2 is now related to this *Y*0, and the transport is sideways in relation to the body, and diagonally away from the observer.

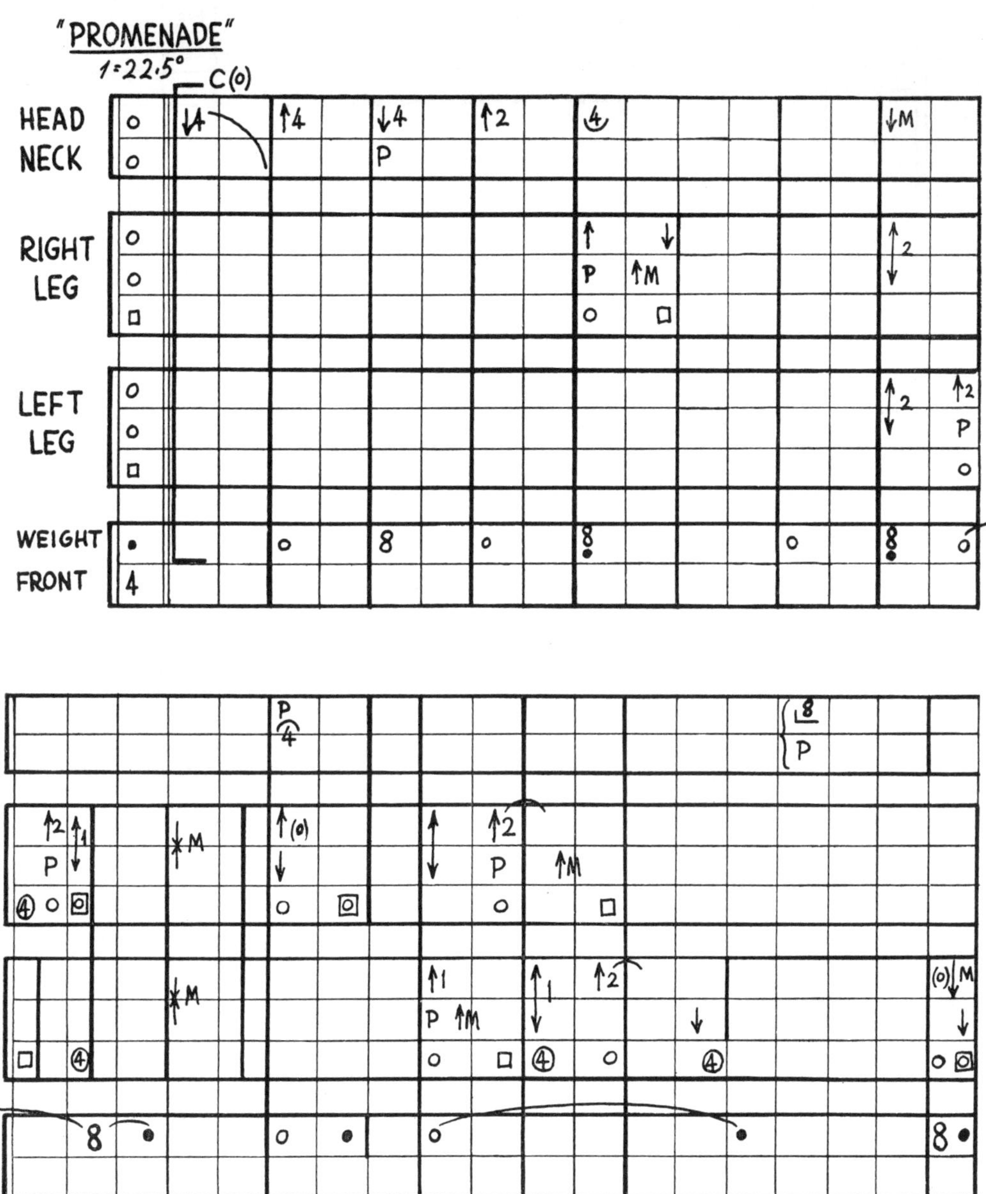

(continued on following page)

Ex. XX. A Study performed by the Chamber Dance Group directed by Noa Eshkol.

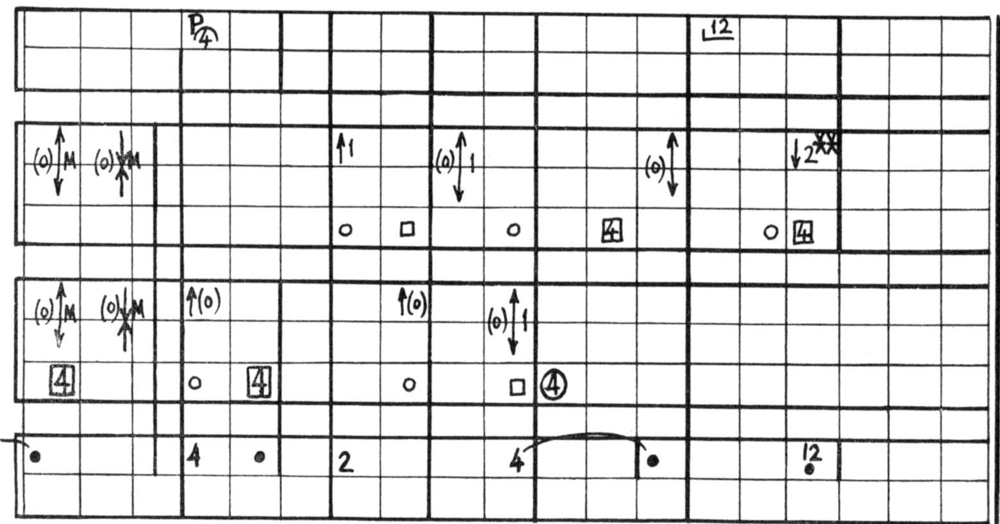

Ex. XX. (*cont.*) This study is divided into two parts. It should be noted that the first part is preceded by the heading *C*(*o*)—a key signature—and that the number in the Front space is 4. The key signature *C*(*o*) relates to this front number—i.e. coordinate (*o*) is directed towards the 'absolute' direction of coordinate 4.

In the second part of the study, following a negative rotation of the whole body through two units of magnitude, there is a change of front from 4 to 2, and also the interpolation of a new key signature *C*(4) for the legs and weight. If no change of front had taken place, movements now written in *C*(0) in the second part would have had to be written as occurring in *C*(4), because they would still be referred to a System of Reference orientated so that *Y*0 is diverted towards front number 4. For the same reason, had there been no change of front, those movements now written in *C*(4) would have had to be written in *C*(2).

Note.—A single asterisk indicates that the leg passes in front of the other; a double asterisk, that it passes behind. In a given work all plane movements not denoted by coordinate numbers are described by the number indicated by the key signature.

CHAPTER 14

The Base of the Body other than the Feet

THERE ARE positions of the body in which the function of base is performed not, as in standing, by the feet, but by some other part. In sitting, this is the pelvis; in kneeling, the lower part of the legs; in lying on the back, the whole surface of the back of the body; and so on. (*See Fig. 44.*) Such positions may occur in one of two ways: either as the starting position of a sequence of movement, or as a position arrived at by gradual stages in the course of a series of simultaneous movements.

The simplest of these positions are those in which the whole body lies on the floor, the limbs remaining in the same relations one to another as when standing in Zero position. Four cardinal variants of lying thus, are: lying on the frontal surface of the body, lying on the back; and on the left and right sides. In order to represent any of these main lying positions as the starting position of a sequence of movement, a Plane movement sign is written in the space representing Shift of Weight; the coordinate gives a direction in which the body may be imagined as having fallen from standing in Zero position, all the relations of the parts of the body remaining as they were in that position. This supposed movement is in fact a maximal shift of weight, resulting in the body's falling to the ground through an angle of ninety degrees, without changing the relations between its limbs from those of Zero position. The direction of this imaginary falling movement, indicated by the given coordinate, determines whether the resulting lying position be on the front, back, or left or right side of the body. (*See Figs. 39 and 40.*) This method of writing such positions is not a fixed principle, but it is a logical way, and any other way would be equally valid provided that the meaning were unambiguous. This way of writing is only valid in the notation of starting positions—and even these *could* be written in the same way as any other positions.

By writing the appropriate positional signs in the spaces representing arms, legs, and other limbs, following one of these cardinal lying positions, various other positions are obtained, according to the requirements of the writer.

Any limb which is used as the base or part of the base, is given the sign of contact with the ground—□. This sign always follows the symbol representing the movement by which the position has been attained. Any limb leaving the ground receives the sign—O.

It is possible (though not obligatory) to place numbers within these signs, as in the case of contact of the feet with the floor (*see Chapter 10*), to represent the side of the part of the body involved. The numbers, as with the feet, are given according to the horizontal coordinates into which the different sides of the limbs face in Absolute Zero Position. Thus the frontal surfaces of the torso, pelvis, or thighs are represented by 0, the back of the head by 4, the outer side of the right arm by 2, &c.

The analysis of movement when the base of the body is other than the feet, is carried out in *exactly* the same manner as in standing; that is, in relation to the System of Reference, of which the Horizontal plane remains parallel to the ground, and the coordinate *X* vertical. Because of this, it frequently occurs that the same movement in relation to the sides of the body is described by means of different planes in standing and in lying. A movement of the arm, rising sideways from the body in Zero Position, will be described as being in coordinate 2 (when 1 = 45°) if the body is standing upright; but, if the body is lying on the back or front, the same movement in relation to the body, will become a movement in the Horizontal plane, which (since the System of Reference remains unchanged) is parallel to the ground. (*See Fig. 45.*)

When in the course of a sequence of movements, a position is arrived at by stages, in which the base is other than the feet, this will become apparent as a result of the written movements. Usually, in such a sequence, there will be a gradual appearance of the sign of 'contact with the ground' in the spaces of all the limbs involved. However, the use of this sign is not obligatory.

When the whole body lies on the floor, the Law of 'Light' and 'Heavy' limbs applies in the same manner as in a jump—i.e. the 'heaviest' limbs are then either the torso or the pelvis. When both move simultaneously, the torso becomes the 'heaviest' limb in relation to the upper part of the body, and the pelvis to the lower.

It is to be noted that when the whole body lies in contact with the ground, a rotation about its longitudinal axis will cause the body to travel on the ground. When single parts lie on the ground (or other surface) and Rotatory movement about their longitudinal axes occurs, they will also be caused to travel. When it is wished to simulate the character of Rotatory movement in which there is no contact with the ground, i.e. in which the limb does not change its position, then the Rotatory movement sign will be written in conjunction with the sign O, signifying that the limb leaves the ground. This sign appearing independently, not as the result of the movement of a 'heavy' limb, denotes the minimal amount of lifting sufficient to allow the rotation to take place without changing its position relative to the System of Reference.

(*See Examples XXI and XXII.*)

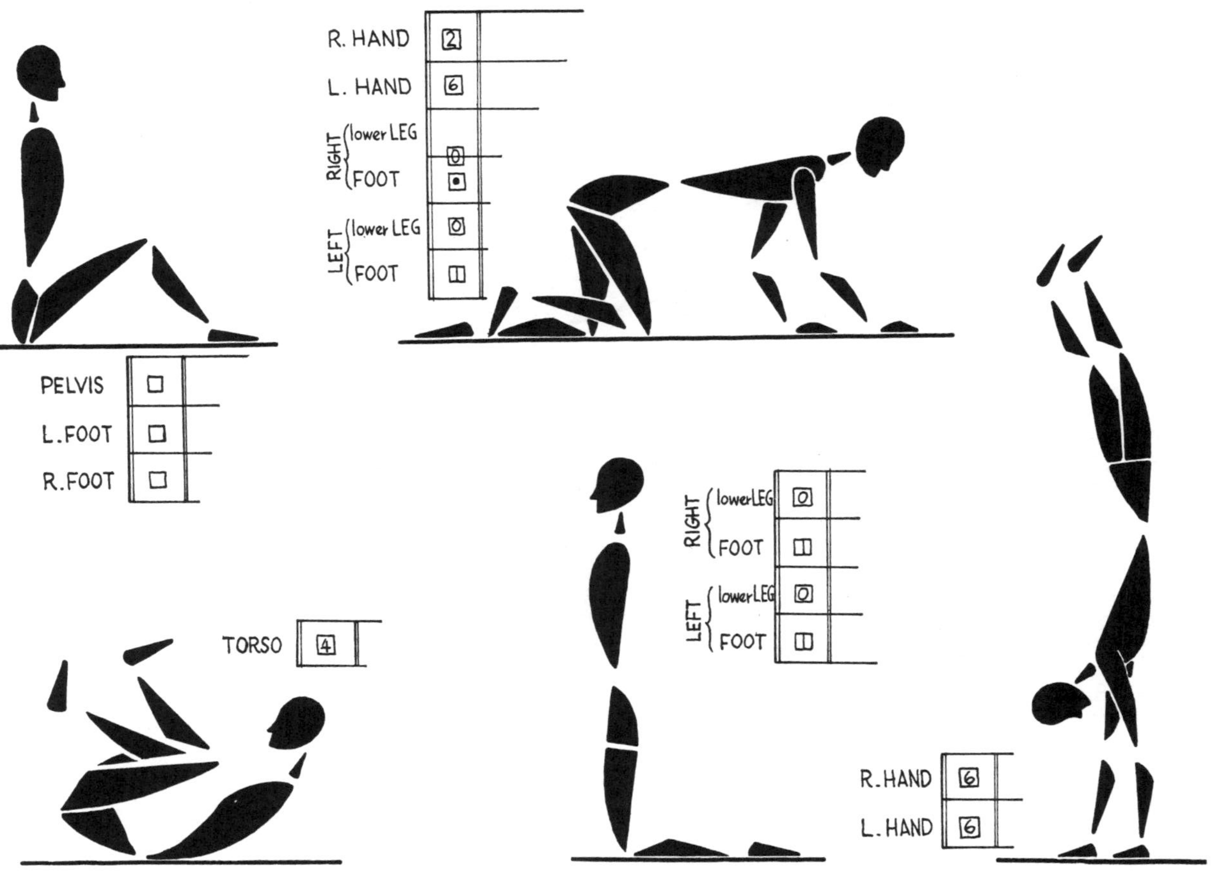

44. Base of the Body other than Feet

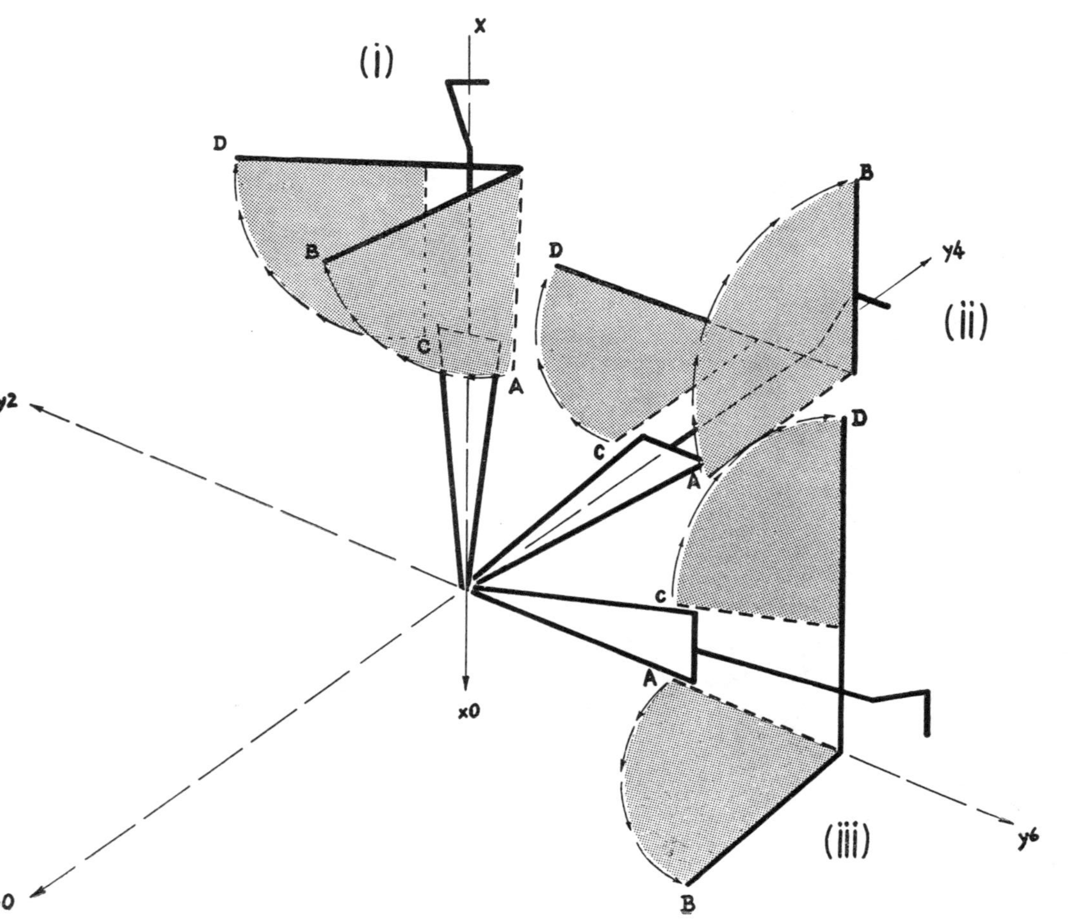

45. *The Influence of the Change of Base on the Analysis of Movement*

The diagram shows three positions of the body. In all positions the arms produce the same movements in relation to the sides of the body. The change of the base of the body from standing to lying on the back, and then on the side, causes a difference in the definition of the movement analysed according to the System of Reference, which remains fixed in relation to its own original position.

In position (i) the right arm moves from *C* to *D*, creating a section of the vertical plane (2) (1 = 45°). The left arm moves from *A* to *B*, creating a section of the vertical plane (0).

In position (ii) the body lies on its back on the floor and the right arm, producing exactly the same movement in relation to the body as in position (i), now moves in a horizontal plane, while the movement of the left arm is still creating a section of vertical plane (0) as in position (i).

In position (iii) the body lies on its side. The right arm creates a section in vertical plane (2), as in position (i), but the left arm creates a horizontal section.

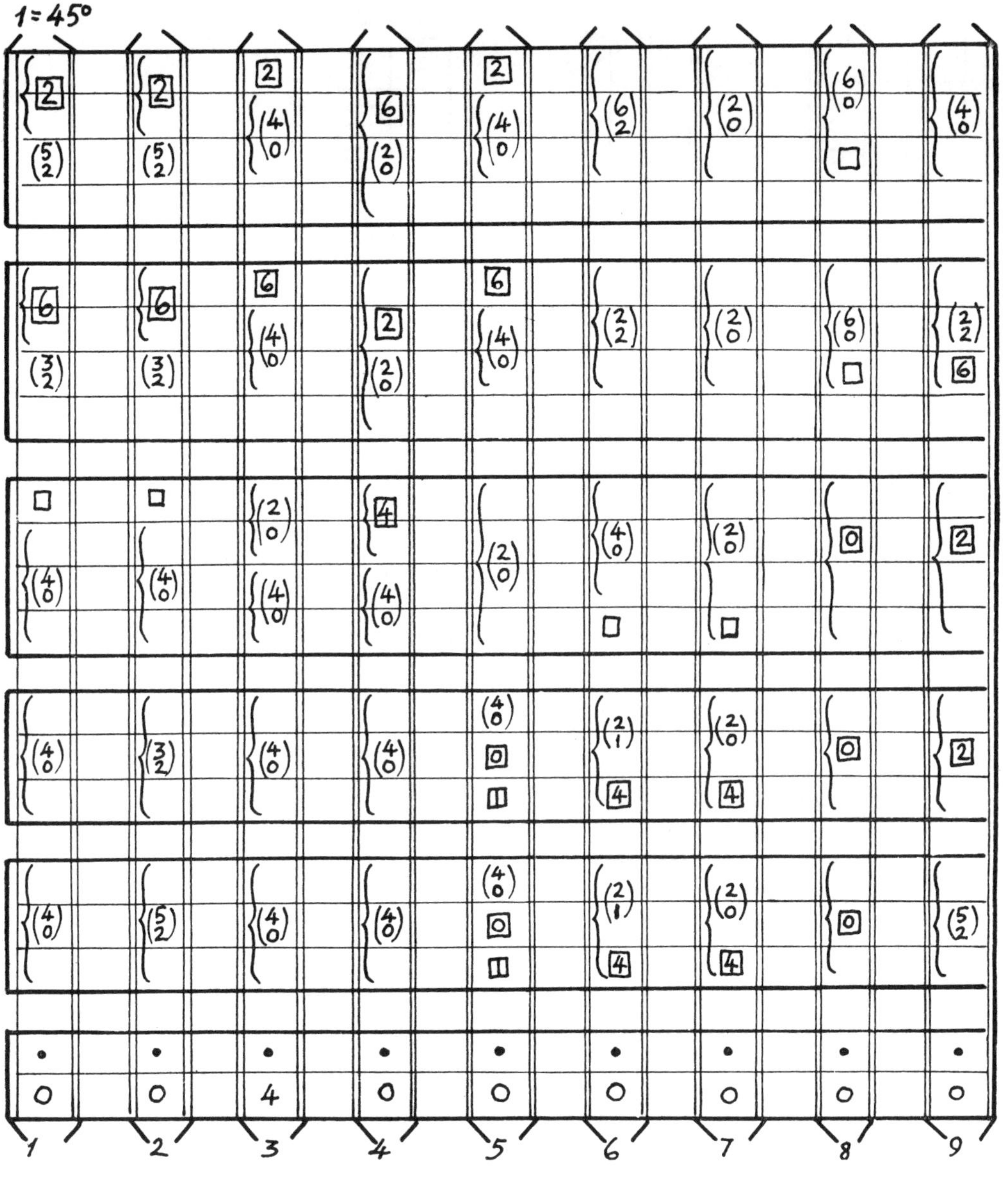

1=45°

1 2 3 4 5 6 7 8 9

Ex. XXI. Nine Positions in which the Base of the Body is other than the Feet. The first three are:

(1) A head-stand, with head, forearms and hands in contact with the ground.

(2) Head-stand, legs apart.

(3) Hand-stand.

1:45° WHOLE BODY : ZERO POSITION [4]

RIGHT LEG	(0)↑1	(0)↑1	(2)↑1	$\overset{3}{(0)}\downarrow 2$					$\overset{1}{\rightarrow}$	(1)↑1	(1)↑1	(0)↓1	$\overset{1}{(2)}\uparrow 2$	$\overset{2}{\leftarrow}$		
LEFT LEG					(0)↑1	(0)↑1	(2)↑1	$\overset{1}{(0)}\uparrow 2$	$\overset{1}{\leftarrow}$	(7)↑1	(7)↑1	(0)↓1			$\overset{1}{(2)}\downarrow 2$	$\overset{2}{\rightarrow}$

RIGHT LEG	(0)↑2	(2)↓2		$\overset{4}{\leftarrow}$	(6)↑4	$\overset{4}{\leftarrow}$	(6)↑4	$\overset{2}{\leftarrow}$		$\llcorner(\frac{4}{0})16$		$\ulcorner(\frac{4}{0})4$	$\llcorner(\frac{2}{0})2$	└2	┌4	$\overset{3}{(0)}\downarrow 2$
LEFT LEG	(0)↑3	(0)↓1	(2)↓2	$\overset{4}{\leftarrow}$	(6)↑2	(0)↓2		$\overset{2}{\leftarrow}$	(6)↑2		$\llcorner(\frac{2}{0})16$		$\ulcorner(\frac{2}{0})2$	┌2	└4	$\overset{1}{(0)}\uparrow 2$

RIGHT LEG:																
thigh	(0)↑2			(7)↓1	(7)↑1	(0)↓1	(0)↑1	(1)↓1	(1)↑1	(1)↓2	(1)↑2	(0)↓2	(0)↑2	(7)↓2	(7)↑2	(0)↓2
lower leg		(0)↓4	(0)↑4	(7)↓4	(7)↑4	(0)↓4	(0)↑4	(1)↓4	(1)↑4		(1)↓4	(0)↑4	(0)↓4	(7)↑4	(7)↓4	(0)↑4

Ex. XXII. The whole body lies on the back, the limbs remaining related to one another as in Zero Position. This is shown by the indication ZERO POSITION [4], given as a key signature. Use should be made of the symbols and conceptions of the notation in such combinations, for the sake of concise writing—care always being taken that the meaning remains unambiguous.

CHAPTER 15

Curved Movement—Non-Conical

THE KINDS of movement which have been dealt with hitherto (Rotatory, Plane, and Conical) have one property in common: namely, that in these movements, all the points on the longitudinal axis of the moving limb create perfect circles. Following from this, it may be said that the longitudinal axis of the limb moves about an axis of movement. The axis of movement is fixed in relation to the System of Reference; that is to say, its position does not change during the movement. There are, however, kinds of movement belonging to the class of Curved movement in which the longitudinal axis of the limb creates complex paths which are not circular. In the analysis of these complex non-circular paths, they may be classified as follows: (1) Elliptical movement, in which the extremity (and all other points) of the limb describes an ellipse; (2) Undulatory movement, in which the extremity (and all other points) of the limb describes waves; (3) Spiral movement, in which a spiral is described. It may be said of these movements that the longitudinal axis of the limb, while moving, approaches and recedes from a fixed axis of movement, or alternatively, the axis of the limb may be imagined as moving around an axis of movement, which does not remain fixed in its position during the movement of the limb around it (as in the case of the three kinds of movement so far dealt with), but which itself moves about another axis, which would be an axis of movement of the second order: the axis of movement of an axis of movement. It is possible to imagine in like manner, a movement of the axis of movement of the second order about *its* own axis of movement, and so on. These complex movements then are the results of a complex relation between the axes of movement.

To sum up: in circular movement, the movement is about a fixed axis (and is one of the three kinds of movement previously dealt with). When the path of the movement in question is complex, the axis of movement is itself moving while the movement takes place.

The above was an explanation according to the axes of movement. The following is a description of the way in which such movements are written.

An *Elliptical movement* is a curved movement in which the extremity of a limb describes an ellipse or part of an ellipse. For the analysis of such a movement, size and relation of either the major or the minor diameter of the ellipse to the System of Reference must be established. This is done by the same method that was employed in defining the relation of the diameter to the System of Reference in the analysis of Conical movements.

Within the Curved movement sign a positional sign will appear—two numbers in brackets, which together with the starting position of the movement express the relation of one of the diameters to the System. It remains to indicate whether the elliptical curve based on the diameter so defined begins as a 'flat' or as a 'high' curve. This will be done by indicating the proportion between the major and minor diameter of the ellipse. Imagine a perpendicular *CD* at the mid-point of the given chord *AB* if the proportion between *DC* and *AC* or *CB* is

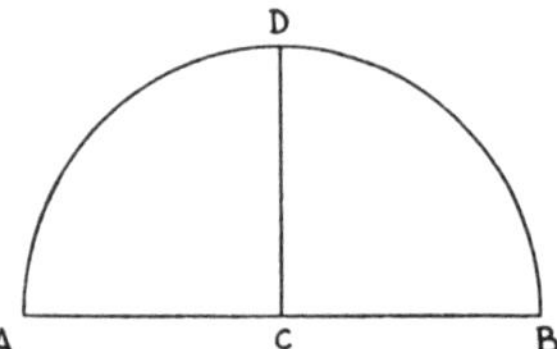

equal: $\frac{1}{1}$, then a curve constructed, on the points *A*, *D*, *B*, will be a semicircle, since equal radii result in a circular path. Whenever the curve is flatter or higher. the relation between the perpendicular and half the diameter will be unequal. In elliptical movement, when the starting position is best understood as being at one end of the major diameter (the movement of the extremity of the limb producing a flat curve in relation to this chord), the height of the perpendicular on the mid-point of the major diameter is given the number 1, and half the length of the major diameter is indicated in porportion to this (because the perpendicular on the mid-point of the major diameter is only *half* the length of the minor diameter, and the length of the major diameter must therefore also be halved to preserve the proportion). The upper term of the proportion represents the height of the perpendicular, and the lower term, half the length of the major diameter: $\frac{1}{2}$, $\frac{1}{3}$, &c.

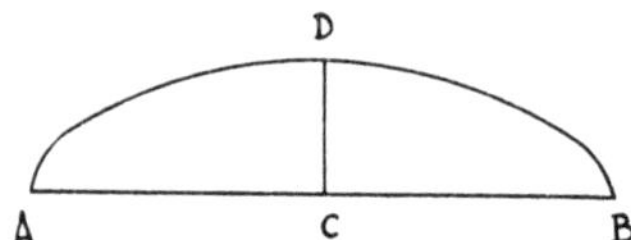

When the starting position is understood as being at one end of the minor diameter (when the curve is a high one), the method of description is identical, except that the base on which the curve is constructed is now the minor diameter, and is represented by the number 1, appearing as the *lower* term of the proportion; the relative height of the perpendicular (which is identical with half the long diameter of the ellipse) is given as the upper term: $\frac{2}{1}$, $\frac{3}{1}$, &c.

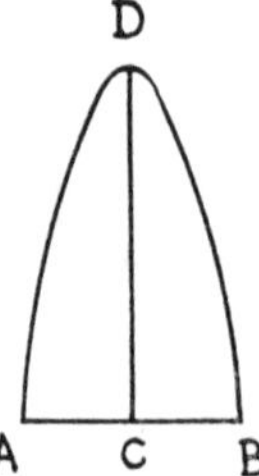

The amount of the ellipse described by the extremity of the limb, and thus also the amount of the curved surface of the elliptical cone, is given by means of a number (taken from the given scale of the composition) indicating the number of degrees of the ellipse to be passed through.

The sign of an Elliptical movement is thus comprised of four units:

(1) The sign of a Curved movement, positive or negative; the sense of the movement is determined by looking from the apex of the elliptical cone towards the base. Clockwise movement is then positive; anticlockwise, negative.

(2) The positional sign, written inside the Curved movement sign, giving in combination with the given starting position of the limb, the size and relation of the base to the System of Reference;

(3) A proportion expressing the relation of the major to the minor diameter, and by this indicating whether the elliptical movement begins with a high or a low curve. When the curve is a high one, the number 1 appears as the lower term of the proportion; when the curve is flat, it is the upper term.

(4) A figure expressing the amount of movement. For Example, $\underline{|\,(\frac{2}{2})\,\frac{1}{3}\,8}$, $\underline{|\,(\frac{2}{3})\,\frac{3}{1}\,8}$, &c. (*See Fig. 46—1, 2, 3, and 4.*)

Undulatory Movement

(a) *Sinusoidal Movement;* (b) *'Half-Barrel' Undulatory Movement*

Undulatory movements are Curved movements appearing in a certain series. Since they appear in a regular sequence, it is convenient to give them a special sign, but they could have been written as a succession of ordinary Curved movements. In the notation of undulatory movement three things must be verified and written:

(i) The nature of the series (sinusoidal, 'half barrel', &c.)—i.e., whether it is composed of waves of equal height, and moving in one sense, either positive or negative; or of waves alternating in their sense of movement, and so on. (*See Fig. 46: 6a, 6b, 7a and 7b.*)

(ii) The range of the Undulatory movement. The range of an Undulatory movement is the extent and location of that plane which may be imagined as lying between the starting position and the final position of the moving limb. This will be written (as in the indication of the diameter of the base in Conical movement) by writing the final position of the limb, the starting position being always known.

(iii) The number of waves actually performed within the specified range. Within the range of movement given, the extremity of the limb performs a number of half-waves which in conjunction become an Undulatory movement. The number of waves performed will be indicated by a figure—preceded by a comma—which represents exactly the number of waves. The size of the waves, when they are exact semi-circles, is inferred from the number of waves performed within the given imaginary plane: the length of the path described by the extremity of the limb, divided by the number of waves, gives the diameter of each half-circle.

Therefore, the greater the number of waves, the smaller each will be—and *vice versa.* When the Undulatory movement is composed not of half-circles but either of 'higher' or 'flatter' curves, an additional indication is given, showing the proportion of the larger chord to the smaller, precisely as in the notation of elliptical curved movement.

(*a*) *Sinusoidal Movement*

In Undulatory movement which is sinusoidal the sense of each curve is contrary to that of the preceding—a positive movement being followed by a negative, which is again followed by a positive, and so on. The symbol for this kind of movement is composed of three signs.

(i) A sign representing the final position of the limb.

(ii) A number preceded by a comma indicating the number of waves.

(iii) A sign expressing the kind of movement, and sense of the movement in the *first* of the curves (positive or negative).

Example $'\widetilde{5\binom{2}{2}}$. A Sinusoidal Undulatory movement, containing five curves; range of movement up to position $\binom{2}{2}$; the movement starting in positive sense.

The same movement, starting in negative direction: $'\overset{\frown}{5\binom{2}{2}}$.

When the curves described by the extremity are higher or lower than semicircles, the symbol is comprised of four signs.

Examples $'\widetilde{5\binom{2}{2}}\,\frac{1}{3}$, $'\widetilde{5\binom{2}{2}}\,\frac{2}{1}$.

The additional sign expresses the degree of 'height' or 'flatness' of the curve, as in the case of an ellipse.

(*b*) *'Half-Barrel' Undulatory Movement*

Here, unlike the previous type, the movement is composed of semicircles all having the same sense—either positive *or* negative—the sign for positive being $\curlyvee$ and for negative $\curlywedge$.

Example $'\overset{\curlyvee}{5\binom{2}{2}}$.

A 'Half-barrel' movement containing five curves; range of movement up to the position $\binom{2}{2}$; the movement starting in positive sense.

The same movement, starting in negative sense: $'\overset{\curlywedge}{5\binom{2}{2}}$.

When the curves described by the extremity are higher or lower than semicircles, the symbol is comprised of four signs.

Examples $'\overset{\curlyvee}{5\binom{2}{2}}{}^{1}_{3}$, $'\overset{\curlyvee}{5\binom{2}{2}}{}^{2}_{1}$. The additional sign again indicates the degree of 'height' or 'flatness' of the curve.

When it is wished either to augment or diminish the size of the waves in the course of either of the two types of Undulatory movement described above, this is indicated by the use of the sign $<$ for augmentation and the sign $>$ for diminution.

Examples; $'\widetilde{5\binom{2}{2}}<$ Augmentation $'\widetilde{5\binom{2}{3}}>$ Diminution.

Spiral Movement

A spiral movement is a Curved movement consisting of several cones which gradually become either larger or smaller. These cones may be either regular or elliptical.

In order to establish the relation of the Spiral to the System of Reference use will be made of the same device of defining the relation of the base of the cone to the System of Reference, which is used in the analysis of ordinary conical movement. In a diminishing spiral, the size and position of the first (outer) cone will be defined in relation to the System of Reference by means of the diameter of its base, and indicated by a positional sign. In an augmenting spiral, the radius is used and not the diameter, because, in an augmenting spiral, the diameter of the first (inner and smallest) cone gives no indication of the size and position of the final cone. The radius of the outer cone (that is, the straight line between the starting and final positions of the limb producing the spiral movement) is known, and this is used in order to establish the position and size of the largest cone, the starting and final positions being identified in the usual way by positional numbers.

The number of the cones to be performed will be indicated by a number preceded by an apostrophe (to distinguish these numbers from those indicating amount of movement). The actual size of each cone will be determined according to the relation between the size of the largest cone and the number of cones to be performed. The diameter of the largest cone will be the same number of times bigger than the diameter of the smallest cone, as the number of cones contained in the Spiral (e.g. when the Spiral consists of two cones, the diameter of the small cone will be half the size of the large).

When the Spiral is an elliptical spiral, the fractional number expressing the relation of greater and smaller chords of the elliptical base will be added to the sign.

(a) When the Spiral is conical, the sign for a Spiral movement consists of:

(1) The sign of a Curved movement, positive or negative.

(2) A positional sign defining the size and relation of the diameter or radius in the base of the largest of the cones.

(3) A number preceded by an apostrophe, indicating the number of cones contained in the Spiral.

(4) A sign of diminution $>$ or of augmentation $<$.
For example: $\lfloor\underline{\binom{2}{2}\text{'}2 <}$ $\lfloor\underline{\binom{2}{2}\text{'}2 >}$ $\lceil\overline{\binom{2}{2}\text{'}5 >}$

(b) When the Spiral is elliptical, the fraction will be added expressing the proportion of the greater to the smaller chords in the base of the ellipse.

For example: $\lfloor\underline{\binom{2}{2}\text{'}2 < \frac{1}{3}}$ $\lceil\overline{\binom{2}{3}\text{'}5 > \frac{3}{1}}$

It is important to remember that the cones and ellipses in a Spiral movement are not of the ordinary kind, for each one does not close on itself, creating a complete circle or ellipse, and their actual curvature changes all the time. But, for the notation of this kind of movement it is possible and sufficient to deal with them as if they were perfect, especially in defining the largest cone.

The exactitude of performance of Spiral movement, in respect of the proportion of its changing curvature, is the responsibility and sensibility of the performer.

(*See Figs. 46—7a and 7b*, *47 and 48* and *Examples XXIII and XXIV*.)

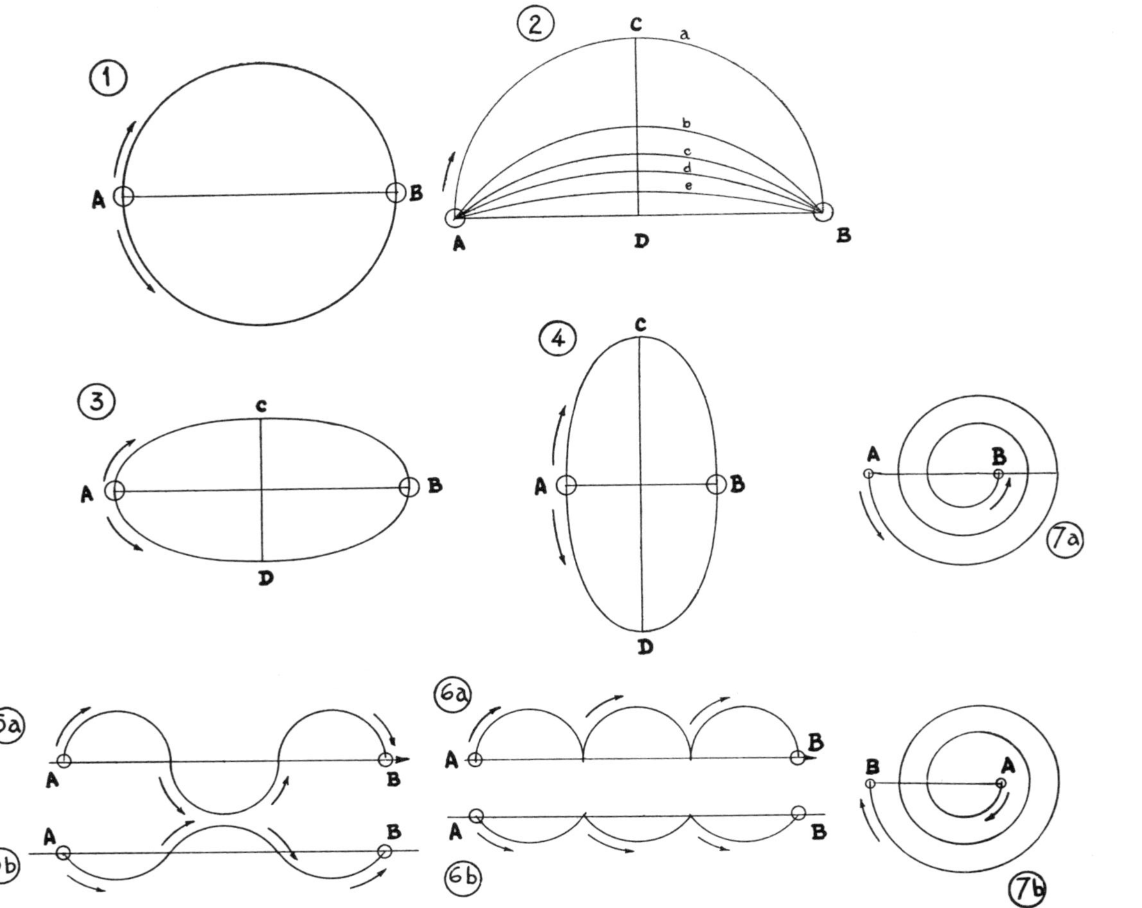

46. *The Path of the Extremity of the Limb in the different types of Curved Movement*

(1) Conical Movement.

(2) Various degrees of height of curves:

(a) semicircle;
(b) curve in which the proportion of height and half the chord is:
(c) proportion $\frac{1}{3}$
(d) proportion $\frac{1}{4}$.
(e) proportion $\frac{1}{n}$.

(3) Elliptical movement in which the limb starts moving from one end of the greater diameter.

(4) Elliptical movement in which the limb starts moving from one end of the lesser diameter.

(5) (a) A sinusoidal movement built on semi-circles.
(b) A sinusoidal movement built on flat curves.

(6) (a) A 'Half-Barrel' movement built on semi-circles.
(b) A 'Half-Barrel' movement built on flat curves.

(7) (a) Diminishing Spiral composed of three cones.
(b) Augmenting Spiral composed of three cones.

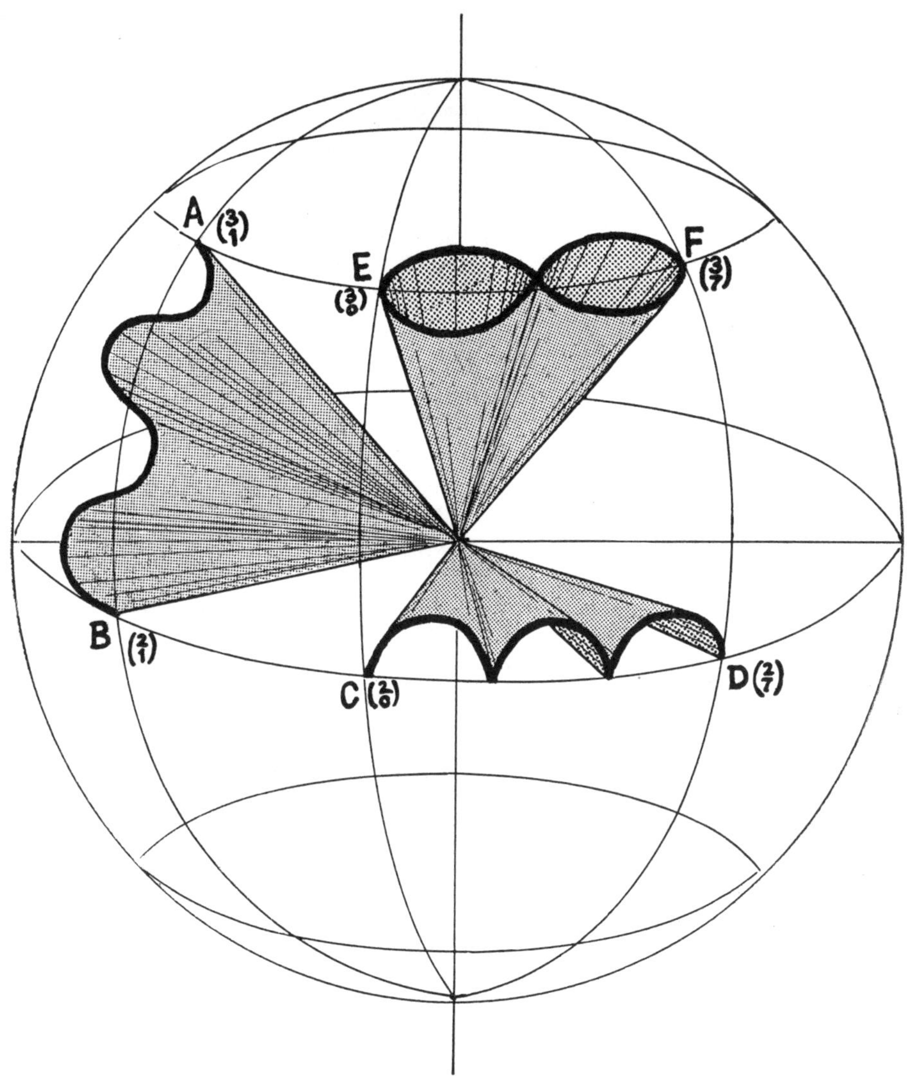

47. Undulatory Movement

In the diagram three kinds of Undulatory Movement are represented:

(1) *Sinusoidal Movement*—the limb moves from *A* to *B*. The position at *B* is $\binom{2}{1}$. The limb creates four half-cones, the first curve being in negative sense. The movement will be written thus: $'\overline{4\tbinom{2}{1}}$.

(2) *Half Barrel Movement*—the limb moves from *C* to *D* creating three half-cones; the position at *D* is $\binom{2}{7}$, the sense of movement, negative. The movement is written thus: $'\widehat{3\tbinom{2}{7}}$.

(3) '*Figure Eight*' *Movement*—the limb moves from *E* to *F* and returns to *E*. The position of the limb at *F* is $\binom{3}{7}$. The movement consists of two Sinusoidal movements, the first beginning in positive sense, and the second in negative sense. The movement is written: $'\widetilde{2\tbinom{3}{7}}$ $'\overline{2\tbinom{3}{0}}$.

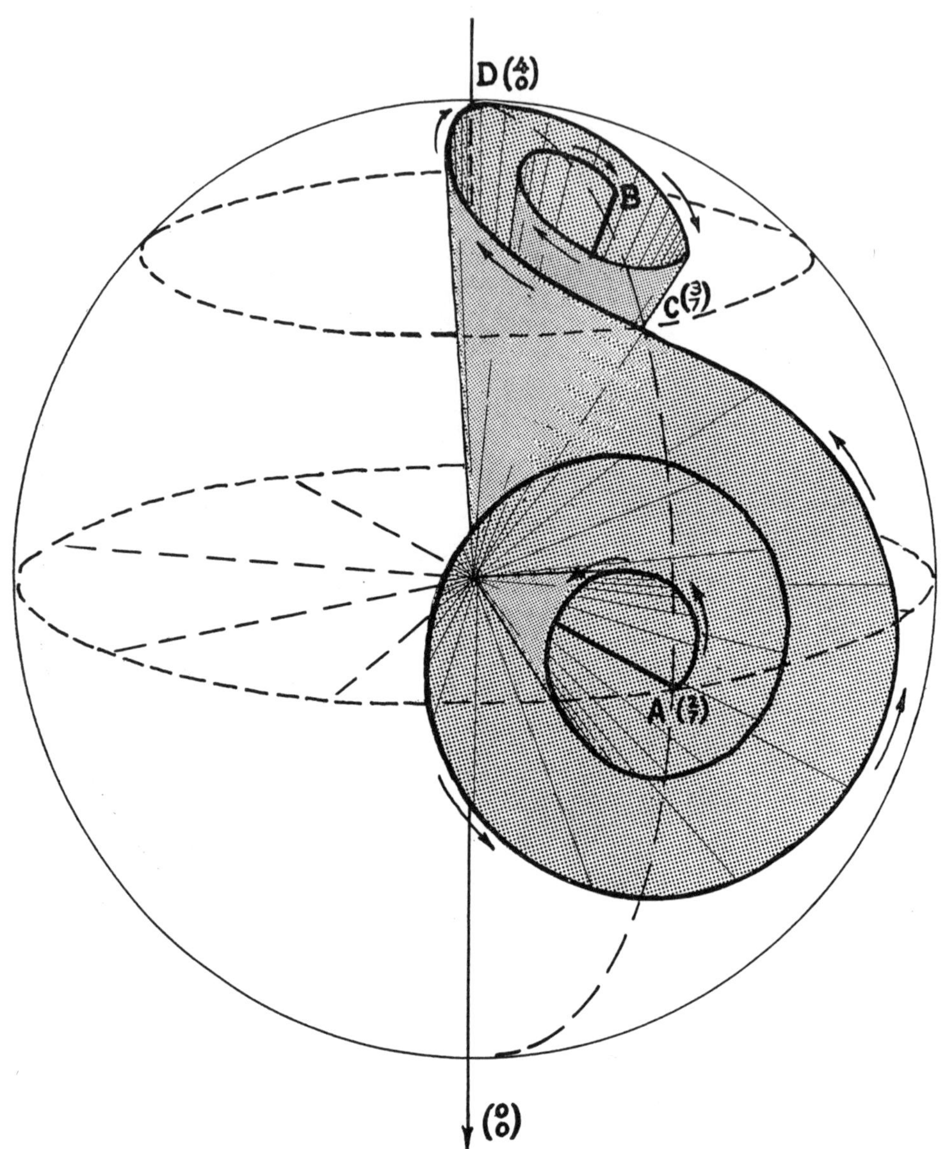

48. Spiral Movement

The limb begins to move from A, through points C and D and ends at B. From A to C the limb produces an augmenting spiral; from C to B a diminishing spiral. These movements will be written in two stages.

(1) The augmenting Spiral. The position at A is given; the position at C is $\binom{3}{7}$. AC is the 'radius' of the outer cone. The movement is in positive sense and the number of cones three. (Every section of a conical envelope which is more than a quarter of a cone is taken into account in calculating the number of cones.) The augmenting spiral movement from A to C is written thus: $\underline{|\ \binom{3}{7}\ '3\ <}$.

(2) The diminishing Spiral is analysed according to the diameter of the outer cone of the spiral. If the scale is $1 = 22{\cdot}5°$, the position of the limb at B is $\binom{7}{14}$ the direction of movement negative; and the Spiral contains two conical envelopes. The movement is written thus: $|\overline{\binom{7}{14}\ '2\ >}$.

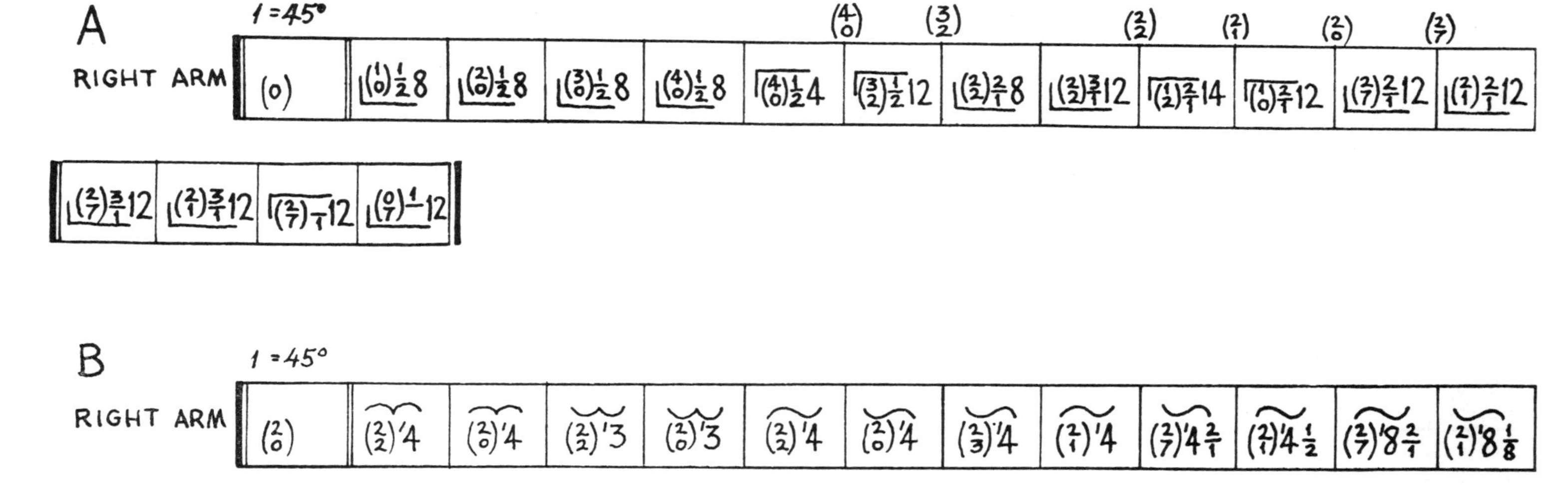

Ex. XXIII. Two Simple Reading Exercises:

(*A*) A sequence of Elliptical Movement.

(*B*) A sequence of Undulatory Movement.

1 = 15°   WHOLE BODY: (0) - [2]

LEFT ARM	6 →	(0)↑6	(6/18)'4	(6)↓12	← 6	(12/0)24	(12/0)½24	(12/0)'6			(6/21)'6	(6/18)'3	5 (6)↑12	4 (6)↓12
LEFT LEG	6 →	(0)↑6	(6/18)'2	(6)↓6	(0)↓6	(12/0)24	(12/0)½24		(6/15)'6	(6/18)'3			5 (6)↑6	5 (6)↓6

3 (6)↑12	2 (6)↓12	1 (6)↑12		(6)↓12	(6/0) 5/1 '6		3 (0)↓6	6	12	(6/18) 1/3 12	← 3	(3)↓12	3 (3)↓12	(6/3)'3	(6/18)'4
3 (6)↑6	3 (6)↓6	1 (6)↑6	(0)↓1	(6)↓6		(6/0)'6	3 (0)↓6	6		(6/18) 1/3 12	← 3	(3)↓12	3 (3)↓12	(6/3)'3	(6/18)'4

Ex. XXIV. A sequence of movement, providing Reading Exercise. The given time-values are arbitrary. The whole body is imagined as laid on its right side: [2] (1 = 15°), all the limbs remaining in the relations in which they stand in Zero Position. The left arm and leg are thus not in contact with the ground.

This example includes every pure (as distinct from auxiliary) movement sign encountered in the notation method. Note that at the end of each section the body arrives again at the starting position.

CHAPTER 16

Simultaneous Movement

(*a*) *Explanation according to the Axes of Movement*

THE PATH of a moving limb in space (i.e. its continuous change of position) is an inevitable result of the movement of the limb itself only when that limb *alone* moves in relation to the System of Reference, without being carried by any 'heavier' limb connected to it (either directly or indirectly). In such a case, the movement performed by the limb (its kind, amount, and relation to the System of Reference) is identical with the continuous change of *position* of the limb in relation to the System of Reference. However, the case is entirely different when the limb is carried by limbs 'heavier' than itself, whether the 'light' limb be at rest or moving while being carried.

To facilitate understanding of the principle involved, only circular movements will be spoken of at present—movements wherein the axis of movement is at a fixed angle to the axis of the limb during one movement.

When a limb moves alone about any axis of movement, and carries a 'lighter' limb, this 'lighter' limb moves about the same axis of movement. That is to say, every point on the longitudinal axis of the 'light' limb turns about the same axis around which the 'heavy' limb turns, although the axis of movement does not pass through the joint of that 'light' limb. Both limbs together may then be seen as one single moving unit (not necessarily as one straight line, but having perhaps an angular shape). When a single unit moves about any kind of axis, every point on the unit creates a circle about that axis. It may therefore be said that the 'light' limb creates a certain circular path which is the direct result of the relation of the long axis of the 'light' limb to the axis of movement of the 'heavy' limb, for this relation remains constant during the movement since the relation between the 'heavy' limb and the 'light' limb remains unchanged.

The nature of the path, the spatial surfaces, created in the above case, would be identical in *kind*—plane, cylindrical (rotative), or conical—with that which would have been created if the 'light' limb had been moving around an axis of movement parallel to the given axis of movement but passing through its own joint. But it would be different in size and shape.

For example, in a movement of the upper arm in the horizontal plane, carrying the forearm in a fixed angular relation of 90° to it, the path created by the 'light' limb, the forearm, is cylindrical in form. The axis of movement passes through the joint of the 'heavy' limb, i.e. the shoulder, and is perpendicular to the horizontal plane. If now the axis of movement were to pass instead through the joint of the forearm, while remaining parallel to its former position, it would coincide with the longitudinal axis of the 'light' limb, and any independent movement of that limb about the newly placed axis of movement would produce a cylindrical path, although of far smaller proportion—that is, a Rotatory movement.

Again, if the upper arm, moving in the horizontal plane, were to carry the forearm at a fixed angle of 45°, the surface created by the passive movement of the forearm would be in the form of a cone, the upper part of which had been cut off. The axis of movement would pass as before through the joint of the 'heavy' limb, namely the shoulder joint. If the axis of movement be again caused to pass through the elbow (the joint of the 'light' limb), but remaining parallel to its previous position, the path of any independent movement of the forearm about the axis will then be conical; the cone being in this case, however, complete, with the apex situated in the elbow joint.

When the 'light' limb moves independently in relation to the 'heavy' limb which carries it at the same time, the 'heavy' limb may easily be imagined as carrying in its movement, not only the 'light' limb, but also all the potential axes of movement of the 'light' limb. When a 'light' limb moves about a certain axis of movement, and is at the same time carried by a 'heavy' limb it will continue to move about its own axis of movement, but both the limb itself *and* its axis of movement, will be carried by the 'heavy' limb. It will be a complex movement wherein the 'light' limb moves about a certain axis of movement, and this axis moves about *another* axis of movement. The path of such a movement will thus be complex, despite the fact that the movement of the 'light' limb alone is a simple circular movement. The explanation of the nature of Elliptical movement according to the axes of movement, should be recalled. From this it follows that the independent movement of a 'light' limb cannot be determined by direct observation of its change of relation relative to the System of Reference (its path of movement); one must subtract from it that change which is caused by movements of 'heavier' limbs which carry with them the 'light' limb and its axes of movement. Only that movement which the limb performs about the axis of movement which passes through its own joint (i.e. its movement in relation to the 'heavier' limb) is its own individual, independent, movement. The change of position in relation to the System of Reference is the inevitable result of the movement of a limb only when it moves singly or when it is the 'heaviest' of a group of moving limbs. Otherwise, its path of movement is the result of its own movement, together with that of all the 'heavier' limbs which move and carry it at the same time.

If it is required to fix the *position* of a limb relative to the System despite the movement of a 'heavier' limb a certain action must be performed. The axis of movement of the 'lighter' limb must be moved about an axis of movement which is parallel to the axis of movement of the 'heavy' limb, the amount of movement being the same as that of the heavy limb but in the opposite sense, the axis of the 'light' limb creating a cylindrical surface. This complex movement of axis of limb and axis of movement results in the 'light' limb remaining in the same position in relation to the System of Reference.

N.B. Cylindrical movement is different from Rotatory movement in that the axis of the limb in cylindrical movement moves parallel to the axis of movement, thus creating a cylindrical surface, whereas in Rotatory movement the axis of the limb turns about itself. *Cylindrical movement cannot be performed by the independent movement of a limb, but only by axes.* Since every limb is connected by a joint to another limb, and the axis of movement always passes through the joint of the moving limb, no limb can create a surface parallel to its own axis of movement, as this would require that its axis of movement should at all points be at some distance from the axis of the limb.

If it is wished that the *movement* of the 'light' limb should not be effected by the movement of the 'heavy' limb, an action must be performed by which the axis of movement of the 'light' limb is prevented from moving about the axis of movement of the 'heavy' limb. That is to say, the axis of movement of the 'light' limb now remains indeed fixed in relation to the System of Reference, whereas in the writing of ordinary Simultaneous movement, the axis of movement of the 'light' limb is only *imagined* as being fixed in relation to the System of Reference for the sake of analysis.

(*b*) *Simultaneous Movement, explained according to Positions and Change of Positions*

When the movement of one limb only is concerned, or when the limb dealt with is the 'heaviest' in a group of moving limbs, its *change of position*, from the beginning to the end of a movement, is the result of the movement of that limb alone; for example, if the limb is in the position $\binom{2}{2}$ and moves in $\xrightarrow{2}$, its position will then change to $\binom{2}{4}$. In other words, the limb's horizontal coordinate will move from 2 to 4. If the limb moves from $\binom{2}{2}$ in $2 \uparrow 1$, then its vertical coordinate will change by one unit and its position will be $\binom{3}{2}$. If the limb moves in an Intermediate plane, its two coordinates will change in proportion to its movement.

But in the case of the change of position of a 'light' limb (a limb carried by the movement of another limb), whether this limb itself be stationary or moving in relation to the 'heavy' limb, its change of position will be at least in part the result of the movement of the 'heavy' limb.

So long as the 'light' limb is merely being carried and is itself stationary in relation to the 'heavy' limb, its change of position will be entirely a result of the movement of the 'heavy' limb and proportionate to the kind and amount of movement of the latter. For example, assume the right upper arm raised at a right angle in the Vertical plane 0 (i.e. forward) from Zero Position. Being the 'heavier' limb in relation to the forearm it carries the forearm with it. When $1 = 45°$, this is written:

Right Forearm		$\binom{2}{0}$	
Right Upper Arm	$(0) \uparrow 2$	$\binom{2}{0}$	

The resulting positions of both limbs are the same.

If the limb which is carried is at the same time moving in relation to the 'heavier', then its change of position is a result of both movements—its own movement, and the movement of the 'heavier' limb. In that case, the 'heavy' limb is only *partly* responsible for the change of position of the 'light' limb in relation to the System.

In a case where several limbs attached to each other move simultaneously, the change of position of each limb is the result of its own movement and of the movement of *all* limbs 'heavier' than itself.

The movement of any limb has two aspects: one, the change of relation of the limb to a 'heavier' limb, and the other, its change of position in relation to the System of Reference.

When the limb is moving singly or is the 'heavier' one, the analysis of its movement according to the System of Reference presents no problems. But, in order to ascertain the movement of the 'light' limb, it is necessary to *imagine* the movement of the 'light' and that of the 'heavy' limb as performed not simultaneously but consecutively. In the following example, the movement is performed by the right arm, starting from a position in which it is stretched directly forward from the shoulder. The upper arm moves through a right angle to the right side, parallel to the ground; the forearm flexes until at right angles to the upper arm. As a result the forearm reaches a position in which it is not only perpendicular to the ground and in front of the body, as it would be in an independent movement, but also to the right of the body and in a new relation to the System of Reference, because it is carried by the movement of the heavier limb:

	Starting Position	Movement	End Position
Right Forearm	$\binom{2}{0}$	$(0)\uparrow 2$	$\binom{4}{2}$
Right Upper Arm	$\binom{2}{0}$	$\overset{2}{\rightarrow}$	$\binom{2}{2}$

The actual change of position according to the System of Reference cannot be understood from reading the movement signs of any one limb singly. It is necessary to read the manuscript page 'vertically' in order to obtain a complete and exact picture of the various changes of position of the limbs in relation to the System.

The two aspects of the movement of the body—that of the change of relations between the limbs, which is expressed by pure movement signs; and that of the change of position relative to the System of Reference, expressed by positional signs—are both given expression in the notation.

In a simultaneous movement a change of relation of a 'light' limb to a 'heavy' is expressed by the usual movement signs, which have been explained already. But it may be wished to express the change of relation of a 'light' limb, not to a 'heavy' limb but to the System of Reference, without taking into consideration whether it is the result of simultaneous movement or not (i.e. as if its change of position were the result of its own movement only).

When it is wished to indicate that a limb remains in a fixed *position* in relation to its Private System of Reference, regardless of its being carried at the same time by a heavier limb, a positional sign will be used in a special way. The position of the axis of the 'light' limb in relation to the System of Reference is written, with the addition of the symbol *f* which signifies that this relation remains fixed in spite of the movement of the heavy limb. For example, the right arm may begin to move from a position in which it is stretched straight forward from the shoulder, parallel to the ground: the upper arm moves, remaining parallel to the ground, through 90° to the right until pointing sideways, but the forearm remains pointing forward all the time, that is, parallel to its starting position. An angle of 90° will have been created between forearm and upper arm, but instead of writing the change of relation of forearm to upper arm (movement) it is simply indicated that the relation of the forearm to its Private System of Reference (position) remains fixed, and the movement is written thus:

	Starting Position	Movement	End Position
Forearm	$\binom{2}{0}$	$f\binom{2}{0}$	$\binom{2}{0}$
Upper Arm	$\binom{2}{0}$	$\overset{2}{\rightarrow}$	$\binom{2}{2}$

Again, it may be that a 'light' limb moves in a certain relation to its System of Reference, which it is desired should remain unaffected by the simultaneous movement of the heavier limb which carries it: that is to say, the axis of movement of the 'light' limb remains in fixed relation to the Private System of Reference. Suppose for example, that the right arm rises from Zero Position upward and forward, passing through 180°, and at the same time the Upper Torso is tilted 45° to the left. If the movement of the arm were carried out in relation to the torso and according to the law of 'light' and 'heavy' limbs, at the end of the movement it would be at an angle of 45° to the ground, continuing the line of the tilted torso. But if the symbol *f* is added to the movement sign which denotes the movement of the 'light' limb, then it will rise forward, always keeping in the Vertical plane 0, which it has started to create, and reach a position in which it is perpendicular to the ground and at an angle of 45° with the torso. This movement is then written:

	Starting Position	Movement	End Position
Arm	$\binom{0}{0}$	$f(0) \uparrow 4$	$\binom{4}{0}$
Torso	$\binom{0}{0}$	$(2) \uparrow 1$	$\binom{5}{2}$

In both the above cases in which the symbol *f* is used, the law of 'light' and 'heavy' limbs is momentarily suspended, the 'light' limb becoming a 'heavy' limb in its own right.

(*See Figs.* 52 *and* 53)

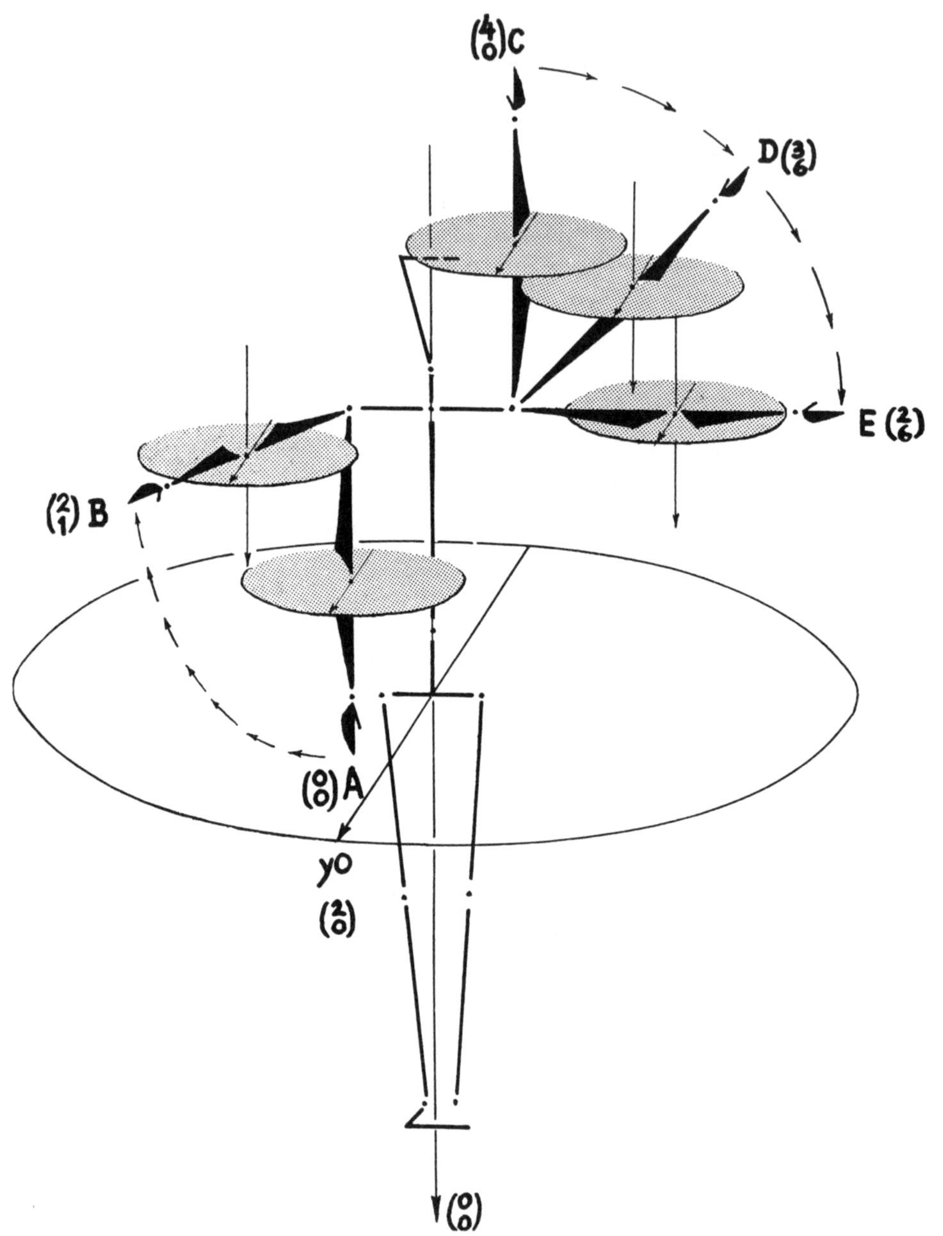

49. A Change of Relation of a 'Light' limb to the System of Reference, caused only by the movement of a 'Heavy' Limb

The position of the forearm at *A* is $\binom{0}{0}$. Supposing the upper arm to move $(1) \uparrow 2$, the scale 0 being $1 = 45°$, then the position of the forearm at *B* will be $\binom{2}{1}$. The position of the forearm at *C* is $\binom{4}{0}$ and it will change its position because of the movement of the upper arm; at *D* its position is $\binom{3}{6}$; at *E* it is $\binom{2}{6}$.

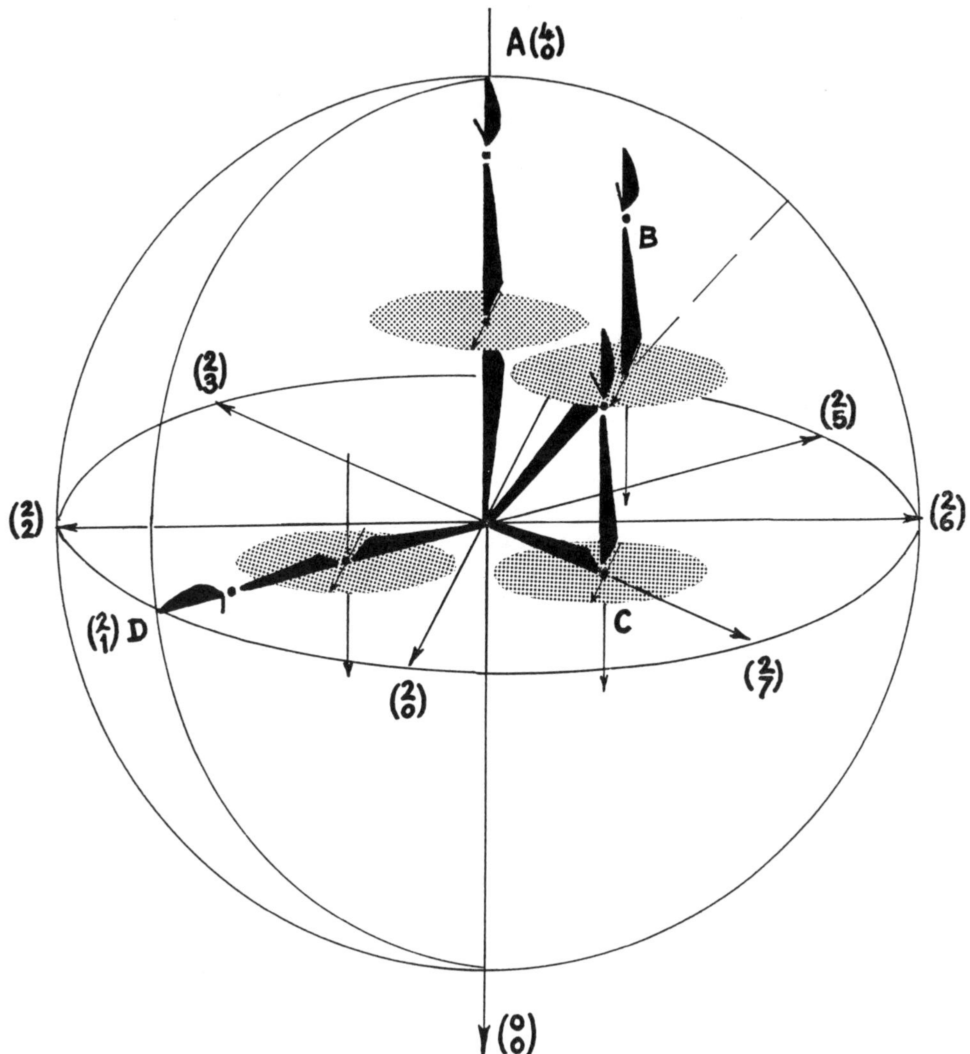

50. The Influence of a Simultaneous Movement on the Change of Position of a 'Light' Limb in relation to the System of Reference

The position of the forearm at A is $\binom{4}{0}$. The upper arm moves: (2) ↑ 1; the forearm moves (2) ↓ 1. The position of the forearm at B is unchanged, remaining $\binom{4}{0}$. The upper arm moves $\binom{1}{7}$ ↑ 1, the forearm moves (2) ↓ 1. The position of the forearm at C remains unchanged $\binom{4}{0}$.

In the notation of these two movements, the movement of the forearm is not written, but only its proper positional sign together with the sign f indicating that it remains in that position relative to the System of Reference.

Forearm	$f\binom{4}{0}$	$f\binom{4}{0}$
Upper Arm	(2) ↑ 1	$\binom{1}{7}$ ↑ 1

119

The upper arm continues to move, from C to D, and the forearm moves (7) ↓ 2. (Should the upper arm not have moved at all, the position of the forearm at the end of its movement would have been $\binom{2}{7}$. However, as the result of the simultaneous movement of the upper arm, its position at the end of this movement is $\binom{2}{1}$).

Examples

All of the following group of studies are reading examples, and may also be performed. This distinction between reading and performance is made because it is not necessarily possible to perform everything that can be written. A coherent composition may be constructed and written, which cannot be performed because of the physical limitations of the body. To illustrate: it may be imagined that such compositions are written for fantastically-limbed marionettes in which the capacity of movement is of the same character as in the human body, but without limitation in range or weight; so that, for example, the head or foot may make full rotations, etc. Or the written notation may represent the movements of an animal or of machinery constructed on the same principles as the human body.

A few signs are used which have been mentioned in the text but not yet fully explained; they are discussed in greater detail in Chapters 17 and 20.

Note the use of the bow ⌢ to indicate that a movement is continued across a thick bar-line which would normally indicate the end of a movement.

In Ex. XXVII signs of contact appear in the spaces of the hands; these are linked by a tie. This is one way in which it is possible to indicate that the hands are in contact wih one another.

In Ex. XXVIII note the change of scale indicated in square brackets; this applies only between the two thick bar lines. The study is composed with the scale 1 = 45°, and in order to emphasize the character of these comparatively very small movements, only they are written in the scale of 1 = 15°, rather than writing the whole work in that scale.

Ex. XXVII and Ex. XXVIII are each the part of one performer in a duo. The part of the second performer in each is given later in the book.

The names given to the studies are suggestive of the source from which motivic shapes or movements were derived. No other significance is to be attached to them.

Careful note should be taken of all key signatures written in the margins and within the page during the course of a work; and of alterations of the value of the time unit, indicated at the bottom of the notation page.

Note that whenever a number is written on the line between two spaces, it applies to each of the parts of the body represented in those spaces.

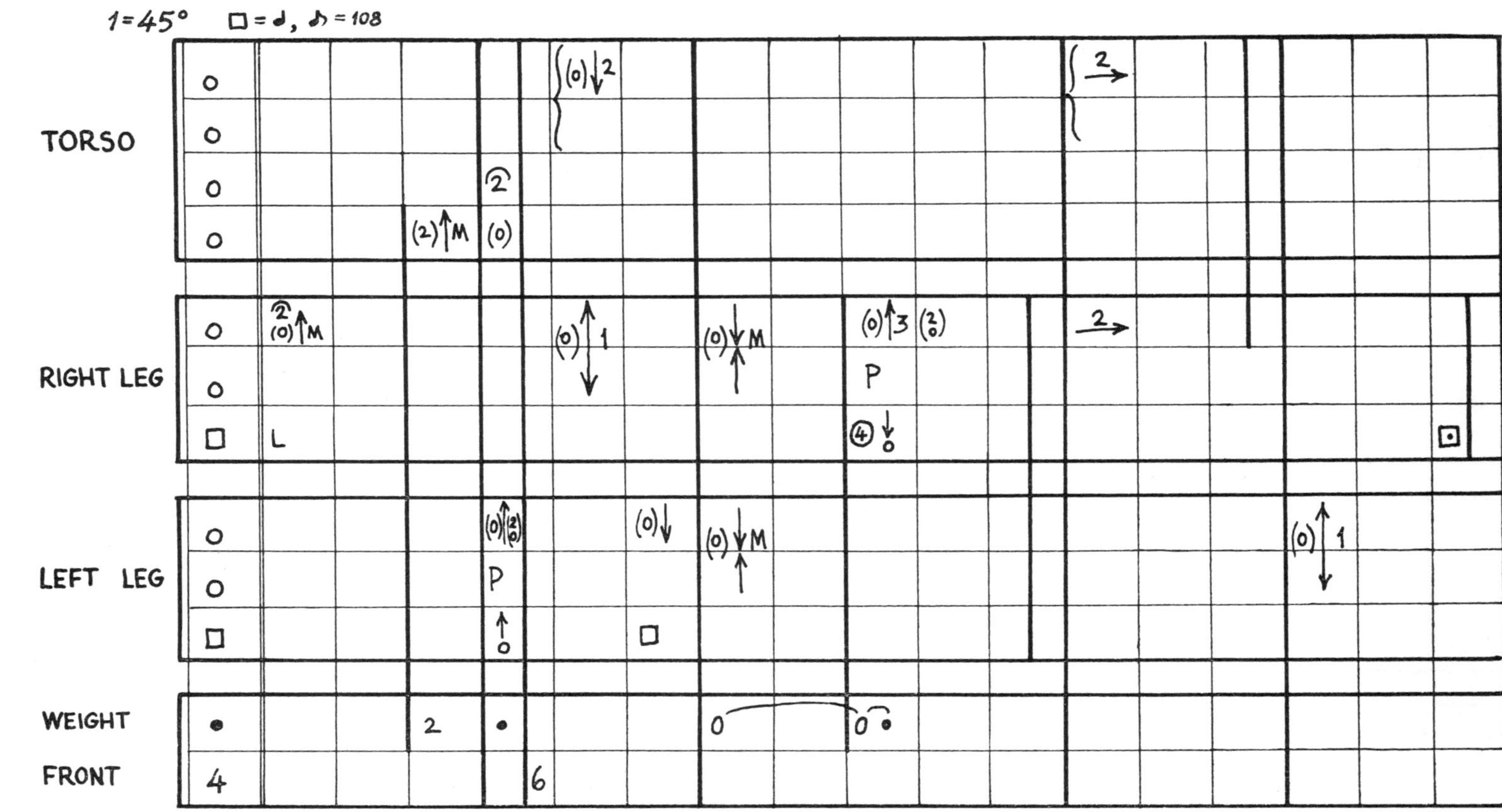

(continued on following page)

Ex. XXV

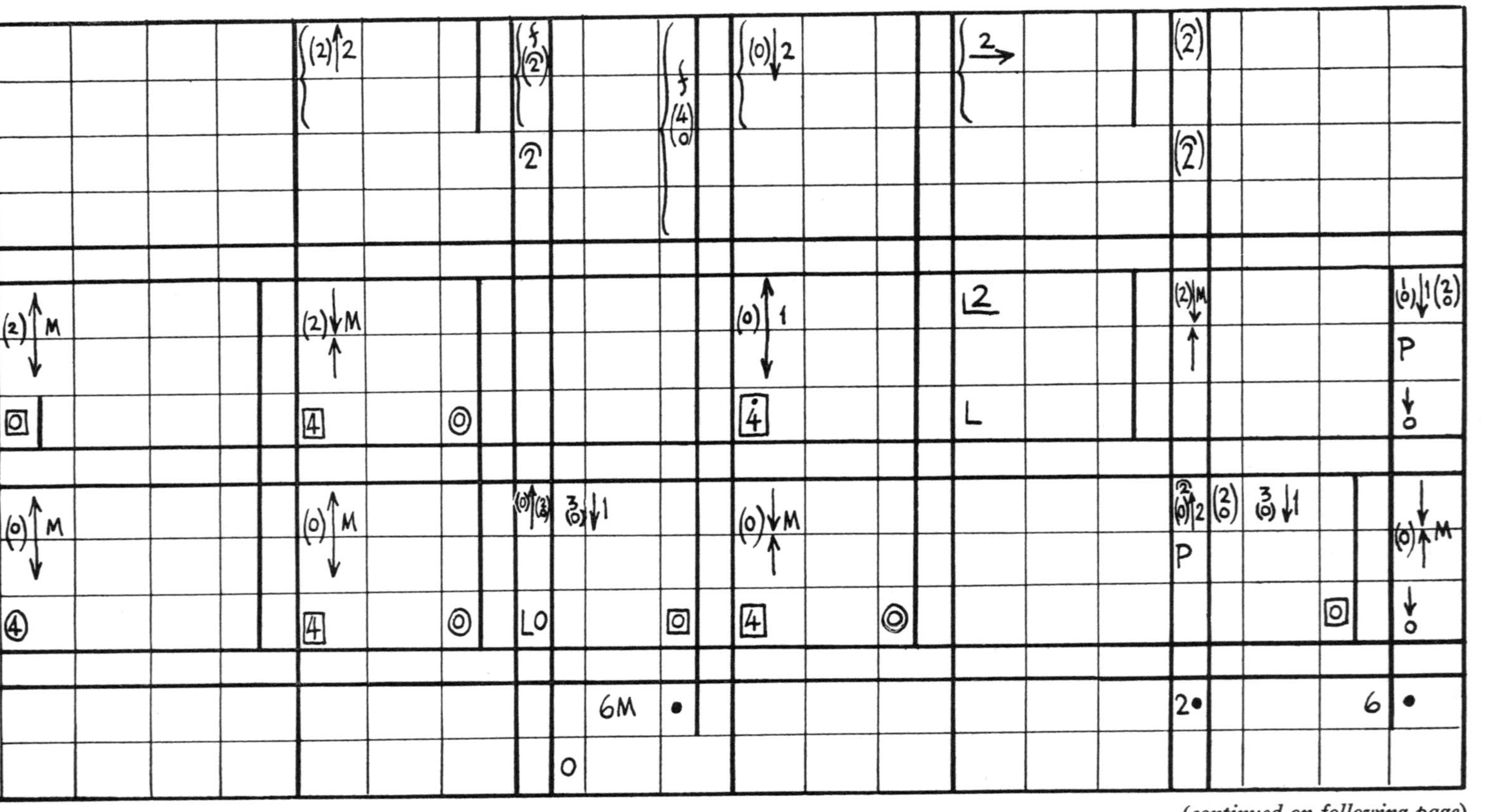

(continued on following page)

Ex. XXV (cont.)

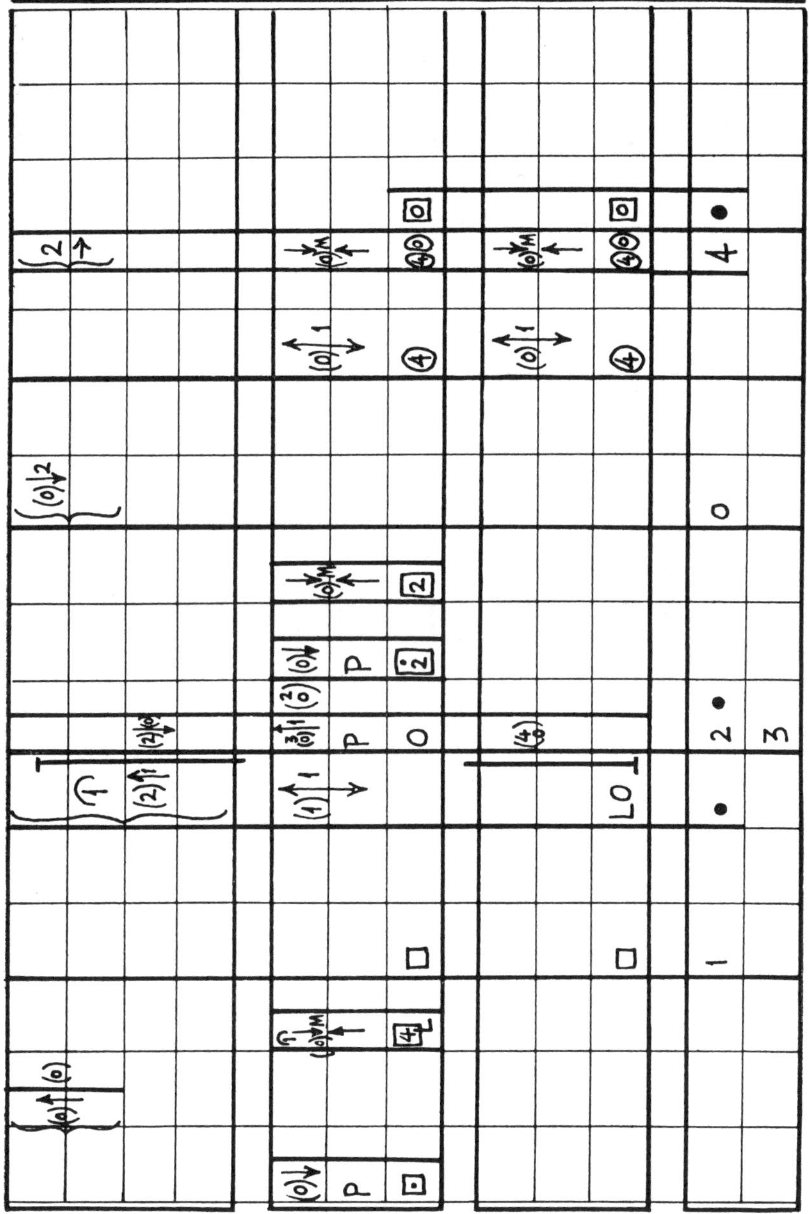

Ex. XXV (cont.)

1: 45°. □ : ♩ : 58

		0	1	2	3	4	5	6	7	8	9	10	11	12	13	14	15	16	17
LEFT	hand	o																	
	forearm	o																	
	upper arm	o									P		$\overset{②}{(0)}$↑2						
RIGHT	hand	o				I													
	forearm	o						(0)↑4											
	upper arm	o				②													
TORSO		o																	
		o																	
		o									(0)↓1								
		o																2↑	↓(0)
RIGHT LEG		⫯			⫰			(0)↕1					(0)↓M ↑					(0)↓	
		□			L ④													o	⊡
LEFT LEG		⫰			⫯			(2)↓1			$\frac{3}{(2)}$↑2		(0)↕1					(0)↓M ↑	
		□			L ④			o				□	④						
WEIGHT		•	o		•	2	•						O						•
FRONT		o																	

(continued on following page)

Ex. XXVI

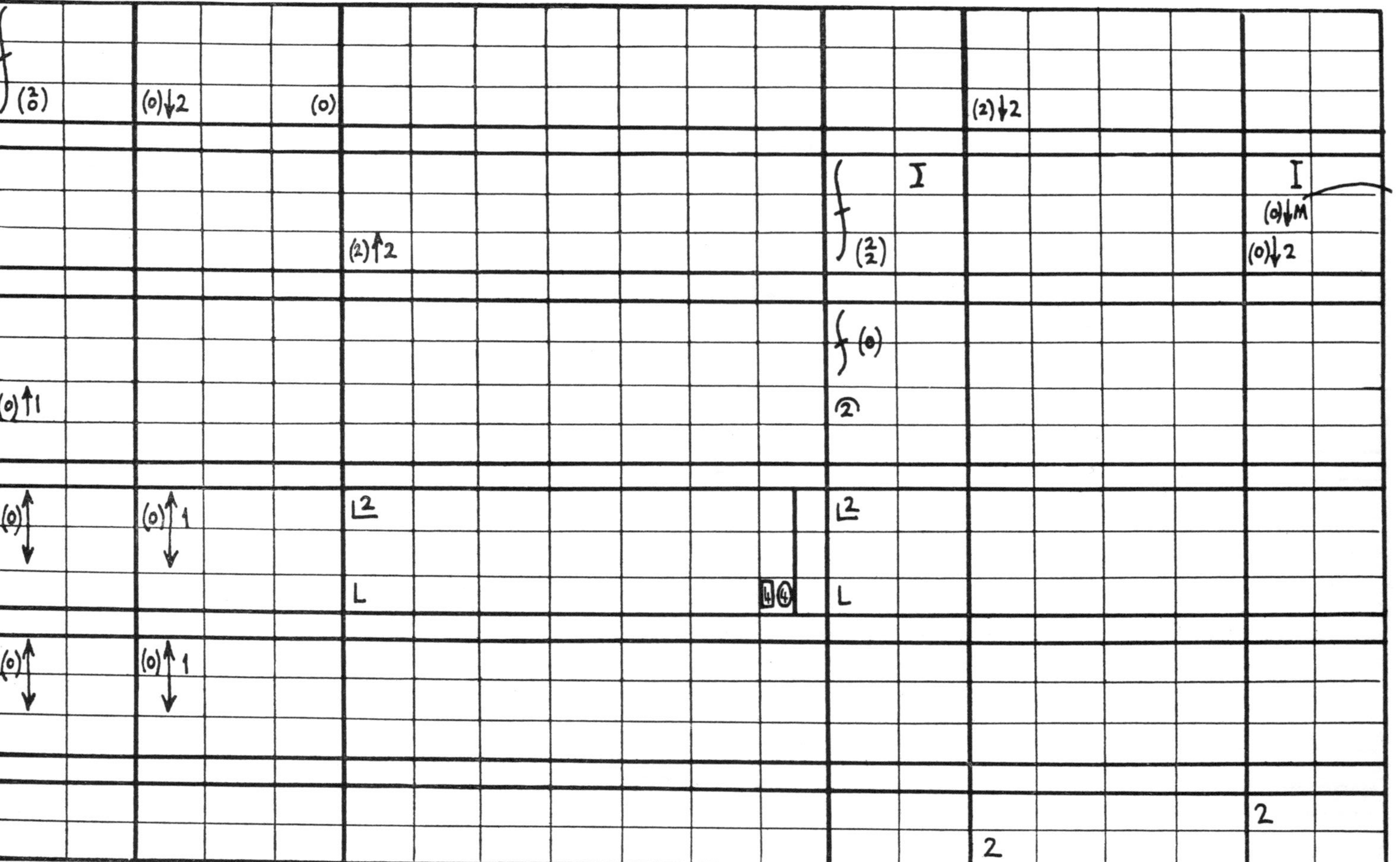

Ex. XXVI (cont.)

(continued on following page)

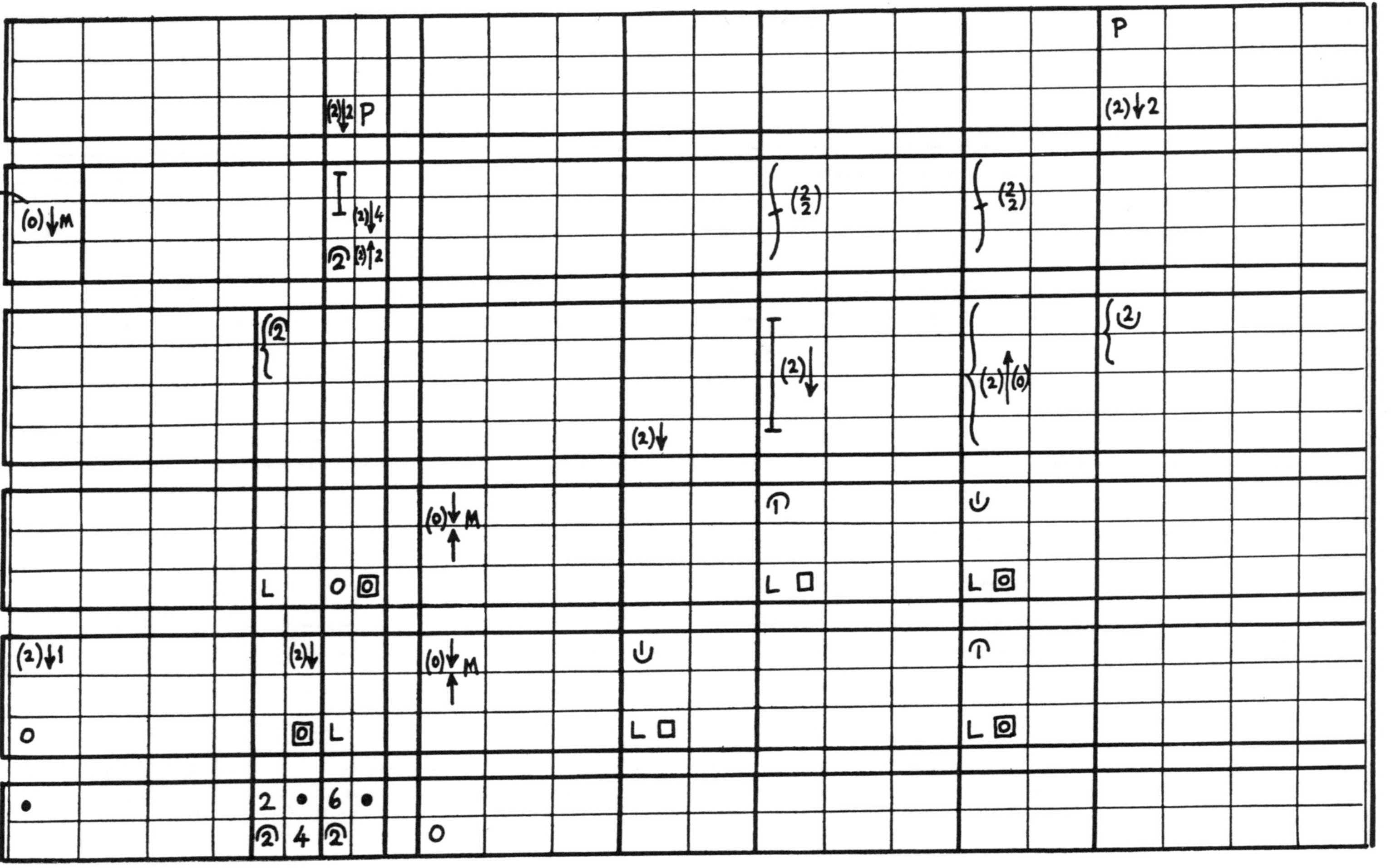

Ex. XXVI (cont.)

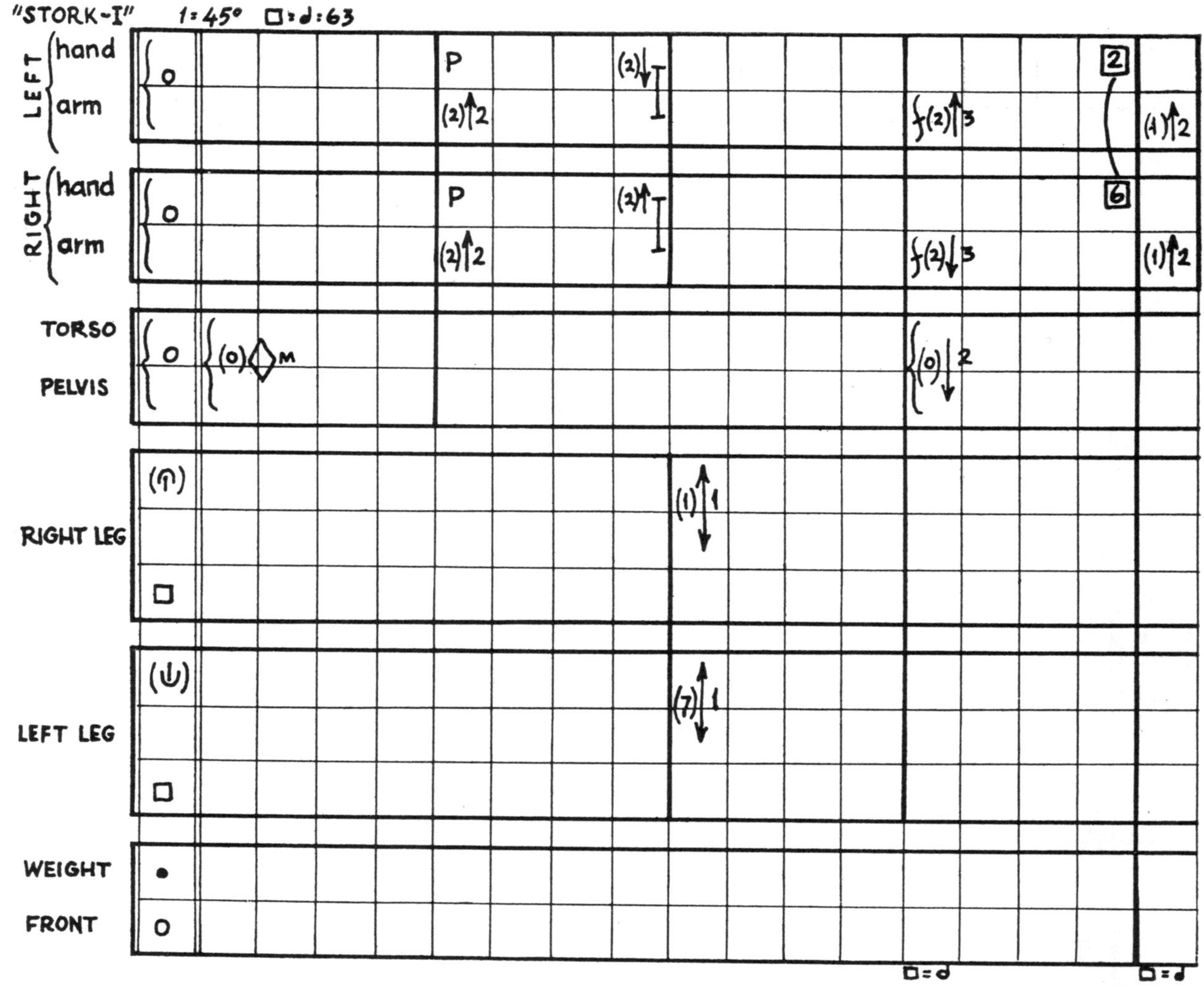

Ex. XXVII

(*continued on following page*)

Ex. XXVII (cont.)

(continued on following page)

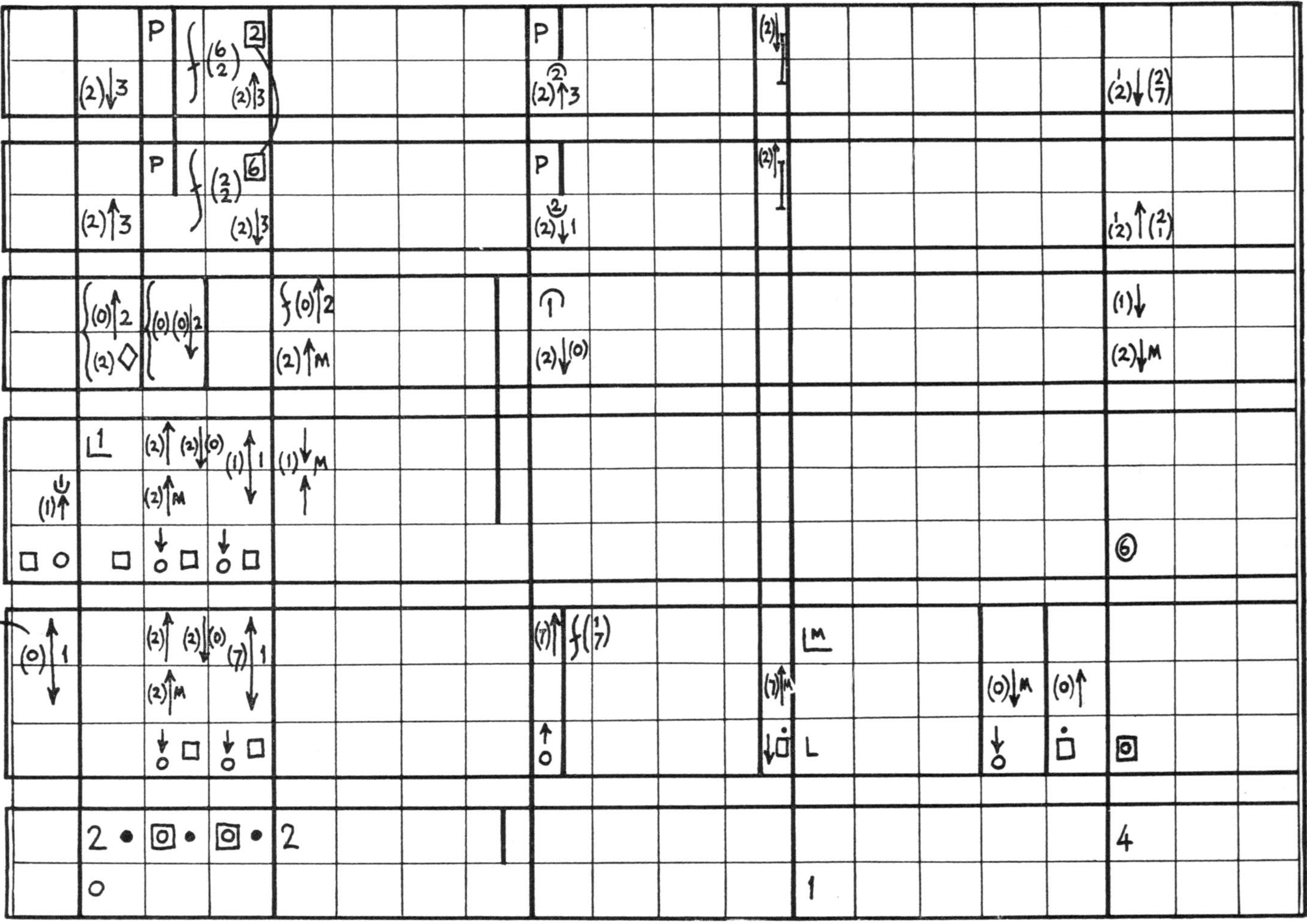

Ex. XXVII (cont.)

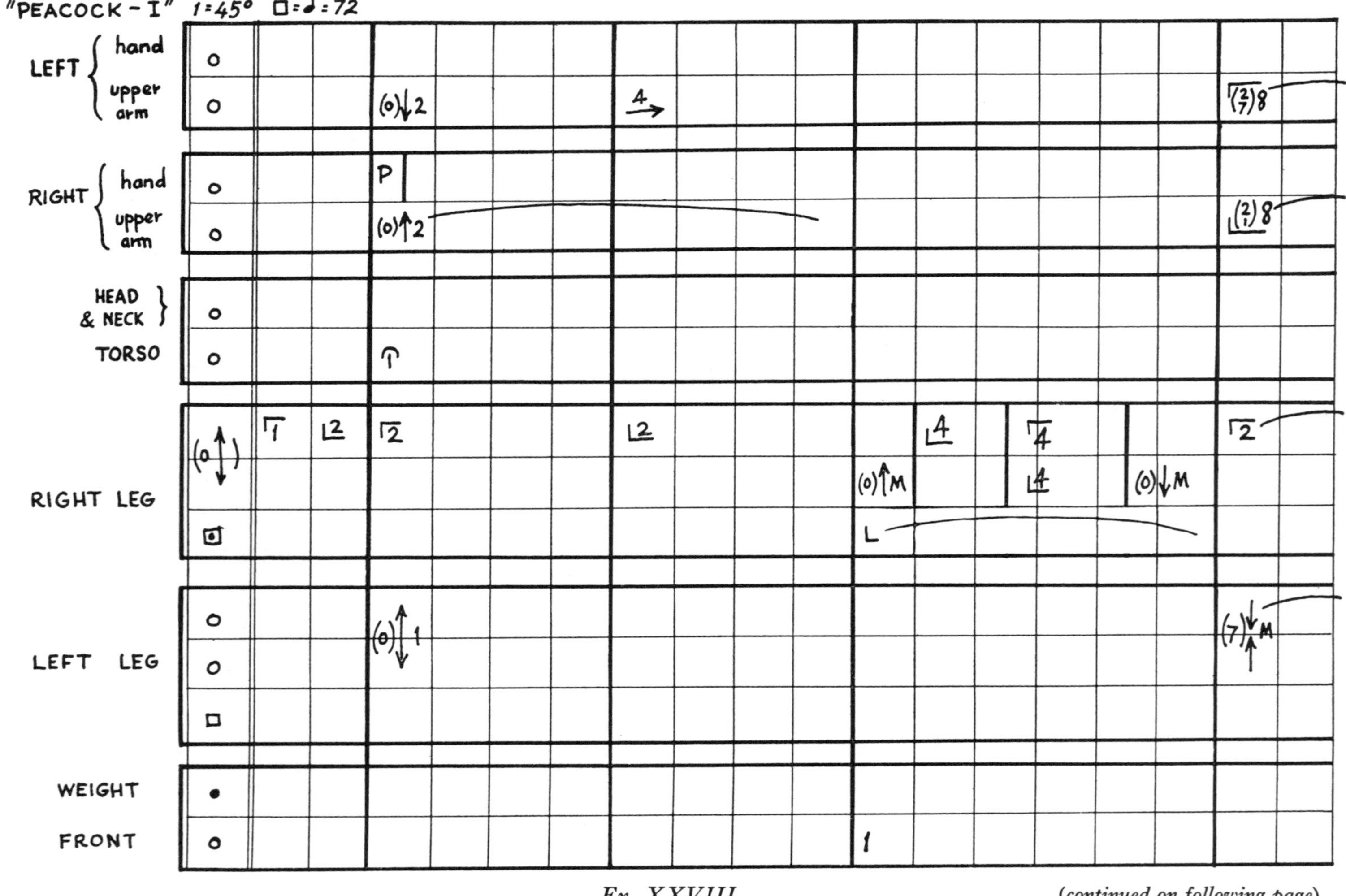

Ex. XXVIII

(continued on following page)

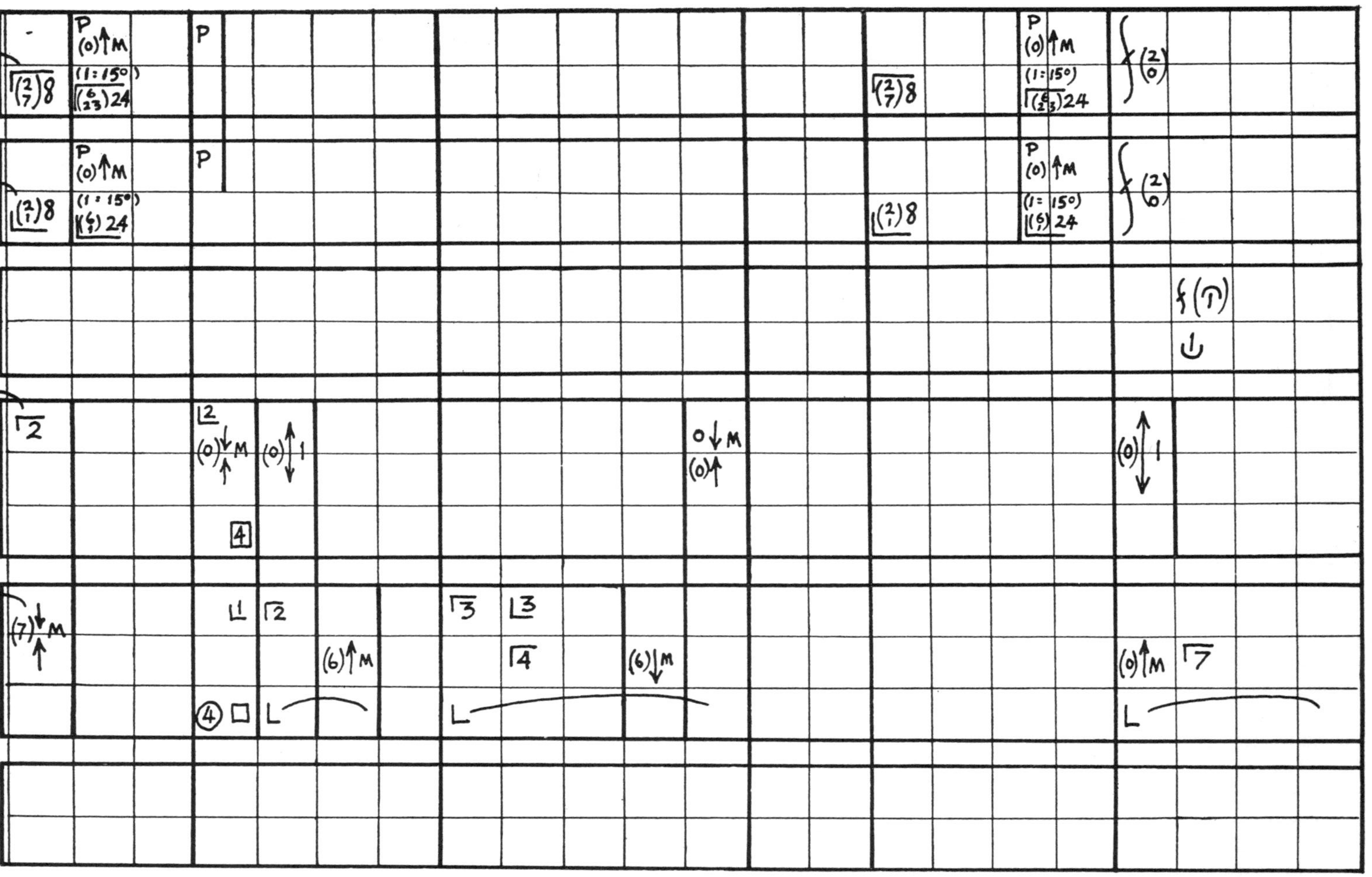

Ex. XXVIII (cont.)

(continued on following page)

Ex. XXVIII (cont.)

(continued on following page)

Ex. XXVIII (cont.)

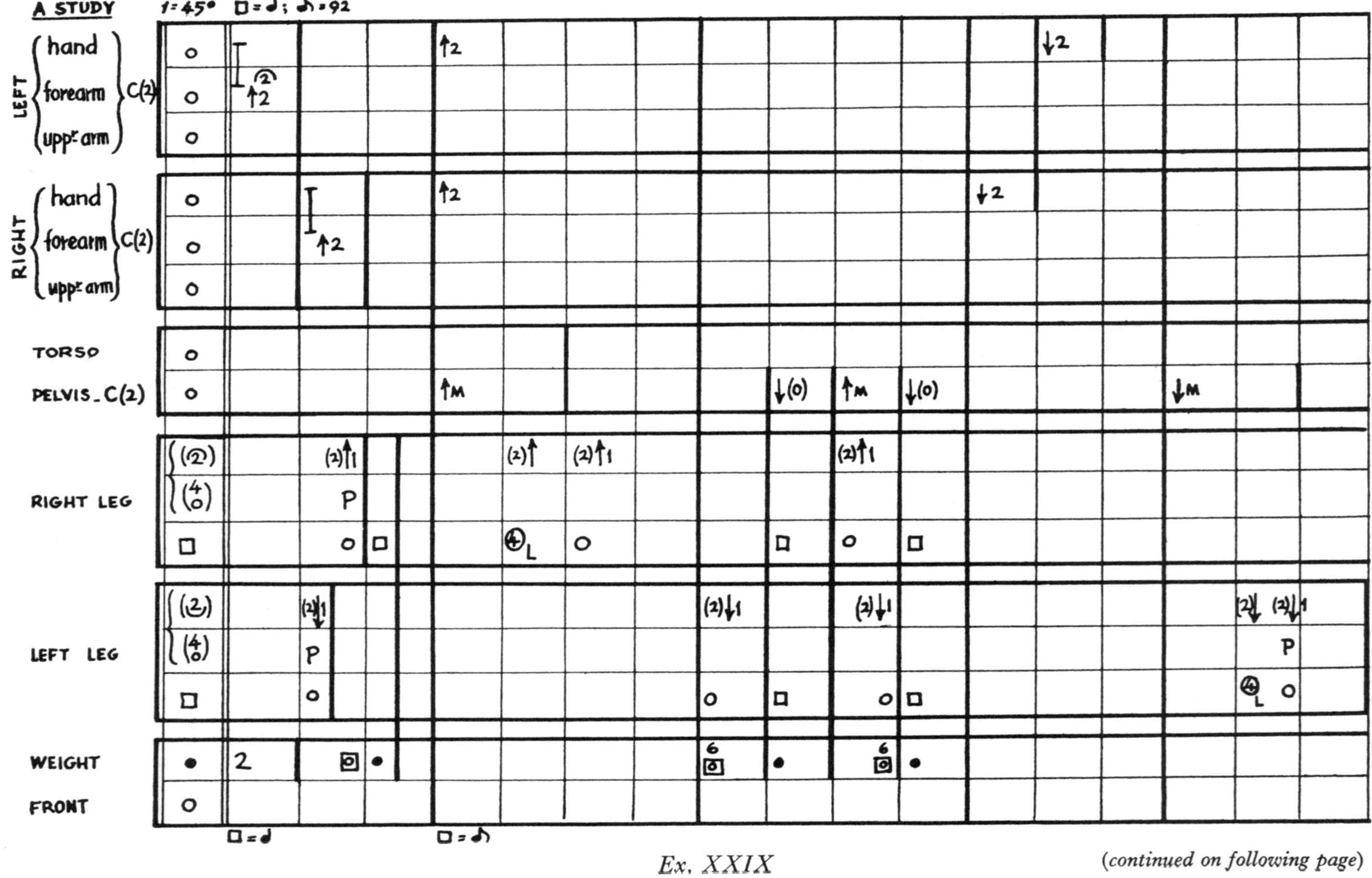

Ex. XXIX

(continued on following page)

Ex. XXIX (cont.)

(continued on following page)

Ex. *XXIX* (*cont.*)

(*continued on following page*)

Ex. XXIX (cont.)

(continued on following page)

K

Ex. XXIX (cont.)

(continued on following page)

Ex. XXIX (cont.)

CHAPTER 17

The Parts of the Body

(Some notes on the characteristics of certain limbs)

THE BODY may be likened to an orchestra, and its limbs to the instruments comprising it. The range of movement, that is, the type and extent of the movements which these instruments can produce, is determined by the structure of the articulations between the parts of the body.

The notation is concerned solely with the visual aspect of the movements of the parts of the body, and the anatomical side is not in any way represented in the written score. There are many small adjustments of the body which are unavoidable in the execution of certain movements: for example, movements of the pelvis in raising the leg more than a certain amount; or of the shoulder-blade in movements of the upper arm. Unless these are deliberately exploited as motifs in the composition, they do not appear in the notation at all, any more than the sound of the breathing of the flautist is represented in an orchestral score. In short the dancer is both performer and instrument, and the notation does not give expression to that which appertains to the performer, but only to the material of dance composition itself.

1. *The Feet.* The feet were discussed in Chapter 10.

2. *The Lower Leg.* In conjunction with Rotatory movement of the thigh, the lower leg is capable of producing conspicuous, apparently curved, movements. The actual rotation of the thigh being comparatively unnoticeable, it is usually practical to write these movements as Curved movements of the lower leg, unless compositional reasons dictate the separation of the physical elements of the movement.

3. *The Pelvis.* The pelvis is capable of Plane, Rotatory and Curved movements, although their range is limited; this is a result of its being connected with other limbs at both sides. The two distinct Plane movements of which the pelvis is capable are those in planes (0) and (2) from Zero Position when 1 = 45°.

All the signs are used in the normal manner, excepting that of Curved movement. In any given position of the body whatsoever, the Curved movement of the pelvis is possible in *one relation only* to the System of Reference; this is the single relation which is conditioned by the positions of the other limbs. It is therefore necessary only to write the sign of Curved movement, with the amount of movement inside it; it is unnecessary to indicate the relation of the base to the System of Reference.

In Zero Position the longitudinal axis of the pelvis is central, being a continuation of the vertical line of the longitudinal axis of the torso. When, however, the weight of the body is shifted onto one leg, the longitudinal axis of the body also shifts so as to be above the new base. Rotation of the pelvis now takes place about this new axis, and has an appearance different from rotation of the pelvis in Zero Position, and different from rotation of other members. In normal Rotatory movement the axis of movement coincides with the longitudinal axis of the limb. This special case is the exception to the rule, insofar as the axis of movement moves away from the axis of the limb, and in any subsequent rotation of the pelvis, the axis of the limb moves about the new position of the axis of movement, creating a cylindrical surface. The explanation of this lies in the fact that the pelvis is exceptional in possessing three joints. The same shift occurs when the base of the body is a part other than the feet. When, for example, the body lies on the back, the longitudinal axis of the pelvis is central, but when the body lies on one side, the axis shifts so as to lie parallel to, and nearest to, the ground. (*See Fig. 51.*)

4. *The Torso.* The torso has two characteristic ways of moving. In the first, it moves as one unit, all the small constituent parts remaining fixed in the relations obtaining in Zero Position. The usual movement signs are used in the normal way and are written either in the horizontal space allotted to the upper torso, or in that of the pelvis.

However, because the torso is built on a chain-like structure of bones—including the pelvis, the vertebrae of the spinal column and the head—it is also capable of changes in its own form. If, during its usual movement in the hip joint, the force of gravity is allowed to act on the torso, its parts will flex towards one another, the straight line of the torso in Zero position will be destroyed and the flexing of head towards the vertebrae of the neck, neck towards vertebrae, and these in turn flexing towards the pelvis, which tilts in relation to the thighs, will result in a slightly curved relaxed position of the whole torso, brought about by the force of gravity pulling all parts in one direction so that each inclines towards its neighbour. The usual movement signs are used to represent this bending movement, but are preceded by the sign *P*, which indicates that the movement is passive; that is to say, muscular tension in all parts of the torso is relaxed, allowing the movement to occur as a result of the force of gravity; the limb or limbs will then tend to hang vertically to the System. This movement may begin in various parts of the torso. When the relaxation and consequent bending are begun at the head, ending at the pelvis, the movement sign is written in the space representing the head, and a curved line is written, sloping diagonally downwards, so as to pass through the spaces of the intervening members, and end in the space which represents the pelvis. This curved line is also written in such a way that it passes through the number of vertical spaces which represent the time taken by the complete movement.

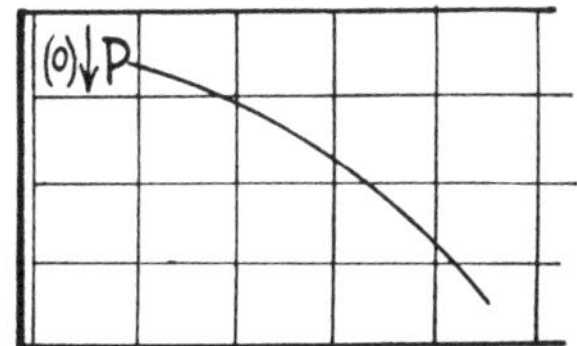

When it is wished to write a movement in which the torso is straightened from a bent position such as is reached by the kind of movement just described, the proper movement or positional signs are superimposed upon the sign of a straight line when the straightening is a simultaneous movement of all parts of the torso; when the movement is graduated, this is indicated by a curved line used in similar manner to the representation of bending.

In the passive movement described above, all the parts of the torso move in an identical movement, producing a curved shape. There is, however, an active physical *curving* movement which may be produced by the movement of the upper and lower ends of the torso, or of part of it, in the same plane but in *opposite* senses. The two extreme points of the long axis of the torso (or the part of it involved in the movement) approach one another on a straight line, producing thereby a curve throughout its whole length, either convex or concave in relation to a given side of the body. This curving may be performed in any direction, but it can be executed and seen in a clear and unmistakable manner, as a deviation from Zero position, in coordinates 0 and 2 (when 1 = 45°). Even when this type of curving movement occurs together with a tilting movement of the whole torso as one unit, or when the position of the torso is not that of Zero position, it is analysed and written as if it had occurred in Zero position.

As the curving movement consists of movements in the same plane but in opposite senses, the sign for it consists of a combination of signs for positive and negative Plane movement. The shafts of the arrows are abandoned and the heads juxtaposed so as to form either a cross × or a diamond shape ◇. The plane is indicated by its proper number. The position of this number relative to the sign shows which part of the curve is to be emphasized.

◇(0) or (0)◇; (0)× or $\overset{(0)}{\times}$ but *not* ×(0) which would indicate a position to be reached.

The use of convex and concave curving movement is confined to the torso and to those members which are comprised of small parts. Whenever curving takes place, the sign is written in the horizontal space representing the upper torso. When it is wished to include the head or pelvis in the movement, the sign is extended to include their spaces by means of a bracket.

When a curving movement is required in the upper part of the torso alone, thus separating the torso into two parts, a line is written above the sign $\overline{◇}$ $\overline{\times}$. When a similar movement is required in the lower part of the torso only, a line is written beneath the sign $\underline{◇}$ $\underline{\times}$.

When it is wished to begin a curving movement from the pelvis, and, moving upward, finish it at the upper end of the part, the sign is a curved line drawn, starting in the space representing the pelvis and passing through the spaces of the other parts, in the order in which they begin to take part in the movement.

Movements may be produced by the separate parts of the torso—the head, neck, chest, or pelvis; these are then written in the horizontal spaces allotted to them. A movement involving the whole torso, even when it is accompanied by independent movements of its parts, is expressed by a movement sign in the space representing the pelvis, or in that representing the upper torso, the effect of this sign being extended, by means of a bracket, to include all the other parts. (*See Figs. 52, 53.*)

5. *The Head and Neck.* Although grouped together here as a single unit, these two members are in fact separable, being capable of very distinct independent movement. The movements of the head *by itself* are very limited, and the movement of both is therefore written in the space which represents the head or neck, *excepting* when the head and neck move in opposition to one another. Together the head and neck can execute Plane, Rotatory, and curved movements. (*See Fig. 54.*)

6. *The Shoulders.* The shoulder blades can move in clear Plane movements in coordinate 2 (1 = 45°)—movements usually referred to as 'raising' and 'lowering' the shoulders; they can move in the Horizontal plane, producing what are commonly called 'inward' and 'outward' or 'forward' and 'backward' movements of the shoulders; they can also produce a type of cylindrical movement combining these two. More than these the shoulders

cannot produce. The movements are analysed and written as if the System of Reference were carried with the shoulders, not maintaining parallel relationship to the main System, but perserving its relation to the upper torso—the 'heaviest' part which carries the shoulders.

Thus, for the right shoulder, raising is written: (2) ↑ ; lowering: (2) ↓ ;
For the left shoulder, raising is written: (6) ↑ ; lowering: (6) ↓ ;
Forward movement of the right shoulder is written: ← ; backward movement → .
Forward movement of the left shoulder is written: → ; backward movement: ← ;

The curved movement of the shoulder, the combination of forward, backward, raising and lowering movements, is represented as a conical movement, the direction of which is determined by looking from the apex towards the base (i.e. outward from the centre of the body). The size of the base is given as either maximal (indicated by *M*) or no indication is given, and minimum size is understood. E.g. positive, maximal: |8 *M* ; negative, minimal; |8 . In any other case the signs given would express conical movement with the base parallel to the ground, but here it indicates the only conical movement of which the shoulder is capabe.

Note that the longitudinal axis of the shoulder is parallel to the ground.

7. *The Forearms.* The apparent Curved movement of the forearm produced in conjunction with the upper arm being very marked, and the actual rotation of the upper arm being usually distinguishable only with difficulty, it is in most cases practical to write such movements as Curved movement of the forearm, just as in the case of apparent curved movement of the lower leg, unless for a particular compositional reason it is wished to keep the elements separate.

8. *The Hand.* Moving as a single unit, the hand is capable of a limited amount of Plane and Curved movement. The richness and variety of movements of the hand are actually derived from movements of the forearm and of the fingers simultaneously with movements of the hand. All movements of the hand are written in the usual manner.

Curved movement of the hand is a result of Plane movement combined with Rotatory movement of the forearm, as in the similar cases of lower leg and thigh, and forearm and upper arm. Being very limited in size, curved movement of the hand may be regarded as of one kind only (a starting position being given), and is adequately represented by indicating the sense and the amount of movement; the sense (positive or negative) is determined by looking at the base of the cone from the apex—which is located in the wrist. If greater variety is demanded, the movements may be represented by using the coordinates, in the normal way.

An infinite variety of subtle differences in the shape of the hand is obtainable by means of the possible change of relation between the small components of the limb. The movements of the separate fingers will not be dealt with here, but there also exist many possible variations of the shape of the whole hand:

The sign of passive movement *P*, appearing in combination with a movement sign, represents the relaxation of muscular tension, resulting in a flexing of all the parts of the hand, brought about by the force of gravity. The effect on the hand is to give it a relaxed appearance.

The 'Straight Line' sign ⊤ indicates that the closed fingers are in one plane.

The sign of a 'Curved Limb'), expresses flexing of all the parts of the hand, of an extent only sufficient to give the whole a 'curved' form.

Maximal concave curving of the hand is seen as a closed fist, ◇M. The sign *M*, appearing alone, represents the stretching apart of all the fingers.

The sign of convex, ×, indicates that the fingers (remaining straight) and the palm of the hand, form an angle of less than 180° between the back of the fingers and the back of the palm. The ends of the fingers, and the wrist, approach each other, remaining on the same straight line on which they lay in Zero Position. The concave sign, ◇, indicates that the fingers and the palm form an angle of less than 180° between their inner sides. Ends of fingers, and wrist, again approach one another on the same straight line.

If a particular composition demands movements of the separate fingers, additional horizontal spaces allocated to the fingers are added to the usual manuscript page, and their movements written therein, in the usual manner, using the normal movement signs.

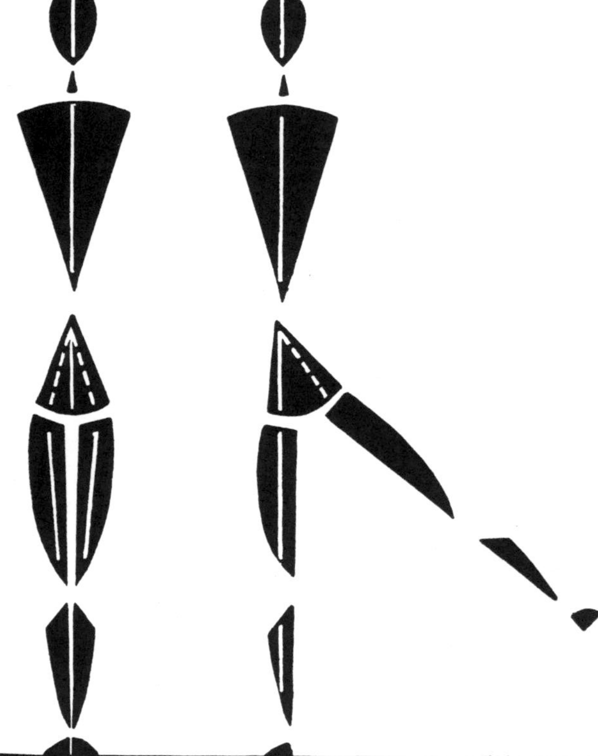

51. The Shift of the Longitudinal Axis of the Pelvis

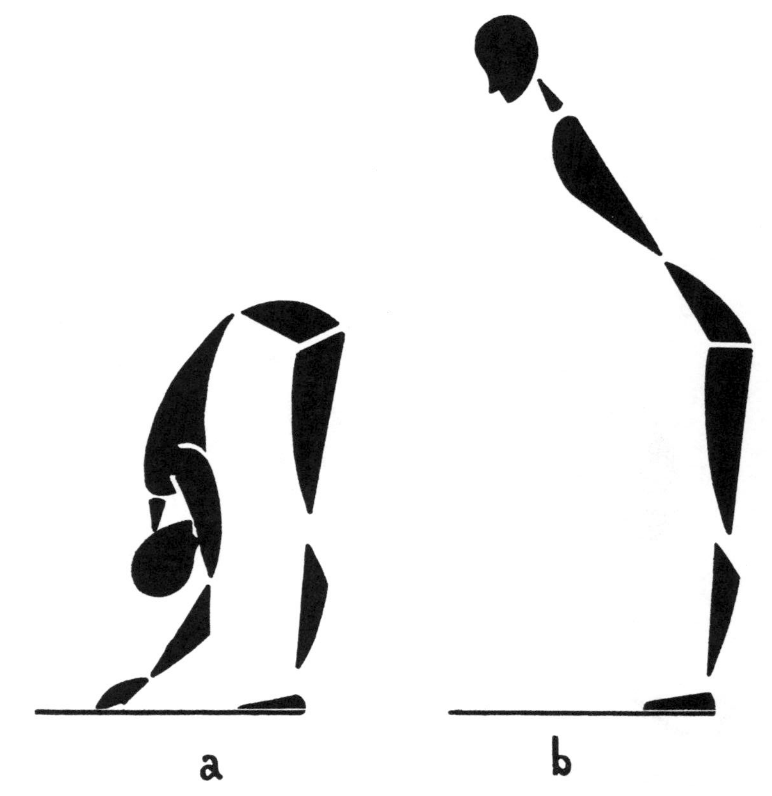

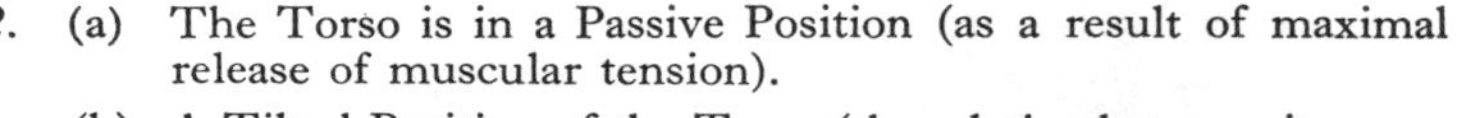

52. (a) The Torso is in a Passive Position (as a result of maximal release of muscular tension).

(b) A Tilted Position of the Torso (the relation between its component parts remaining as in Zero position).

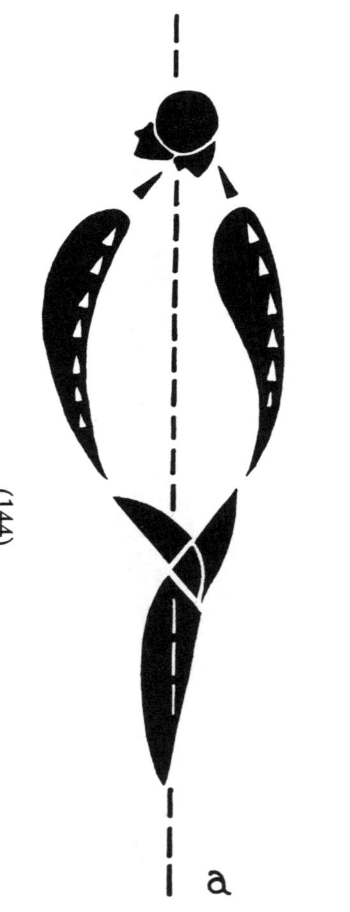

53. (*a*) *Concave and Convex Movement* (involving all the parts of the Torso)

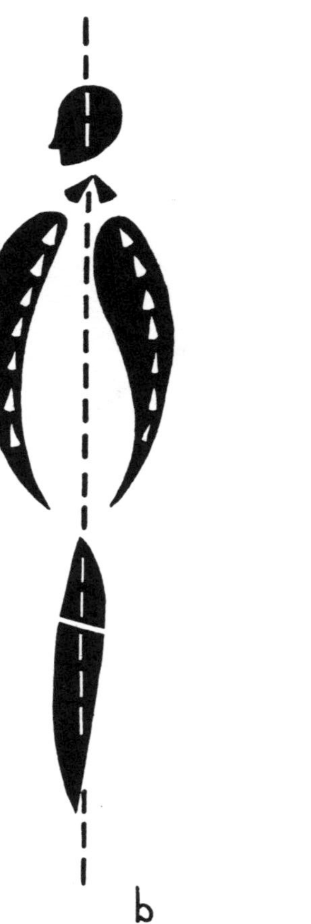

53. (*b*) *Concave and Convex Movement* (excluding Head and Pelvis)

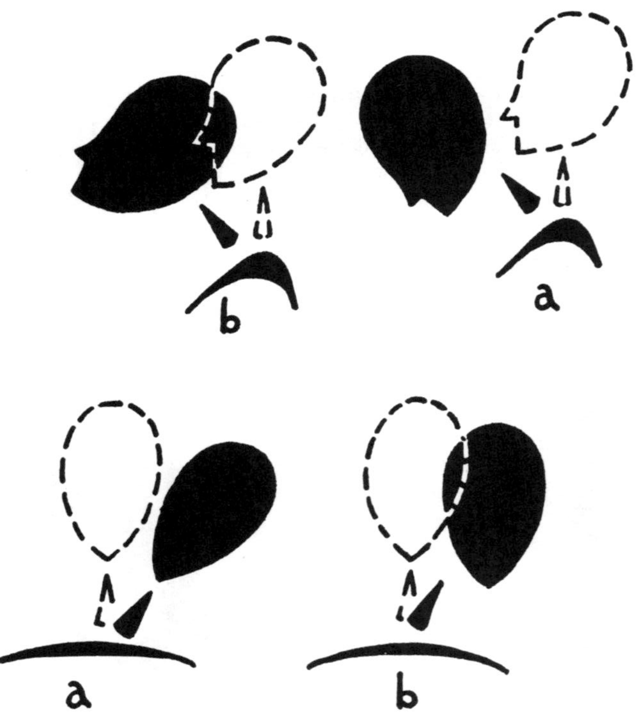

54. (*a*) *Head and Neck moving in the same direction*
(*b*) *Head and Neck moving in opposite directions*

Examples

Examples XXX, XXXI and XXXII are reading examples which may also be performed.

In Ex. XXX one recurring motif is the use of the torso in which its chain-like structure is exploited, and the separate parts flexed towards one another in movements commonly called 'bending' or 'relaxing' the back; and counter-movement of the head and neck in relation to the torso.

In Ex. XXXI there appear flexing movement of all parts of the torso ('bending' of the back), and movement of the torso from the hip-joint ('tilting' with straight back). Throughout this example positional signs are given at the end of most movements of the torso and arms. These are statements of the position reached at the end of each bar, and are intended as a help in reading. This is a practice which may be used in the writing of any piece of notation.

Note that in conical movement there is a continuous change of the side of the limb which faces towards the axis of movement. When a complete cone is created, all sides of the limb will face towards the axis of movement in succession.

In Ex. XXXII the hands play a major part. It will be noticed that occasionally a line divides the hand space into two parts. The upper half of the space is then given to movements of the fingers from their roots outward, and the lower half of the space to movements of the remainder of the hand, between the wrist and the fingers. Because of the use of the small limbs of the body, and of intricate rhythmical patterns (with the value of the time-unit continually changing throughout the composition), this is a delicate work, and special care should be taken in its proper performance.

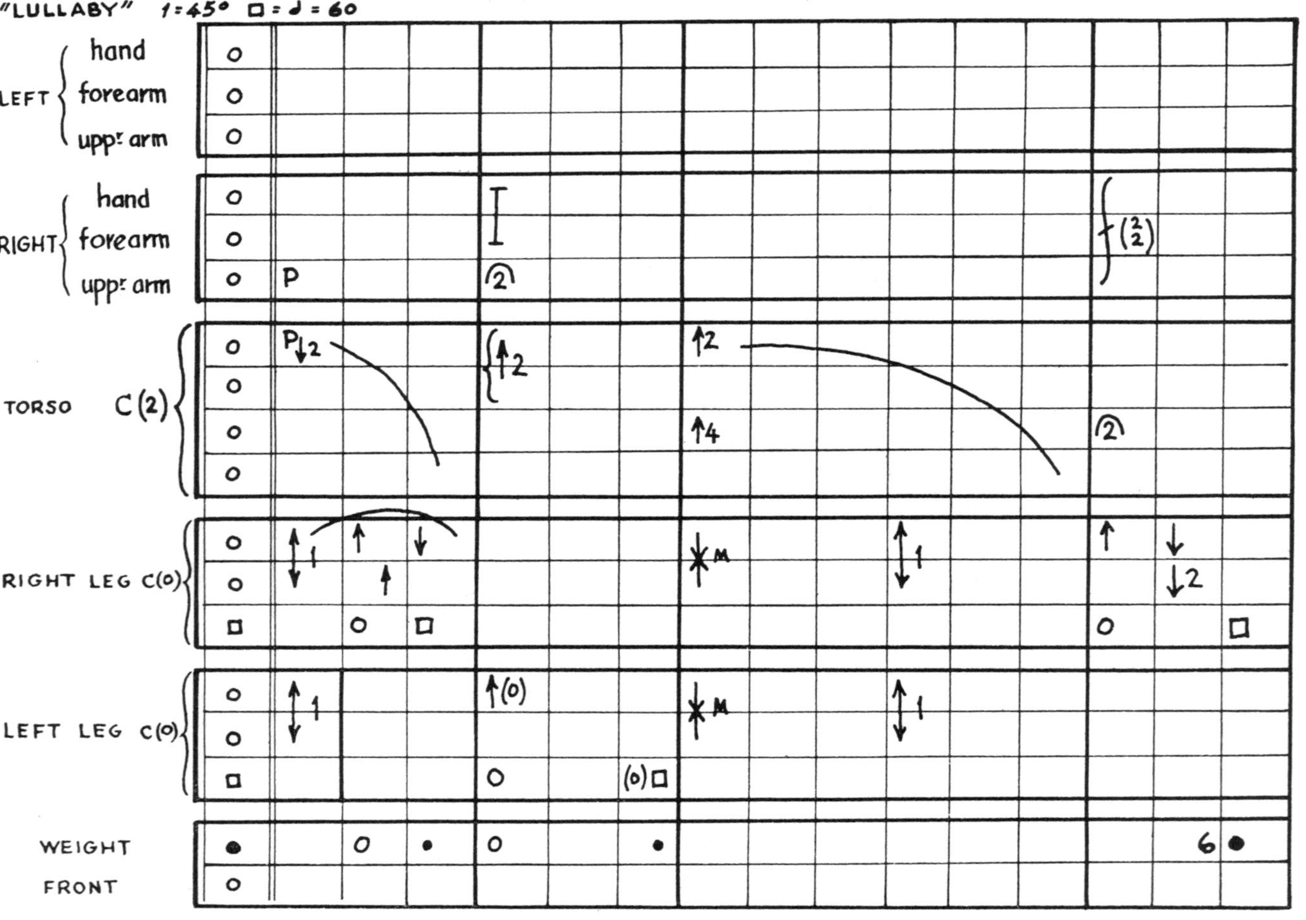

(continued on following page)

Ex. XXX

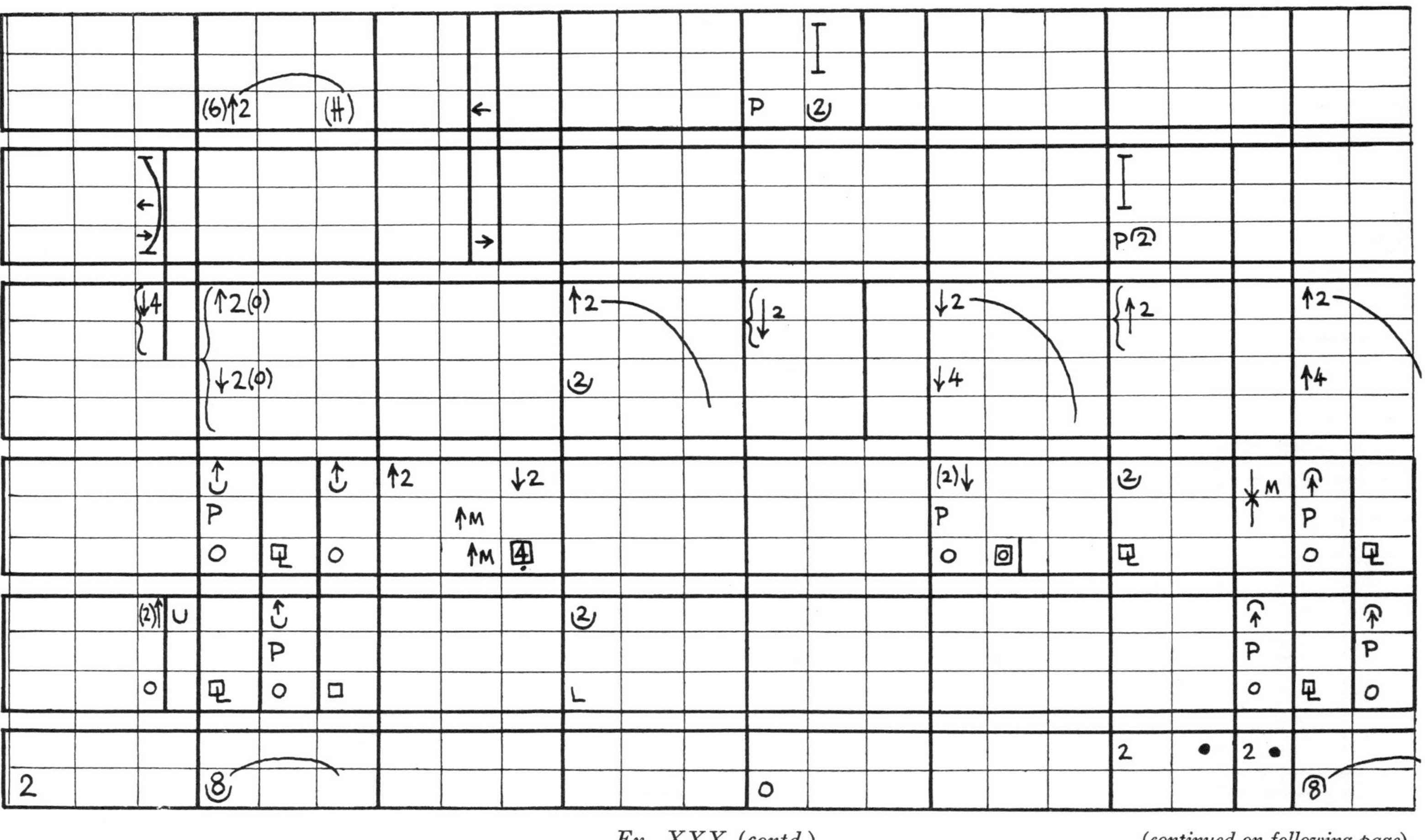

Ex. XXX (contd.)

(continued on following page)

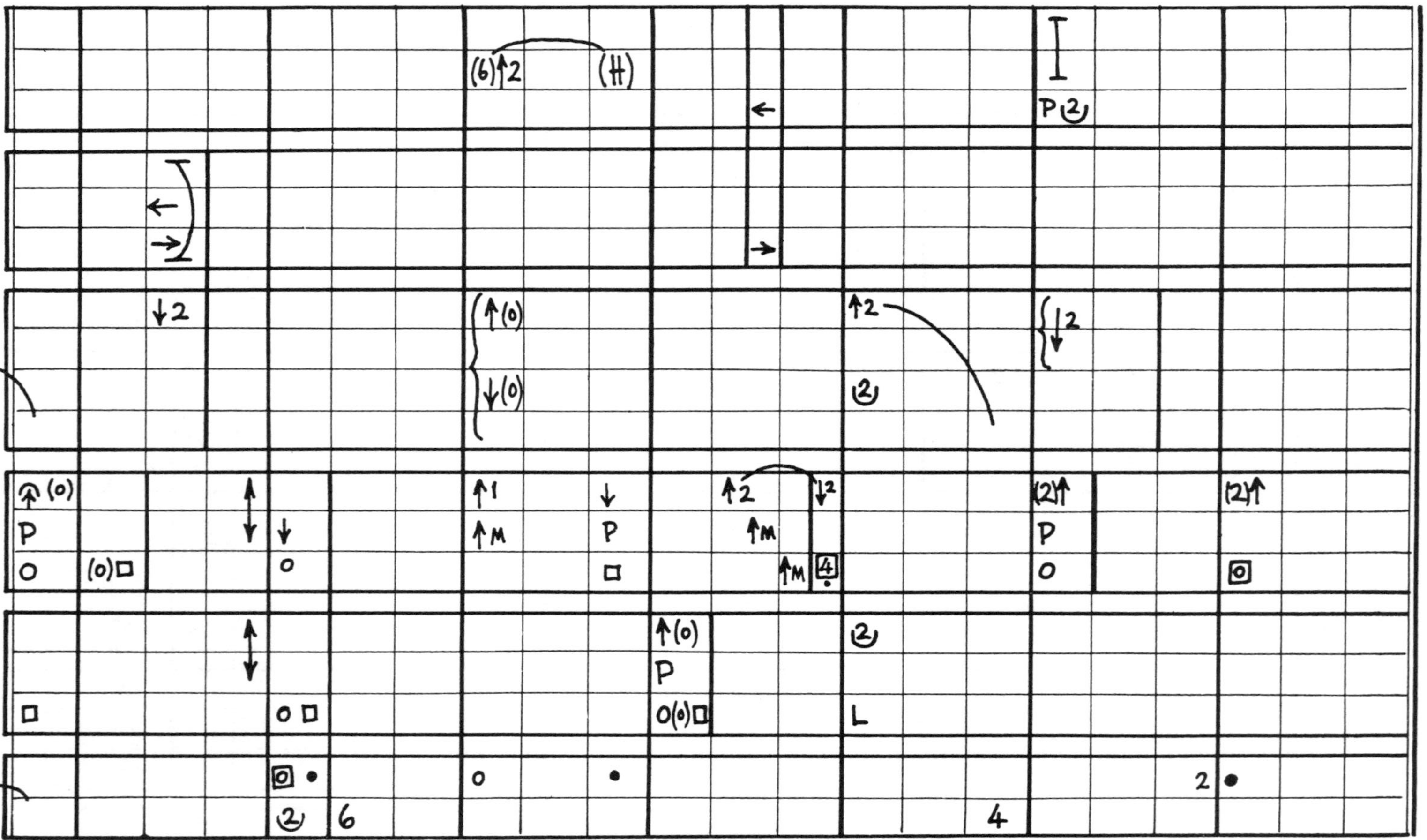

Ex. XXX (cont.)

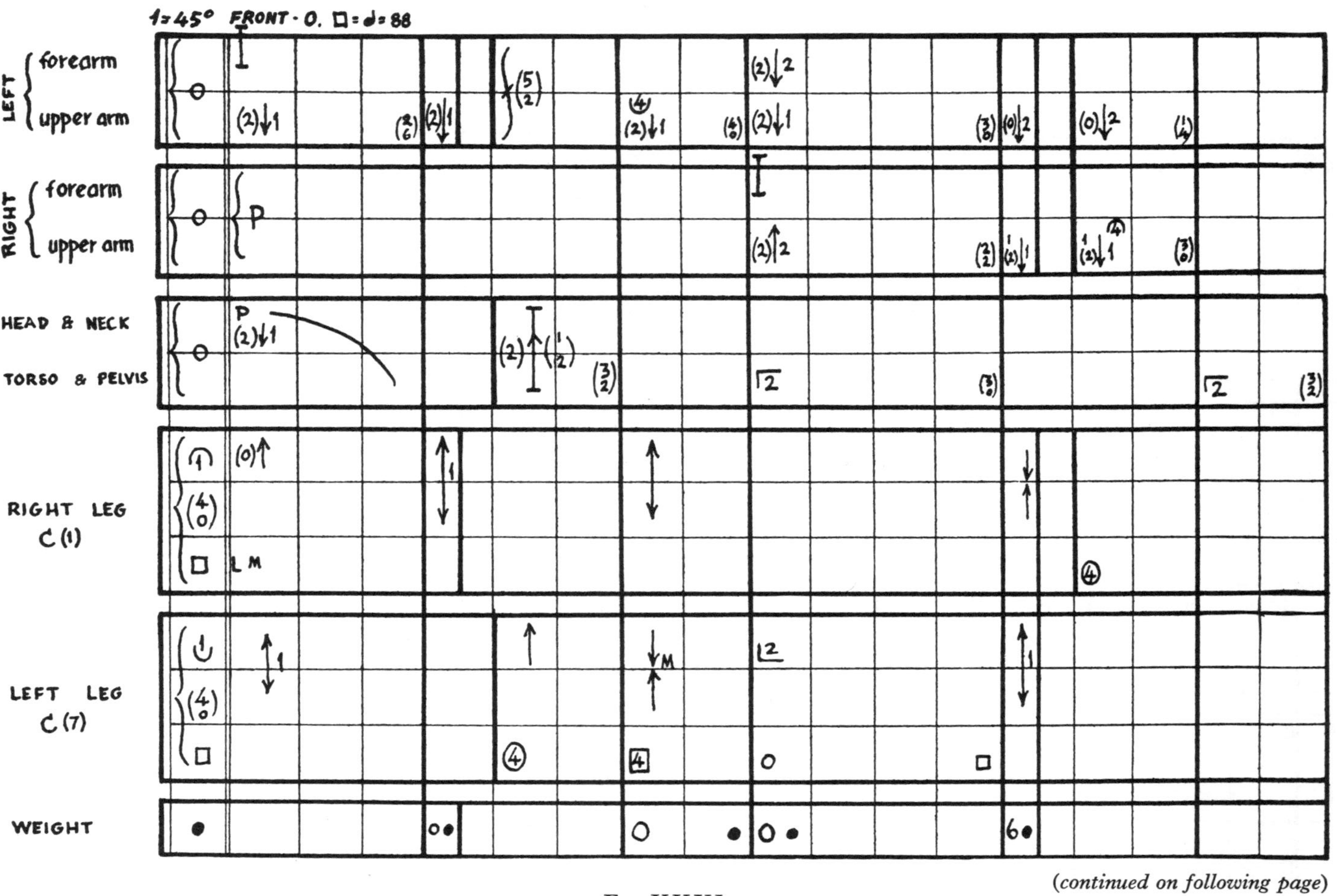

(continued on following page)

Ex. XXXI

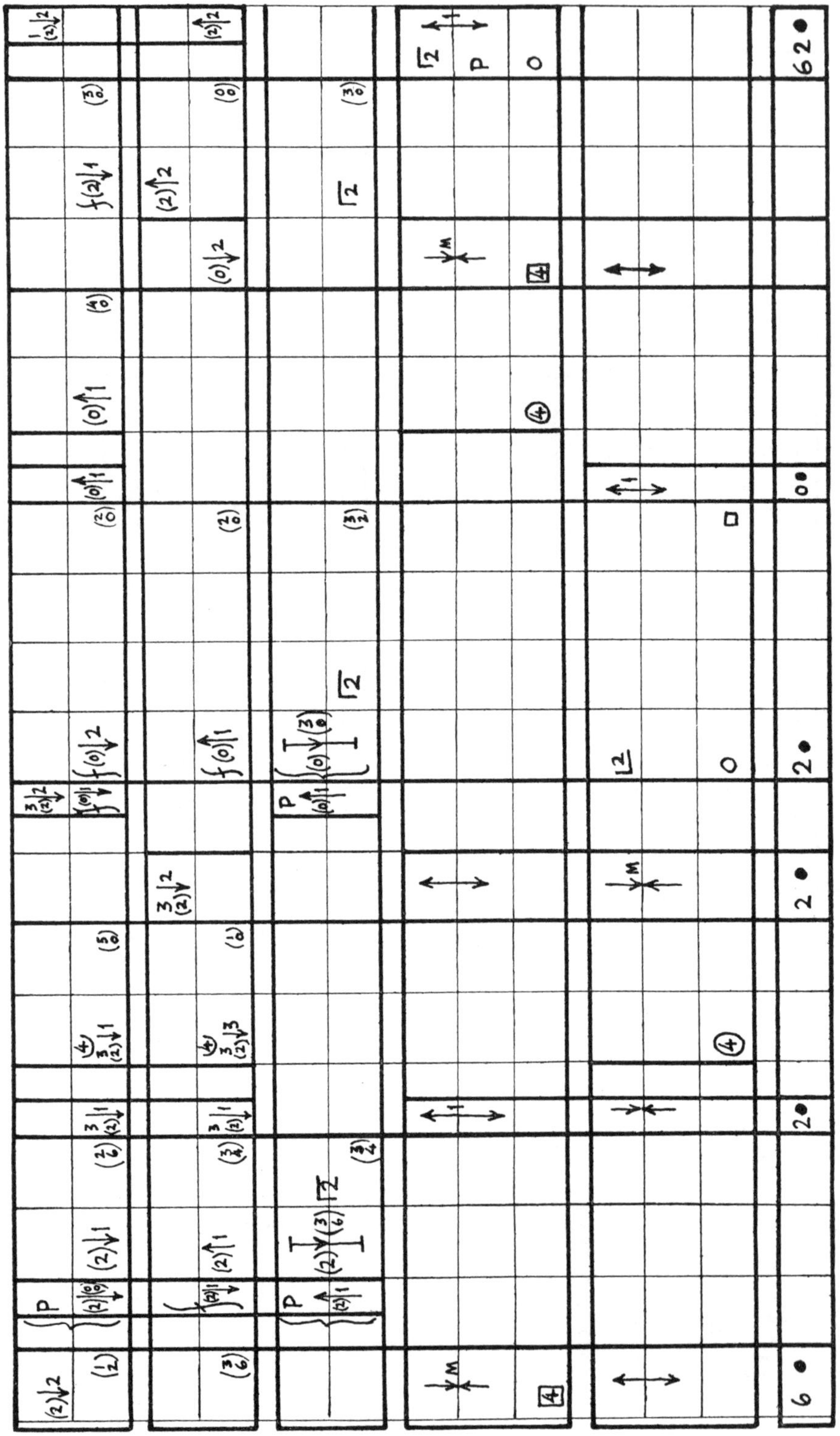

Ex. XXXI (cont.)

(continued on following page)

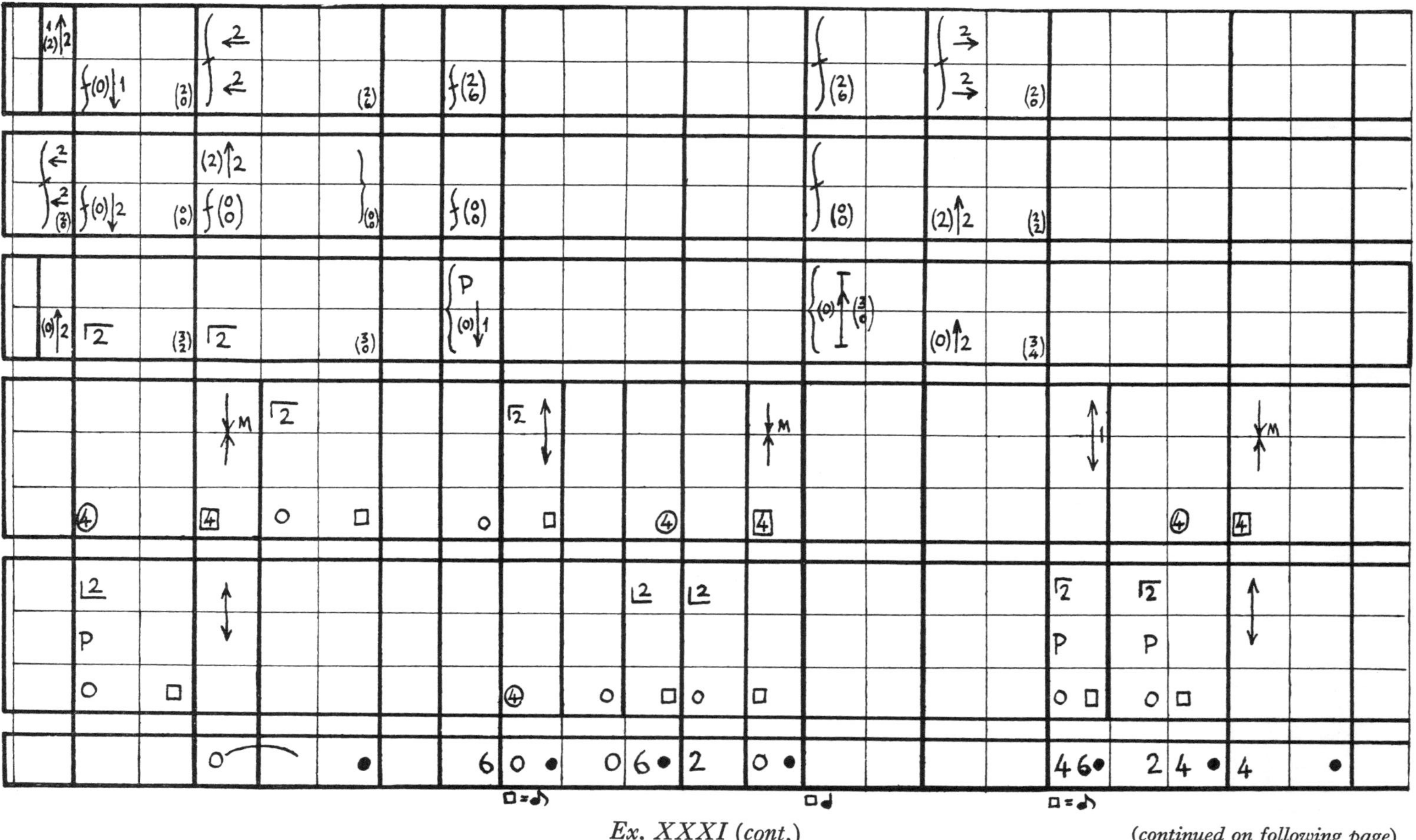

Ex. XXXI (cont.)

(continued on following page)

L

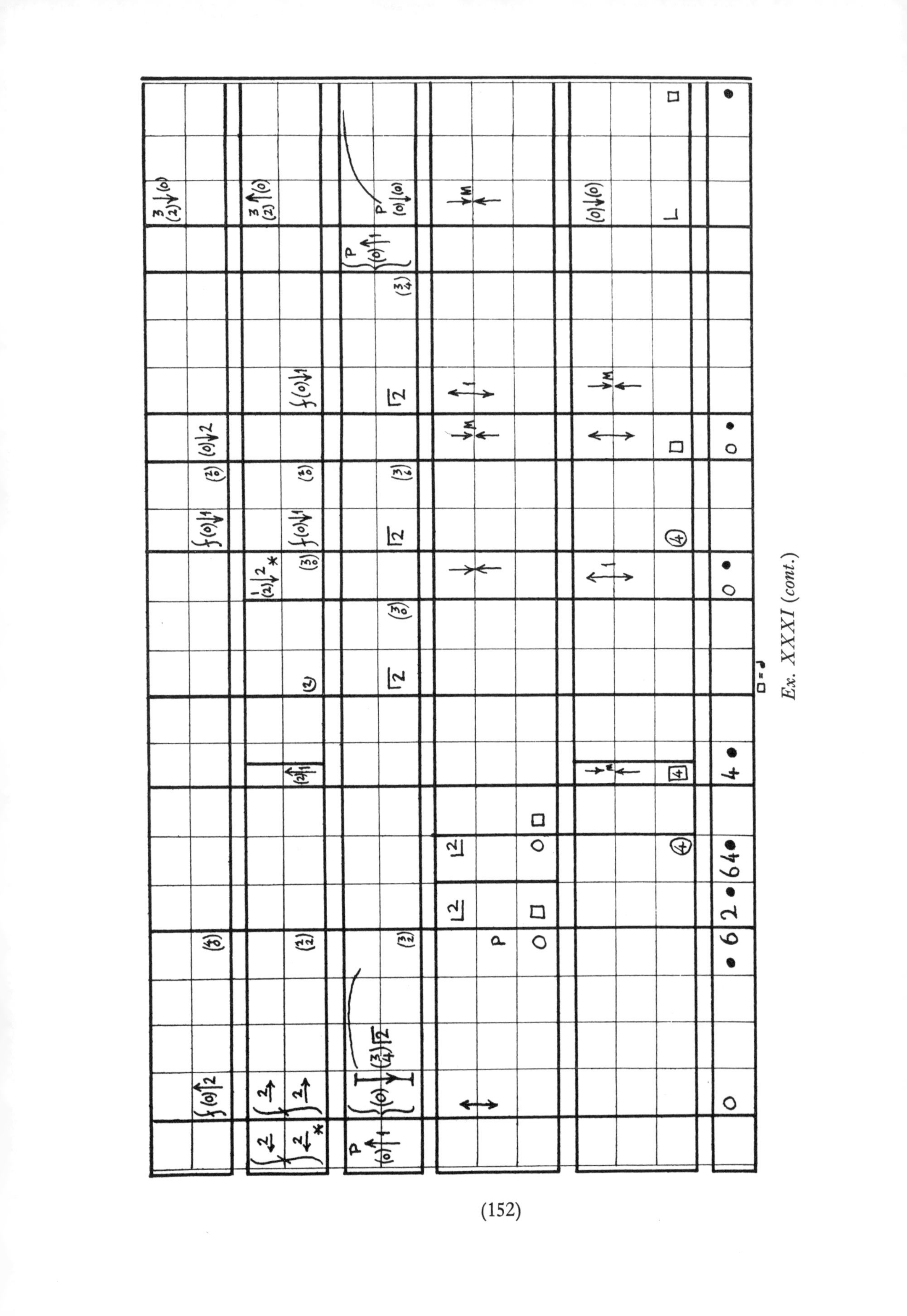

Ex. XXXI (cont.)

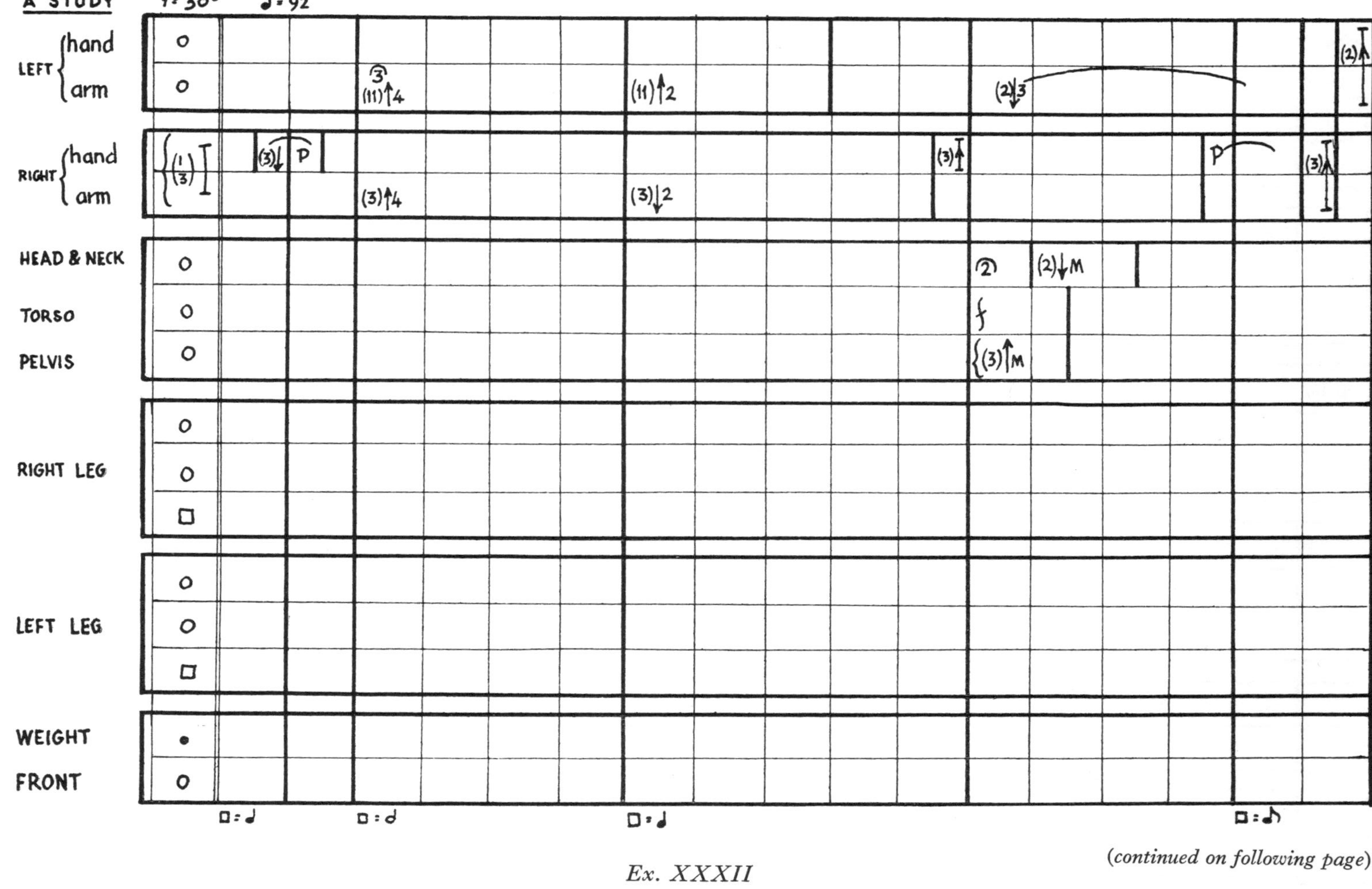

Ex. XXXII

(continued on following page)

Ex. XXXII (cont.)

(continued on following page)

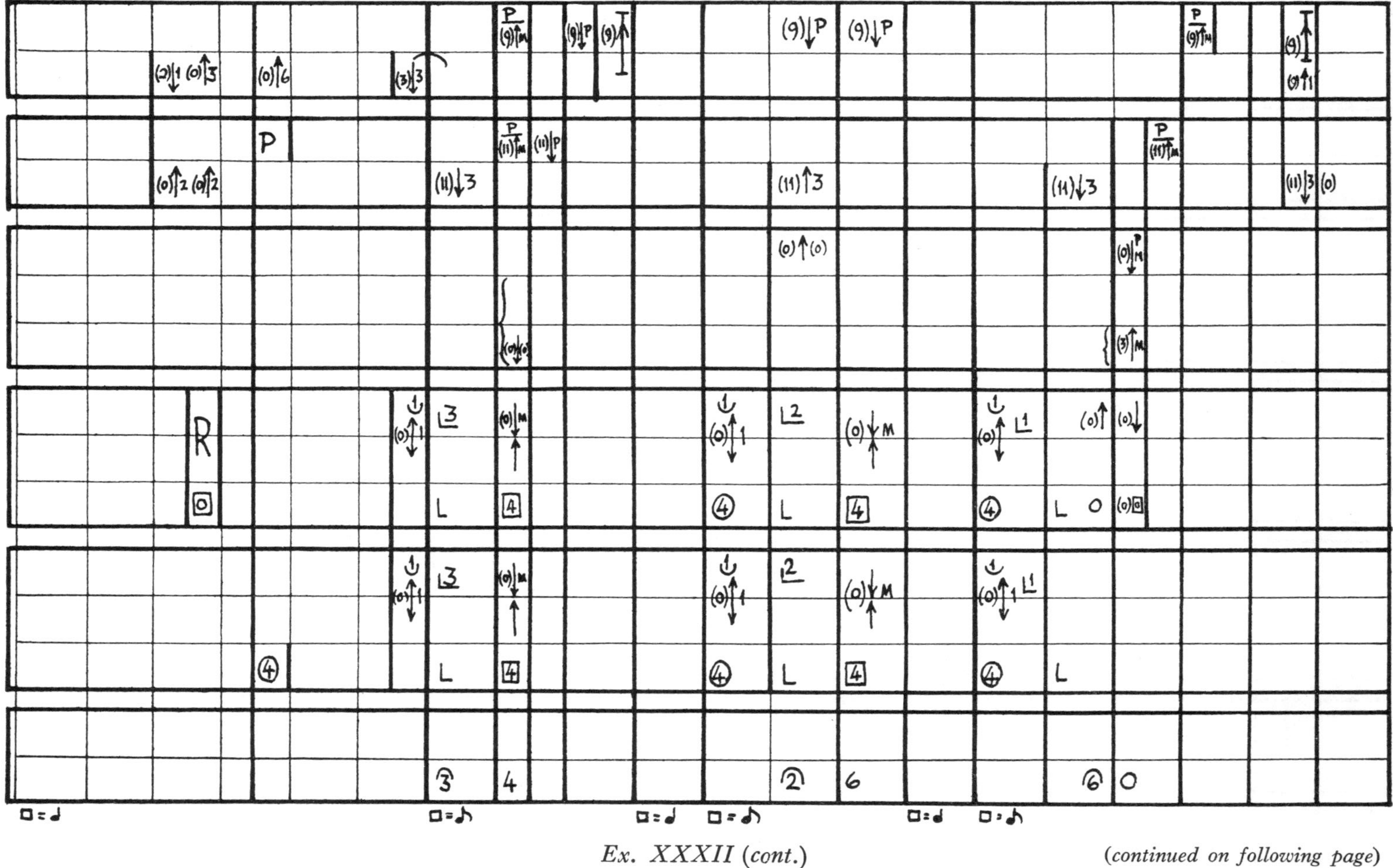

Ex. XXXII (cont.)

(continued on following page)

Ex. XXXII (cont.)

CHAPTER 18

Transport

TRANSPORT is the change which occurs when the body occupying one place changes it for another place. Transport of the body is always the inevitable result of certain complex movements, occurring in the limbs forming the base of the body, referred to in daily life as 'steps', 'jumps', &c. The transport of the body is therefore inferred from the notation of the actual movement.

However, when a dance composition involves more than one moving body, it is necessary to provide an indication of the places occupied by the several bodies (or even of one body) in relation to the plane or space allotted to that dance. Since this space may be of any shape whatsoever, it is necessary to draw up a plan indicating the kind of space to be used and the *starting places* of all bodies occupying this space, in relation to each other and to the space. All the relations between the bodies—human or non-human—will be the inevitable result of the movements performed by them. This plan may be described either geometrically or verbally, as convenient. A verbal description might run:

> '*The Space:* Rectangular, 4×2 metres; the side nearest the audience a long one.
> '*First Performer:* Stands 1 metre from back of rectangle and 1 metre from observer's left side of rectangle.
> '*Second Performer:* half-metre from back, one and half metres from left side of rectangle.
> '*Third Performer:* half-metre from front, 1 metre from right side of rectangle.'

It is to be stressed that only one such plan—a starting plan—is needed for any one composition, however complex that composition may be. When for any reason it seems desirable, more than one such plan may be introduced in the course of a notated composition.

For this notation, choreography is of interest when it is a result of the movements of the human body exclusively, and the choreographic plan is implicit in the notated score together with the starting plan.

(*See Fig. 55.*)

The Path of Transport

The Path of Transport is not the path created by the moving body or its parts, but the path traced on the ground by the contact of the base of the body with the ground which bring about transport of the body. This is sometimes referred to as the 'floor-pattern'. Any such path is the inevitable result of some movement which is performed by the body. (Cases in which this path is the result of any cause exterior to the body are not the concern of the present notation).

Any deviation of this path from a straight line will be found to be the result of rotation of the limbs during the transport. Supposing a leg to have been lifted from the floor, and at the same time as a rotation of the pelvis. The lifted leg will be carried by this rotatory movement, and the place to which it descends will be the result of the simultaneous movements of the leg and of the pelvis. If this movement be repeated several times in the same sense, some kind of circular path will be traced on the ground by the movements. When the amount of rotation in each movement is equal, the path will be exactly circular. To the extent that the amount or sense of rotation is changed in each movement, the path traced will be elliptical, spiral, undulating—in fact any path composed of arcs.

The path will be the inevitable result of the movements taking place during transport, and it would be sufficient to write the movements comprising the step, jump, &c., the movement signs including in the normal way the amount of any rotation which occurs. However, when it is possible to find in these movements a regular sequence in which the amount of rotation is equal in every step, or when it is found that the change of rotation is regular (e.g. every so many steps) this is expressed in the notation, not by writing the whole sequence, but by indicating the overall characteristics of the sequence. A simple example is that of walking in a circle, with steps equal in size, and an equal amount of rotation in each step, the circle being completed in twenty steps. There is no need of repeating the twenty steps and the rotation occurring in each. It is sufficient when the successive movements of the two legs are written, with a sign of repetition indicating that these movements are repeated ten times. The size of the circle will be partly the result of the size of the movements which comprise these steps. The sign of rotatory movement, positive or negative, with the number 8 (when $1 = 45°$) within it, written in the space representing the Front, will indicate that in the course of twenty steps there is a rotation of 360 degrees of the whole body—or, in simple words, the performer walks in a circle. If only part of a circle is performed, then the numbers 4 (half a circle) 2 (a quarter of a circle), &c., will be written inside the rotation sign in the Front Space.

This sign does not indicate exactly how much and in what manner the rotation is performed on every step; the exact amount of rotation is, however, the result of the division of the overall rotation by the number of steps during which it is completed. Precision in the execution of this amount is the task of the performer, upon whose accuracy it depends.

The same principle is applied when the transport follows other curved paths:

e.g. an elliptical path: $\underline{\lfloor \tfrac{2}{1} \qquad}$
an undulatory path: $\widetilde{'3}$ $\overset{\omega}{'2}$ &c.
an augmenting spiral path: $<$ '4
a diminishing spiral path: $>$ '5.

These signs are borrowed from the movement signs which bear the same names. Since it is unnecessary to give the relation to the System of Reference, but only the path created on the flow, that part of each sign is omitted which normally indicates this relation.

See Examples: XXXIII and XXXIV.

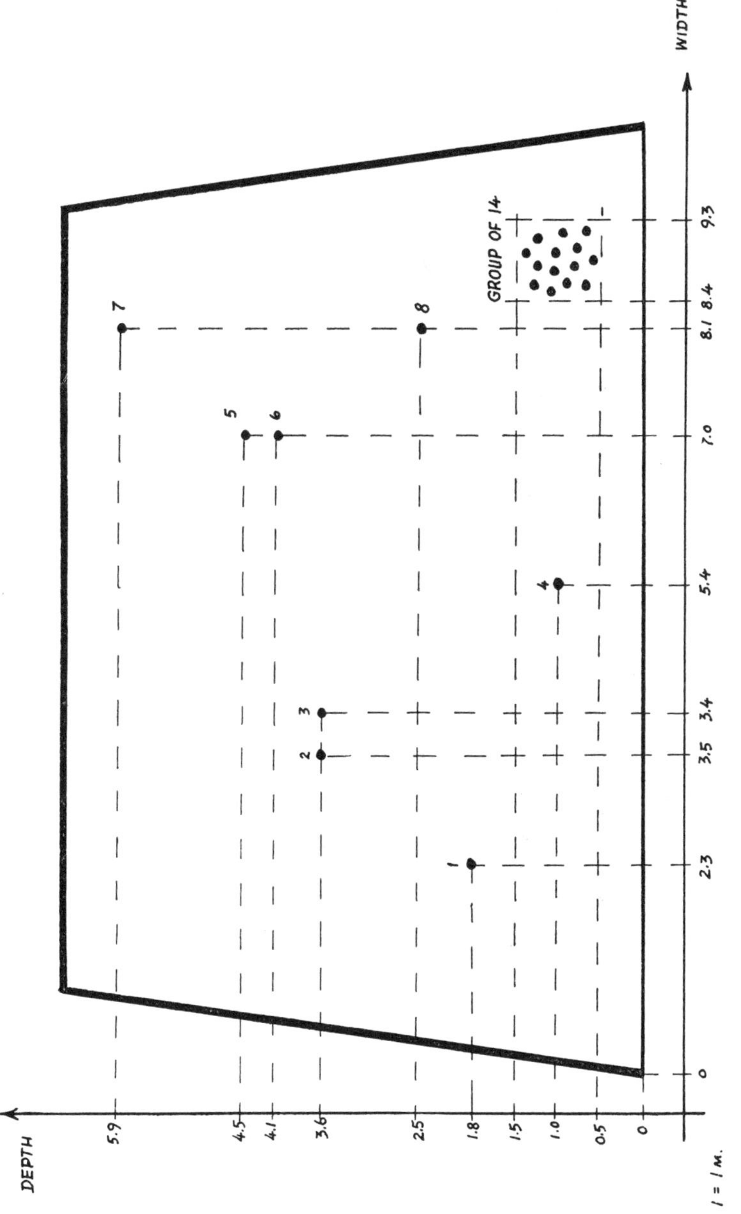

NUMBER ON PLAN	1	2	3	4	5	6	7	8	GROUP
WIDTH	2.3	3.5	3.9	5.4	7.0	7.0	8.1	8.1	8.4 – 9.3
DEPTH	1.8	3.6	3.6	1.0	4.5	4.1	5.9	2.5	0.5 – 1.5

55.

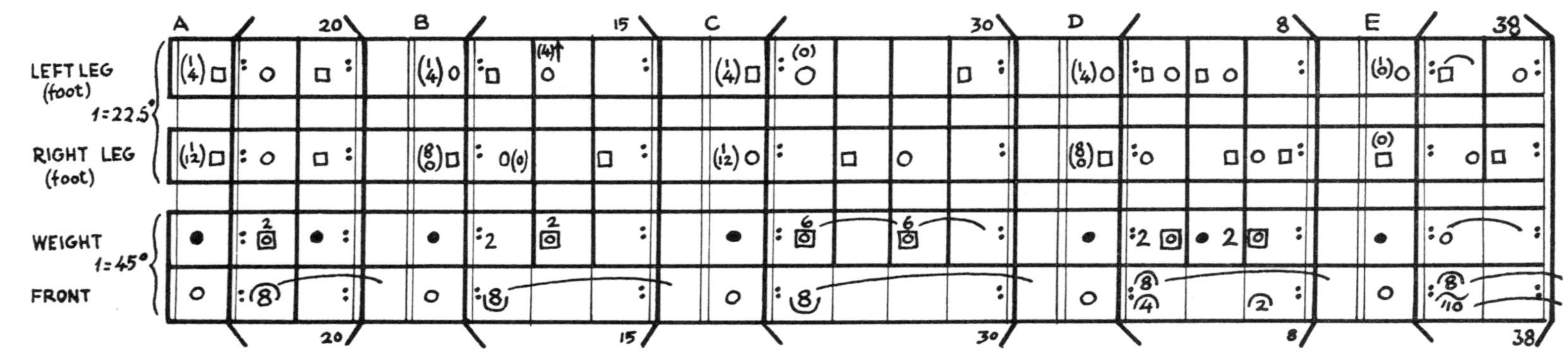

Ex. XXXIII. Paths of Transport. The patterns are the result of the movements written in the appropriate places, in conjunction with rotation signs in the Front space which express the overall rotation taking place during these movements. The example is a shorthand notation of combinations of known 'steps'; only one space is provided for each leg, and this is used mainly to indicate contact with the ground. The signs of contact are given for the feet, but the positional and movement signs apply to the whole leg. In each section a whole circle is created; note that the rotation sign in the Front space is carried over the repeat sign, indicating that a whole circle is completed only during the performance. of all the repetitions of the written movements. In *D* and *E* two signs appear in the Front space, one above the other. The upper sign, carried over the bar, indicates the overall pattern created by the steps; the lower indicates the separate rotations performed by the body within the overall rotation.

A: consists of twenty-one jumps with legs astride ('in second position'); the performer's back will be toward the centre of the circle created.

B: a sideways 'galop'; the front of the body will be toward the centre of the circle.

C: a sequence of hops.

D: a sequence of skips, with half a turn of the body on each.

E: walking forward, a closed curved path is completed, whose circumference consists of ten sinusoidal waves.

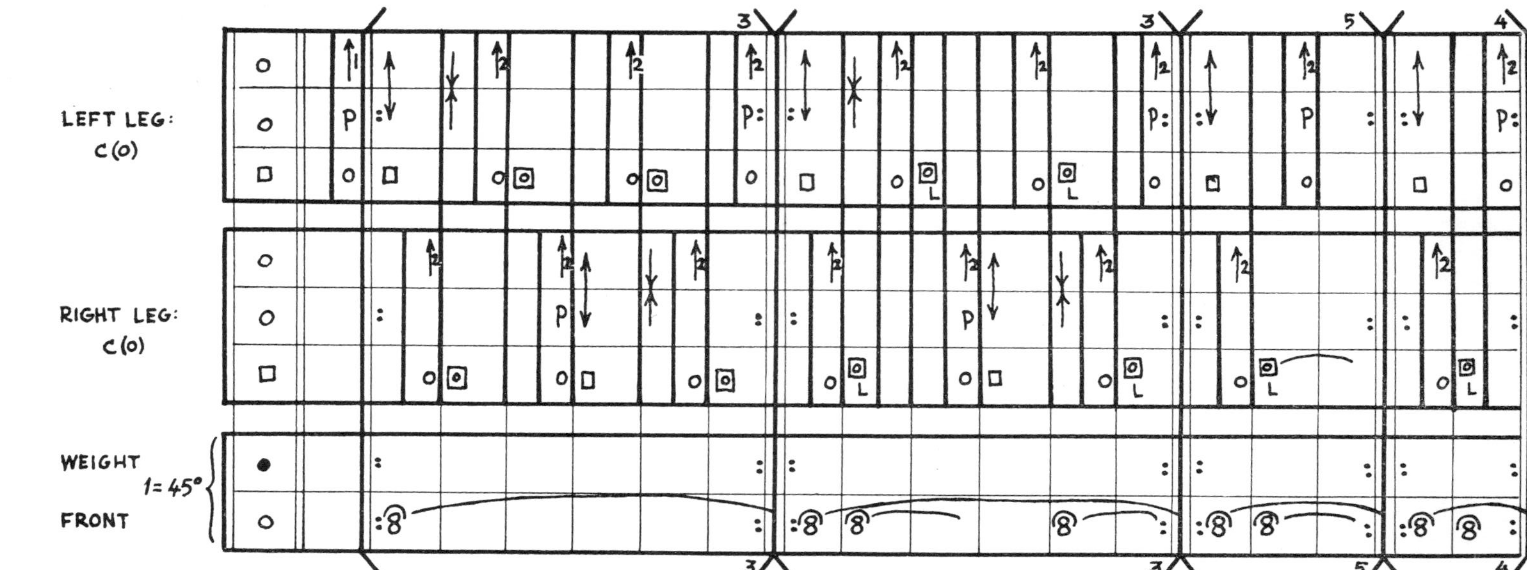

Ex. XXXIV. A Waltz. The sequence is divided into four parts; in each, a complete circular path is performed during all the indicated repetitions of that part. The first is a simple waltz step. In the second part the same sequence is given with the addition of a whole turn of the body during the second and third steps, half a turn on each. In the third part only two steps occur; a whole turn of the body takes place on the second step, which has a duration of two units. The last section is a contraction of the waltz step and has a duration of two units only, with one step on each; on the second there is a whole turn.

Note that no scale of amount of movement is given for the legs. All movements are plane movements in coordinate (0) and any magnitude may be used which is physically possible, ranging from very small to very large.

CHAPTER 19

Auxiliary Movement and Positional Signs

SIX SIGNS will be dealt with in this chapter: they are the signs for:

(1) Symmetrical Movement $\frac{\|}{\|}$
(2) Symmetrical Position ($\frac{\|}{\|}$)
(3) Repeat ||:   :||
(4) Reverse *R*, *Ra*, *Rb*
(5) Parallel Movement ||
(6) Parallel Position (||).

(1) The sign for a 'Symmetrical' movement $\frac{\|}{\|}$ appears in the horizontal space reserved for one of the paired limbs, and indicates that this limb produces in symmetrical manner the movement written for the corresponding member of the other side of the body. The movement is transposed from one side of the line of symmetry of the body to the other, in mirror fashion. When symmetrical movements occur simultaneously, the sequence is written for the limb on one side of the body, and the symmetrical movement sign is written in the corresponding limb on the other side of the body. But when a 'Symmetrical movement' sign is found and no movement sign appears in the space of the paired limb, the corresponding movement is the last one written for that limb. This principle applies not only to single movements, but also to complete sequences. The numbers of bars to be repeated is indicated by a figure in square brackets written beside the sign of 'Symmetrical movement'. The number of bars must always be that of the original sequence, but their individual time values may be varied; in this case empty bars must be drawn representing the new rhythmical pattern, and the Symmetrical movement sign written at the beginning.

It will be found that a sequence of movement having been symmetrically transferred to the paired limb, will yield a new sequence from the point of view of its positional relation to the System of Reference and of the notated signs. This new sequence may now be interpreted by any limb—including the limb which originally performed it—starting from any position. This is a theoretical possibility and perhaps a means of composition, for in such a manner are produced variations in a chosen defined material.

(2) When the sign of Symmetrical movement appears enclosed in brackets in the horizontal space of one of the paired members ($\frac{\|}{\|}$) it is to be understood as a positional sign. It then means that the limb is to move by the shortest possible path to the position symmetrical with that of the corresponding limb on the other side of the body, or that the limb *is* in such a position.

(3) Repetition of a sequence of movements is indicated by enclosing it with Repeat signs ||:   :||. The *exact* recapitulation of a sequence in relation to the System of Reference is possible only when the last movement brings the limb back to its position at the beginning of a sequence. When the repeated sequence begins from a different starting position from that of the original sequence, the path of movement, which will still consist

of the same order and same amount, kind, and sense of movement, will differ from the original in its positional relationship to the System of Reference. The Repeat sign then expresses the repetition of the kind, amount and sense of movement only, in fact, the repetition of those elements of movement whose nature is relational and not those aspects which are specific—that is to say, positional.

(4) After a sequence of events has occurred, it is possible to review the events in the same order in which they took place—following step by step their occurrence in time from the first event to the last. In the notation, this kind of reviewing of a sequence of events—that is, a sequence of movements—would consist in re-reading (and perhaps rewriting) the written sequence in the same direction in which it was originally written—from left to right—in the normal direction of axis *T*, which represents the flow of time on the manuscript page.

However, once a sequence of events has been established (performed—noted—noticed—recorded) the *direction* of reviewing this sequence is not necessarily the original direction in which they happened, but may be one of many other directions which are suggested in each recorded material by the complexity of the record itself which it is to be assumed expresses the material. It is to be likened to acts of memory which, while passing over the same events, organize them into a new pattern, thus creating new imaginary events. These patterns will always be the result of the 'form' or 'direction' in, and by which, it has been decided to review the sequence of events.

The simplest of all reversals of the direction of reviewing a sequence of events is the reversal of their order of appearance, beginning with the last and retracing step by step the whole sequence until the first is reached (the first having now become the last of the series). When these events are notated *positions*, the reverse order of reading them would exactly express the required new order. However, this notation is essentially a movement notation, a notation of change, and change implies that there are at least two points (positions) from which the change could have been inferred, namely, the position just preceding the change, and the one arrived at when the process of transition has ended. In other words, every pure movement sign implies a position from which the movement begins and a position in which the movement terminates. Therefore, in order to reverse a single movement expressed by one movement sign, it is necessary to invert the sense of the movement sign, that is, a positive sign becomes negative and vice versa—and in this way the terminating stage of the original movement becomes the first stage of the reversed movement.

Thus the reverse order of a sequence of movement is obtained by the reading of the sequence in the reverse direction to the original together with the inversion of each movement symbol.

These two devices—the reversal of the order of the signs of a sequence of movement, and the inversion of the sense of the signs representing a sequence of movement—are devices suggested by the notation system itself, that is, derived from the nature of the symbols, which it is to be assumed express the properties of the material; devices for the treatment of the actual material, which is movement. They are therefore logical means by which movement may be composed.

It is thus possible to read any notated sequence of movement in the reversed order from the original *without* inverting each movement sign; and it is possible to recapitulate the *original* sequence with inversion of the sense of the movement signs. The resulting new movement patterns will be recognizable referable variations on the first sequence.

The variations provided by these two methods are always and only variations in which amount and kind of movement remain constant; in other words, they are spatial variations on a theme of magnitude (intervals). The new movement patterns created by the transformation of the original sequence by the means suggested can never stand in the same spatial relationship to the System of Reference as that of the original; hence the point of creating these new patterns. Only the first-mentioned of the three types of reversal can be applied to a sequence so that the resulting variation stands in the same positional relation to the System of Reference.

Reversal of the order of the signs of a sequence, together with sense inversion of the signs, is represented by the sign *R* written in the horizontal space of the limb to which it is applied.

Inversion of the sense of the movement by inversion of the movement signs, when the order remains unchanged is represented by the sign *Ra*.

The reversal of the order of the signs of the sequence, without inversion of the separate signs, is represented by the sign *Rb*.

When more than one movement is involved in the reversal, double bar lines are written at the beginning and end of the sequence.

(5) Parallel Movement. When a movement or sequence of movements appearing in the horizontal space of a limb is identical with that appearing in the space of another limb, the two are said to be sequences of 'parallel movement'. That is to say, the relation of each movement to the Private System of Reference of the limb producing it is identical with that of the corresponding movement of the second limb. The movement produced by one of the limbs is represented by the parallel movement sign: ||. When Parallel movement occurs in the limbs which are not paired members, the Parallel movement symbol should be followed by a letter in square brackets, and the same letter should appear in the space of the appropriate limb. When the Parallel movement continues over more than one bar, the sign is extended by means of a tying bow ⌒.

It will be noted that there is a similarity to the function of the Repeat Sign, except that in the case of Parallel movement, the movement may be repeated by a different limb from that which originally performed it; and furthermore, the movement may also be reproduced by the second limb simultaneously with its performance by the first.

(6) The sign for 'Parallel movement', when enclosed by brackets, also becomes a positional sign, but this positional sign, unlike the Parallel movement sign itself, is used only with paired members of the body. The limb in whose horizontal space it appears, is to be brought to a position parallel to that of the corresponding member on the other side of the body: (||)

(*See Examples following* Chapter 20.)

CHAPTER 20

More Auxiliary Movement Signs

(1) Passive Movement: P
(2) Straight Line: Ī
(3) Curved Line:)
(4) Zero Position as a Position: (0)

(1) Passive movement is movement in which muscular tension is released and the force of gravity is allowed to act upon a limb. The tendency of any limb, when acted upon by the force of gravity, is to fall into a position in which its longitudinal axis is perpendicular to the ground. When the Passive movement sign P appears alone in the horizontal space of a limb, it represents a movement of this particular 'falling' character, the limb dropping by means of the shortest possible path until it reaches a hanging position. In cases where there is more than one possible direction in which the limb may fall, such as that in which an arm held vertically upward is allowed to drop, the passive movement sign is followed by a movement sign indicating the specific path chosen—in this example, whether by way of passing forward and downward, sideways and downward, &c.

P(0) ↓, P(2) ↓, &c.

In the larger single limbs a slow release of tension is not seen, until the critical moment at which the limb is no longer held in position by the muscles and falls at the speed dictated by the force of gravity. In members which consist of many small jointed parts (such as the hands and torso), this slow release has an immediate visible effect on successive parts, and this gradual effect is represented by writing the Passive movement sign in the horizontal space of the first part of the limb affected, and continuing it by means of a curved line written so as to pass through the other parts of the limb in turn, as they are affected.

The sign may be used to indicate release of tension alone. When, for instance, an arm is in Zero position and stretched downward to form a straight line, the passive movement sign will indicate that the muscles of the limb are relaxed and the arm merely hangs in the same position.

(2) The sign of a Straight line: Ī. This is used when it is wished to bring the longitudinal axes of a number of parts into one straight line. The movement requisite in order to reach this position could be written in full, in the usual manner; but when this movement is minimal, or when it is not considered necessary to indicate the exact path of the movement, the Straight line sign is used as an abbreviation, standing in place of the pure movement signs. It may also be used together with movement signs in order to emphasize the occurrence of the shape of a 'Straight line'. The sign can only be used in limbs adjacent to one another, such as hand and forearm, thigh and pelvis, &c.

(3) 'Limbs in Curved Line': $\overline{)}$. This is a positional sign. Each part whose horizontal space is included by the sign, is at maximal obtuse angle to its neighbour, so that the overall visual result is a 'rounded' shape: the arm positions of the Classical Ballet provide a typical example, all the parts of the arm being flexed so as to produce obtuse angles at all the joints, the total effect being that of a softly curved arm.

(4) The position of zero position: (0). Zero position is a theoretical position consisting of given relations between the parts of the body. It can therefore also be used (for purposes of abbreviation or exactitude) during the course of a movement sequence, when a limb assumes or passes through a position identical with the Zero position. When used in this way, appearing either alone or in combination with movement signs, it is enclosed in brackets. Care should always be taken to write this sign *after* the movement sign, to avoid confusion with the numbers denoting planes. This sign can only be used as a positional sign when a limb is in the same relation to the adjacent limbs as it is in Zero position *and also* in the same relation to the Horizontal plane of the System of Reference, as it is when the whole body is in Zero position. For example, an arm may be perpendicular to the floor, but if the torso be tilted out of the vertical, it cannot be written that the arm is in Zero position, since the relation of the arm to the torso is not then that of Zero position.

Auxiliary movement signs are not essential to the notation. Every sequence of movement could be written without their help. However, in cases where the writer does not consider a full description indispensable, they provide an abbreviated method of writing certain movements. They also help towards an additional exactitude in the performance of a written work and one may find that some bear the nature of dynamic indications. Again, they may facilitate the understanding of a composition by emphasizing the recurrence of typical shapes, pointing out the composer's choice of specific forms.

(*See following Examples.*)

Examples

Some of the following studies are parts of duos or larger works; since, however, they are intended chiefly as reading exercises and not for finished public performance, no plan is given for the relative starting positions of the performers. The main purpose of these examples is to illustrate the signs and principles explained in Chapters 17, 19 and 20.

Note that the form of the manuscript page varies according to need, spaces being provided for the active limbs only.

Ex. XXXV and XXXVII are parts of duos, the first parts of which have already been given; Ex. XXXVIII and XXXIX are complete duos. The parts of each should be compared because in each case the corresponding parts are recognisable variations of each other, In Ex. XXXV, for instance, the whole leg sequence is identical with that of "Peacock—I" but with variation in the manner of contact of the feet with the ground, and with rhythmical variation. On this are superimposed the new motif of movements of the pelvis, and a new motif of arm movements. In this example note that conical movement is written for the lower leg, according to the convention explained in Chapter 17. In Ex. XXXVIII the part of the second performer is the exact reversal of the sequence of movement of the first; it could in fact be notated by writing the letter R after the first performer's part. The part of the second performer is obtained by reading that of the first performer backwards, and with inversion of the signs. In Ex. XXXV, XXXVI and XXXVII there is a simple use of symmetrical movement and positional signs, and reverse signs, the first two always referring to the movement or position—either preceding or simultaneous—of the appropriate paired member, and the latter to the limb's own preceding movement. In Ex. XXXVI, note that a rotated state of the legs is given as a key signature. This rotated state of the limb limits and determines plane movements of the legs, especially when they are in contact with the ground; the coordinate will be that of the half-plane towards which the frontal surfaces of the limb face, and therefore no coordinate number is given before the sign of Plane movement. In reading the example many familiar steps from the Classical Ballet may be recognised, such as *assemblé*, *sisson*, *pas de chat* and others.

Ex. XXXVII, XXXVIII, XXXIX and XLI provide examples of the use of the repeat sign. In Ex. XXXVIII the repeated sequence begins from a position identical with that of the initial starting position. and the ensuing sequence will then be identical with the original; this is the simplest form resulting from a repeat sign. An identical starting position in repeated sequences means only that the relations between the parts of the body are the same; it does not imply that the Front is the same in both. When a change of Front has occurred in an original sequence, the repetition will begin with the Front prevailing at the end of the original. Any rotation of the body taking place in the repeated sequence will be of the same amount as before, but the body will face new 'absolute' directions whose numbers will be proportionate to the amount of rotation. In Ex. XXXVII the repeat is used in a different manner; a symmetrical repeat sign is written for the leg movements, which means that the sequence is repeated in mirror fashion by the other side of the body, while an ordinary repeat sign is written for the arm movements. The resulting pattern is thus a further modification of the first by the change of intra-body relationships. The result of the fact that a repeat sign involves repetition of intervals only, may be seen in Ex. XXXIX (second part) and XLI. In these the repeat sign occurs on a different position from the initial starting position. By repeating all the intervals of the original sequence, each repetition will yield a completely new sequence from the point of view of the positional relationships of the limbs to each other.

Ex. XL provides an instance of the writing of the curving movements described in Chapter 17.

N.B. In the light of a natural tendency observed in the movements of the body, it has been found advisable in the practice of writing, to make an amendment to the Law of 'Light' and 'Heavy' limbs. According to the principle as it has been stated, when the feet are anchored to the floor, the thighs are 'heavy' in relation to all the parts above them. There is, however, an overwhelming tendency to keep the upper parts of the body vertical—or in whatever position it may be, prior to the movement of the legs—and not to allow it to be carried by flexion or extension of the legs, which are anchored to the ground. For instance, according to the Law of 'Light' and 'Heavy' limbs, if the legs are flexed from Zero position, and there is no independent movement in the torso, the torso will be carried by the movement of the thigh and its position at the end of the movement will be identical with that of the thigh. But in fact the tendency is to keep the upper part of the body vertical unless there is a special reason for doing otherwise. In the notation, therefore, unless otherwise stated, the position of the torso remains unchanged by flexion and extension of the legs. This amendment applies to all notated material in this book.

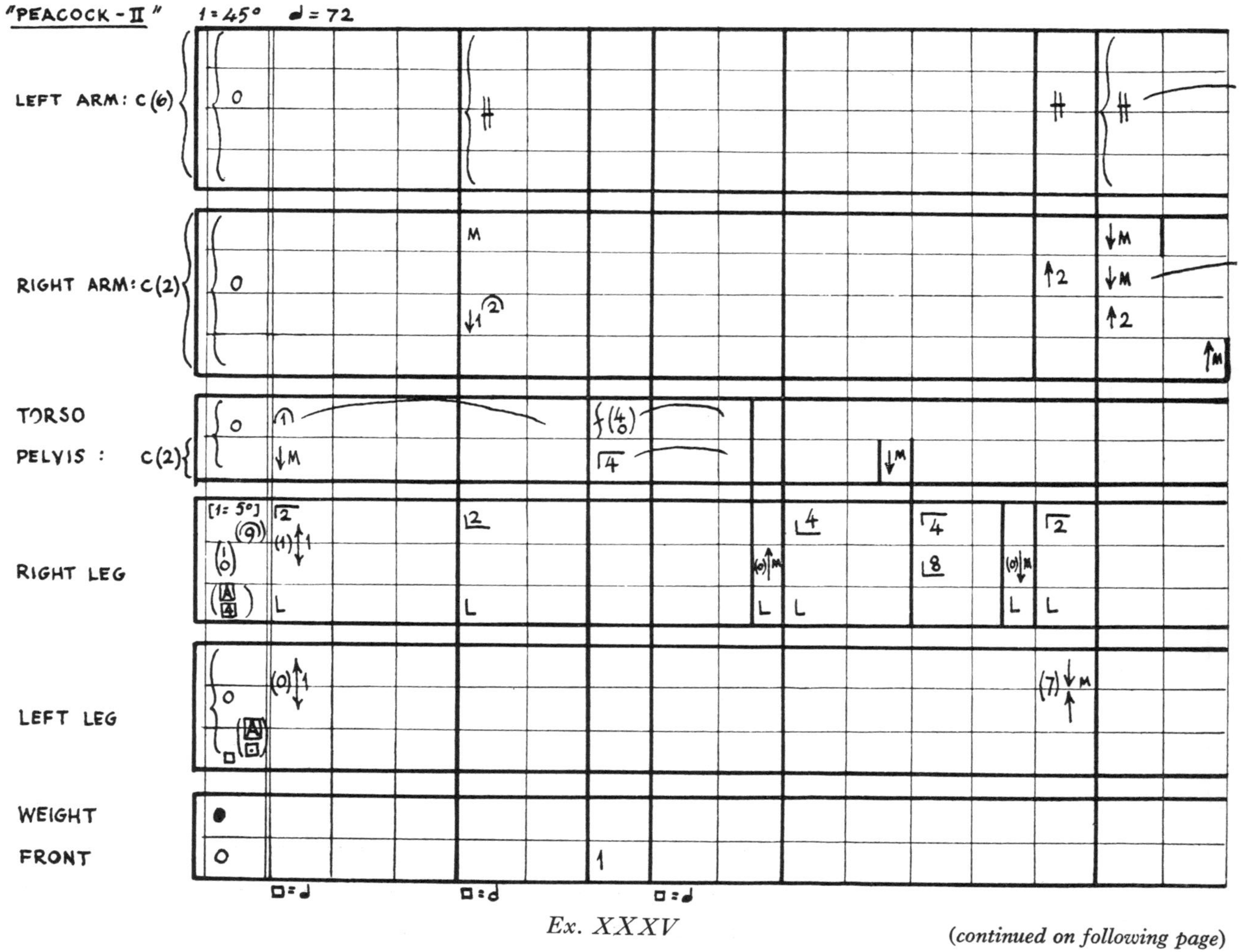

Ex. XXXV

(continued on following page)

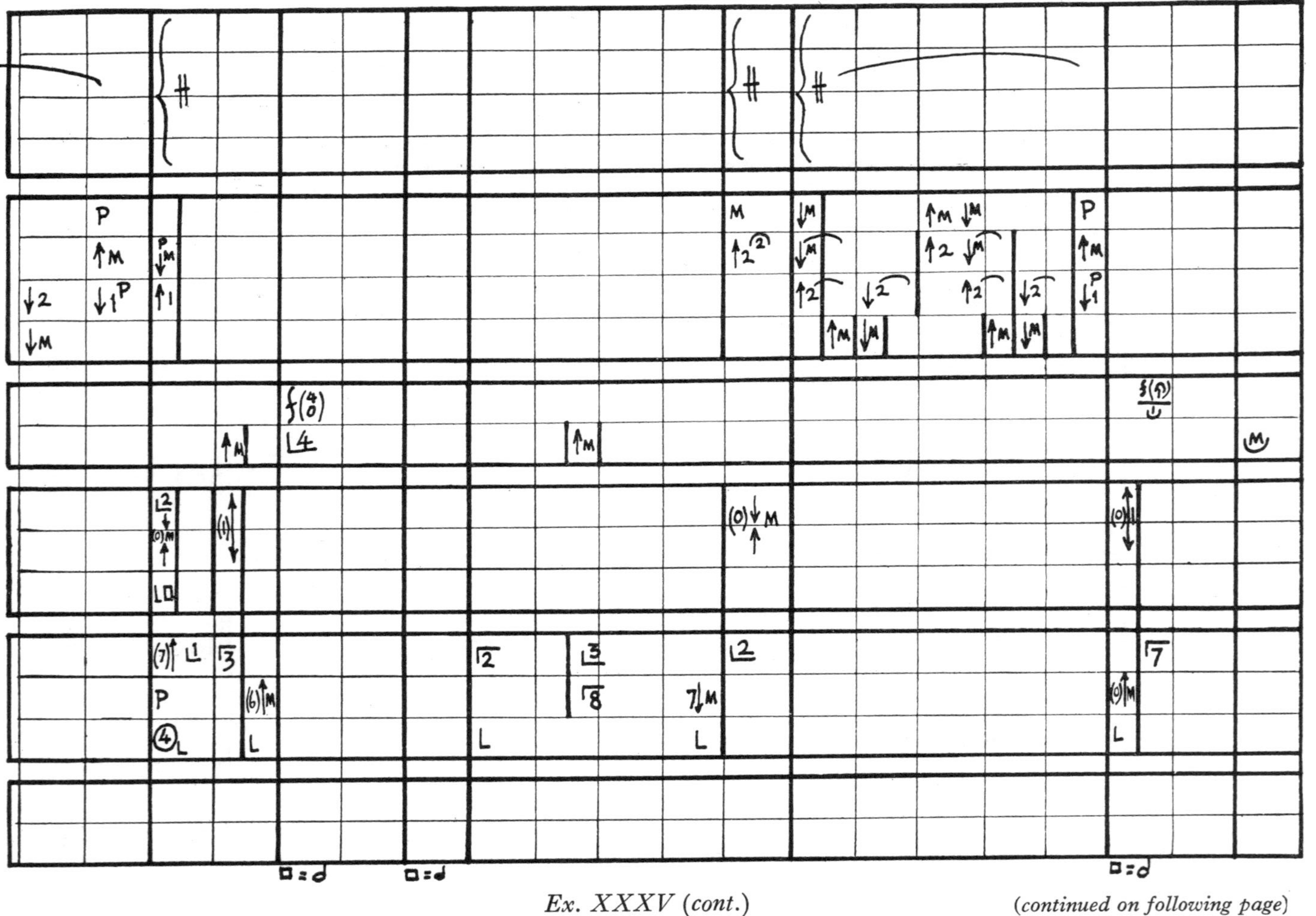

Ex. XXXV (cont.)

(continued on following page)

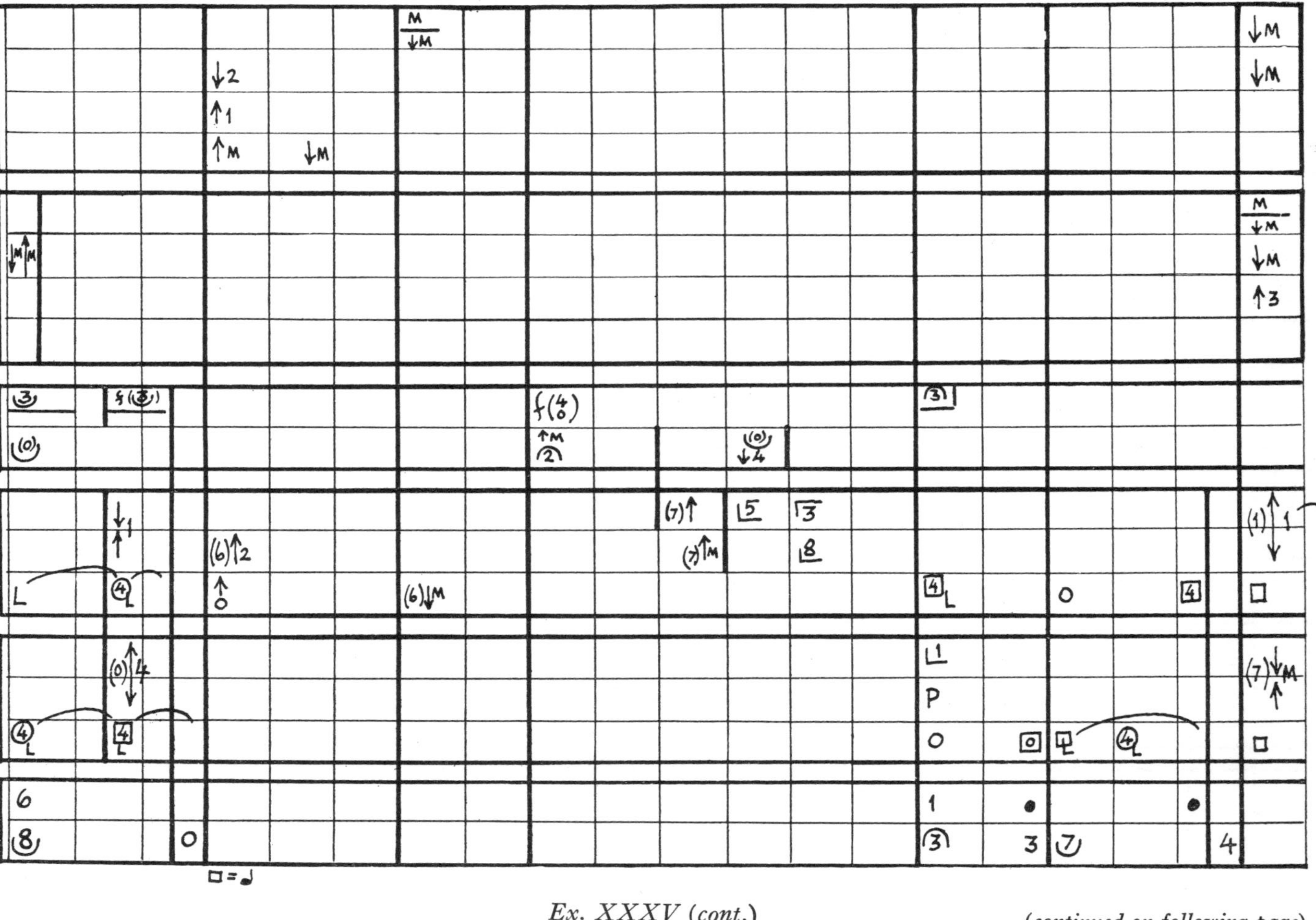

Ex. XXXV (cont.)

(continued on following page)

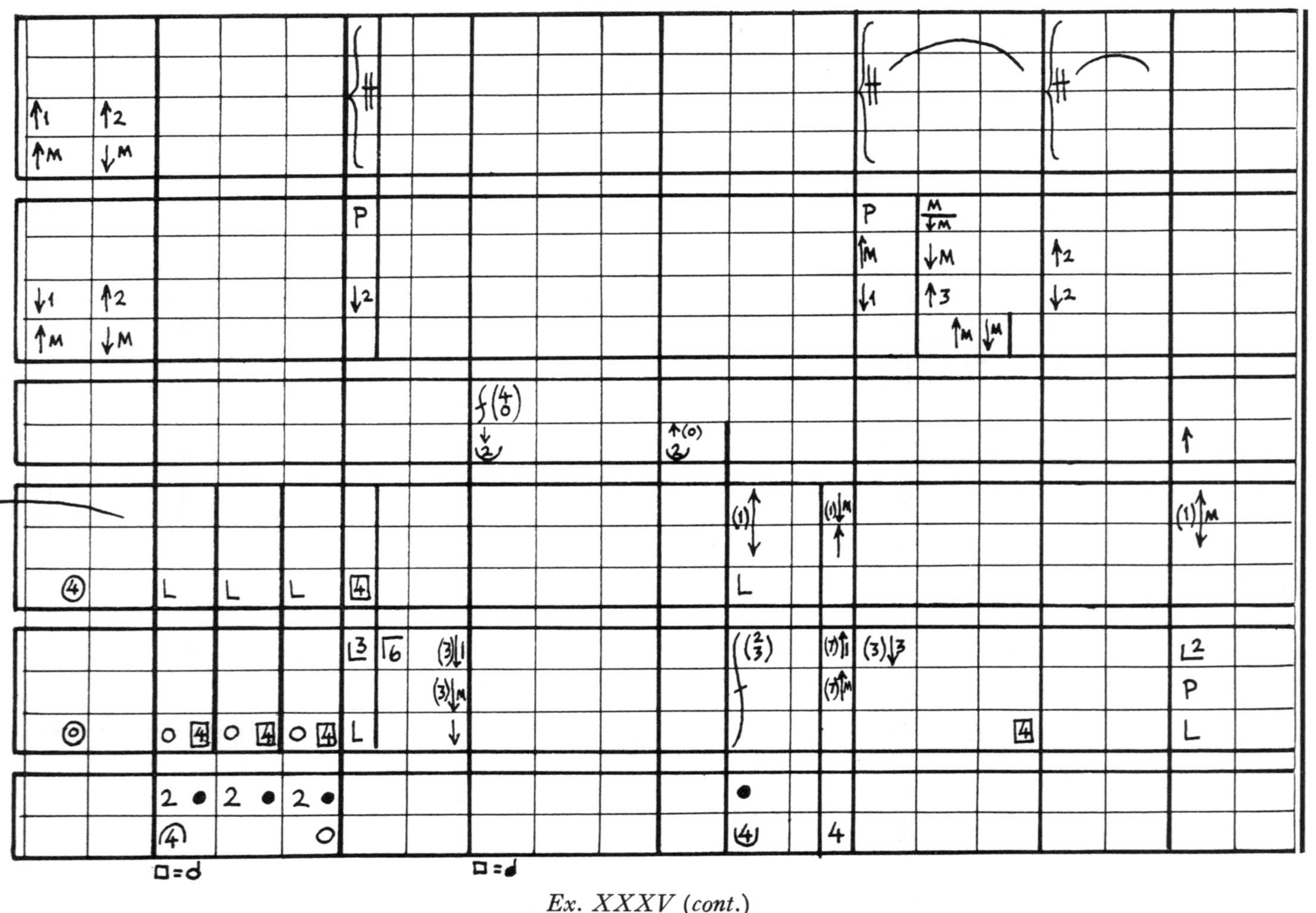

Ex. XXXV (cont.)

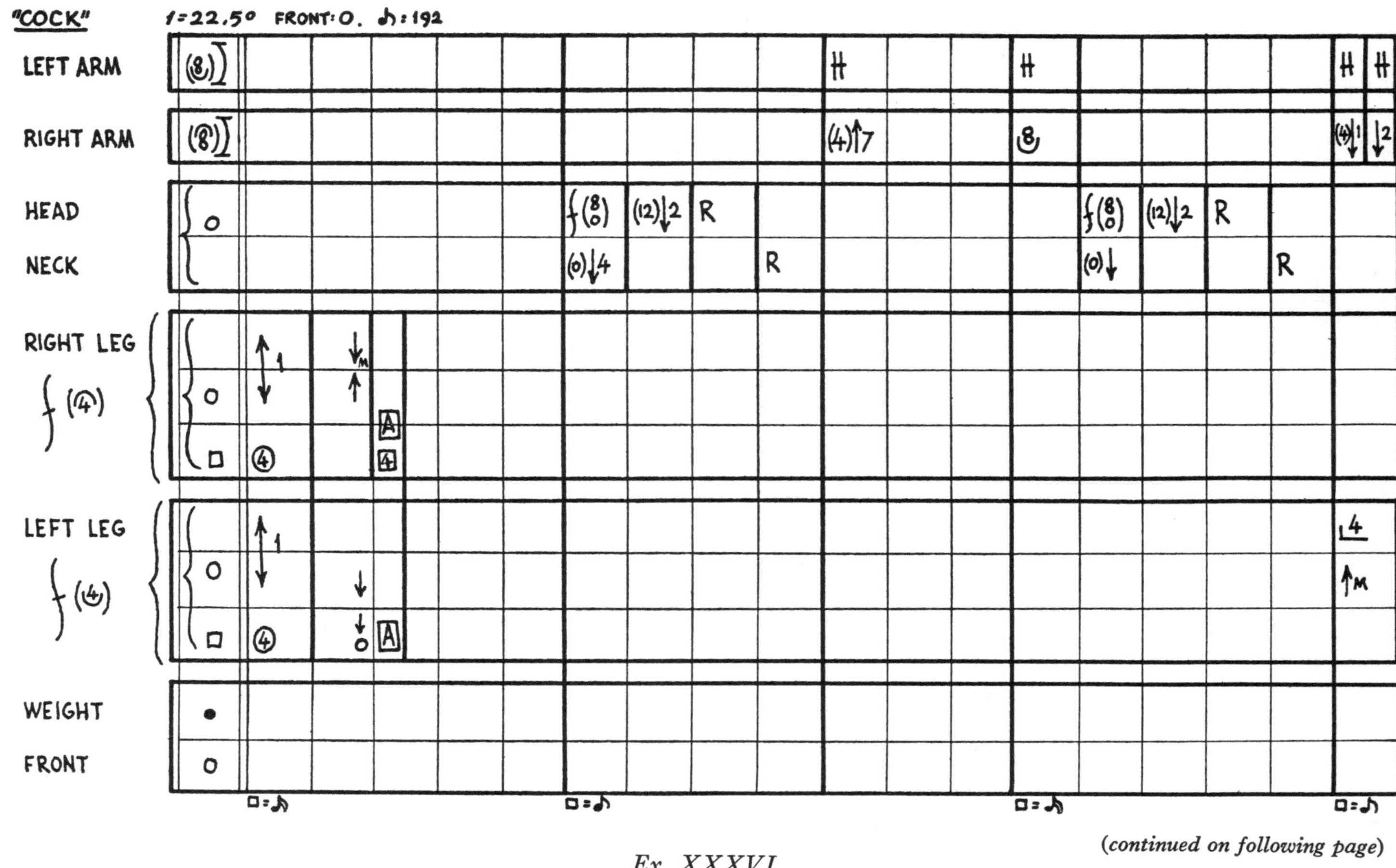

(continued on following page)

Ex. XXXVI

(□ = ♪)

□ = 𝅘𝅥𝅯

Ex. XXXVI (cont.)

(continued on following page)

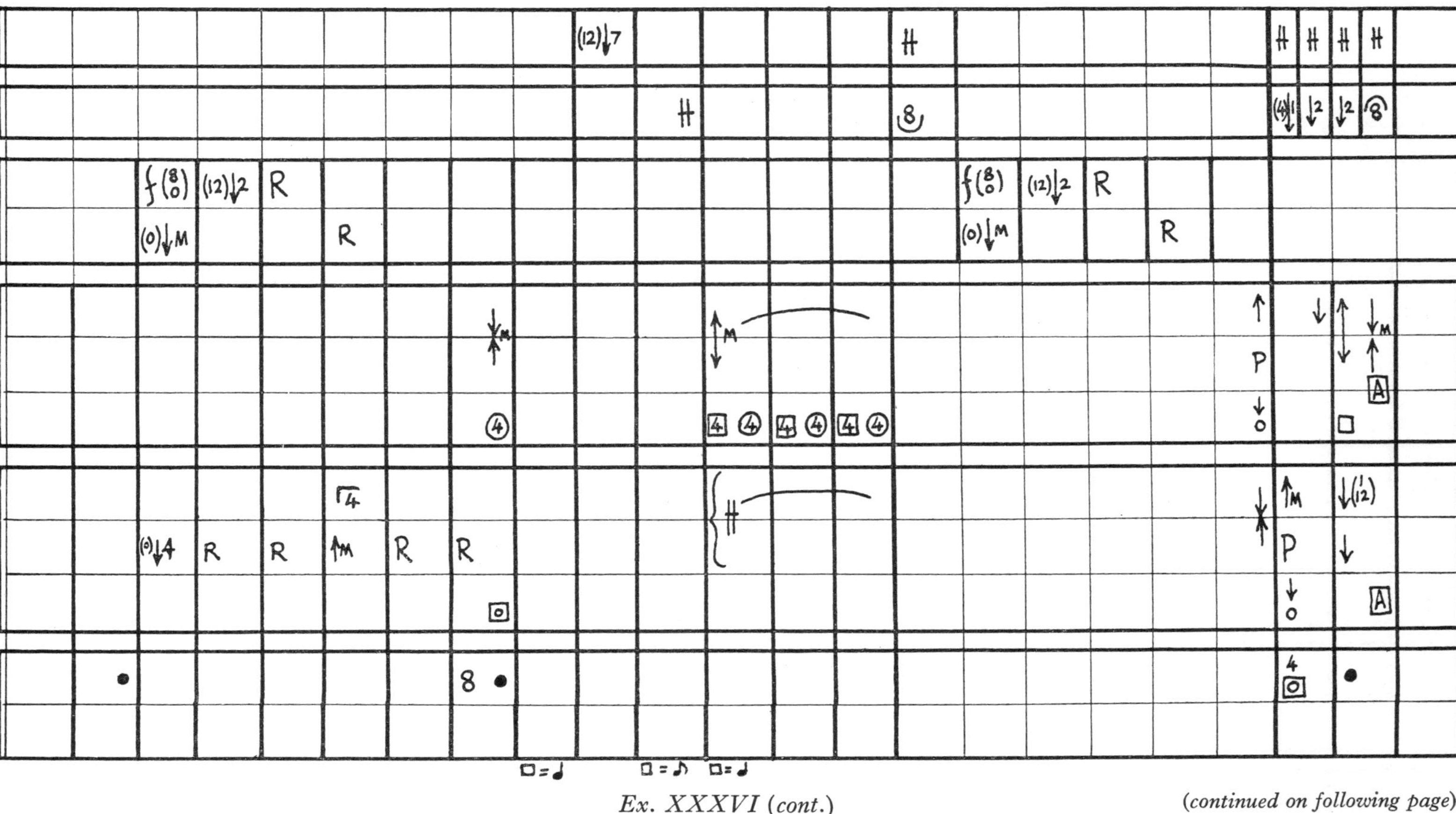

Ex. XXXVI (cont.)

(continued on following page)

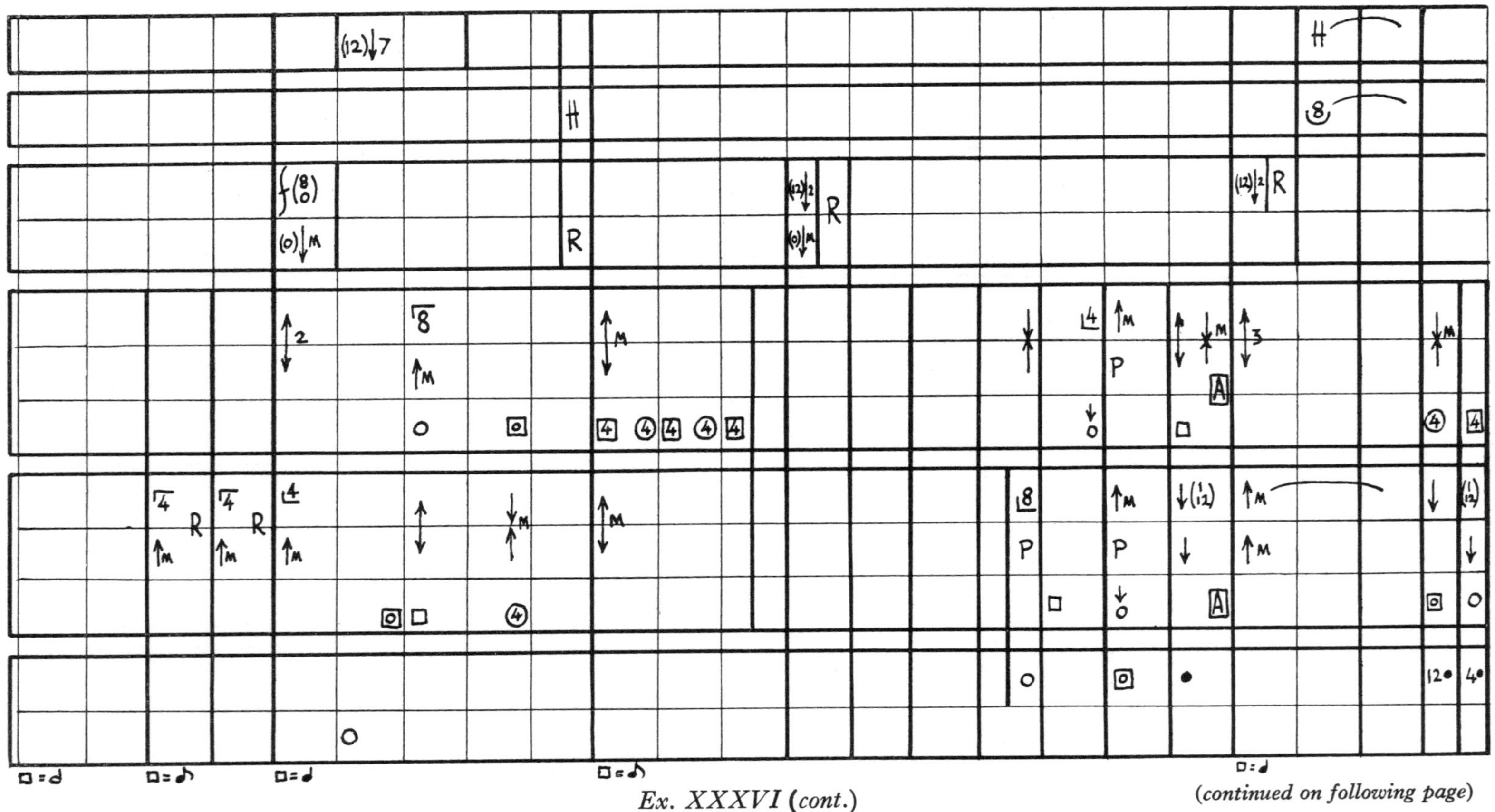

Ex. XXXVI (cont.)

(continued on following page)

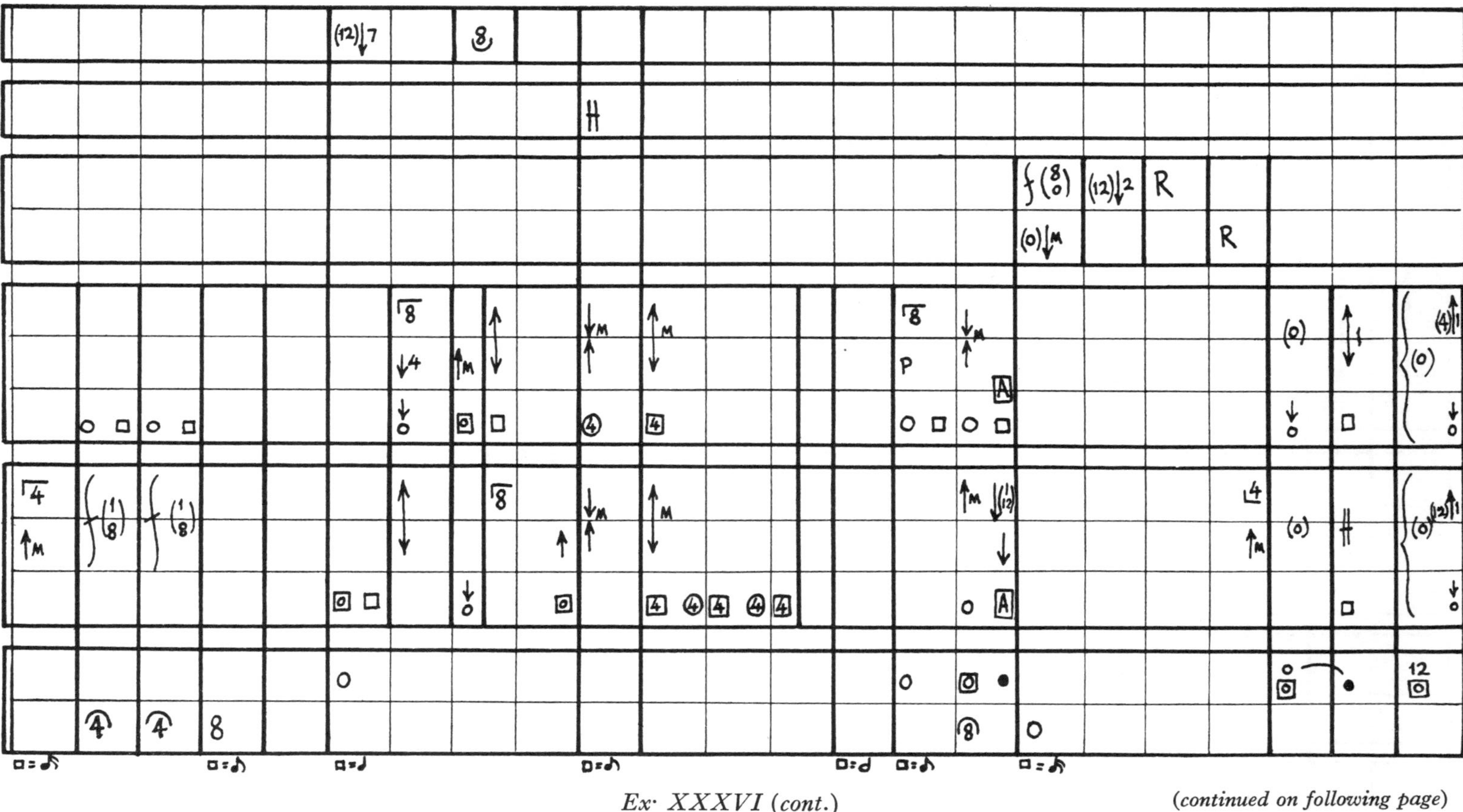

Ex· XXXVI (cont.)

(continued on following page)

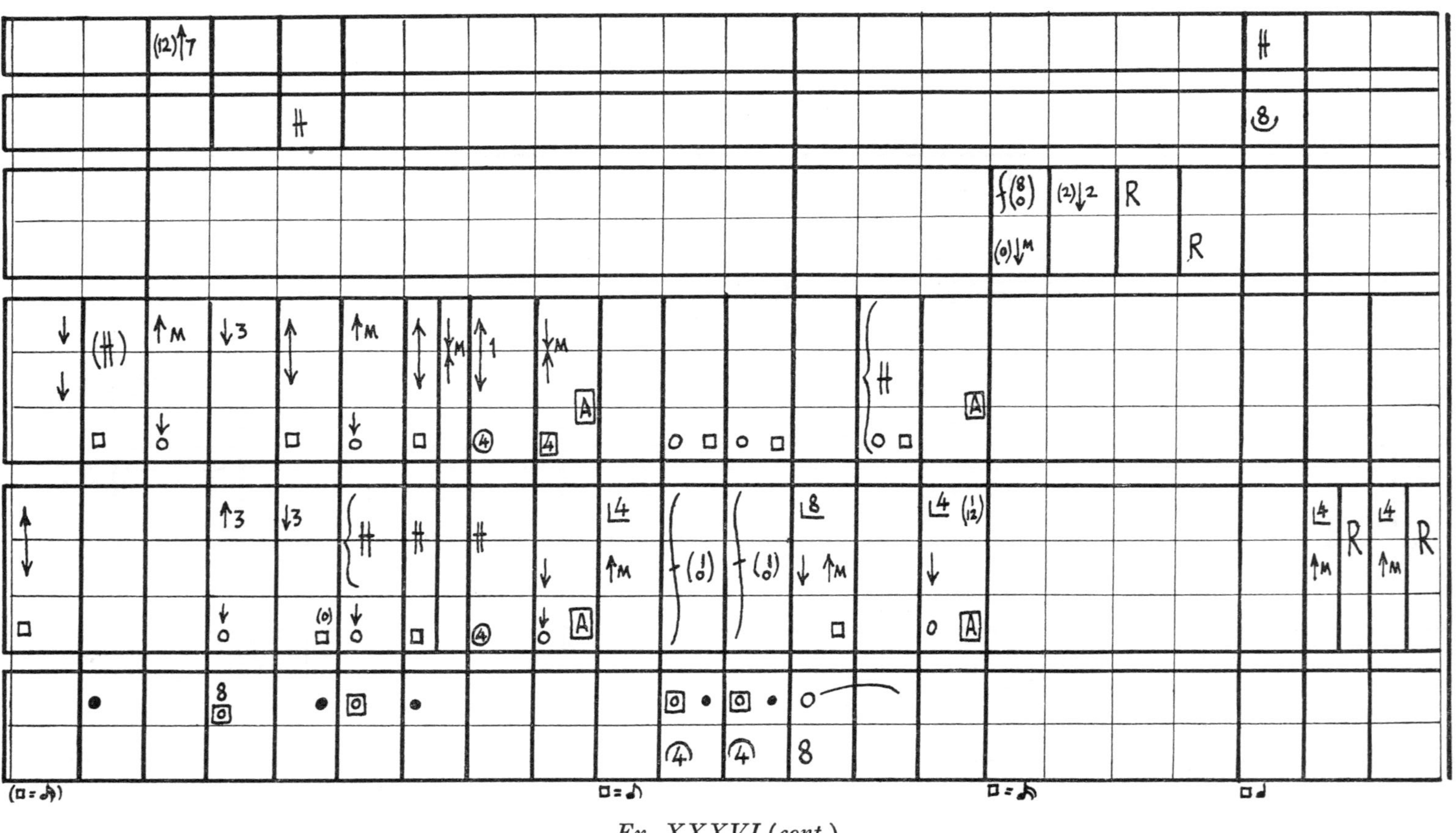

Ex. XXXVI (cont.)

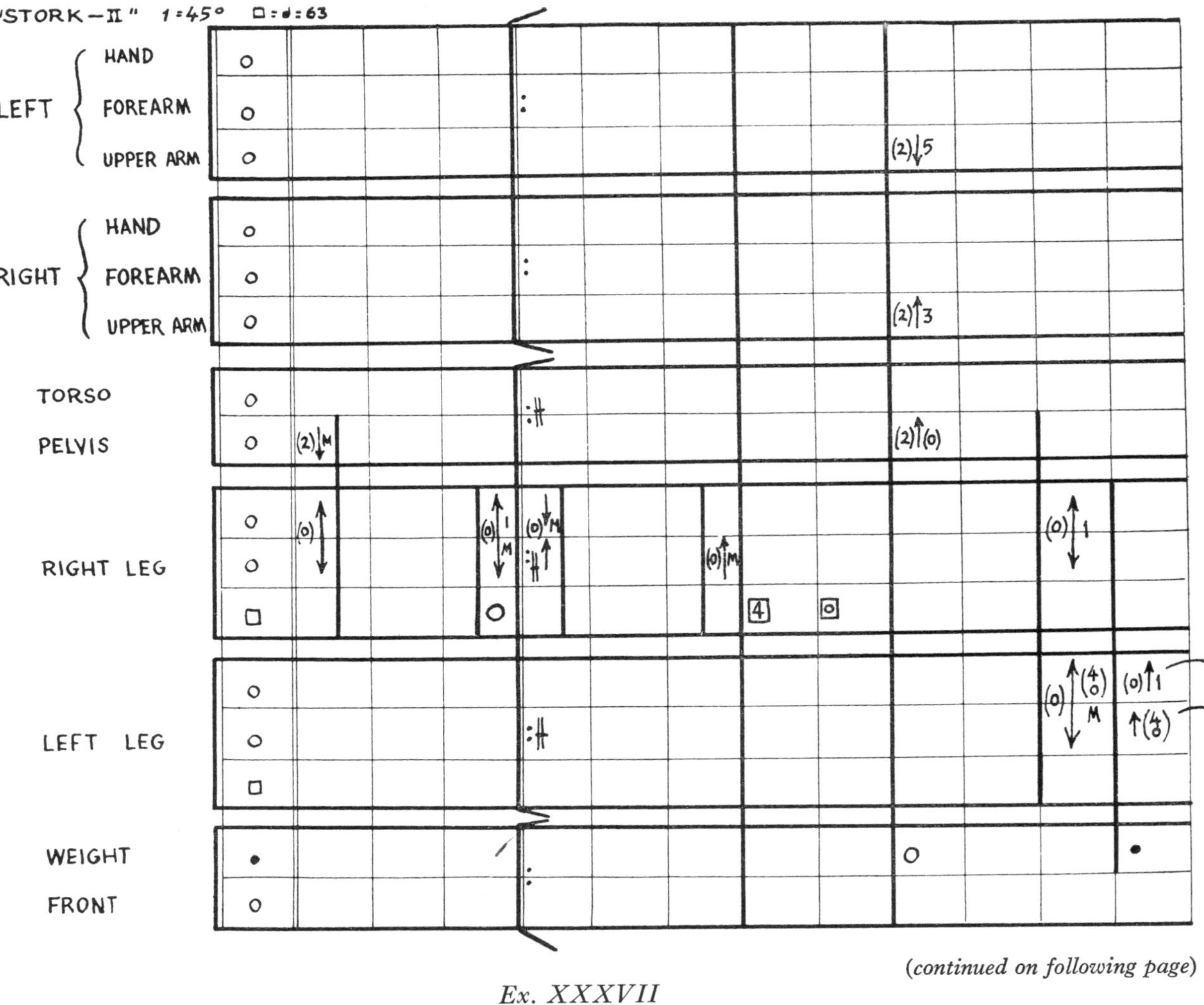

(continued on following page)

Ex. XXXVII

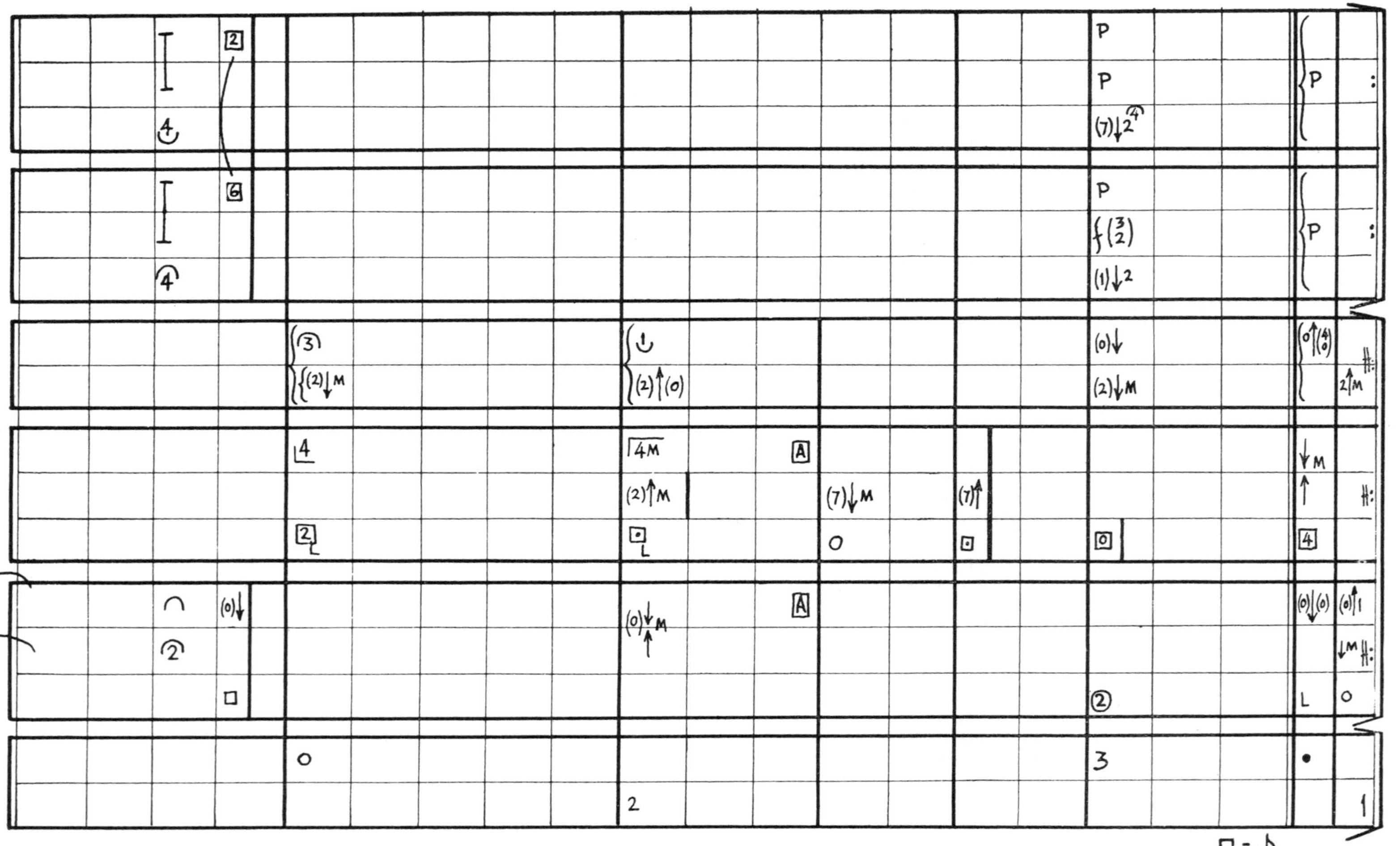

Ex. XXXVII (cont.)

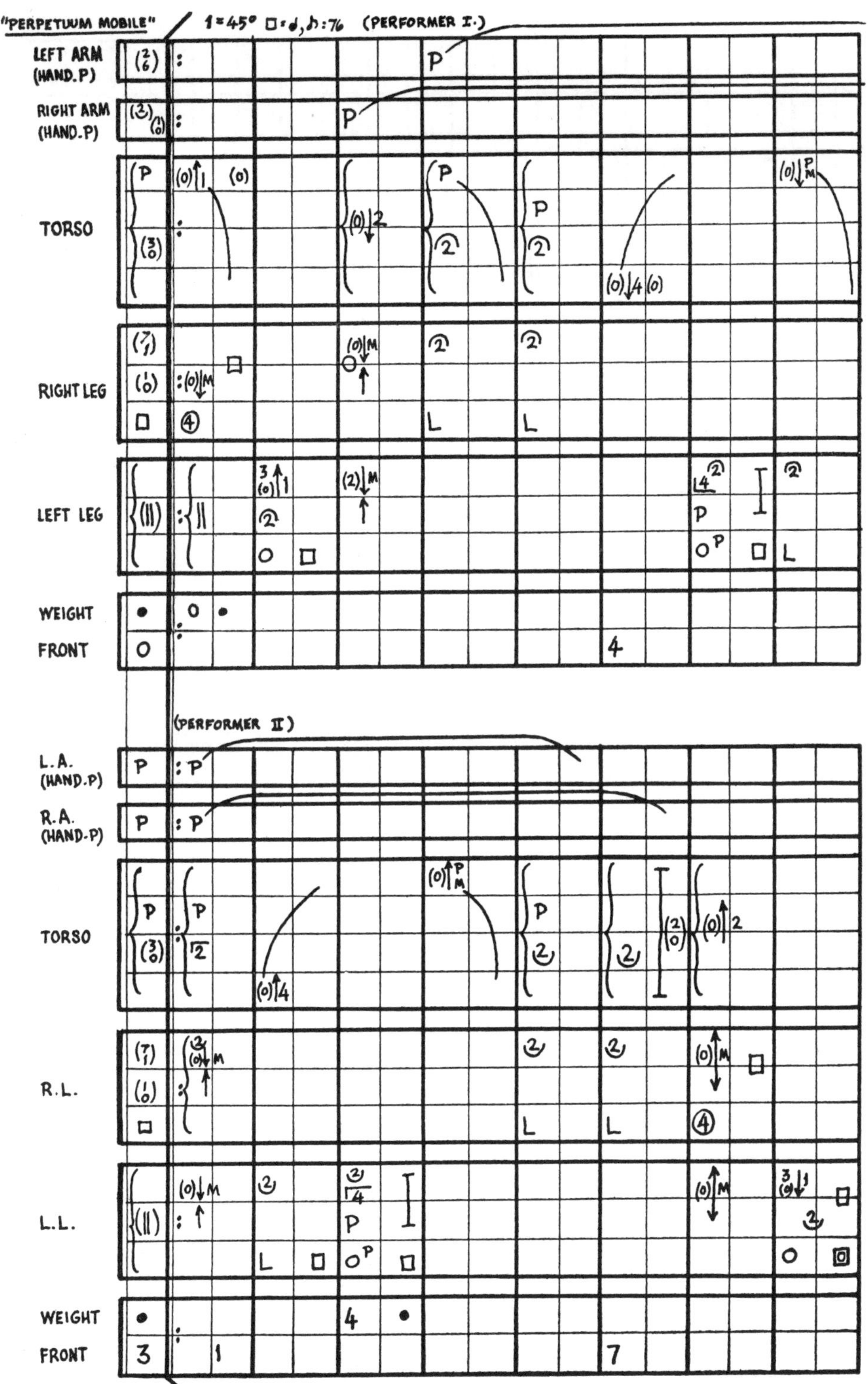

(continued on following page)

Ex. XXXVIII

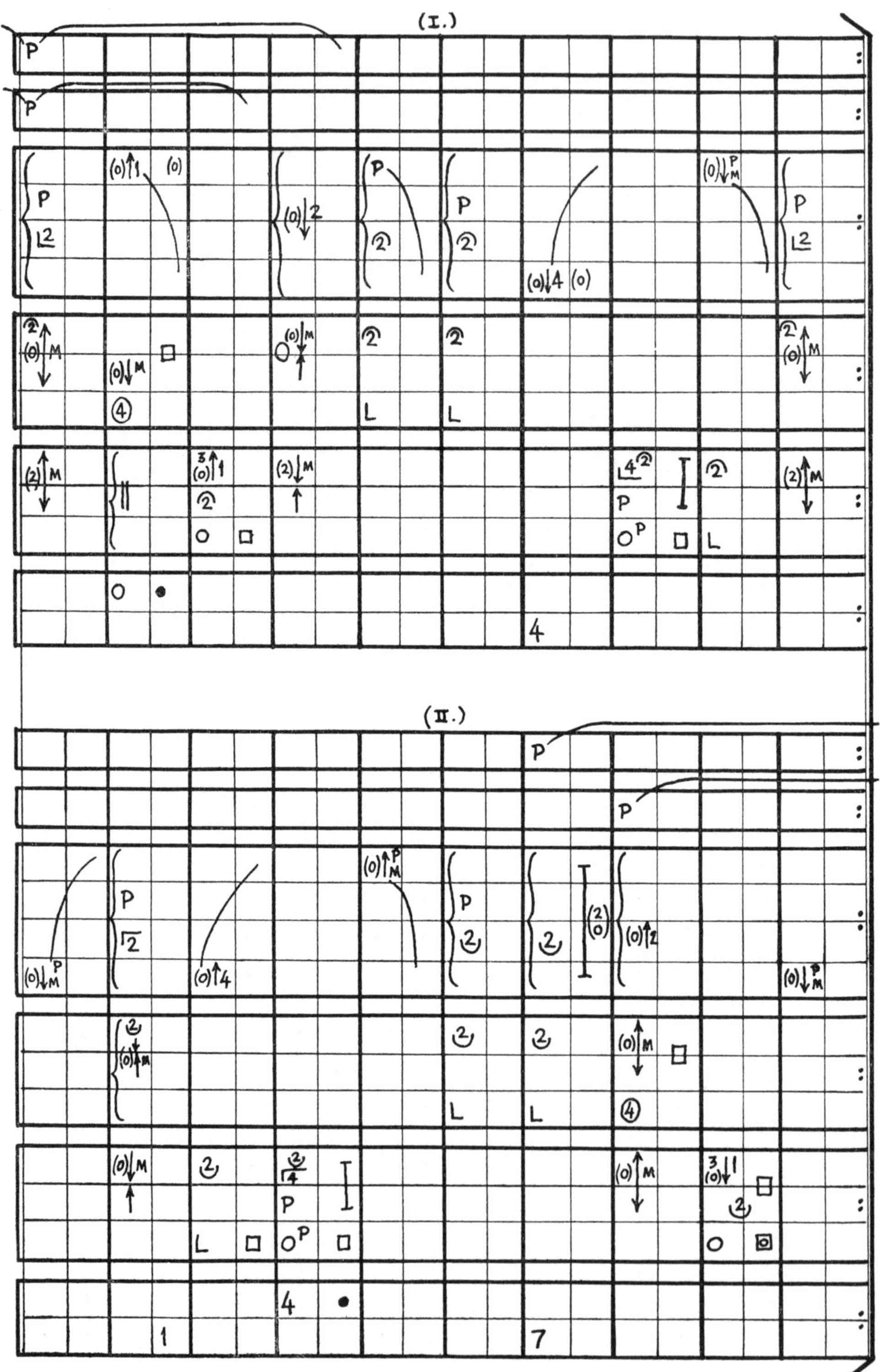

Ex. XXXVIII (cont.)

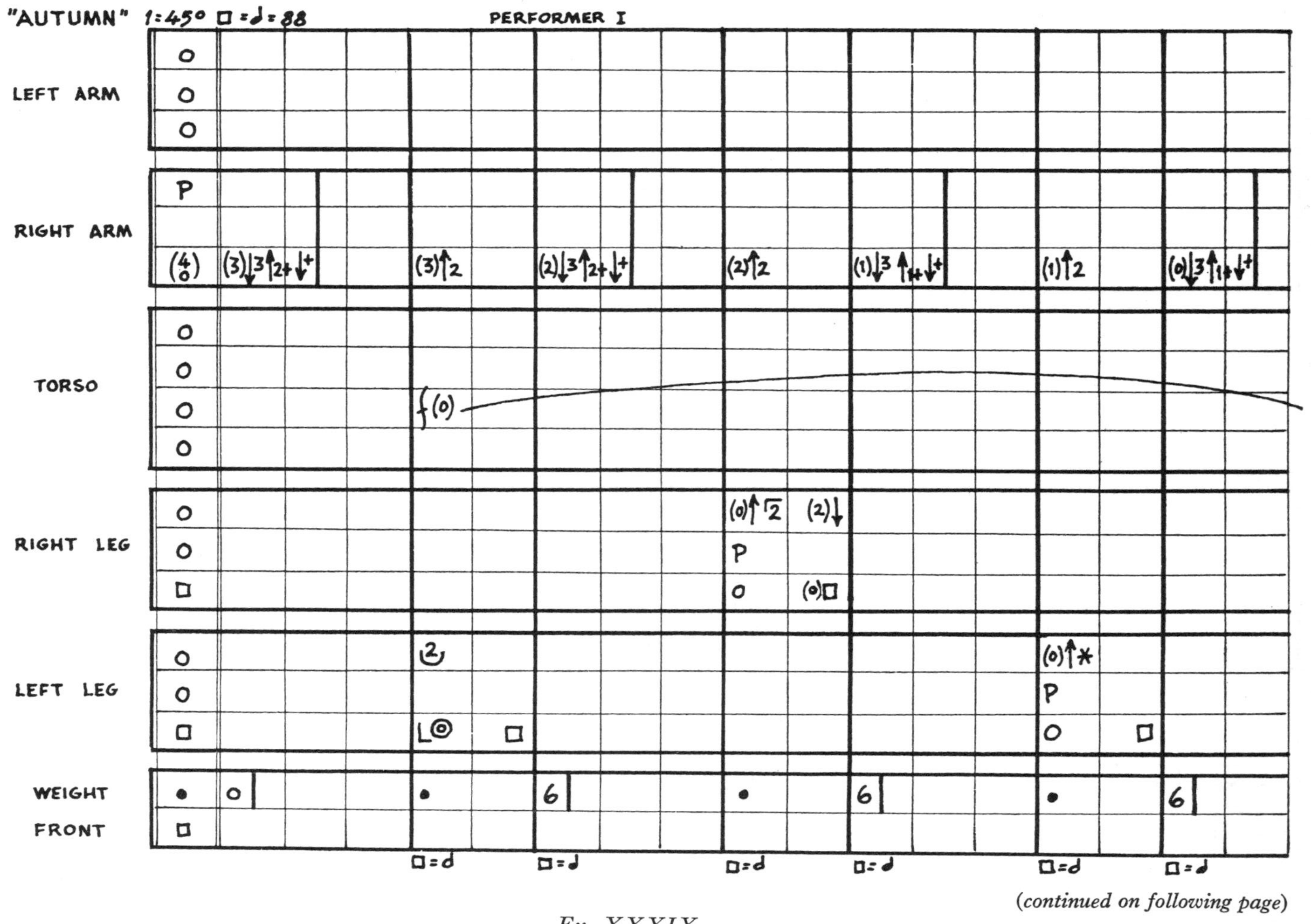

(continued on following page)

Ex. XXXIX

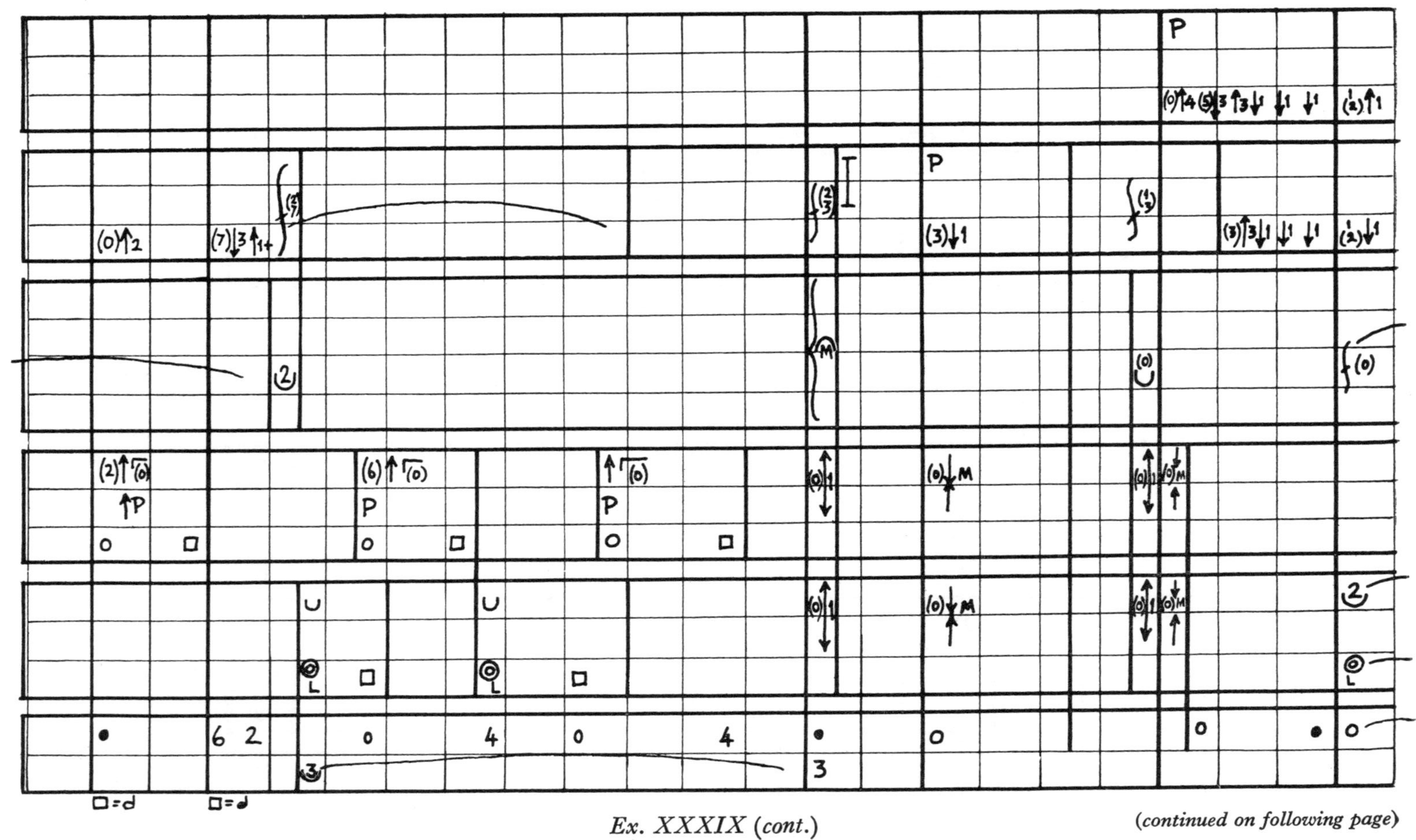

Ex. XXXIX (cont.)

(continued on following page)

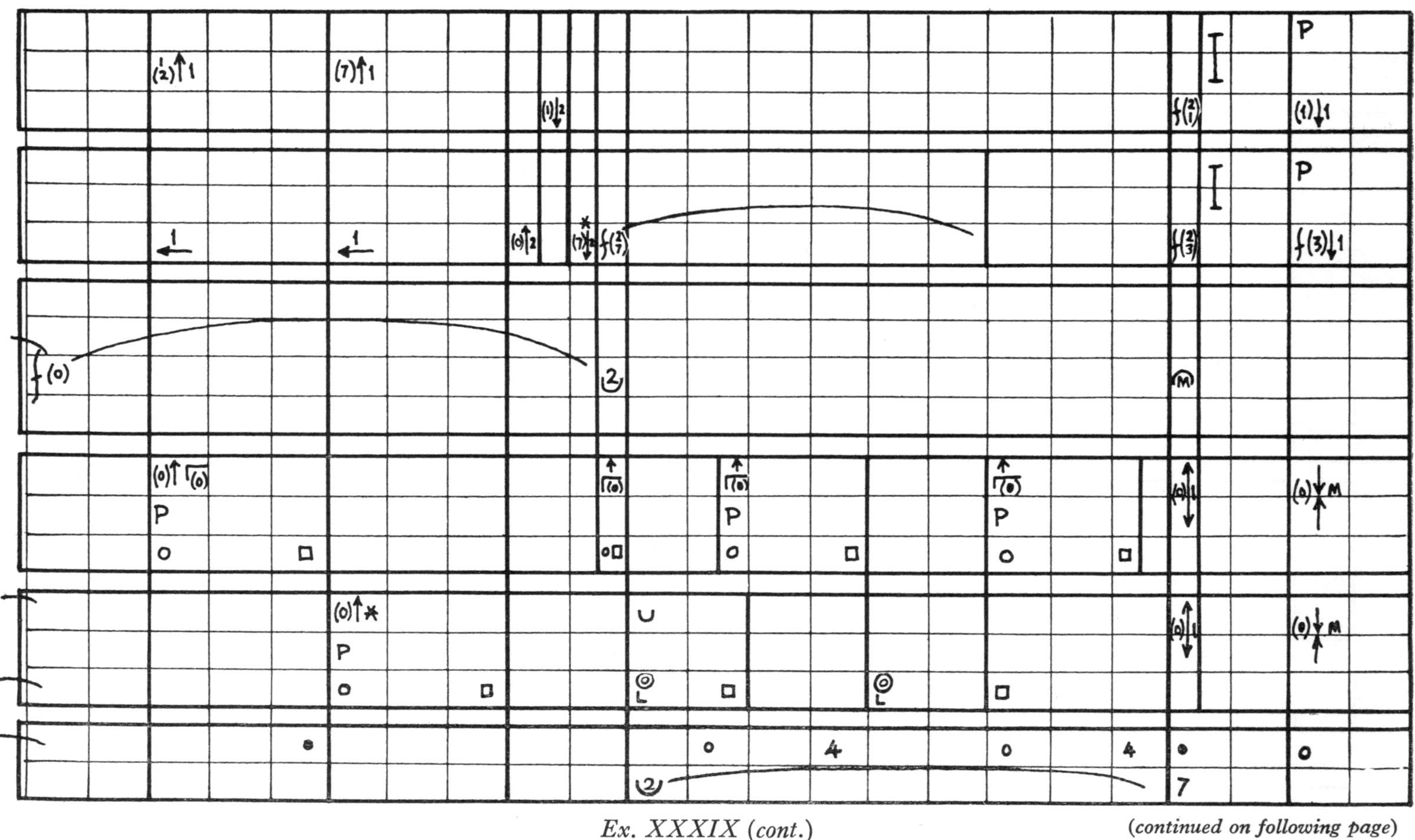

Ex. XXXIX (cont.)

(continued on following page)

Ex. XXXIX (cont.)

(continued on following page)

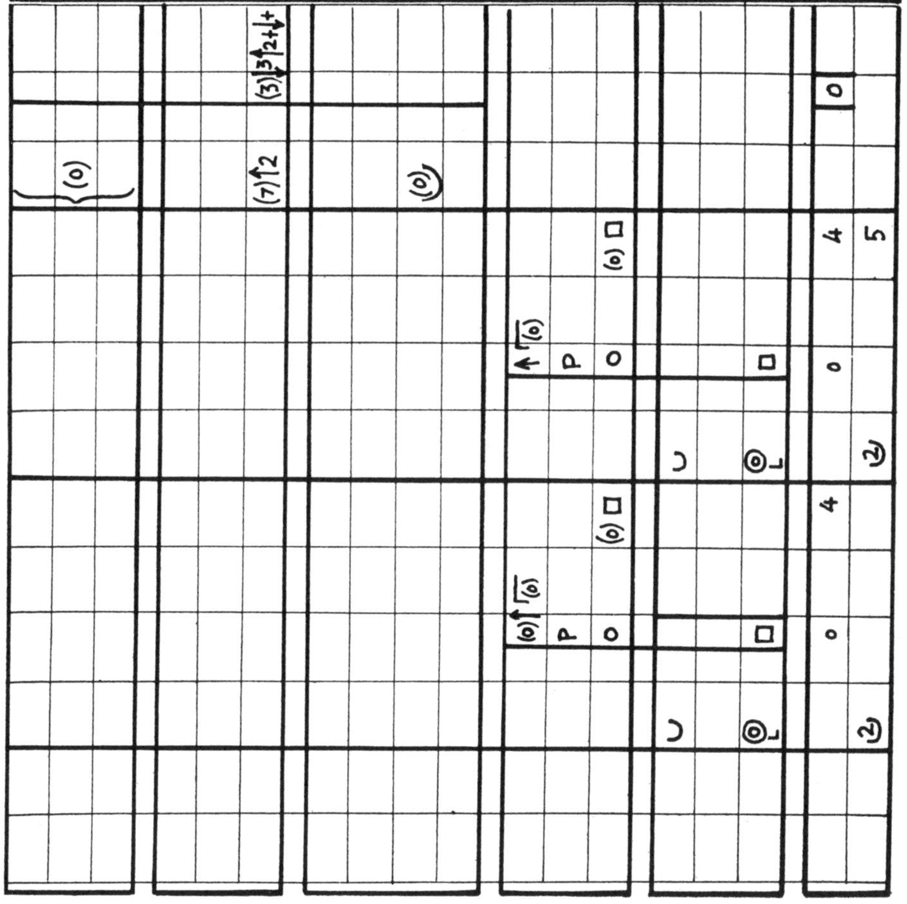

(For second performer's part *see following page*)

Ex. XXXIX (*cont.*)

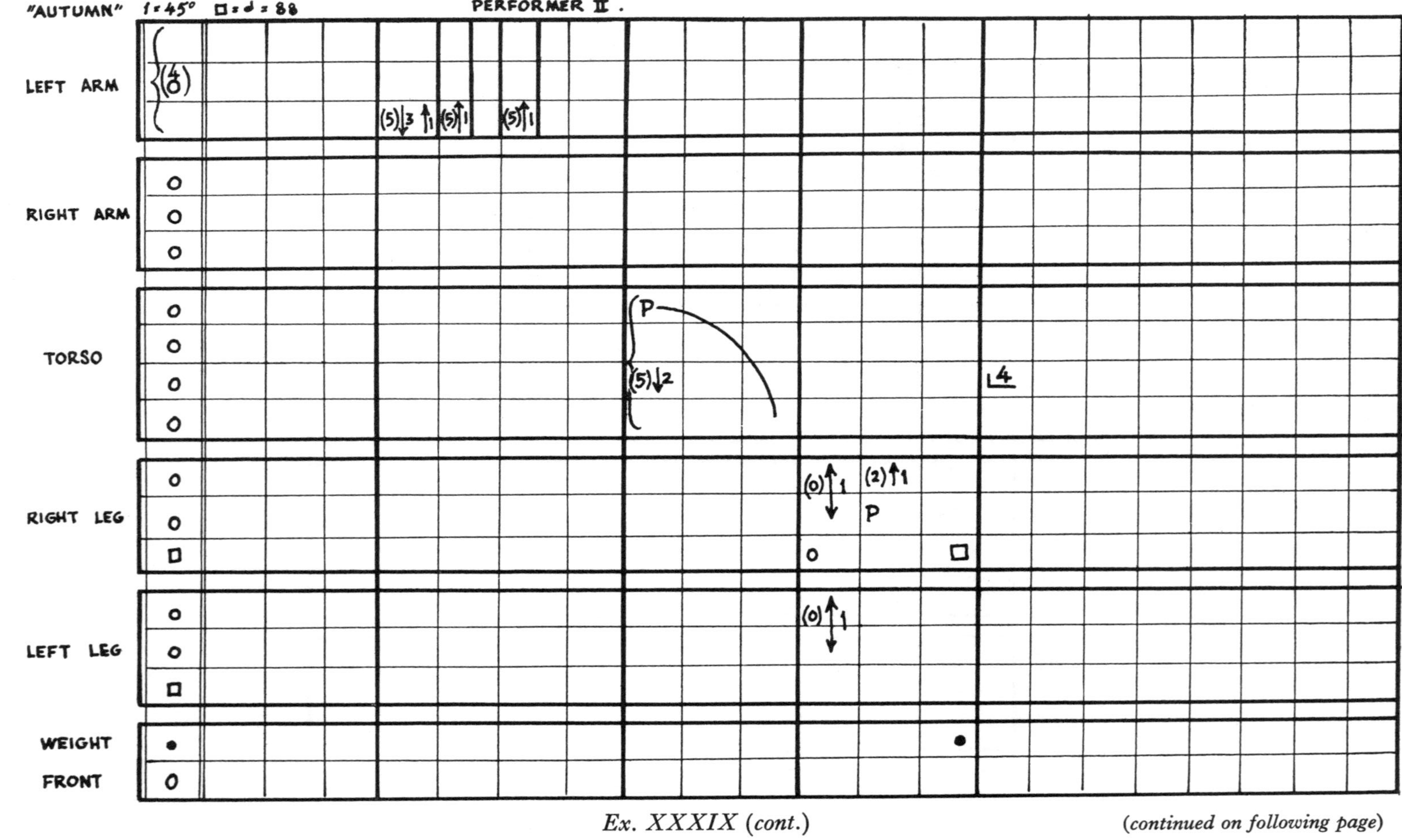

Ex. XXXIX (cont.)

(continued on following page)

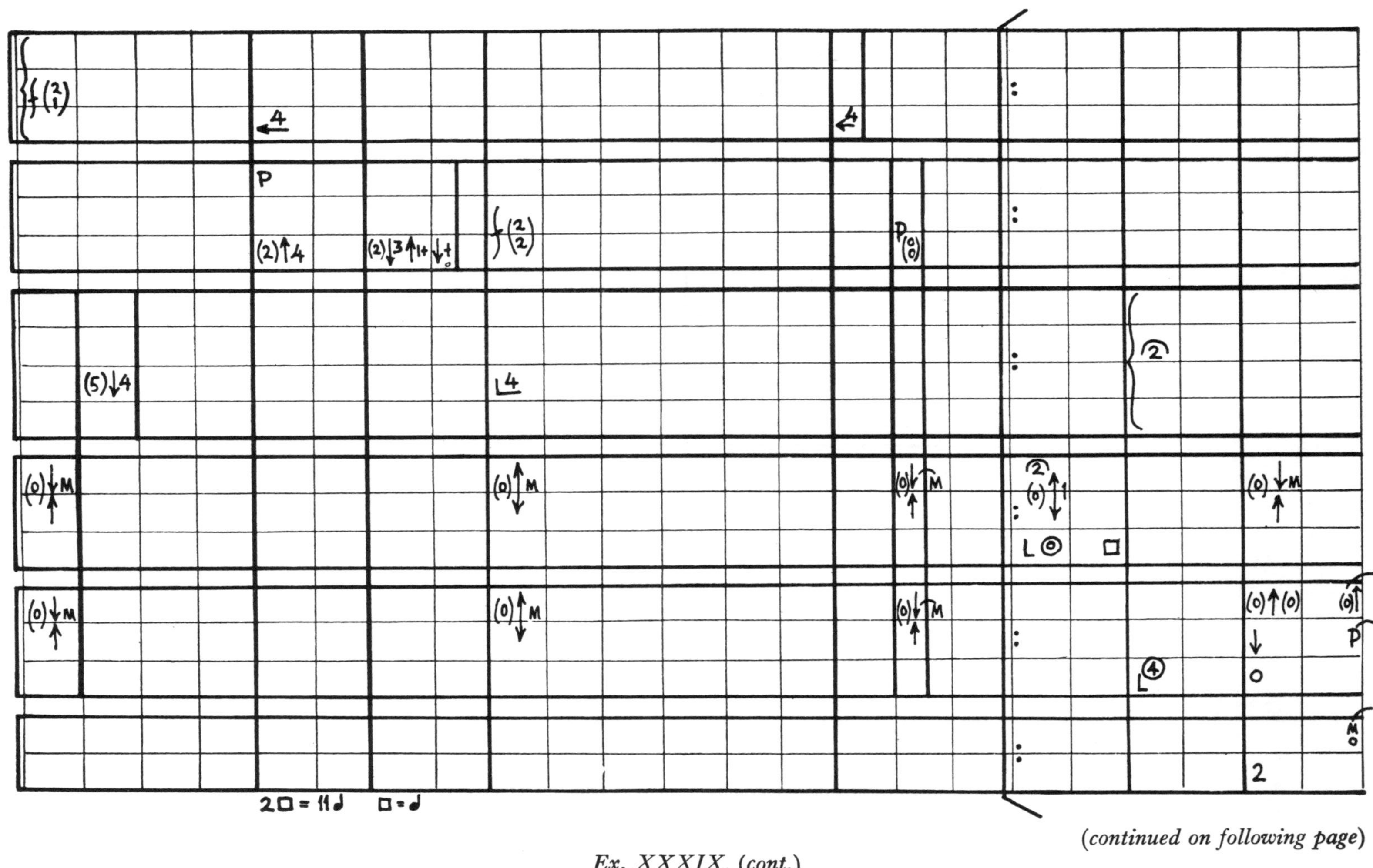

(continued on following page)

Ex. XXXIX. (cont.)

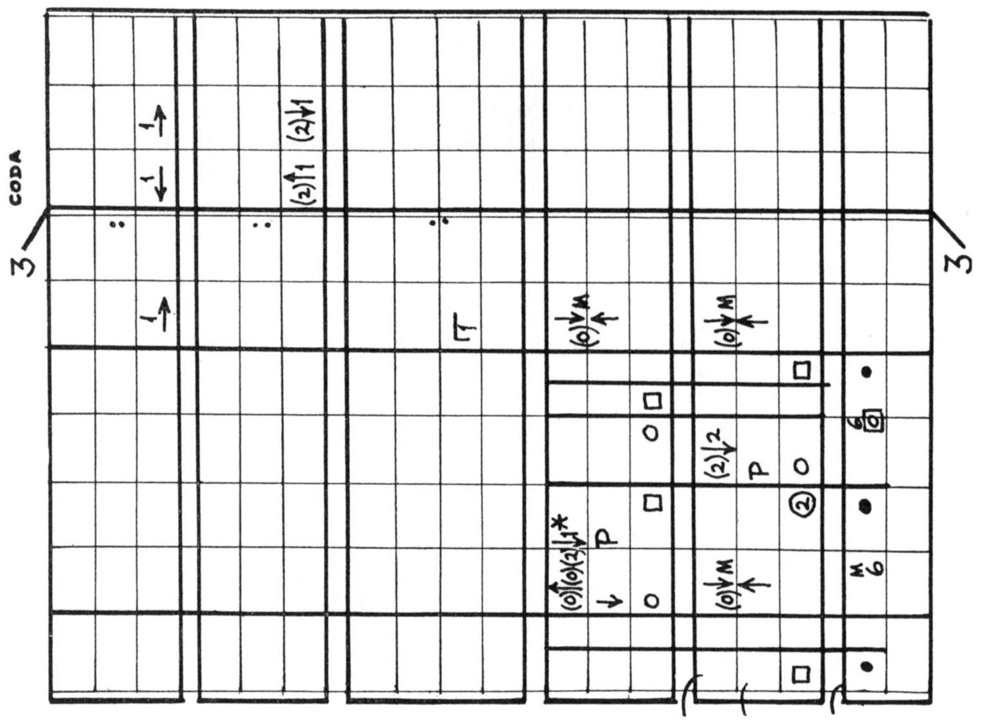

Ex. XXXIX. (cont.)

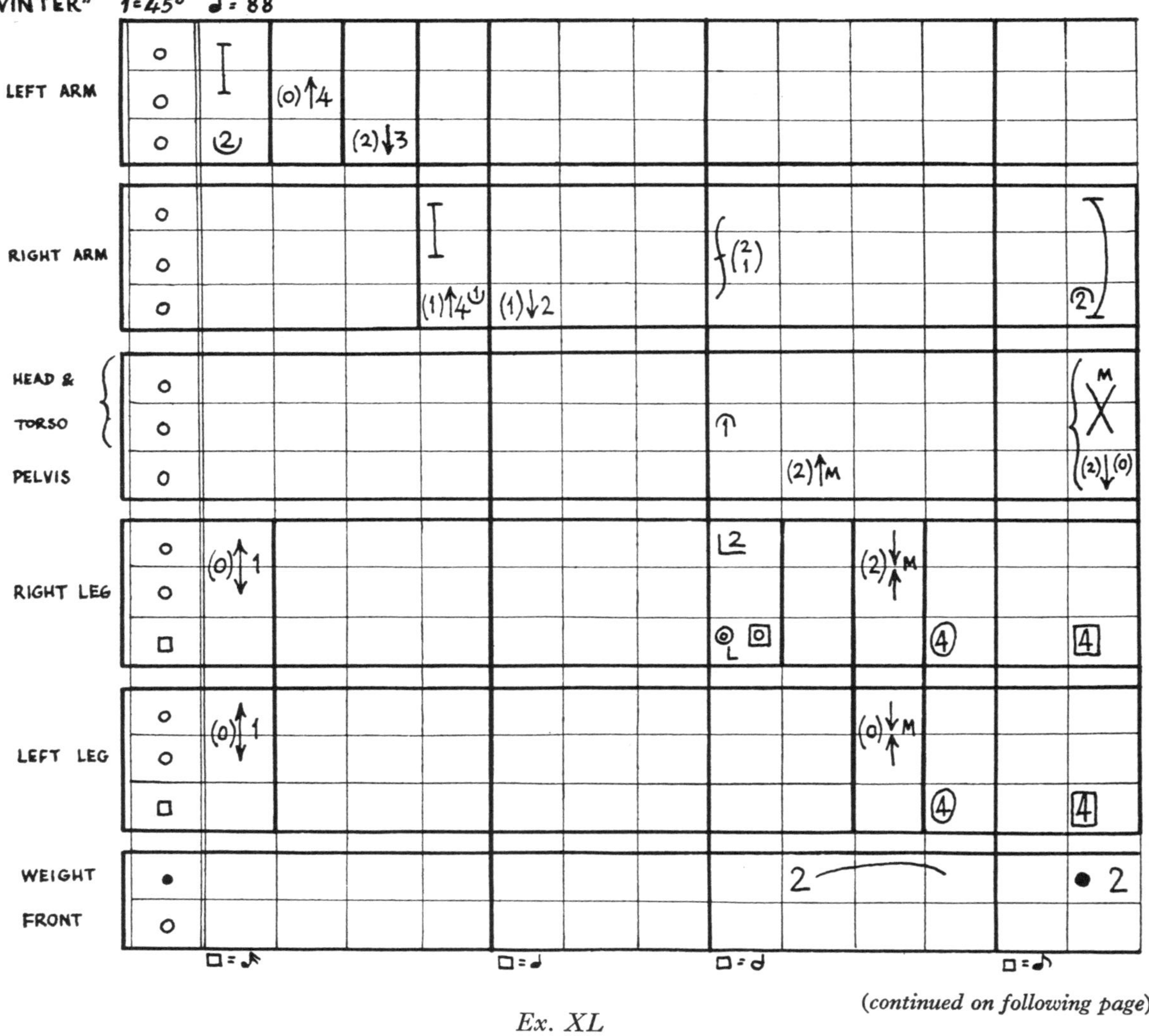

(continued on following page)

Ex. XL

(continued on following page)

Ex. XL. (cont.)

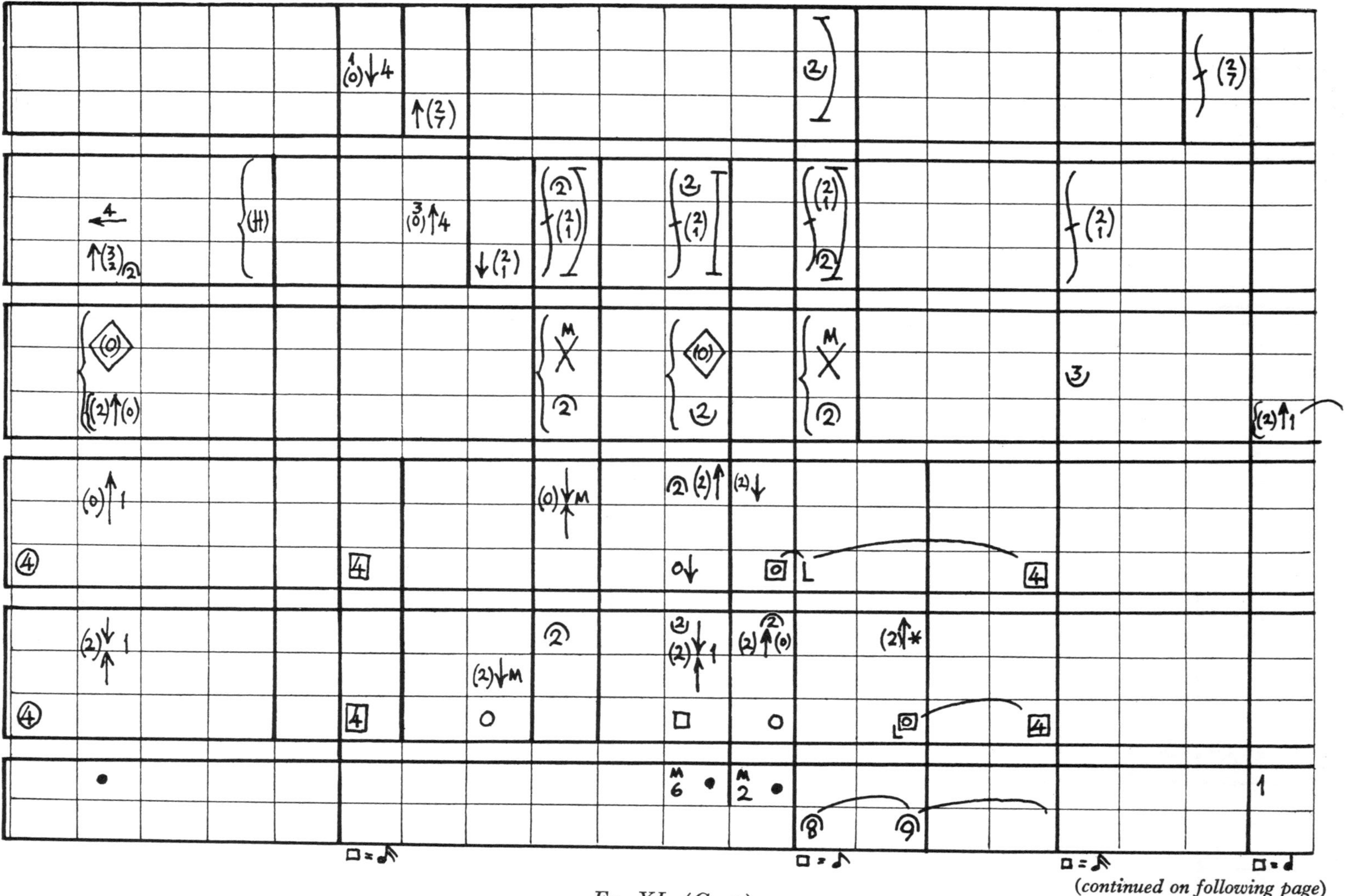

(continued on following page)

Ex. XL. (Cont.)

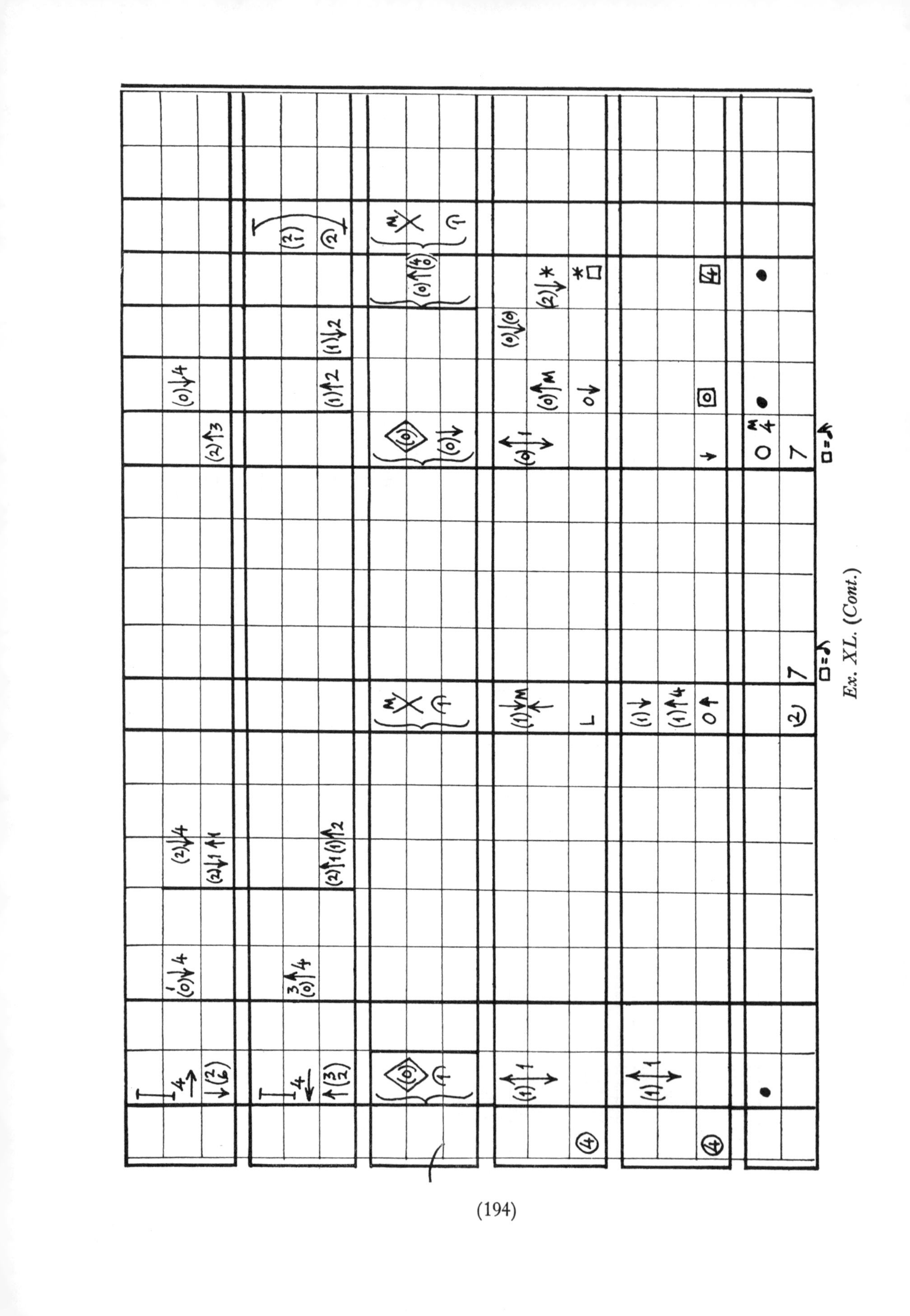

Ex. XL. (Cont.)

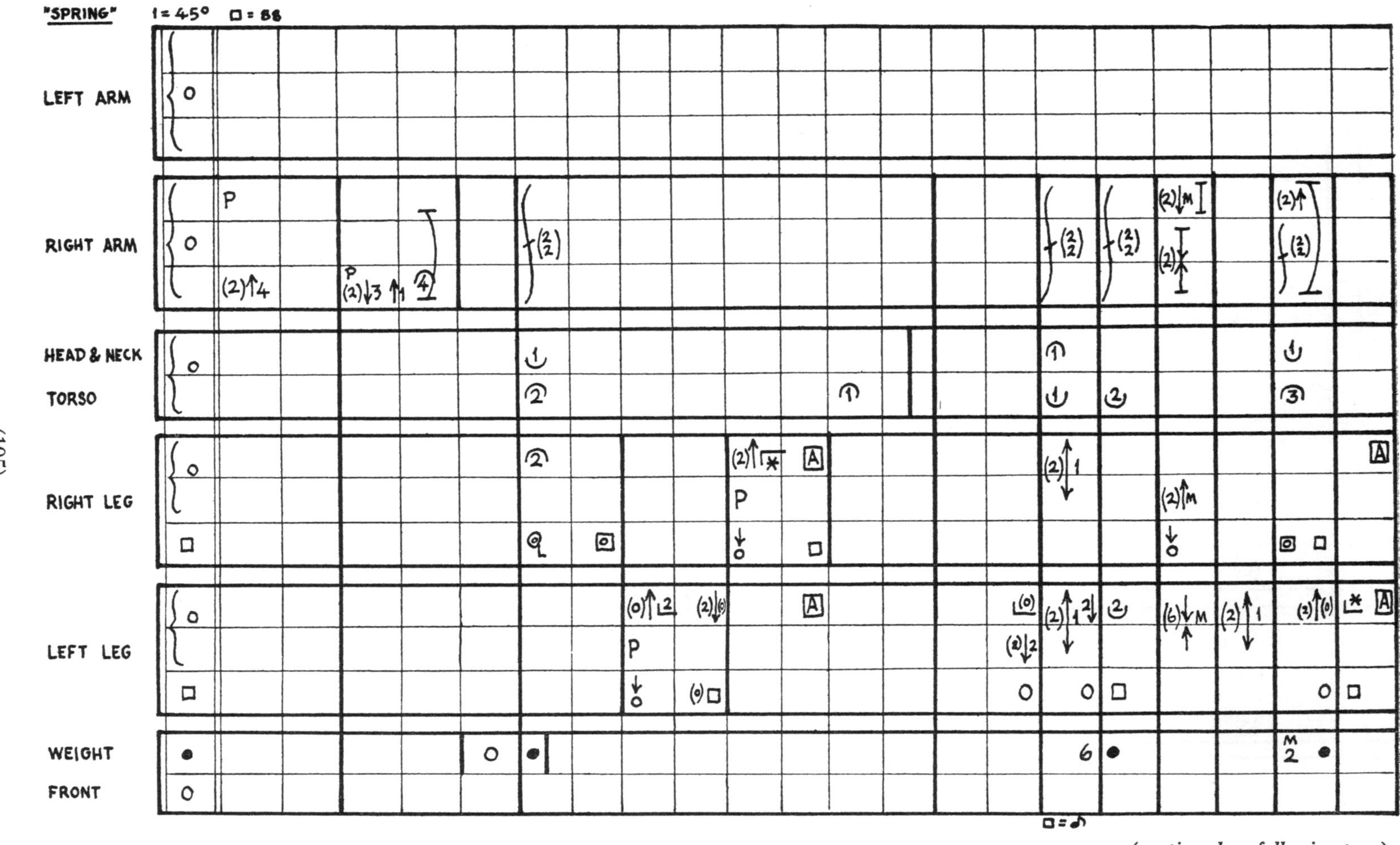

Ex. XLI

(continued on following page)

Ex. XLI. (cont.)

(continued on following page)

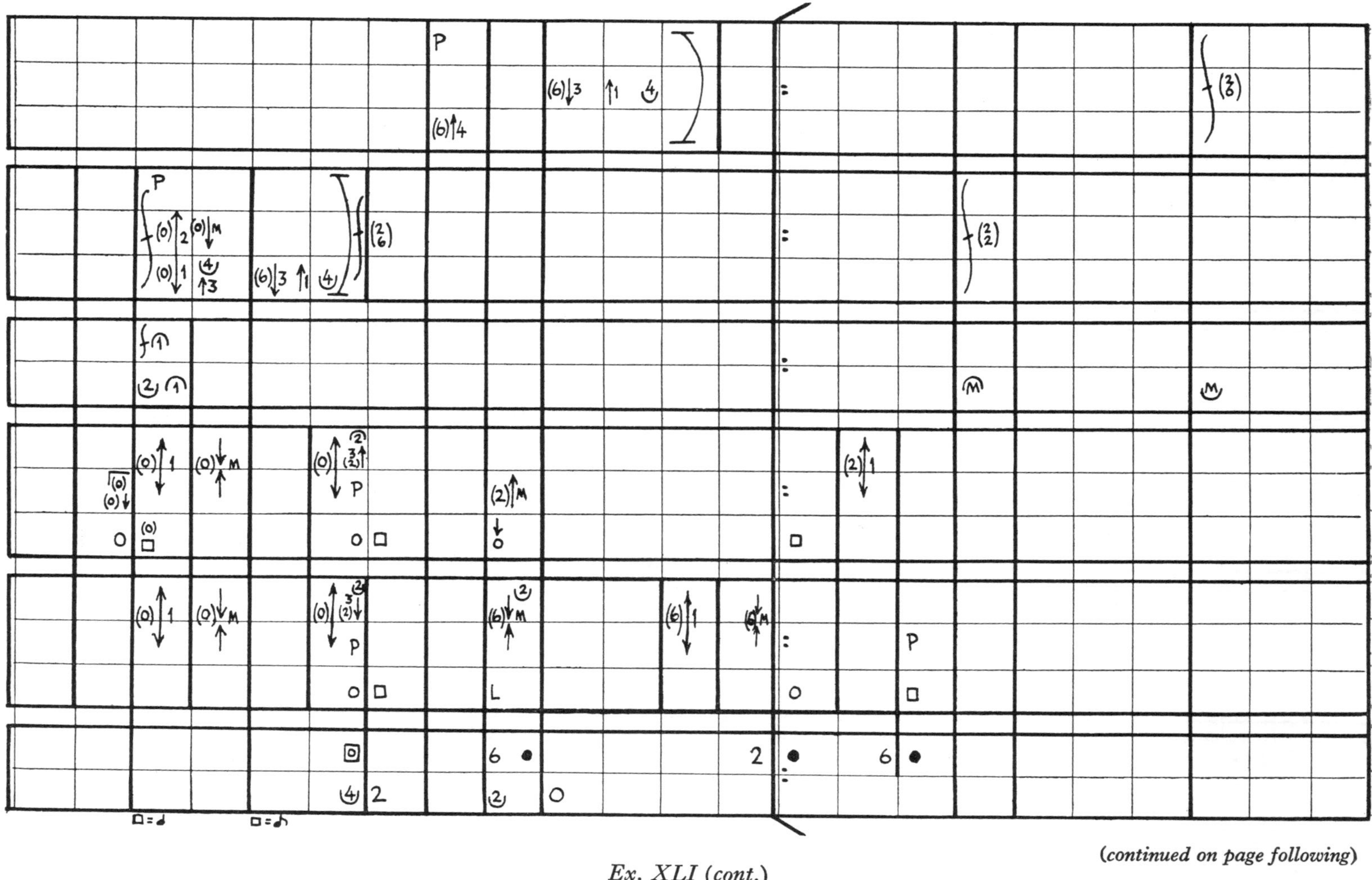

Ex. XLI (cont.)

(continued on page following)

Ex. XLI (cont.)

CHAPTER 21

The Axis of Movement

THE MOVEMENTS of the parts of the human body are circular in essence; every point on the axis of a limb moves in a certain circle. If a line be supposed perpendicular to the plane of that circle and passing through its centre, it may be said that this line is the axis about which the point moves whatever kind of movement the limb produces, all points on the limb move about the same straight axis.

N.B. For the sake of simplicity in the following discussion, when 'a movement' is spoken of, the movement meant will be that of a single limb.

In *Plane movement* the circles of all the points on the axis of the limb are on the same plane and concentric, that is, have a common centre, and a line perpendicular to the movement plane in this central point serves as an axis about which move all points on the axis of the limb.

In *Conical movement* all the centres of the circles in which the points on the axis of the limb move, combine to form a straight line. This line is the axis of the cone, i.e. it connects the apex to the centre of the base, and is perpendicular to the base.

In *Rotatory movement* the axis of the limb serves as an 'axis of movement' about which the limb turns.

The line about which all points on the limb move, will be called the *Axis of Movement.*

The idea and term 'Axis of Movement' has already been used in the explanation and definition of the three 'kinds of movement' and it has been stated that:

(a) In a *Rotatory movement* the axis of the limb is identical with the axis of movement —i.e., the angle between axis of limb and axis of movement is 0°.

(b) In a *Conical movement* the moving axis of the limb is at an acute angle (less than 90°) with the axis of movement.

(c) In a *Plane movement* the axis of the limb and the axis of movement are perpendicular to each other (at an angle of 90°).

The Axis of Movement is then an imaginary straight line passing through the joint of the moving limb, and serving as the geometrical focus of all the points on the axis of the limb during its movement; i.e., on this line are all the centres of the circles of movement of the points on the axis of the limb. The Axis of Movement is perpendicular to these circles at their centres.

Since every line which *passes through the joint* of a given limb passes through the centre of its Private System of Reference, therefore the axis of movement, which also passes through the joint, can be defined as in defining positions, according to two coordinates. From any given position a limb may theoretically move (if physical limitations are not considered) about any given defined axis of movement.

At the beginning of a process of movement the position of a limb is given: either as Zero Position or any other starting position. From any position in which the limb may be, it may move around a chosen defined axis of movement which is in a fixed angle to it in one definite way only. The definition of the positions of axis of movement, plus the starting position of a limb, will establish the *kind* of movement which can be produced. From this it follows that it is possible to render any movement into symbolic language by means of the analysis and definition of the axis about which that movement takes place. When the change of relations of limbs to one another (movement) is symbolically expressed according to the analysis of axes of movement, the three 'kinds of movement' will not possess each a distinct symbol, as in the method hitherto described in this book; one movement symbol will suffice for all three types of movement. In this case, the complete movement symbol will contain three elements at least, namely (1) the position of the axis of movement, understood in conjunction with the axis of the limb, will express the 'kind of movement' and the relation of the movement to the System of Reference; (2) amount of movement; (3) sense of movement.

From all that has been proposed and demonstrated in this book it follows that the analysis and composition of movement may be approached in two ways; i.e. a choice is given between two alternative ways of reviewing and symbolizing movement, each way emphasizing more strongly a different aspect of movement:

(a) *Establishment of the Axis of Movement.* If, in any given position of the limb, it is decided to move it about a certain axis, the 'kind' of movement will be the result of the relation between the position of the axis of the limb and the position of the chosen axis of movement. When the angle between the two axes remains unchanged, the movement can be in one path only, in one of two possible senses.

(b) *Establishment of the 'Kind of Movement' and its spatial relationship to the System of Reference.* If it is decided to move the limb in a given 'Kind of movement', that axis of movement must be chosen which will result in the required type of movement when the limb moves about it. It will be found on investigation that, for any position of a limb, it may be moved in a given 'Kind of movement' around many axes; that is to say, in any given position of a limb, it is possible to move it with the intention of producing a certain kind of movement, about one of a whole 'family' of axes. For example, if it is wished to move the limb from any given position in a Plane movement, this movement may be produced about any axis perpendicular to it. The total of all these axes is the plane which is perpendicular to the axis of the limb. Similarly with Conical movement: if it is wished to move the limb in a Conical movement in which the angle of movement is (for example) 45°, for this purpose any axis of movement may be chosen which is at an angle of 45° to the axis of the limb. The total of these axes is the surface of a cone of which the angle of the apex is 90° (45°+45°); and the axis of the limb represents the axis of this imaginary cone.

(From these two examples it is seen that, in movement from a given position of a limb, the 'kind of movement' alone does not in itself define the relevant axis of movement, since this is one out of a complete 'family'. The spatial relationship of the required movement to the System of Reference must be known so that the correct axis may be chosen from this family of axes.)

Hitherto the three 'kinds of movement' (Rotatory, Curved and Plane) have held a very venerated place in the method of notation offered, both as basic tools of analysis and—consequently—also in the symbolic representation. After the identification of a movement according to its kind, its further properties were ascertained—its location relative to the System of Reference, its sense, and amount.

The act of identification of a movement was, however, no more than a 'natural' act. It was simply discerned in direct observation by the naked eye that there is a marked difference in the manner in which limbs change their relations to one another on various occasions, with regard to the appearance of the actual change. These differences were classified into three axiomatically distinct types of movement, and the concept 'axis of movement' was used rather to emphasize their distinctness. (This kind of 'natural' discernment may be likened to the primitive awareness of the differences of pitch among tones, or differences between various colours, before the organization of each in a comprehensive system wherein the differences are simply different *degrees* of the same event.) Every method of analysis strives to arrive at laws of the material which can be considered fundamental. It is possible to be satisfied that a law is fundamental when in its light seemingly distinct aspects of the material dealt with appear as but different *degrees* of the same event; the material thus being rendered into an organized whole by correlating its parts. The fewest possible principles which can be found that will express both what is common and what is peculiar to seemingly distinct, sometimes unreconciled, events in one defined field of interest, may be considered as fundamental laws.

By using the imaginary Axis of Movement as the basic means of definition of movement a further step is taken in the direction of generalization and abstraction in the understanding of the behaviour of limbs when changing their relation to one another. In this manner events are stripped of the seemingly real, axiomatic difference which was assumed when the three 'kinds of movement' were regarded as essentially different and given, because of this, different symbols; by using the imaginary Axis of Movement they are conceived in their similarity and dis-similarity at one and the same time: that is, they are conceived as various degrees of the same event. This has aleady been noted, but not emphasized by the actual notation.

By using the Axis of Movement as the means of definition, the various appearances in the event of one limb changing its relation to another are explained by one principle only—by the relation between axis of limb and axis of movement. As has already been remarked, instead of the three symbols (in conjunction with numbers) which were hitherto necessary for the notation of movements, only one main symbol (with numbers) will be required in order to express all the possible changes of relation between the parts of the human body, which are the subject of this book.

(*See Example XLII.*)

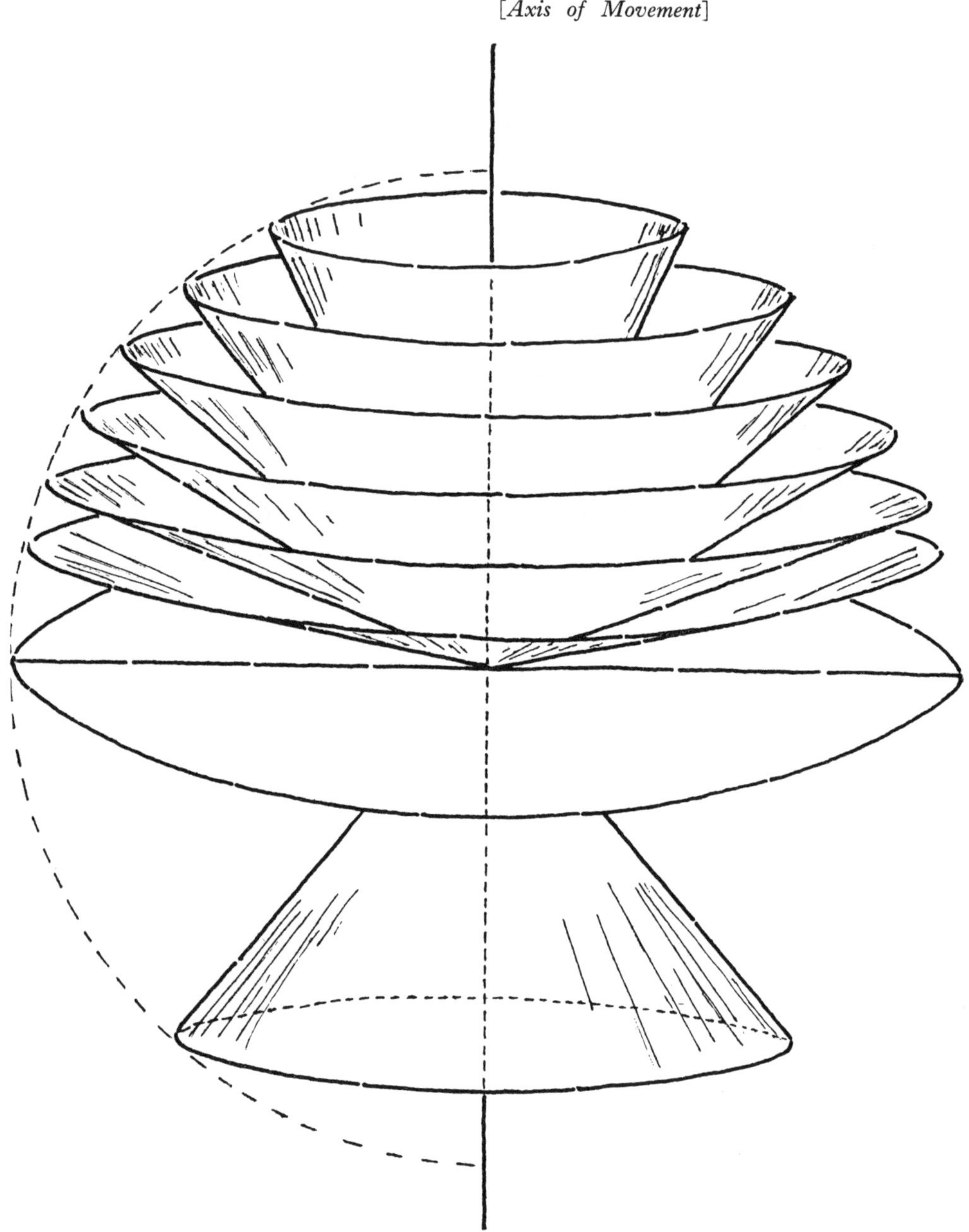

56. Different Surfaces created by Movement about the same Axis of Movement

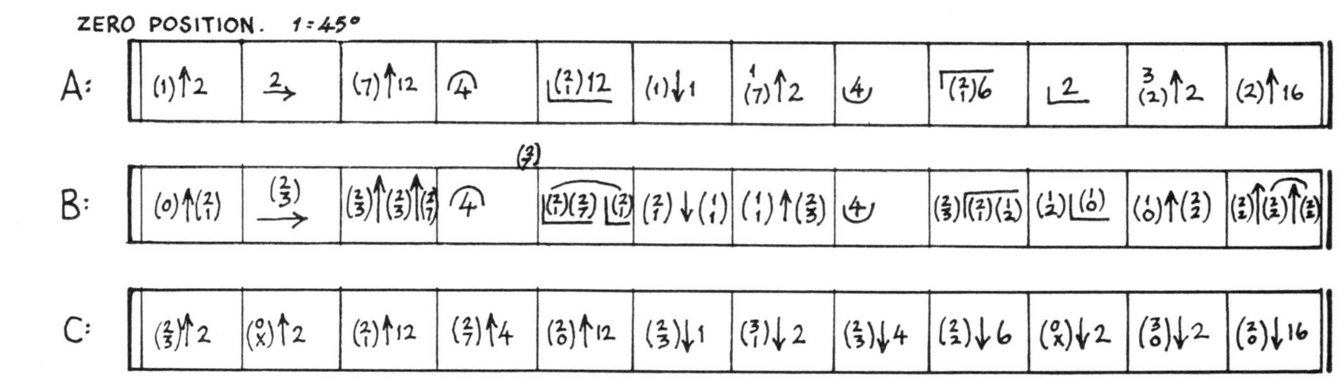

Ex. XLII. One sequence of movement written in three different ways.

A: A movement is denoted by defining kind, sense, and amount of movement. (The usual manner of writing.)
B: A movement is denoted by defining the starting position, kind and sense of movement, and final position.
C: A movement is denoted by defining the axis of movement and amount of movement about this axis. The positional number preceding the arrow denotes the position of the axis of movement around which the limb moves; the arrow in this case does not denote kind of movement, but only sense of movement. ↑ denotes positive (clockwise) and ↓ denotes negative (anticlockwise) movement, determined looking outward along the axis of movement from the joint in which the movement takes place. The number following the sign gives the amount of movement, i.e. the size of the section of a circle performed by the extremity of the limb in its movement.

Published on the occasion of the project
Pause: Noa Eshkol Chamber Dance Group
at KW Institute for Contemporary Art, Berlin
August 25–27, 2023
Curator: Krist Gruijthuijsen

and the exhibition
Noa Eshkol. No Time to Dance.
at Georg Kolbe Museum, Berlin
March 15–August 25, 2024
Curator: Kathleen Reinhardt

Originally published by
Weidenfeld & Nicolson, London, 1958

Publication
Editors: Mor Bashan, Krist Gruijthuijsen
Assistant Editor: Dror Shoval
Editorial Management: Nikolas Brummer
Texts: John G Harries, Michal Shosani and
Humi Einbinder, Mor Bashan and Dror Shoval
Images: The Noa Eshkol Archive for Movement Notation
Copyediting: Anita Iannacchione, Jayne Wilkinson
Proofreading: Z. Harris
Translation: Anna Shraer, Lihi Paul
Design: Marc Hollenstein
Lithography: Holger Herschel
Printing and Binding: Lösch GmbH & Co. KG

Published by
KW Institute for Contemporary Art
KUNST-WERKE BERLIN e. V.
Auguststraße 69
10117 Berlin

Verlag der Buchhandlung Walther und Franz König
Ehrenstraße 4
50672 Köln

In collaboration with
Georg Kolbe Museum
Sensburger Allee 25
14055 Berlin

Distributed by
Buchhandlung Walther König
Ehrenstraße 4
50672 Köln
Tel: +49 (0) 221 / 20 59 6 53
verlag@buchhandlung-walther-koenig.de

ISBN 978-3-7533-0602-5
Printed in Germany

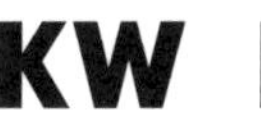

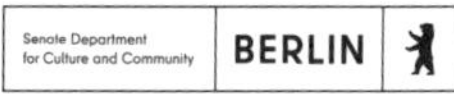

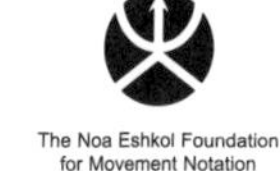

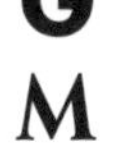

Funded by the German Federal Cultural Foundation

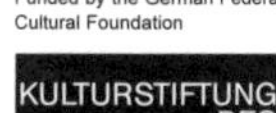

Funded by the Federal Government Commissioner for Culture and the Media

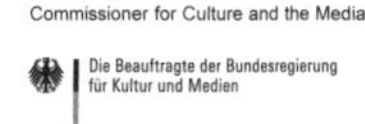

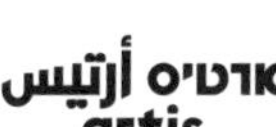

Freundeskreis
Georg Kolbe Museum

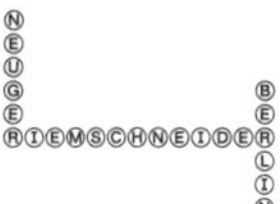

KW Institute for Contemporary Art is supported by the Senate Department for Culture and Community

The exhibition *Noa Eshkol. No Time to Dance.* at George Kolbe Museum is generously supported by Kulturstiftung des Bundes, Artis, New York, and Freundeskreis of the Georg Kolbe Museum, Berlin

The publication *Movement Notation* is generously supported by Artis, New York, and neugerriemschneider, Berlin